THE WORLD ENCYCLOPEDIA OF
FOSSILS &
FOSSIL-COLLECTING

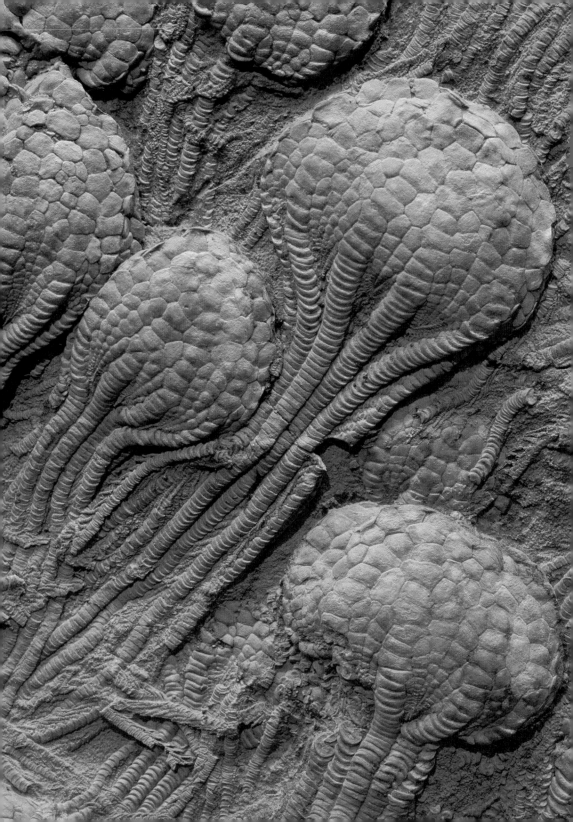

THE WORLD ENCYCLOPEDIA OF

FOSSILS &

FOSSIL-COLLECTING

An illustrated reference guide to over 375 plant and animal fossils from around
the globe and how to identify them, with over 950 photographs and artworks

STEVE PARKER

southwater

This edition is published by Southwater,
an imprint of Anness Publishing Ltd, 108 Great Russell Street,
London WC1B 3NA; info@anness.com

www.southwaterbooks.com; www.annesspublishing.com

If you like the images in this book and would like
to investigate using them for publishing, promotions or
advertising, please visit our website www.practicalpictures.com
for more information.

© Anness Publishing Ltd 2014

A CIP catalogue record for this book is available from
the British Library.

Publisher: Joanna Lorenz
Editorial Director: Helen Sudell
Project Editors: Ann Kay, Tim Jollands and Catherine Stuart
Production Controller: Pirong Wang
Consultants: John Cooper (Booth Museum, Brighton)
Contributors: Vivian Allen, Julien Divay, Ross Elgin, Carlos
Grau, Robert Randell, Jeni Saunders and Matt Vrazo
Book and Jacket Design: Nigel Partridge
Artists: Andrey Atuchin, Peter Barrett, Stuart Carter, Anthony
Duke, Samantha J. Elmhurst and Denys Ovenden (for these and
other picture acknowledgements, see final page)

PUBLISHER'S NOTE
Although the advice and information in this book are believed
to be accurate and true at the time of going to press, neither the
authors nor the publisher can accept any legal responsibility or
liability for any errors or omissions that may have been made.

*Page 2 image shows fossilized crinoids. These creatures,
which include sea lilies and featherstars, are members of one
of the oldest animal groups on Earth.*

CONTENTS

INTRODUCTION

Fossils have been treasured since ancient times. Long ago, people gathered these strangely shaped lumps of stone for many purposes – as objects of worship, signs of their worldly wealth and power, evidence of their god's handiwork, or simply as beautiful and elegant items to display and admire.

Fossil collectors of the ancient world could not have understood how their curiosities were formed. They could not know the enormous contribution of fossils to the development of modern scientific knowledge, about the Earth and the living things that have populated it through time. Had they understood the significance of fossils, they might well have been even more amazed at what they had collected.

More than 2,000 years ago in Ancient Greece, natural philosophers such as Aristotle mused on fossils and their origins. Some explanations were inorganic – fossils were nature's sculptures, fashioned by wind, water, sun, ice and other non-living forces. Some explanations were supernatural – fossils were the work of mythical beings and gods, placed on Earth as examples of their omnipotent powers. Aristotle himself described how fossils developed or grew naturally within the rocks, from some form of seed which he called 'organic essence'.

Below: Reconstructions from fossils of dinosaurs such as the famous Tyrannosaurus rex *continue to fascinate.*

In the 1500s, firmer ideas took root. In 1517 Italian physician-scientist Girolamo Frascatoro was one of the first on record to suggest that fossils were the actual remains of plants, creatures and other organisms or living things. In 1546 German geologist Georgius Agricola coined the word 'fossil', but not as we now understand it. His 'fossils' were almost anything dug from the ground, including coal, ores for metals and minerals, and what he believed to be rocks that just happened to be shaped like bones, teeth, shells and skulls. In 1565 Swiss naturalist Konrad von Gesner's works contained some of the first studied drawings of fossils. However, like Agricola, von Gesner believed that they were stones which, by chance, resembled parts of living things.

A fashion for fossils began in the 1700s in Europe. Wealthy folk established home museums where they displayed fossils, stuffed birds and mammals, pinned-out insects, pressed flowers and so on. Around 1800, scientists began to ponder more deeply on the true origins of fossils. It was suggested that they may indeed be the remains of once-living things. But as all life had been made by God, and

Below: Palaeontologists from the Natural History Museum, London, excavate 380 million-year-old tetrapod fossils in Latvia.

*Above: The rotting carcass of a spotted hyaena (*Crocuta crocuta*). Fossils begin like this – as the parts of living things that endure and are preserved in sediments.*

Below: This fossilized lower jaw of an extinct hyaena species is recognizably dog-like in character.

God would not allow any of his creations to perish, fossils could not actually be from extinct organisms. They must be from the types of living things which are still alive today.

Famed French biologist Georges Cuvier broke ranks. He studied the huge, well-preserved skull of a 'sea lizard' that looked like no living reptile, which he named *Mosasaurus*.

Above: Museum collections and exhibitions, especially well-designed displays like this one at the National Museum of Wales in Cardiff, are an excellent place to learn more about fossils.

Cuvier also examined fossil mammoth bones and saw their differences from those of living elephants. His new explanation was that these fossils were the remains of creatures that had indeed become extinct – in the Great Flood of Noah's time, as described in the Bible. As more and more varied fossils were dug, from deeper rock layers, the explanation grew into the story of Seven Floods. Each deluge

saw a great extinction of living things. Then God re-populated the Earth with a new, improved set of organisms.

In 1859 English naturalist Charles Darwin's epic work *On The Origin Of Species* brought the idea of evolution to the fore. Fossils fitted perfectly into this scientific framework. Indeed they were used as major evidence to support it. In the struggle for survival, species less able to adapt to the current conditions died out, while better-adapted types took over. However the process never reaches steady state or an end point, since conditions or

environments change through time – forcing the organisms to evolve with them. This explains not only the presence of fossils in the rocks, but also why these fossils exhibit changes over time.

Today the origins of fossils are well documented. And fossils are central to the story of Life on Earth – from the earliest blobs of jelly in primeval seas, to shelled creatures that swarmed in the oceans, enormous prehistoric sharks, the first tentative steps on land, the time of the giant dinosaurs, and the rigours of the ice ages with their woolly mammoths and sabre-toothed cats. A recent spate of discoveries now allows us to trace the origins of our own kind, back to ape-like creatures in Africa several million years ago. Yet, in addition to this scientific basis, we can still regard fossils as ancient people did – with wonder and appreciation of their natural beauty, while holding a part of Earth's history in our hands.

Left: The idea that fossils were the remains of long-extinct, fantastical creatures – such as this giant sea serpent in Charles Gould's Mythical Monsters, *published in 1886 – sparked some enduring myths.*

FOSSILS AND FOSSIL-HUNTING

Fossils are usually described as parts of living things which died long ago, and were preserved in the rocks, turned to stone. The processes of fossilization can happen in different ways, as described over the following pages. But they all share three main features.

First, the original objects preserved are from all kinds of living organisms – not only animals, but plants, fungi and even microbes. Second, the process takes a very long time – at least many thousands of years. Indeed, the majority of fossils are millions of years old. Third, most fossils are not the actual substances and materials from those once-living organisms. Fossilization gradually replaces living or organic matter with inorganic minerals and crystals. So, in general, a fossil is a lump of stone or rock. However its shape is taken from that of the original organism. This is summarized in the phrase 'bone to stone'.

Fossils themselves are fascinating, but many people gain even greater enjoyment by searching for them. It involves the thrill of the chase, and anticipation of an exciting new discovery. Fossil-hunting is an active outdoor pursuit, in the fresh air amid often beautiful scenery. It allows us to expand our basic understanding of geology and biology, from the way landscapes form and erode, to the shapes of snail shells and sharks' teeth.

Fossil-hunting always produces results. For some, the greatest satisfaction lies in creating a well-thought-out display. For others, it's about making a contribution to local or even national museums and to existing paleontological knowledge. For the few who come across a spectacular find, the attraction may even lie in fame and fortune.

Left: Rocks within the Earth's crust are subject to dramatic movements over a very long period of time, crumbling and slipping into the oceans or being raised into towering mountain ranges. These footprints were originally made by a carnivorous dinosaur upon an ancient Cretaceous shoreline, but have since been lifted, over millions of years, to form part of a near-vertical fault in the Andes. The palaeontologist measuring the stride of the creature has had to overcome some difficulty in access to record this information.

FOSSILS THROUGH TIME

Fossils trace the evolution of life from the tiniest, simplest scraps of living matter, to huge and complex creatures like dinosaurs, whales and mammoths. It is a very long story, spanning billions of years, with many surprising events along the way.

The oldest known fossils are microscopic shapes in rocks dating back more than 3,500 million (3.5 billion) years. That's 3,500,000,000 years – a very long time. In fact it's more than two-thirds of the time that our planet has been in existence.

Like the other planets of the Solar System, the Earth probably formed from a cloud of dust and rocks whirling in space around the embryo Sun, some 4,600 million (4.6 billion) years ago. About 1,000 million years later, signs of life were appearing as microscopic organisms in the 'primeval soup' of the early oceans. However for more than 2,000 million years after these beginnings, life stayed very small and very simple.

Changing Earth

The earliest living things probably resembled the organisms called bacteria and cyanobacteria (blue-green algae) today. They are the simplest forms of life and make up a kingdom

Below: As the present day continents began to take form during the Jurassic Period, reptiles dominated all habitats, with dinosaurs ruling the land and crocodiles presiding over freshwater lakes and rivers.

Above: A well-preserved trilobite fossil (Calymene blumenbachii) from Silurian times.

of organisms known as the Prokaryota. It's believed that their activities helped to change the nature of early Earth. At first the atmosphere was rich in poisonous gases such as methane. However the biochemical activities of the first life-forms pumped increasing amounts of oxygen into the air. This was a source of ozone which began to shield the surface from the Sun's harmful ultra-violet rays (as it still does today). These changing conditions allowed the next steps in evolution – see Burgess Shales, pages 14–15.

Jelly to shells

From 2,000 million years ago, microorganisms grew in layered mounds of minerals in shallow water. These became well preserved as the objects known as stromatolites (shown in later pages of this book). Some stromatolites have been through the process of silicification, to form the kind of rock known as stromatolitic chert. Within these can be found amazingly preserved remains of the microbes. From about 1,000 to 800 million years ago there are increasing and tantalizing signs of multicellular organisms, perhaps resembling simple jellyfish: these might be called the first true 'animals'.

Fossils start to appear in appreciable numbers in rocks formed after about 540 million years ago. This was the

time that shelled creatures evolved in the seas. Shells, being hard and resistant to decay, fossilize fairly well. Living things before this time, from about 1,000 to 540 million years ago, had evolved greater size and complexity. But they were mostly jelly-like. Their soft bodies fragmented and rotted before preservation could occur. Only a few rare and precious fossils give glimpses into this misty phase of life's history.

From water to land

At first, life flourished only in the seas. Fossils form well in water, as organisms die and sink, and are

Origins of names

The names of the geological time spans called periods were mostly established in the 1800s. Some originate from the area where rocks of a particular age were first surveyed and studied. The Cambrian Period (540–500 million years ago) takes its name from Cambria, an old Roman-Latin term for Wales. Geologist Adam Sedgwick introduced the name in 1835 after describing rocks from North Wales. Other period names have their origins in the main types of rocks formed at the time. For example, the Cretaceous Period (135–65 million years ago) is so called from the huge thicknesses of chalk laid down as it progressed – *creta* ('kreta') is an old Latin term for 'chalk'.

Below: The ammonite Mantelliceras *is preserved in chalk typical of the Cretaceous Period.*

covered by silt, mud, sand and other sediments on the bottom. From the sea, plants moved into freshwater, and animals followed them. Their fossils show an increasing variety of forms. By 400 million years ago another major habitat was being conquered – the land. Until that time the ground had been barren, with no covering of soil as we recognize it. Pioneering plants and animals spread over the mud, sand and rocks, leaving their fossils as they colonized new areas. Their remains show that plants needed stiff stems to hold themselves up, since they were no longer buoyed by water. Animals could wriggle or squirm. But the more complex types changed their fins for limbs, and took their early steps over the ground.

Reptile domination
By 350 million years ago a new group of creatures had appeared, with scaly skin and waterproof-shelled eggs. These were the reptiles, and their fossils trace their climb to dominance.

Above: An early Palaeozoic plant, Moresnetia zalesskyii.

Below: Mesozoic brittlestars, Sinosura sp., from the late Jurassic Period.

Above: The remains of a woolly mammoth and straight-tusked elephant being excavated from a clay pit in Sussex, England, in 1964. These large herbivores existed within the last 1.75 million years.

By 200 million years ago they had given rise to the major large animals in all three major habitats – on land, as the dinosaurs; in the air, as the pterosaurs; and in the sea, as plesiosaurs and ichthyosaurs. Startling fossils of these great beasts, including their eggs and babies, and the animals and plants that shared their time, show how they lived and died.

Above: Early Cenozoic (Palaeocene) seedling Jaffrea speirsii, a relative of the living katsura tree in the magnolia group.

Below: Cenozoic mammoth hair dating from the Quaternary Period.

Towards the end of the 'Age of Reptiles', plants underwent a revolution. Conifers, ginkgos and similar trees had dominated for much of the era. But by 100 million years ago a new group, the angiosperms, were becoming established. These include the dominant plants we see around us today – flowers, herbs and broad-leaved bushes and trees.

Mass deaths
About 65 million years ago there was a great change in the types and varieties of living things. Dinosaurs, pterosaurs, plesiosaurs and many other groups of animals, and many plants too, all abruptly disappear. This is known as a mass extinction. It marked the end of the great time span known as the Mesozoic Era, 'Middle Life'. This era had begun with an even greater loss of life 250 million years ago, which had in turn marked the end of the previous era, the Palaeozoic or 'Ancient Life'. Following the Mesozoic came our own era, the Cenozoic or Cainozoic, 'Recent Life'. Each of these huge phases of life is documented by the types of fossils in the rocks, and the make-up of the rocks themselves.

THE GEOLOGICAL TIME SCALE

Fossils are records of life in the past. But when, exactly – how many thousands or millions of years ago? Palaeontologists and other scientists use a dating system known as geological time to put the various time spans of the past into perspective.

Rocks and the fossils they contain are dated in various ways, to find out how old they are in millions of years. These dates are fitted into a framework known as the geological time system. Its divisions are based on significant changes in the rocks and the types of fossils within them, as various kinds of life came and went throughout evolutionary history.

Eras and periods

As described on the previous page, the major divisions of geological time are termed eras. First is the Precambrian, when living things were mostly specks, although larger and more complex creatures resembling jellyfish and worms appeared towards the end. The Precambrian was followed by the Palaeozoic, Mesozoic and Cenozoic Eras – Ancient, Middle and Recent Life respectively. In turn, each of these great eras is divided into spans called periods. Most of these periods lasted a few tens of millions of years. Again, the transition from one to the next is marked by important changes in fossils, as extinctions of previously dominant organisms occur and new types take over.

Epochs

As we progress from the past towards the present, the amounts of fossils, and their details of preservation, generally increase – because earth movements, erosion and other forces have had less time to destroy them. Also, the technologies used for finding the age of a rock or fossil are more accurate with younger specimens. This allows increasing accuracy of dating in the Cenozoic Era. So the next-to-last and current periods, the Tertiary and Quaternary, are subdivided into shorter time spans known as epochs. Further subdivisions do exist, but are often used to date rocks on a more local scale.

Useful shorthand

The names of the eras, periods and epochs act as 'shorthand labels' to enable palaeontologists to define and communicate a fossil's place in the past.

Precambrian Era
4,600–540 million years ago

Palaeozoic Era
540–250 million years ago
• Cambrian Period
540–500 million years ago
• Ordovician Period
500–435 million years ago
• Silurian Period
435–410 million years ago
• Devonian Period
410–355 million years ago
• Carboniferous Period
355–295 million years ago
• Permian Period
295–250 million years ago

Mesozoic Era
250–65 million years ago

• Triassic Period
250–203 million years ago
• Jurassic Period
203–135 million years ago
• Cretaceous Period
135–65 million years ago

Cenozoic Era
• Tertiary Period
65–1.75 million years ago
  • Palaeocene Epoch
  65–53 million years ago
  • Eocene Epoch
  53–33 million years ago
  • Oligocene Epoch
  33–23 million years ago
  • Miocene Epoch
  23–5.3 million years ago
  • Pliocene Epoch
  5.3–1.75 million years ago
• Quaternary Period
1.75 million years ago – present
  • Pleistocene Epoch
  1.75–0.01 million years ago
  • Holocene Epoch
  0.01 million years ago (10,000 years ago) – present

Variations in dating

There are several variants of the geological time scale, used in different fields such as basic palaeontology, mainstream geology, geological surveying, and prospecting for fossil fuels. For example, in some systems the Cambrian Period starts 570, 560 or 543 million years ago, and the Jurassic Period begins 144 million years ago.

Also, in the US the Carboniferous Period is sometimes known by two other names, the Mississippian Period or System followed by the Pennsylvanian, with the split at about 320 million years ago. However the sequences of the names for the eras, periods and epochs remain the same in all of these time scales.

Right: Exposed rock in the Ouachita Mts, Missouri. The mountains formed in what US geologists would term the Pennsylvanian.

Palaeogene and Neogene

In recent years, some amendments have been suggested to the traditional dating system outlined above. These affect the Tertiary Period (65–1.75 million years ago) and its various epochs, which together account for almost all of the Cenozoic Era. Traditionally, the Tertiary was followed by the Quaternary Period – the tail-end of the Cenozoic – which ran to the present day. In the revised system, the Cenozoic Era is divided into two more equal time spans, the Palaeogene and Neogene Periods. The former takes in the Palaeocene to Oligocene Epochs, which remain unchanged. The Neogene includes the Miocene and later epochs to the present, which again remain unaltered. So in the scheme depicted below, the Palaeogene Period would run from 65 to 23 million years ago, and the Neogene from 23 million years ago to the present. Thus the familiar labels 'Tertiary' and 'Quaternary' are superseded. However, many areas of palaeontology move rather slowly, and numerous exhibitions, museums and collections still exhibit Tertiary specimens. For this reason, we have added 'Tertiary' and 'Quaternary' to the chart below, as they remain a point of reference for fossil enthusiasts.

Further amendments also affect the boundaries between recent time spans, such as shifting the end of the Eocene Epoch and start of the Oligocene from 33 to 34 million years ago, and likewise the end of the Pliocene Epoch and start of the Pleistocene from 1.75 to 1.8 million years ago.

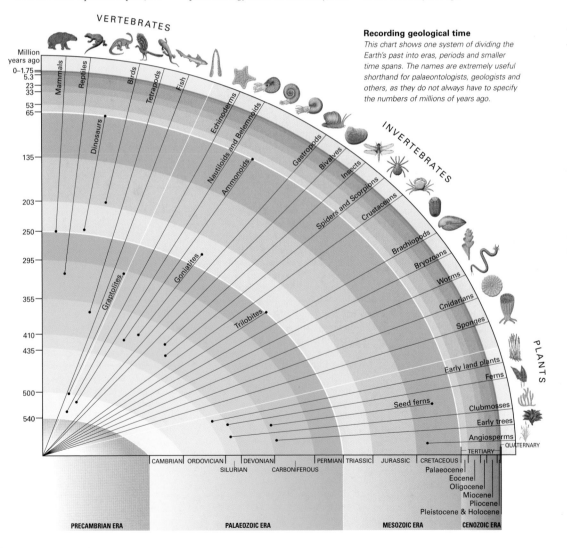

Recording geological time
This chart shows one system of dividing the Earth's past into eras, periods and smaller time spans. The names are extremely useful shorthand for palaeontologists, geologists and others, as they do not always have to specify the numbers of millions of years ago.

MAJOR FOSSIL SITES – THE AMERICAS

Some of the greatest fossil discoveries have been in the 'Badlands' of the North American Midwest – especially Alberta (Canada), and Montana, Wyoming, Colorado and Utah (USA). This is typical fossil-hunting country with bare rocks swept of soil by winds and rain, so that remains are easily spotted.

The landscape of the Badlands is subject to hot sun in summer, and freezing rain in winter, meaning plenty of erosion in the rocks as they weather, crack, peel and split, and fragments tumble down steep slopes or are washed away by flash floods. This ongoing geological activity continually exposes new layers with fresh fossils.

An embarrassing error

Perhaps the biggest 'fossil gold-rush' occurred in the Badlands region towards the end of the 19th century. It involved dinosaurs, of course, as well as many other reptiles, and plenty of other creatures, plus plants too. It was partly a result of bitter rivalry between two eminent palaeontologists, Edward Drinker Cope and Othniel Charles Marsh, and their respective teams of prospectors, workmen, restorers and benefactors. Their conflict began in about 1870, as an early wave of 'dinosaur-mania' was sweeping North America. Cope invited Marsh to view the remains of a long-necked, tubby-bodied, four-flippered, sea-going reptile, a plesiosaur called *Elasmosaurus*. Marsh noticed that Cope's reconstruction had the skull on the tail rather than the neck! From this time the two men were locked in competition to find the best fossils.

Below: Excavating dinosaur fossils on the Patagonian plains.

The first fossil gold rush

The intense antagonism of Cope and Marsh continued until their deaths in the late 1890s. Between them they named about 130 new kinds of dinosaurs and well over 1,000 other animals, from sharks to mammoths. Some of these finds have not stood the test of time, due to the race, rush and confusion of the so-called 'Bone Wars'. However the energy of the two men enthused many fellow fossil-hunters, and today North America vies with Asia (mainly China) to have the most fossil plants and animals described and catalogued.

The Burgess Shales

In 1909 eminent American palaeontologist Charles Walcott explored a quarry high in the Rocky Mountains near the town of Field, British Columbia. He came upon an astonishing treasure trove of fossils now know by the general name of 'the Burgess Shales'. The remains dated back to the Cambrian Period, some 530 million years ago. Walcott was astounded at the detailed state of preservation, which had occurred so fast that it entombed not only hard-shelled animals but also soft-bodied creatures like worms before they had time to rot away.

The Cambrian explosion

However, Walcott was less able to accept the incredible diversity of living things at such an early time – worms, sponges, jellyfish, arthropods related to crabs, and many more. According to beliefs of the time, creatures from that long ago should not be so diverse or varied. Life should have had started small and simple, and gradually worked up to the complexity and variety we see today. This idea is embodied in the concept of the 'evolutionary tree of life'. The tree

Above: A fossilized bee, more than 35 million years old, found in Colorado, USA.

began, long ago, with a trunk and a few branches, then expanded and diversified to the myriad twig ends of the present time. But finds such as the Burgess Shales show that this was not the case. Rather than a tree, an unkempt hedge might be a more apt comparison, with many branches appearing here and there throughout evolutionary time, some dying out rapidly but others enduring for much longer. The Burgess Shales represent one of these early bursts of evolution, which included the first shelled creatures. The time is often called the 'Cambrian explosion'.

South America

The number of significant fossil finds in South America has increased considerably since the 1960s. In particular, this continent lays claim to possibly the earliest, one of the biggest meat-eating, and the biggest of all dinosaurs – *Eoraptor*, *Giganotosaurus* and *Argentinosaurus*. Many other fascinating finds have come to light, often as a result of modern mining operations – in particular in Bolivia. Specimens include insects, frogs, small mammals and other creatures from the Tertiary Period, encased in amber.

Right: Map of the Americas, showing some of the major fossil discovery sites.

1. Colville River, Alaska, USA
2. Red Deer River, Alberta, Canada
3. Burgess Shales, Field, British Columbia, Canada
4. Hagerman Fossil Beds National Monument, Idaho, USA
5. Dinosaur National Monument, Utah/Colorado, USA
6. Como Bluff, Wyoming, USA
7. Kansas Inland Seas, USA
8. Joggins, Nova Scotia, Canada
9. Rancho La Brea, Los Angeles, USA
10. Texas Red Beds, USA
11. Santana Formations, Araripe Basin, north-east Brazil
12. La Paz Oligocene beds, Bolivia
13. Valley of the Moon, Ischigualasto Park, Argentina
14. Cerro Condor and Chubut, Argentina

MAJOR FOSSIL SITES – EUROPE, AFRICA

Collecting and displaying fossils as objects of beauty and intrigue – 'nature's sculptures' – gained popularity in Europe in the 1700s. So fossil-rich sites became well known even before people appreciated that these items were the remains of once-living things.

One of the first people known to make a living from fossil-hunting was a young woman, Mary Anning (1799–1847). Mary lived and worked in Lyme Regis, Dorset, South West England. Here, the coast is continually being eroded as waves eat into the cliffs. The region is sometimes referred to as the Jurassic Coast; many of its rocks were formed on the sea bed during this period, as countless marine creatures died and sank and were subsequently buried. The curly patterns of preserved ammonite shells are especially plentiful. Mary was one of those people who easily developed a 'good eye' for the best fossils, spotting tell-tale signs that enabled her to quickly distinguish fossilized creatures from ordinary rocks.

Fossil fame

Mary Anning spent her days on the Lyme Regis foreshore with her geological hammer and basket, gathering impressive specimens which were sold to private collectors and museums. She has a remarkable record of finds, including one of the first ichthyosaurs (dolphin-shaped sea reptiles) to be unearthed, in 1814; a virtually complete plesiosaur

Below: The 'Jurassic coast' of Dorset, UK.

(tubby-bodied, long-necked sea reptile) in 1824; and probably the first discovery in Britain of a flying 'pterodactyl' or pterosaur, in 1828. The shorelines near Lyme Regis still throng with fossil-hunters today.

Exquisite quality

Some of the world's most well known and valuable fossils come from the Solnhofen quarries of Bavaria, Germany. The limestone here is very fine-grained, known as 'lithographic' limestone since it was formerly quarried for use in printing. The seven or so preserved specimens of the first known bird, *Archaeopteryx*, were discovered in the area. So were the fossils of one of the smallest dinosaurs, *Compsognathus*. The amazing detail and quality of preservation allows study of their minutest features, including the feather structures of *Archaeopteryx*. These suggest that this bird, rather than being a clumsy glider, could truly fly – although probably not as aerobatically as most birds today.

The Karoo

Great Karoo Basin, centred around Victoria West in south-central South Africa, houses one of the largest and most important sets of fossil deposits in the world. Most of the rocks date

Above: After World War I, a team of scientists from the British Museum travelled to Tendaguru, Tanzania, to study and remove dinosaur fossils, including Brachiosaurus. *The main excavations had been done by German palaeontologists prior to this.*

from 270 to 230 million years ago – Permian to Early Triassic Periods. The rocks are divided into layers or series, which are (from oldest to youngest) the Dwyka, Ecca, Beaufort and Stormberg series. Long ago the climate was much damper than today. Ancient reptiles, in particular, roamed the luxuriant shrublands and swamps, and included mammal-like reptiles, pareiasaurs, titanosuchids and the smaller gorgonopsians.

Cradle of humankind

The vast continent of Africa is still relatively unexplored by fossil experts, but many palaeontologists accept that humans evolved here. Fossil remains of several kinds of prehistoric humans have been recorded. They range from smallish ape-like types who walked almost upright some five million years ago, to the first of our own kind, *Homo sapiens sapiens* or anatomically modern people, beginning around 150,000 years ago. Some experts recognize five or six main kinds of ancient human in Africa, while others contend there were twice as many.

Right: Map of Europe and Africa, showing some of the major fossil discovery sites.

1. Elgin, Scotland
2. Isle of Wight, England
3. Bernissart, Belgium
4. Neander Valley, Germany
5. Messel Quarries, Germany
6. Solnhofen, Bavaria, Germany
7. Beziers, France
8. Teruel, Spain
9. Tenere, Niger
10. Hadar, Ethiopia
11. Lake Turkana (Rudolf), Kenya
12. Olduvai Gorge, Tanzania
13. Tendaguru, Tanzania
14. Mafetang, Lesotho
15. Karoo Basin, South Africa

MAJOR FOSSIL SITES – ASIA, AUSTRALASIA

The tropical zones of the world, especially southern and South-east Asia, tend to be covered with lush vegetation and so have yielded few fossils. However, arid regions such as the Gobi and Australian deserts, with their exposed, eroded landscapes, are much more productive.

The vast arid stretches of Mongolia's Gobi Desert were first explored for fossils in the 1920s. Expeditions organized by the American Museum of Natural History visited the area, in the quest for the 'missing link' between apes and humans. One of the group's leaders was Roy Chapman Andrews, a larger-than-life taxidermist-turned-adventurer who always wore a ranger hat and carried a gun. The expedition sent back regular reports of exciting, perilous encounters with bandits and sandstorms – rather different from the usual staid world of palaeontology. Andrews is often identified, having been transplanted from palaeontology to archaeology, as the inspiration for the fictional movie hero Indiana Jones.

Remarkable finds
The Gobi rocks explored by the American expedition were far too old for human remains. Some dated to the Oligocene Epoch, 30–25 million years ago. Others were even more ancient, having formed in the late Cretaceous Period, some 70 million years ago, towards the end of the Age of Dinosaurs. However the expedition did

Below: Dinosaur egg fossil discovered in Mongolia – the first such egg to be found.

Above: Cambrian sponge fossil found in Archaeocyathid limestone, South Australia.

score some tremendous finds. One was the first known nest of dinosaur eggs, associated with the pig-sized, plant-eating horned dinosaur *Protoceratops*. One of the richest fossil sites in the Gobi became known as the Flaming Cliffs and continues to reveal major finds. Another exceptional find at Hsanda Gol was the remains of what is still the largest known mammal to have dwelt on land, *Paraceratherium* (formerly called *Indricotherium* and *Baluchitherium*). This vast Oligocene beast stood almost five metres tall at the shoulder and weighed 20 tonnes.

Scales and feathers
Some of the most astonishing fossil finds in recent years are from China's north-eastern province of Liaoning. Many are from the Early to Middle Cretaceous Period, 130 to 90 million years ago. They include some of the strangest dinosaurs ever found, and an incredible diversity of birds. Many of these creatures were covered in feathers, including some of the dinosaurs. The small predatory dinosaur *Microraptor gui* had feathers on all four limbs – the only known animal to exhibit such a feature. Exceptional preservation conditions in fine-grained rocks have helped to reveal the secrets of how and why feathers evolved.

More surprises
In addition, Liaoning has yielded fossils of mammals larger than any others dating from the Cretaceous Period. It was long believed that no mammal from the Mesozoic Era, the Age of Dinosaurs, was much larger than a rat. *Repenomamus gigantus* was dog-sized, resembled a small bear, and weighed in at about 15 kilograms, thereby overturning the accepted idea. Fossils of its cousin, the possum-sized *Repenomamus robustus*, reveal the remains of a small young dinosaur called a psittacosaur inside its body region – presumably its last supper.

Ediacara
In 1946–47 Australian geologist Reg Sprigg was surveying the Flinders Range of mountains in South Australia, seeking new deposits of the valuable metal ore, uranium. In the Ediacara Hills, Sprigg began to dig up strange fossils, the like of which had never been seen before. They dated back to Precambrian times, some 575–560 million years ago. They were soft-bodied life-forms, so unlike anything else in the fossil record, or alive today, that it's still not clear if some are plants or animals. Only a chance event meant they were buried rapidly and preserved swiftly, and then survived more than half a billion years to the present. These organisms, from a time before limbs or shells or fins, are now known by the general name of Vendian life. In contrast, the Riversleigh Quarries of Queensland have only been studied since the 1980s. They contain one of the world's densest concentrations of fossils, from the Late Tertiary Period, including kangaroos and marsupial predators resembling big cats.

Right: Map of Asia and Australasia, showing some of the major fossil discovery sites.

1. Hsanda Gol (Shand Gol), Mongolia
2. Nemegt Basin, Mongolia
3. Beipiao, Liaoning, China
4. Chaoyang, Liaoning, China
5. Umrer, India
6. Lufeng, China
7. Guangxi, China
8. Riversleigh Quarries, QLD, Australia
9. Muttaburra, QLD, Australia
10. Roma, QLD, Australia
11. Ediacara Hills, SA, Australia
12. Lightning Ridge, NSW, Australia
13. Dinosaur Cove, VIC, Australia
14. Mangahouanga, New Zealand

WHAT BECOMES A FOSSIL?

In theory, almost anything that was once alive could become a fossil – even a scrap of the jelly-like tissue from the soft body of a sea creature. In practice, most fossils are formed from hard parts of animals and plants, such as teeth, bones and shells, or tree bark and cones.

There are a number of popular misconceptions about what makes a fossil. Some people automatically think of dinosaurs, and ignore everything else. At the other end of the spectrum, the term 'fossil' once referred to any natural mineral object like a stone, rock or pebble. Today the accepted definition of a fossil involves an organic origin – an object that was once living. This includes all organisms or life-forms and parts thereof, from microbial organisms, tiny plants and

Above: The formidable killing claw of Dromaeosaurus albertensis was carried on the second toe of each foot.

Above: A Tyrannosaurus tooth dating from the Cretaceous Period, recovered near the Red Deer River, Alberta, Canada.

Above: In modern terminology, all 'fossils' have originated from once living matter.

Below: The scales, fins and tail of this fish, Notaeus laticaudatus, have been particularly well preserved in marl.

insects such as ants and gnats, to the greatest trees, sharks, dinosaurs, whales and mammoths.

Disappeared without trace
When most living things perish, they begin to rot and decay. Their remains may be decomposed by fungi and bacteria, and torn up, burrowed into or crunched to pieces by all manner of scavengers, from maggots to hyaenas. What is left weathers into fragments by the action of sun, rain, wind, ice and other elements of weather. In the water similar decay occurs, aided by waves and water currents, and the decomposing actions of fungi, worms, bacteria and others. So the vast majority of living things die and disappear without trace. They are recycled by natural processes back into the ground, lake or river bottom, or sea bed. They leave no fossils.

The harder, the better
Fossilization usually takes a long, long time, and is a chance-ridden process. As a result, usually only the harder parts of living things are preserved as fossils. These are the parts that resist decay, rot and scavenging, and which persist long enough for preservation to begin. Again, popular myth says that only bones form fossils, and perhaps teeth too. But there is a long list of other parts which are prime candidates for fossilization, as follows.

Plant parts
• The ribs or veins of plant leaves. (These are sometimes seen in winter, when the fleshy areas of the leaf have disintegrated to leave a 'skeleton' of harder, woodier veins.)
• The bark and wood of trees and other tall plants with trunk-like main stems.
• Roots, which are often among the hardest parts of a plant, and are usually underground, away from rotters and scavengers.
• Plant seeds, many of which are designed to resist harsh conditions such as winter, and then spring to life as they germinate when their surroundings improve.
• The woody cones of trees such as firs, pines and spruces.
• The thin, stiff, needle-like leaves of these various conifer trees.
• Pollen grains, which are tiny but tough, and resistant to most physical damage. Many are microscopic but

Above: The fossilized shells of bivalves.

Above: Unearthing the remains of a 40 million-year-old giant whale, now in the desert at the Wadi Hitan 'Whale Valley' reserve, 150km/ nearly 100 miles south-west of Cairo, Egypt.

they are produced in countless quantities, which improves the chances that some will be preserved.

Animal parts

• Shells or hard body cases, especially of molluscs such as snails and in the past, ammonoids and nautiloids. This includes the outer body casings or exoskeletons of insects, although these are usually only thick and resistant enough in certain examples, such as the hardened wing-cases, known as elytra, of beetles.

Spines
This very variable category of parts that might fossilize includes any long, narrow, sharp body projections. Spines occur on creatures as distantly related as sea urchins, spiny sharks (ancient fish), hedgehogs and porcupines. Often they fall from the main body after death and are preserved singly or in jumbled heaps.

Below: Whereas the spines of smaller creatures such as sea urchins may be relatively small, others – such as the ancient spiny shark Ctenacanthus *– boasted pretty sizeable protrusions. The specimen below is a preserved spine (or ray) from one of* Ctenacanthus's *enormous fins, and it measures some 19cm (7.6in) across.*

• Bones. Only the vertebrate or backboned animals possess true bones, which make up a skeleton. But then, not all vertebrates have bones – a shark's skeleton is made of cartilage or gristle, which is softer, bendier and more likely than bone to disintegrate.
• Scales, especially of fish and certain types of reptiles. In particular the large, hardened, bony scales, known as scutes, which covered certain dinosaurs, crocodiles, and fish such as sturgeons, are usually good candidates for fossilization.
• Teeth. These are possessed by most vertebrates, and certain other creatures like sea urchins also have tooth-like structures. For instance, in some snail-like molluscs the tongue is known as the radula and has hundreds of micro-teeth for scraping and rasping food. At the other end of the size range, the tusks of mammoths and other elephants were giant overgrown teeth.
• Horns. Usually these have a bony inner core covered with the hard, tough but light substance which itself is called horn (or keratin – see below). Various prehistoric mammals such as antelopes, cattle and rhinos had horns. There were also horned dinosaurs, or ceratopsians, such as *Triceratops*.
• Antlers, which are possessed chiefly by male deer and which are different from horns. They are formed of skin-covered bone and are shed each year to regrow the next, unlike horns, which are generally permanent and grow through life.

• Claws, nails and hooves, which are all formed from the same horny material as horns, known as keratin. Cats and birds of prey have sharp claws, the hoofed mammals or ungulates possess hoof-tipped toes, and most monkeys and apes have flattened nails similar to our own.

Above: The veins of a leaf Delesserites *from the Palaeocene Epoch.*

Below: Fossilized animal bones in a cave.

HOW FOSSILS FORM

Fossilization is a very variable process. It depends not only on the physical nature and chemical composition of the parts being preserved, but also on the nature of the sediments which bury them, water content, temperature, pressure, mineral availability and many other factors.

Fossils form in several ways. The 'normal' method is described here, and variations are included over the following pages, according to different habitats and conditions. The standard process occurs when a whole organism – or more often, parts of it – are buried. This usually happens in the sea, when a dead animal sinks to the bottom. It is covered by mud, silt or other small bits known as sedimentary particles. These are washed along by water currents or float down from above as the fine 'rain' of tiny fragments that settles continuously on the ocean floor. In general, the faster this initial burial, the better the state of preservation will be, since the animal or plant has less time subjected to decay, scavenging and disintegration.

Below: How a fossil forms, stage by stage.

Sediments and minerals

More sediments build up on top of the buried parts. This increases the thickness of the layers and the depth to which the parts are covered, and so increases the pressure on them. Gradually the pressure and squeezing begin to force together the particles, compressing the sediments harder and harder. Gradually, too, water seeps or percolates through these sediments, carrying with it natural minerals. These minerals slowly replace the organic substances or materials in the buried parts. The ongoing process of mineral replacement is known as permineralization.

Turned to stone

The original parts may be squashed, distorted and shattered during this phase, in which case the fossils are destroyed. In other cases the parts

Above: Soft-bodied, brittle-shelled creatures such as trilobites are often found fossilized in a squashed shape. These, of the genus Angelina, were recovered from the Late Cambrian Tremadoc Beds of Merioneths, Wales.

retain their original size and shape, and even their detailed inner organization, as their organic molecules and microstructures are replaced, one by one, by the inorganic minerals of rock. If the process continues to completion, then the original parts become completely

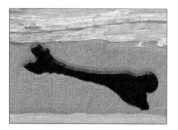

Stage 1: A hard part of a once-living thing, here symbolized by a single animal bone, resists weathering, scavenging and decay.

Stage 2: The part is washed into a river and sedimentary particles such as sand, mud or silt slowly settle and cover it.

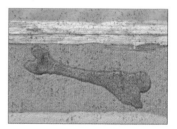

Stage 3: Over time, more sedimentary layers collect on top. The part and its layer are squashed by the increasing weight.

Stage 4: Minerals in the original part are dissolved and washed away, leaving an empty space or hollow chamber – a mould.

Stage 5: The space is filled by further minerals which trickle or percolate in from the surrounding rocks, forming a cast.

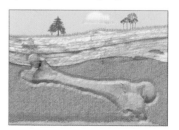

Stage 6: Earth movements, erosion and other processes gradually remove the upper layers, so that the fossil is eventually exposed.

Above: Rock strata are beautiful exposed in the iconic, partially eroded sedimentary landscape of western North America's canyons. The geology of these canyons is rich in the fossilized remnants of plant life and vertebrate animals.

inorganic or rocky. This is called petrification and is summarized in the handy but limited phrase 'bone to stone'. Meanwhile the rock around has been buried and compressed, and its grains and particles are cemented together by natural minerals too. As a result, the original parts of the plant or animal have become rock encased in rock.

Rocks that contain fossils
Because of the way fossils form, they are found only in certain types of rocks, known as the sedimentary group because they began as layers of sedimentary particles. Sedimentary rocks include sandstones, limestones, siltstones, mudstones and shales. In addition to sedimentary rocks, there are two other major groups of rocks: igneous and metamorphic. Igneous rocks form when original rocky material melts under great pressure and temperature and then cools again. Molten lava that flows from volcanoes hardens into igneous rock. The original rocky material may be sedimentary rock containing fossils, but melting in

the igneous phase destroys them. Likewise, metamorphic rocks form when original rocky material is transformed by tremendous pressure, heat and chemical changes, but without actually melting. Again, if the original material had fossils, these are usually destroyed during the metamorphosis. The practical result of all this means that it's no use looking for fossils in igneous rocks, like basalts, granites or rhyolites, or in metamorphic rocks, like marbles, schists or gneisses. Usually, only sedimentary rocks will do, as shown on geological maps.

Moulds and casts
On occasion, as sedimentary rock forms around a piece of an animal or plant, the percolating mineral-laden water dissolves the part and washes it away. The result is a hole, space or chamber in the rock, of the same size and shape as the original part. This is a 'negative imprint' or impression, which paleontologists often refer to as a mould fossil. At a later time, this space may itself be filled by more minerals seeping in from the water and rock around. Now the result is a cast fossil, again of the same size and shape as the original organism part, but composed of a different selection of minerals and crystals.

Tiny part of a tiny part
It should be emphasized that at any time, in any of these processes, pressure and temperature and general earth movements can warp, twist, fragment and destroy fossils. Only a tiny proportion of plants and animals begin the preservation process. Only a tiny proportion of these end up as still-recognizable fossils. And only a tiny proportion of these fossils actually see the light of day, when we find them – the rest lie deep and undisturbed.

Trace fossils
Fossils which are not preserved actual parts of an animal or plant, but objects or signs made by them, or left by them, are known as trace fossils. Examples are footprints, burrows, nests, feeding marks and tail-drags. Perhaps some of the most unlikely are coprolites – fossilized droppings, lumps of dung and similar animal excreta. In their original state, coprolites would be squishy and smelly. But the preservation process turns them into hard objects made of rocky minerals.

Below: Fossilized fish coprolites originating from the Triassic Period.

FOSSILS IN THE SEA

Seas have covered most of the Earth's surface for most of its history. Sediments may be washed from land into the sea, where they settle on the bottom. The result is that the majority of fossils are from sea creatures, plus a few marine plants too.

It may seem strange that fossils found on high ground, such as the Burgess Shales in the Rocky Mountains, or the Vendian creatures of Australia's Ediacara Hills, came originally from life at the bottom of the sea. The answer lies in 'dynamic Earth' and its geology. The hard outer shell or crust of our planet is never still. Some of its activities are sudden and awesome, like a volcanic eruption, or an earthquake that sets off landslides, or an underwater earthquake that triggers tsumanis (giant fast-moving waves). But many other activities are too slow for us to see. Huge jagged sections or plates of the Earth's crust slide and drift, push into each other, or grind under or over their neighbours. Where plates collide, the rocks fold and buckle to build mountains. The forces of erosion such as sun, wind, rain and ice counteract by wearing away rocks. These changes may occur at the rate of just a few millimetres each year. But they have continued over the vast span of geological time.

Ancient seas on dry land

As a result rocks are continually on the move, forming and drifting, distorting and twisting, and being worn away or destroyed by the forces of erosion. This is how sediments that were once on the sea bed may be uplifted into mountains, and then eroded to expose their fossils. The layers or strata of sedimentary rocks always form horizontally, with level surfaces as particles settle under the force of gravity. But later earth movements can ripple and fold these rock layers like

*Above: These 'chain coral' of the Silurian period (*Halysites *genus) are shaped like the links in a bicycle chain.*

Left: Parkinsonia ammonite recovered from Dorset, UK.

Below: A stunning example of fossiliferous limestone rich in the remains of ammonites.

paper, and even twist and turn them upside down. Usually the youngest or most recently formed sedimentary rocks are nearer the surface, so that as we excavate down to deeper strata, we 'dig back in time'. Inverted layers can confusingly reverse this sequence.

The most fossils

As previously described, conditions for fossilization are most likely in the seas, because of the way sedimentary rocks form. Also, compared to land, seas and oceans have always covered much more of our planet. (Today, the proportion is about 71% for seas and oceans.) Both these factors mean that the vast majority of fossils are from sea creatures – especially hard-shelled ones. Indeed, some sedimentary rocks are almost entirely composed of fossils. They began as piles of dead shelly sea organisms. The fossil remains may be recognizable items or fragments of the organisms, such as the shells of limpets and sea-snails. These rocks are sometimes known as fossiliferous limestones. There are three main types:
• Biohermal limestones – formed by living things growing in situ, such as the tiny stony cup-like skeletons of corals, or accumulations of creatures anchored to the sea bed, such as crinoids (sea-lilies) or mussels.

Above: Shells are usually smashed by wave action, but in sheltered bays they are often more likely to be buried intact.

Right: Very muddy seashores may discourage scavengers, which also boosts the chances of marine life being preserved.

• Biostromal limestones – mainly shells and other fragments of dead animals washed about and generally piled up, such as brachiopods, trilobites, oysters and other bivalve molluscs, and sea-snails like whelks.

Ediacara mudslide

The amazing fossils of Ediacara, South Australia, are from soft-bodied organisms, which usually rot away far too quickly for preservation. Scientists have concluded that this Precambrian community must have been surprised by a sudden mudslide, perhaps triggered by an earth tremor. Suffocating mud covered the area so fast, and there was no escape for its inhabitants. The blanket of mud kept away scavengers, and the low-oxygen conditions within it prevented the action of bacteria and other microbes which normally cause soft-tissue decomposition.

Below: The puzzling fossil Mawsonites *was one of those recovered from the Ediacara Hills, northern Flinders range.*

• Pelagic limestones – mainly tiny floating life-forms whose individual shells are often too small to make out. These die in their billions and sink to the sea bed, forming the greater proportion of ocean-floor ooze, which gradually hardens into sedimentary rock. As a result, pelagic fossiliferous limestones usually have a smoother, fine-grained appearance compared to the lumpy texture of the other types.

Bigger sea creatures

Most fossils are bits and pieces of organisms. Rarely a plant or animal is preserved whole, with its parts still together, in the positions they were in life. For a vertebrate animal like a fish, this is known as an articulated specimen. Stunning articulated fossils of fish show us their exact size and shape when alive. Sometimes even the

positions of their fins are visible. Even the remains of what they last ate may be preserved in the stomach and gut region. In general, the bigger the organism, the more likely it is to come apart during preservation. So complete articulated skeletons of sea reptiles like ichthyosaurs and plesiosaurs, perhaps metres in length, are truly exceptional finds. It's likely that the original animals died in calm waters and their carcasses settled quietly on the sea bed, to be covered quickly but gently by sediments.

Below: Whole specimens such as this spiny-finned fish Diplomystus dentatus, *recovered from Wyoming, USA, and dating to either the Palaeocene or Eocene Epochs, can tell us much about the habits of the creature. This lake species was a relative of the herrings, and its upturned mouth suggests that it fed on insects at the water's surface.*

FOSSILS IN SWAMPS

Swamps, marshes and bogs are good preservers. Their still waters are usually low in oxygen, which inhibits microscopic decay by organisms such as bacteria. Also, mud and quicksand are excellent traps for unwary animals, which are 'swallowed' whole by the mire, ripe for preservation.

At times in the Earth's history, more than half the world's land area was freshwater wetlands. Mosaics of swamps, marshes and bogs were interspersed with pools, creeks and islands of drier land, constantly changing their pattern and shape as water levels fluctuated with the seasons and passing centuries. Perhaps the best known time for such conditions was the Carboniferous Period, 355 to 295 million years ago. The climate was also much warmer then. Tropical floodplains were home to vast forests of lush vegetation, where huge insects dwelt, and giant amphibians lurked in the steamy dark pools.

Dominant plants

There were no broad-leaved trees in Carboniferous times, as there are in tropical jungles today. The dominant Carboniferous plants were huge clubmosses and horsetails. Both of these groups still survive, but now they are much smaller in size and numbers. The enormous Carboniferous clubmoss *Lepidodendron* grew to 40m/130ft – as

Above: Coal being mined in China. This rapidly industrializing nation depends on fossilized carboniferous plants for much of its energy.

tall as the typical modern rainforest tree. Fossils of *Lepidodendron* are common worldwide and often show the characteristic 'scaly' bark with its kite- or diamond-shaped old leaf attachments. One of the largest horsetails was *Calamites*, at 15 and sometimes 20m/50–65ft tall, also with a woody strengthened stem. Its fossils are found mainly in Europe and North America.

Above: One of numerous fern impressions recovered from the Late Carboniferous Coal Measures, Illinois, USA.

Below: The 'coal swamps' formed during the Carboniferous supported giant insects and early tetrapods (four-legged vertebrates).

Above: Swamps remain productive habitats today. Since Mesozoic times, alligators have been among their most dominant carnivores – as here, in the Cypress National Reserve, USA.

The coal forests

These vast green swamps of clubmosses, horsetails, ferns, seed-ferns, and the newer groups of coniferous trees and cycads, produced vast amounts of vegetative growth during the Carboniferous. As the plants lived and died, their remains toppled and sank into the shallow bogs and marshes. Decomposition was slow, since warm water is low in oxygen, and the organisms of decay soon used up what was left of the oxygen for their life processes. So the slow-rotting plant matter piled up thickly, and was compressed under the weight of more layers above. Today's results of these 'Carboniferous coal forests' are various forms of coal and similar fossils fuels. They took tens of millions of years to form. We mine them with eye-blinking speed. When we burn these fuels, we are actually releasing the Sun's light energy, which those plants trapped more than 300 million years ago.

Giants of the swamps

Lumps of coal sometimes split open to reveal patterns of leaves such as ferns and clubmosses, and occasionally, animal remains. These were from creatures trapped in the semi-rotting vegetation and turned to fossils. The Carboniferous swamps were home to the biggest flying insect ever, the dragonfly *Meganeura*, with a tip-to-tip wingspan of 70cm/28in. It was probably snapped up occasionally by a new and enlarging group of four-legged, land-dwelling 'amphibians' such as temnospondyls and anthracosaurs. The fossils of these are also numerous in some regions. A well-known temnospondyl was *Eryops* of North America. At 2m/7ft long, it was one of the early large predators, resembling a huge and fierce salamander. Also in the Carboniferous, the first reptiles appeared as small, slim creatures outwardly resembling modern lizards.

Very special fossils

In rare cases, the fleshy body parts or soft tissues of a living thing are preserved as carbon-film fossils. The organic molecules of the ex-living tissue decay very slowly in an unusual way, into a thin dark film of carbon-rich substances. The resulting fossils themselves may look like a smear of oil or a scrape of soot in the rock – and that is approximately what they are. Carbon-film preservation can show the outlines of whole soft-bodied creatures, and the shapes of tentacles, flaps and fins around harder fossilized parts of animals such as fish, amphibians and reptiles.

Below: A carbon film impression of a Redwood tree leaf (Sequoia), from the natural history archives of Humboldt State University, California, USA.

Slow decay

The same processes that occurred most abundantly during the Carboniferous Period have happened in other times and places, and continue today. The Jurassic Period, in the middle of the Mesozoic Era, also saw a warm, damp climate and luxuriant plant growth, which fed the enormous dinosaurs of the time. Their legacy is some of the largest single fossils ever produced – huge limb bones and vertebrae (backbones) bigger than a person.

After the mass extinction at the end of the Cretaceous Period, 65 million years ago, the first phase of the Tertiary Period – the Palaeocene Epoch – was another span of moist and temperate conditions. This may have been one factor in the burst of evolution which saw new kinds of mammals and tall, flightless, predatory birds rise to prominence on land, in place of the once-ruling dinosaur-like reptiles.

Left: A Lyrocephaliscus euri frog skull recovered from Spitsbergen, in the Arctic Circle – a land once part of the tropics and rich in swamp life and lush vegetation.

FOSSILS IN FRESHWATER

Rivers and lakes support a variety of freshwater and semiaquatic life, ranging from fish to snails, worms, amphibians and reptiles. Yet they are also magnets for thirsty land animals. Heavy rain and floods wash remains from the land into these bodies of water, making preservation more likely.

It's a quiet day in the prehistoric world. Creatures have come down the steep riverbank to drink, bathe and cool down in the placid waters. Suddenly the river surges – a flash flood from torrential rains upstream crashes around the bend and sweeps all before it. The fitter, more agile animals can leap up the steep bank to safety. The young, old, sick and infirm have no chance, and the rushing torrent soon carries away their struggling bodies. Hours later, when the main flood has eased, the carcasses lap onto a sandbank downstream. Scavengers gather and the rot sets. A few days later, another flash flood covers the partly bared bones with sandy sediments. The process of preservation begins – and we dig up the resulting fossils millions of years later.

The science of taphonomy

It's exciting to speculate how ancient animals and plants met their ends, especially when large groups of remains are all preserved together. This applies through all eras and periods of geological time. Land animals need to drink, and so pools and rivers have always acted as magnets for wildlife. How did a herd of prehistoric mammoths or a flock of ancient birds all end up in the same place, entombed together? The science of taphonomy delves into the gap between death and rediscovery. It examines the processes by which dead organisms become fossilized, and how the circumstances, surroundings and other chance events all contribute to the groups or assemblages of fossils which we eventually uncover.

Above: Stegoceras *dinosaur vertebra of the Pale Beds, Alberta, Canada.*

Below: Freshwater habitats have supported animal life for millions of years. In some freshwater habitats, the remains of creatures were preserved in the base rock beneath the substratum, or lake bed.

Above: An amalgamation of pond snail fossils (Paludina) preserved in rock.

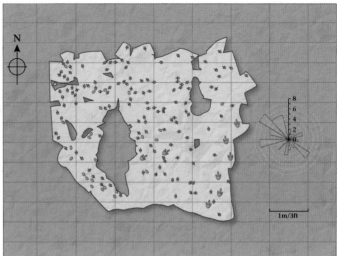

Prints on the bank

Footprints or paw tracks have created some of the most valuable trace fossils. They often occurred after animals had walked along riverbanks or lakesides, or across floodplains. The creatures made impressions with their feet, paws, hooves, claws, nails, tails and other parts, in the damp, soft clay, silt or mud. The indents were then dried and baked hard in the hot Sun. As the rains returned, another flood brought further sediments which filled the indentations, and so the fossilization process could begin. Many trackways of larger animals, such as dinosaurs, mammal-like reptiles and mammals, have been uncovered. In an area near Winton in Queensland, Australia, some 130 dinosaurs have left more than 3,200 prints in one rocky slab as they moved swiftly across the territory.

• The spacing of the prints (stride length) can suggest walking and running speeds.
• Print depth related to the firmness of the underlying sand or mud, and speed of movement, give valuable clues to body weight.
• Prints of many animals of the same kind and size, jumbled but all facing the same way, indicate a loose herd or family group on the move.
• Prints of the same kind but different sizes usually show a mixed-age group, with youngsters and adults.

The matrix

Close examination of fossils and the rocky material in which they are encased, called the matrix, reveals many clues. If the surrounding particles of sediments in the matrix are all aligned in a similar direction, and the fossils are a dense amalgamation of remains from just one kind of animal or plant, this may be due to flash flooding and powerful currents which swept away and drowned a herd or group. More jumbled and randomly oriented particles, with a mixed assemblage of fossils from various animals, could indicate a slower, more gradual process of accumulation.

Freshwater life

In lakes and rivers, fossils usually formed as described previously, when remains were covered by sediments. There are fossils of freshwater fish, amphibians such as frogs and salamanders, and aquatic insects like diving beetles and dragonfly nymphs. As usual, hard-shelled creatures are among the most numerous fossils, such as pond snails and freshwater mussels. Apart from the details of the animal remains themselves, plant fossils preserved with them can help to distinguish between the freshwater of inland sites and the saltwater habitat of seas and oceans. Preserved stems of

Above: Plotting footprints onto a map offers a clearer perspective of the movements of the animal, and points towards behaviour – perhaps that it is seeking food or trying to escape from a predator.

reeds and rushes, leaf 'skeletons', and hard seeds and cones all indicate freshwater origin. Flat, lobed blades or laminae, and grasping finger-like holdfasts, are distinguishing features of seaweeds.

Below: Fossilized footprints often tell us whether animals travelled in groups, such as this herd of sauropod dinosaurs.

FOSSILS ON LAND

Most terrestrial (land-living) animals and plants which have left fossils were actually preserved in water – usually along the banks of rivers and lakes, or on seashores. Windblown sand or similar particles can also act as sediment to bury organisms in arid habitats.

Examples abound of creatures such as dinosaurs or prehistoric mammals being caught in a flash flood, drowned and buried under sediments on the river bed or lake bottom. Fossilization on dry land, without the role of water in any form, is rare by comparison. However, preservation may take place if the conditions are right.

Mummification

In very dry conditions, an animal carcass or dead plant may lose all its natural moisture and body fluids quite quickly, before decay can progress far. The micro-organisms and chemical processes that cause decomposition rely on the presence of moisture. So, once dried out, the remains may not disintegrate any further, or at least, do so very slowly. Plant scientists and florists use this technique for pressing flowers or making dried versions. This severe drying out of organisms is known as mummification.

Mummification can happen in deserts and drought-ridden conditions, and also in very dry caves. It's usually necessary for the remains to have some kind of physical protection against

Above: The dry, windswept, slowly-eroded Gobi Desert is a rich source of fossils dating especially from the Late Cretaceous Period, such as these dinosaur eggs.

Above: The part-mummified flipper of a crabeater seal, preserved in the Dry Valleys of the Transantarctic Mountains, Antartica – a continent which is largely an 'ice desert'!

wind, large swings in temperature, scavengers, moist air carrying microbes, and other agents which would cause them to degrade. This may happen when a dead animal is covered by sand in a desert storm, or is lost in a deep cave or tunnel.

A prelude to fossilization

Mummified remains of animals which became extinct relatively recently, like moas, mammoths, giant sloths and cave bears, are well known. However,

these specimens would not survive the rigours of geological time without further preservation. Mummification is usually seen as a helpful prelude to proper fossilization, with its entombment by sediments and mineral replacement. In such cases the initial drying out can help to preserve soft tissues such as skin and other features that would normally be lost. The giant tyrannosaur known as 'Sue' was partly mummified before true fossilization took place. So were some of the

Left: The remnants of plants, trees and even animal carcasses may be subject to limited decomposition, or 'mummification', in very dry or barren conditions.

Below: Petrified wood from a coniferous forest of Arizona, USA, from the Triassic Period.

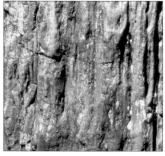

Above: Insect droppings preserved in Dominican amber, from the Late Miocene.

Trapped in tar

Here and there, natural deposits of tar or asphalt ooze to the surface and form pools. If these are covered by rain water, they may look just like waterholes, inviting animals to come and drink. But as soon as the thirsty creatures wade in, they become stuck and start to sink, gripped by the thick, gooey tar. Their struggles may attract predators, who try to approach – and they too are trapped. The animals sink and are preserved by the chemicals in the tar, often in great detail. One of the best-known sites for tar pit preservation is La Brea, in the suburbs of Los Angeles, USA. More than 600 species were preserved from 40,000 to 10,000 years ago, in a cluster of about 100 tar pits. They range from mammoths, mastodons, dire wolves, sabre-toothed cats, bison, giant sloths and short-faced bears to rabbits, rats, birds, lizards, insects and various plants.

Below: The Page Museum at La Brea holds an annual excavation of specimens, where visitors can observe professionals, and volunteers like the two people shown, recovering the bones of animals that drowned in the ancient tar pits here.

remains of dinosaurs such as *Protoceratops*, and their nests and eggs, which were preserved in the dry scrub of what is now the Gobi Desert, some 70 million years ago.

In the freezer

Another temporary mode of preservation is deep-freezing. Some of the best-known examples are mammoths, woolly rhinoceroses, giant deer and other large mammals trapped in the snow and ice of the far north – the tundra and permafrost across Northern Europe and Asia. Specimens are regularly exposed from the ice, especially by mining and exploration for gas, oil and mineral ore deposits across the vast wastes of Siberia. But as soon as the thaw sets in, so does decomposition. It's necessary to melt the remains very slowly and treat with chemical preservatives at once, in an ongoing process, to have any hope of stabilizing them over the long term.

Amber

This substance is the hardened, fossilized resin, gum or sap of ancient plants, especially conifer trees such as pines, firs and spruces. The trees make this resin partly as a form of sealant to cover any cracks, breaks, gashes or 'wounds' in their bark – just as our blood clots to seal a cut in the skin. Sometimes smaller creatures passing by, such as flies and other insects,

Above: 'Dima' the baby mammoth was found in permafrost on the banks of the Kolyma River, Siberia, in 1977. She was believed to be between 6–8 months old at the time of her death, some 40,000 years ago.

spiders, centipedes, even small frogs and lizards and mammals, become stuck in the adhesive, glutinous secretions. So do plant items like windblown pollen, seeds, petals and fragments of leaves or twigs. If the resin or sap continues to ooze fairly rapidly, it may cover and encase the specimen, preserving every tiny detail. Amber contains some of the most beautiful and spectacular of all fossils, giving valuable insight into the evolution of small and delicate creatures that are hardly ever preserved in the usual way. A few specimens of amber date as far back as the Early Cretaceous, but most are from the Tertiary Period. Famous deposits occur in the Dominican Republic, Caribbean and the Baltic region of Europe.

Below: Cold and frozen conditions drastically slow decay and allow time for preservation.

GREAT FOSSIL-HUNTERS

In 1770 Dutch chalk miners unearthed what looked like the huge skull, jaws and teeth of a weird and wonderful creature. It was nicknamed the 'Meuse monster', after the region in which it was discovered. The great find prompted a heated debate about the creature's origins, and captured the public's imagination.

Theories about the Meuse monster's origins prompted more and more speculation. Were there more 'Meuse monsters' still alive in the depths of the sea? Was the beast a victim of a biblical catastrophe? Was the find a fake, put there by pranksters – or even by the Almighty, in order to test people's religious faith?

Monsters and myths

The 'Meuse monster' fossil made headline news around Europe. All of a sudden, ordinary folk began to imagine an exciting long-gone world populated by huge beasts. The specimen was examined by Georges Cuvier (1769–1832), who acknowledged that its kind were probably long extinct, and who named it *Mosasaurus*. Cuvier was the most famous and respected biologist of the time. He began the work of studying, naming and classifying fossils according to the same principles used for living things – a novel and slightly heretical idea at the time. Cuvier was based at the Paris Museum of Natural History, which was then the biggest scientific organization of its kind in the world. His specimens included many fossil reptiles and mammals from the Tertiary rocks of the Paris Basin.

The country doctor

In the 1830s tales began to surface about more great beasts from long ago, which had left fossil remains such as teeth, jaws and bones. Gideon

Above: Dr Gideon Algernon Mantell was a country doctor as well as a palaeontologist. However, his greatest 'discovery', the teeth of the dinosaur Iguanodon *(see below), was probably made by his wife, Mary Ann.*

Mantell (1790–1852) was a doctor from Sussex, England. He consulted Cuvier about some teeth he had found, about 1820, which resembled the teeth of a living iguana lizard but which were much larger. Mantell was a keen collector of fossils, and travelled widely to examine and obtain specimens. He also had a home museum where he proudly displayed his best finds. In 1825 Mantell decided to call his new find *Iguanodon*, meaning 'iguana tooth'. He imagined it as a massive, sprawling, plant-eating lizard.

Above: Sir Richard Owen was responsible for the naming of the fossil group Dinosauria. He is pictured here holding the enormous leg bones of a moa, a flightless New Zealand bird that was ultimately hunted to extinction.

Fossils become fashion

In 1842, Richard Owen (1804–92) produced a report on fossils of great reptiles. Owen was an expert anatomist and would become Superintendent of the British Museum of Natural History – now the Natural History Museum, London. His report suggested that certain reptiles known from fossils should be included in a new group, the Dinosauria, 'terrible lizards'. Its members included Mantell's plant-eating *Iguanodon*, and also *Megalosaurus*. This was named in 1824 from a fossil jawbone with large sharp teeth, by William Buckland (1784–1856), Professor of Geology at Oxford University.

The general public became more interested in dinosaurs as giant fearsome beasts from long, long ago. Their fascination increased sharply when Owen joined forces with sculptor Waterhouse Hawkins to produce life-sized models of the great creatures.

Above: British doctor Gideon Algernon Mantell named one of the first dinosaurs, Iguanodon. *Mantell's fossils consisted only of teeth, and it was more than 50 years before complete skeletons were found in Belgium. The creature is now believed to have been a four-footed herbivore.*

Above: The French palaeontologist and anatomist Georges Cuvier did much to propagate the principles of functional comparative anatomy, and courted controversy by classifying fossils by criteria usually reserved for living things.

These were displayed in the gardens of the Crystal Palace exhibition centre in Sydenham, south-east London from about 1854. People travelled from all around to gather open-mouthed around the reconstructions. Dinosaurs hit the news and fossil-hunting became the latest fashionable pastime among gentlefolk of the period.

Below: The decision to mount life-sized dinosaur models at Crystal Palace, south-east London, was due in part to a surge of public interest in prehistoric creatures.

Fossils go west

During the mid-1800s 'fossil fever' spread to North America. In 1868, life-sized models of dinosaurs such as *Hadrosaurus* were displayed in New York's Central Park. By the 1870s Cope and Marsh (see Major Fossil Sites – The Americas) were racing to see who could recover the most fossils. In the wake of the hunt for dinosaur remains, many other kinds of fossils were also found, studied and named. Some of the greatest contributors to the breadth of information that resulted are as follows.

• **Richard Lydekker** (1849–1915) published a vast 10-volume catalogue of fossils at the British Museum of Natural History (now The Natural History Museum), in 1891. His book *A Manual of Palaeontology* (1889) was for many years the 'bible' of fossil collectors and restorers.

• **Barnum Brown** (1879–1968) was perhaps the greatest collector of fossils in the early 20th century. Working for the American Museum of Natural History, he led explorations to the Red Deer River region of Alberta, Canada from about 1910 to 1915, and further excavations at Howe Ranch, Wyoming in the 1930s. He is perhaps best remembered for finding the first *Tyrannosaurus rex* specimen in 1902.

• **Eugene Dubois** (1858–1940), a Dutch anatomist, shook the world when he

Above: Richard Lydekker's cataloguing of specimens for A Manual of Palaeontology, published in the late 19th century, created an inspirational resource for fossil-hunters seeking a means of identifying and categorizing their finds.

announced his discovery of 'missing link' fossils in Trinil, Java, in 1891. He named the remains as 'upright ape man' *Pithecanthropus erectus*. Today these fossils are included in the profile of the species *Homo erectus*.

The Sternbergs

As families of fossil enthusiasts go, there are few to match the Sternbergs of North America. They were father Charles H (1850–1943) and sons George, Charles M and Levi Sternberg. As well as actively collecting specimens, they assisted both the science and hobby by devising many on-site fossil-hunting techniques, such as encasing fragile specimens in protective jackets or casts, as well as ways of copying fossils using latex rubber.

Below: Charles Sternberg Senior reflects on some of his collected fossils. He was one of the USA's most pioneering palaeontologists and fossil-hunters.

GREAT FOSSIL-HUNTERS (CONTINUED)

If the previous centuries saw the rise of palaeontology as a charismatic science, modern times have certainly kept the pace. During the 20th century, some staggering new finds reshaped many assumptions about the prehistoric world, and also marked a greater involvement for the amateur fossil sleuth.

During the 20th century, fossil-hunting and collecting spread around the world as a popular pastime for many and a profitable profession for a few. Some dipped into it as a hobby, while others retained a lifelong interest. And some known for contributions in other fields have also held a fascination for fossils.

Little-known fossil sleuth

Marie Stopes (1880–1958) is best known as a pioneer and writer on sex education and women's health issues. From 1921 she established Britain's first family planning or 'birth control' clinics. But in her early career Marie studied plants and fossils. In 1905 she became the youngest DSc (Doctor of Science) in Britain, and first female science lecturer at Manchester University. Marie studied cycads and other ancient plants and showed how their remains could decompose and fossilize to form coal.

Lucky find

Rarely, amateur fossil-hunters strike it lucky. Most of these instances involve dinosaurs. In 1983 William Walker was searching a clay pit, as he often

Below: Dr Marie Stopes, palaeontologist and later – more famously – social reformer.

Right: William Walker's story is cheering to all amateur fossil collectors. His famous Baryonyx claw, discovered in 1983, provided important information about the spinosaurids, which were huge predatory dinosaurs. Walker unearthed his 'lucky find' in a clay pit when he was not actively looking for fossils. A reconstruction of Baryonyx appears below.

did. A plumber and part-time quarry worker, at a pit in Surrey he noticed a claw-like fossil – a gigantic one that measured more than 30cm/ 12in. Local experts informed London's Natural History Museum, and staff soon determined that plenty more remains were at the site. The result was *Baryonyx walkeri*, 'Walker's heavy claw', a meat-eating dinosaur some 10m/33ft long. *Baryonyx* was a different kind of carnivore from others known at the time, and so of tremendous scientific value.

Time and experience

Ten years after Walker's discovery, another part-time palaeontologist entered the spotlight. Car mechanic Ruben Carolini was a fossil enthusiast who spent much of his spare time out in the field. While visiting the 'Valley of the Dinosaurs' in Neuquen province, Argentina, Carolini spotted some exciting-looking bones and called in the experts, led by Rodolfo Coria from Carmen Funes Museum. The result – another great meat-eating dinosaur – was named *Giganotosaurus carolinii*, or 'Carolini's giant southern reptile'. It quickly became regarded as one of the biggest terrestrial carnivores – larger even than *Tyrannosaurus rex*. However, a 2006 review of already-known *Spinosaurus* fossils from Africa deduced that this spinosaurid was the world's all-time biggest land predator.

The top full-timers

At the other end of the scale to these chance finds by amateurs, are renowned professionals who regularly turn up breathtaking discoveries. Most work for museums, universities or similar institutions. They have teams of surveyors, diggers and other staff, and resources to plan, equip and finance excavations in great detail. Among the leading professionals of the past few decades are Paul Sereno (1957–) and Dong Zhiming (1937–). Sereno is attached to the University of Chicago and has made discoveries of immense importance in North America, South America and Africa. They included record-breaking dinosaurs such as *Eoraptor* and *Herrerasaurus*, which were among the earliest of the dinosaur group.

China's 'Mr Fossil-finder'

Chinese palaeontologist Dong Zhiming has led expeditions to many sites, including Yunnan Province and the Gobi Desert. He and his teams have unearthed, studied and named hundreds of new species, not only dinosaurs but mammals and other creatures. One of his prize finds was a quarry near Dashanpu, in Sichuan

Unsung heroes

Fossils of dinosaurs and other great beasts usually grab the limelight. But all kinds of fossils are important, and many palaeontologists have contributed enormously to our knowledge of the prehistoric world while remaining relatively unknown. Dorothy Hill (1907–97) was based in Queensland, Australia. She first studied Mesozoic rocks, but then began to analyze fossil corals from the Palaeozoic Era. Corals and their reefs are hugely important in dating remains, as index or indicator fossils (see Dating Fossils, later in this section). Her three-volume *International Treatise on Invertebrates* is still admired by palaeontologists worldwide. Dorothy Hill also became the first woman to be made a professor at an Australian university.

Below: Professor Dorothy Hill is credited with making scientific studies more accessible to women in Australia.

Above: Chicago-based palaeontologist Paul Sereno, who identified a new species of dinosaur from bones collected in India, displays a model of the assembled skull of the 67-million-year-old carnivorous predator at an exhibition in Bombay. Working with Indian students, Sereno pieced together bones collected over a 20-year period from the western and central regions of the country.

Below: Giganotosaurus carolinii has been regarded as the largest known carnivore to roam the earth – a plaudit since taken by Spinosaurus. Amateur collector Ruben Carolini discovered the fossilized bones of this mighty meat-eater in Patagonia, Argentina in 1993, and a subsequent excavation unearthed a skull that was larger than any existing Tyrannosaurus. The reconstructed skeleton of this theropod is about 70% complete. Parts of a larger specimen have since been found, and indicate it was 8–10% greater in size.

(Szechwan) Province. This 'dinosaur graveyard' and has yielded thousands of fossils. At the museum on the site visitors can see large areas of fossils still partly embedded in the rocks.

Apart from dinosaurs, finds of early human fossils, and their relatives and ancestors called hominids, often grab the public's imagination (see also Famous Fossils, later in this section). Louis Leakey (1903–1972) and wife Mary Leakey (1913–1996) did much to establish East Africa as a centre for hominid evolution. In 1964 Louis and associates proposed the name *Homo habilis* ('handy person') for remains found associated with simple stone tools at Olduvai Gorge, Tanzania, from 1960. Mary and her team came upon the famous Laetoli hominid footprints in Tanzania, in 1978. The prints are dated to 3.7 million years ago and show a hominid with a true bipedal gait.

WHO OWNS FOSSILS?

Rules and regulations covering fossil-hunting are often quite vague – and, in any case, vary greatly around the world. This is rarely of consequence if people hunt fossils for pleasure, for their own personal collections and displays, cause minimal damage on site, and make no monetary gain.

Occasionally, there are problems when an unexpected find turns out to be very valuable or scientifically important. For example, assume a marvellous fossil is discovered, which is potentially worth a small fortune. Who gets the recognition and/or the money? In most cases, the actual finder, whether professional or amateur fossil sleuth, receives the recognition. Photographs of the specimen in situ with the person who spotted it are invaluable evidence in this respect, to ensure that credit is given where due. But the actual ownership of the fossil, and any profit arising from it, could be claimed by several parties, singly or in combination. They include:

• The landowner. This may be a private individual, a national or state organization like a heritage trust, or a business or commercial outfit such as a mining company.
• The benefactor or financier who has put up the funds to support the dig and pay for equipment, expenses and other costs.

Below: Fossil experts who lead walks and digs can advise on safety and legality, as can the local museum or palaeontological society.

• The leader, organizer or site manager of the dig, who takes ultimately responsibility for decisions about which fossils are worth excavating.
• The organization or institution which has set up and probably funded the excavation, such as a university, museum or palaeontological society.
• A commercial company which buys and sells fossils, and which may not be involved in a direct or practical way, but which has 'bought the rights' to any or all specimens yielded by the field trip.

Famous fossil battle

For day-to-day finds, such a list may seem fanciful. But there were months of discussions over who owned, and so had the right sell at auction, the enormous *Tyrannosaurus* 'Sue', worth US $8 million. This incredible specimen, the largest and most complete *T. rex* fossil ever discovered, was found in 1990 by dedicated fossil hunter Sue Hendrickson. A volunteer with the Black Hills Institute of Geological Research, South Dakota, Hendrickson was one of a party digging for fossils on land owned by

Above: Although educational trips to fossil sites are generally encouraged, schools should be careful to seek permission and ensure pupils are properly supervised.

Sioux leader Maurice Williams. Peter Larson, president of the Black Hills Institute, bought the rights to excavate the tyrannosaur for a comparatively small sum, but the validity of this sale was later contested by the US Federal Government. While her ownership was under question, 'Sue' spent time in transit under conditions that many palaeontologists argued would have a detrimental effect upon her bones. She was eventually sold in New York by Sotheby's, for the famous seven-figure sum, in October 1997, seven years after her discovery.

Public access

Some fossil sites have open access and can be enjoyed by virtually anyone at any time. The main examples are coasts and shorelines. Specimens can usually be picked up and removed without problems. On areas of 'common land' it may be possible to pick up a loose specimen lying at the surface. But any use of hammers or other tools, to chip and release an embedded fossil, is not advised. It could be viewed as illegal damage to the site, and legal claims of trespass and criminal damage could be brought.

For almost anywhere else, it is wise to obtain written permission from the landowner (see Collector's Code and

Transporting Fossils). This may vary from a quarrying company or private estate owner to a highways authority or district council. The local palaeontology or geology society can help with this, or it may require a visit to the local council or Land Registry office. It is one of many reasons why novice fossil-collectors are urged to join a local club or society.

Many owners of fossil-rich sites have standard agreements ready to sign, date and exchange. Part of the agreement is to absolve the landowner from any risk, and make the fossil-hunter solely responsible for accidents and injuries. Fossil sites may well be steep and rocky, with loose stones – and claims for injury compensation are an all-too-familiar part of modern life, so do observe the general Countryside Code at all times when out and about.

Fossil-rustling

Taking a fossil from a site or collection without proper permission is, in effect, stealing. The recent explosion in prices paid for the best fossil specimens has meant that cases of 'fossil-rustling' have tripled in the past 20 years. One of the most infamous is the so-called Maxberg torso specimen of *Archaeopteryx*, one of only seven or so fossils of this earliest known bird. The only specimen to be held as part of a private collection (in Pappenheim, Germany), the Maxberg mysteriously disappeared following the death of its owner Eduard Opitsch in 1991. Despite police investigations it has not been found and is now believed to have been privately sold.

Below: Other Archaeopteryx *fossils form part of collections in Germany, and at The Natural History Museum, London (shown).*

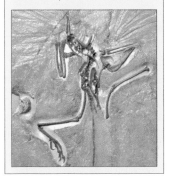

Special cases

Many valuable fossil sites, and other areas of natural beauty and special interest, have been made into national parks, wildlife refuges or heritage reserves. It is usually against the regulations to take any fossils or other items from these places. Some ill-informed amateurs may believe that a small fossil slipped into the pocket could not be traced. But an expert would soon analyze the specimen, its mineral make-up and matrix, and so pinpoint its place of origin.

Above: The gigantic Tyrannosaurus rex *fossil known as 'Sue' is now housed at the Chicago Field Museum, USA. The Museum famously won the bid for the bones, paying US $8.4m – the largest sum ever exchanged for a fossil, making 'Sue' a record breaker in every sense. 'Sue' is not a Jurassic specimen as many assume: rather, she is believed to have died at the end of the Cretaceous Period, possibly the victim of another tyrannosaur aggressor. Her discovery has greatly influenced the way in which palaeontologists perceive the movement and behaviour of these beasts. The fossils of 'Sue' were the subject of a protracted legal ownership battle between the landowner, the expedition sponsors, and the leading fossil-diggers.*

Countryside Code

In addition to various fossil-collecting codes, as detailed on the following pages, everyone is encouraged to observe the general rules of the Countryside Code when accessing rural land, whatever the reasons for doing so. In 2004, following new legislation concerning countryside access and the public's 'right to roam', the code for England and Wales was revised and updated. The rules focus on personal safety and the protection of the land.

- Be safe - plan ahead and follow any signs.
- Leave gates and property as you find them.
- Protect plants and animals, and take all litter away with you.
- Keep dogs under close control.
- Consider other people.

In addition:

- Beware of fire risks.
- Avoid damaging crops or disturbing animals.
- Respect the work of the countryside.

WHERE TO LOOK FOR FOSSILS

It sounds a little obvious, but the best place to look when starting to collect fossils is indeed a map. More precisely, several maps, especially geological maps showing rock types and ages, as well as guidebooks, and perhaps a visit to the local museum, fossil shop or antiquities centre.

The usual countryside map is a helpful starter, showing roads, towns, railways, parks, simple topography and similar features. This is useful for planning the trip and accessing the site. A geological map is also needed. This is available for purchase from specialist map suppliers, or perhaps for loan or hire from a local club or society. Geological maps show the general types and ages of rocks present or outcropping at the surface, as areas of lines and colours. Experts also employ satellite images and remote sensing to locate and survey new sites.

The right rocks

As described earlier, fossils are nearly always found in sedimentary rocks. So regions of igneous or metamorphic rocks are of little interest to fossil hunters. The age of sedimentary rocks is also important. If you have become

Below: The first geological map of Great Britain, drawn by William Smith (1769–1839). Many of his topographical studies were centred around the spa town of Bath in England, where he lived for much of his life.

Above: It is important to take great care when gathering fossils from locations that could present hazards to the collector, such as unstable cliff edges. As a precaution, safety helmets (hard hats) should always be worn.

interested in, say, fossil mammals, then it's little use targeting rocks from the Palaeozoic Era. Likewise if you are looking to build a collection of trilobites or ammonites, then Tertiary rocks are too recent and will not contain them.

Also, the names of rock and mineral types can be bewildering to anyone unfamiliar with them. So it's advisable to read the maps in conjunction with a good rock-and-mineral guide book or identifier. In addition, a general guide book for the locality should describe areas of public access, private land,

Fossil-collector's Quarry Code

- One individual or party leader should obtain prior permission to visit a quarry or mine.
- Visitors should be familiar with the current state of the quarry, and consult the manager for areas which have access or hazards.
- Arrival and departure must be reported to the quarry office on every visit.
- Safety hats are usually compulsory; stout boots are also essential.
- Visitors should keep away from vehicles and machinery.
- All blast signals and warning procedures must be understood.
- Quarry faces and rockpiles are highly dangerous and liable to collapse without warning – stay away.
- Beware of wet sand and lagoons of spoil or sludge.

(See also the general Collector's Code in this section.)

Right: Forbes Quarry was the site of Gibraltar's first Neanderthal human find, in 1848. Five sites for Neanderthal finds have now been identified on 'The Rock'.

Inland cliffs and bluffs

Outcrops of bare rock occur in many drier regions of scrub and desert. Hot days and cold nights alternate to expand and cool the rock, so that it cracks and flakes. Winds may pick up sand or dust and blast the exposed surfaces. Also the winds and occasional flash floods wash away particles to prevent soil formation that would cover the bare ground. So fresh fossils appear regularly at the surface.

River valleys

In some regions, rivers gradually cut their way downwards, exposing layers of rock as they go. Sometimes the layers or strata are clear enough to be 'read like a book', yielding different kinds of fossils from their various ages of formation. However eroded, rocky riverbanks can be steep and slippery, with difficult access.

nature reserves and national parks and similar. This helps to decide when permission may be needed.

Types of sites

In many places, surface rocks are covered up: by soil, trees, crops, roads, buildings, golf courses and many other features. Fossils are most easily identified where rocks are bare and preferably in a continual process of being freshly exposed. This can happen by natural processes such as weathering and erosion, or by a range of human activities. Such sites include:

Coasts and shores

Waves, winds, tides, undercut cliffs, rolling boulders and rockfalls mean that seashores and coastlines are some of the best of all fossil sites. A visit after a storm may reveal marvellous new exposures. However the very agents that erode the rocks can present great danger too. So extra care is needed, especially with an eye on the tides to ensure that you are not trapped or cut off.

Below: The cave of Jebel Qafzeh, Israel, has yielded the remains of several Homo sapiens *up to 100,000 years old.*

Quarries and mines

Some of the best fossil finds have come from mining and quarrying sites. Vast amounts of ores, minerals and rocks are worked, exposed and removed. However the site owners may have strict rules about fossil collecting, so that it does not interfere with the operation of what is an extremely expensive business (see panel).

Cuttings

Artificial 'valleys' cut for roads, railways, canals and even pipelines can present many fossil-hunting opportunities. However the land is owned by someone, and permission should be sought. The noise and activity of a busy road or railway line nearby not only presents hazards such as fast-moving vehicles, but can also be very tiring and distracting.

Caves

Fossil-hunting underground, in caves and tunnels, is a specialist activity that needs expert help. There are many dangers such as lack of light for working, seeping gases, and possible cave-ins or floods. Some professional excavations of caves have unearthed important ancient human remains.

PLANNING THE TRIP

Nearly every region has a geology or palaeontology society, natural history club, local museum and history group, rock-and-mineral association, or similar organization. Both careful consideration and expert advice will help to ensure that the trip does not become a wasted opportunity.

Regional and local groups undoubtedly offer enormous benefits to the keen but inexperienced fossil hunter. They can advise on planning and equipment, likely finds, and perhaps loan items of equipment such as tools and containers. There are also the benefits of shared experience and social interaction. A visit to the local museums also helps, to see the types of fossils found in the locality.

Another way of gaining experience is as a volunteer on an organized dig by a museum, university or similar institution. This can vary from a day or two at a local site, to a longer period in a more exotic location. Some holiday companies specialize in these types of breaks and vacations. It can be an invaluable experience to mix with the experts, and learn from their knowledge with 'on-the-job training'.

Equipment
Proper preparation and equipment make fossil-hunting infinitely more pleasurable and rewarding than when without these items. A collection of tools, bags and other kit can be built up over time. It need not be expensive

Below: The fossil collector's kit should contain items both for personal safety as well as for exposing specimens on site.

Above: With field gear safely tucked away in portable rucksacks, you are free to make and record observations about what you see.

– ordinary household items or do-it-yourself tools will often do, until the proper versions are affordable.

Clothing and safety
Warm, comfortable clothes, that fit loosely and do not chafe, are a must. People today are much less accustomed to spending all day outdoors, with the sun – or rain – beating down. Several layers of shirts and jumpers, plus a hooded waterproof jacket or coat, are ideal. So are stout shoes or boots.

Rocks are usually hard and sharp, so gloves are very important. A safety helmet or 'hard hat' is obligatory in some situations, and always helpful near tall rock faces. Sunglasses or a peaked cap help to shield the eyes from glare, especially from light-coloured shiny rocks. Goggles or a visor protect the eyes from flying shards of rock while hammering. And a mobile phone is an excellent aid in case of accident or injury.

Location and recording
Maps, local guide books, and fossil or mineral field identifiers are invaluable, usually in compact pocket form. A magnetic compass helps to locate the site in detail and orientate the finds, for example, the direction of fossilized footprints. A field notebook with pencil (and sharpener) or waterproof-ink pen is necessary for notes and sketched records. Modern lightweight cameras are a boon for 'point-and-shoot' photographs of fossils.

Safety hat

Safety goggles

Large magnifier

Geological hammer

Various sizes of chisel

Large paintbrush

Small fold-away magnifier

Felt marker pen — Tweezers — Camera — Map
Clear plastic bags — Notebook for recording finds —
Kitchen paper — Selection of writing tools — Compass

Above: The above items are essential for recording the details of finds both in situ and partly removed, and should be present on site.

Field tools

The main hand tools for fieldwork are:
• Geological hammer, with one blunt face and one pick-end.

Construction sites

As builders and construction companies dig footings and foundations, they may expose fossil-containing rocks. However, they may not always welcome fossil hunters. Having extra people on site can cause problems with safety, insurance and the use of machinery. Also a large, urgent construction project is unlikely to pause while a few fossils are recovered. However, it's always worth asking …

Below: An informal chat with construction staff on site may quickly reveal whether or not the type of items being uncovered are likely to be of interest.

• Guarded chisels, usually 'cold chisels' with hardened blades and plastic hand grips which protect against hammer blows to the hand. (Wood chisels are not suitable.)
• A mallet for use with the chisels, although the geological hammer may suffice.
• Trowels, large and small, for lifting and picking at loose items.
• Brushes, generally a small and large paintbrush, for sweeping away fine loose debris. Shaving brushes are excellent.
• Hand lens or magnifier, to study small details.
• Sieves, to separate actual specimens from loose sediments such as fine gravel, sand or silt. These can be lightweight plastic, of rigid or collapsible foldaway design.

Containers

A selection of plastic or canvas bags is ideal for carrying fossils. Newspaper, tissues or kitchen paper can be used to protect them in transit. Smaller specimens are safest packed into lightweight, rigid, plastic lidded containers such as sandwich boxes. See also equipment for plastering or jacketing fossils.

All of this, and more, is best carried in a sturdy backpack or knapsack. This leaves both hands free, is comfortable to wear rather than hold, especially when supporting packages of heavy fossils, and is easier to balance when walking in rough country with uneven terrain underfoot.

Photography and sketching

Some fossil-hunters take a few quick snaps of their finds in situ, but are later disappointed at the lack of clarity in the images. The undulating, random surfaces of rocks, and their often varied colours, mean that it can be difficult to make out shapes and objects. It is advised to take some photographs from directly above, and others from much lower viewpoints and from several angles, so that features can be identified by comparing these images. Shadows can be troublesome if they are from harsh flash or a low sun, but equally, lack of shadows when the sun is overhead also results in lack of definition.

Below: Many local museums display fossils excavated from the surrounding region. Staff are often willing to advise on the origins of particular specimens, which can help in the planning of a field trip to the local area.

DIGGING UP FOSSILS

Before setting out on a day's fossil-hunting, remember to tell someone reliable about where you are going and when you expect to return, supplying the relevant map references where possible. Also check the weather forecast, and revise the plan if it looks bad – digging really does require dry weather.

Think about personal necessities and sustenance before the trip – take food as necessary, and plenty of fluids. Being out in the sun and wind all day is thirsty work. On arrival at the site, carry out a quick survey and decide which areas look best for excavation, by a few short 'test digs' or blows with the hammer. Remains may already be 'eroding out' in some places. Look for shapes and textures that suggest fossils, like smooth curves of bone ends or regular lines and striations on shells, which distinguish them from the surrounding rock. See also the Collector's Code, later in this section.

Above: A pair of protective gloves, that still allow sufficient grip and manoeuvrability, is important when working in the field.

Above: This conifer wood bored by Teredo bivalve (shipworm) is an Eocene specimen from the Isle of Sheppey. It is a good example of a specimen likely to be tough to extract from rock without losing much of the detail.

Big to small

When digging for fossils, there are several basic guidelines.
• Go easy and take care. A too-hard hammer blow could shatter a prize specimen. If time is short or the weather turns foul, you may simply have to leave the fossil where it is, partly excavated. It will still be there tomorrow or the day after.
• Work from big to little, tough to delicate. Use the larger tools to remove unwanted rock, then work more sensitively and in greater detail as the specimen is exposed.

• Work with the rock rather than against it, using its natural splitting or bedding planes to your advantage.
• Remove a block containing the fossil, rather than the specimen itself. Leave detailed exposure and cleaning until later, back at the workroom, where it is more comfortable and proper equipment is at hand.
• Don't forget to wear safety equipment such as goggles and gloves.
• Record each stage of the excavation with a simple map, a few sketches or (if you have brought a camera) photographs, and plenty of notes. The latter should include map reference and the surrounding rock types.

Initial stages

Large quantities of material covering a fossil, known as the overburden, may be loose gravel, sediments or rockfall. It can be removed with a spade or perhaps a pick-axe. (Professionals sometimes use road-drills, jack-hammers, construction diggers or even explosives, but these are beyond most part-timers.) Then hammer and chisels can be employed. Keep an eye on the rock fragments as they are removed. If the fossil is well embedded in matrix, try to assess its overall size and position, and work around this, leaving plenty of room for error. Try a trial few blows on a rock of the same type which does not contain a fossil, to see how the rock reacts and splits or shatters. Do not chip or scratch the fossil itself, which could spoil its appearance and considerably reduce its scientific value.

Later stages

As the fossil is uncovered, switch to gentler methods. A small trowel or dental pick can lever out detached

Left: At a communal site, be careful not to stray onto a neighbouring patch, or damage delicate fossils with boots or piles of debris.

Shall I, shan't I ...?

Faced by a jumble of rocks and fossils at a new site, one of the most vexing questions for the novice fossil hunter is: Which specimen shall I choose? In other words, which ones will be worth the time and effort to excavate? Or even: Is it a fossil or just a weirdly shaped rock? For beginners, the answer is usually quite simple: Choose almost any one, since it will be valuable practice that brings precious hands-on experience.

Also consider: Would I wish to spend time cleaning up this specimen for my collection and perhaps display? It's wise to spend some time giving the whole site a brief survey, rather than stopping at the first attractive fossil. There might be a better-preserved, more complete version just a few metres away.

Below: Use of a geological hammer and chisel will preserve the fossilized specimen while separating it from the rock (and it would be safer wearing gloves).

Above: When uncovering larger fossils, an excavator carefully works around the specimen to remove 'overburden' and detach it from the surrounding matrix.

Left: Both a trowel and metal tray are useful items when sifting through sediment.

fragments. For very fragile fossils, a paintbrush, bradawl or dental-type pick may be suitable. It's best to chisel out a larger lump of rock around the fossil and lift out the whole item. Very fragile or crumbly specimens can be strengthened or stabilized as described later in the section.

Notes

Your notebook should contain plenty of jottings that record details such as locality, date, type of rock, position of fossil specimen, its size, notes on initial identification and other relevant information. All these details help to confirm formal identification later. A sketch can help to pinpoint an unusual feature, such as a spine or claw, that may not be easily visible on a photograph of the complete specimen.

Below: When labelling new specimens, for example by using corrective fluid and a ballpoint pen, be sure to mark the least important area, so that the fossil itself (like this small graptolite, to the right of the label) is not obscured.

COLLECTOR'S CODE AND FOSSILS

Each fossil presents a unique challenge for those tasked with removing it from the site and transporting it back to the workroom. Not least, some fossils are extremely heavy! As when digging up specimens, moving fossils could potentially disturb the local environment and should be conducted with great care.

Palaeontology and geology associations offer codes of behaviour when fossil-hunting. These are based on respect for the countryside and its inhabitants, as well as the need for caution and safety.

Field Collector's Code

1 Obey the Country Code and observe local byelaws. Remember to shut gates and leave no litter.
2 Always seek permission before entering onto private land.
3 Don't interfere with machinery.
4 Don't litter fields or roads with rock fragments that could injure animals or be a hazard to people or vehicles.
5 Avoid disturbing wildlife.
6 On coastal sections, check tides or local hazards such as unstable cliffs, if necessary with the Coastguard.
7 In mountains or remote areas, follow advice given to mountaineers and trekkers. In particular, inform someone of where you are going and when you are due back. Do not go alone.
8 Do not venture underground except with expert help.
9 Never take risks on cliffs or rock faces. Take care not to dislodge rock: others may be below.
10 Be considerate and do not leave hazards or dangers for those who come after you.

Above: A palaeontologist examining a six million year old fossil in Abu Dhabi. The hot and arid conditions, and the sheer size of the fossil, make this a very challenging excavation.

Great weight

Most fossils are solid rock. So they are heavy. A hand-sized specimen is already a considerable weight to carry, especially when trekking on foot. A dinosaur leg bone may weigh several tonnes. So it's vital to be realistic about what can be transported back from a collecting trip. Much depends on whether vehicles can get near to the dig site. If not, it is best to budget for two or three trips on foot, from the site back to the car or truck, carrying sets of specimens each time. Although

you may be tempted to try and save time, if you try to carry lots of heavy specimens in one journey, you risk breaking them – or yourself.

Fragile fossils

Sometimes fossils start to crack or crumble as they are being excavated. The first response is: Is it worth continuing? Is the specimen valuable

Below: Palaeontologists in Nigeria strengthen the weaker areas of a sauropod dinosaur bone before applying a hessian bandage.

Below: Further plaster is then applied to the bandaged specimen to complete the 'jacket' before the fossil is moved.

Below: Once the plaster has hardened the bone must be turned over so that the under surface can be fully encased within the 'jacket'.

Maps and grids

On larger sites, or when many fossils are preserved together, it's important to know their positions in relation to each other. This can help to reconstruct how the original organisms died and were preserved. Sometimes the site is covered by a grid of strings or wires, set at regular intervals such as one metre. Then the position and orientation of each fossil can be measured and plotted. This process continues with the excavation, so that the depth of specimens is also known in order to complete a three-dimensional location.

Below: This excavation of dinosaur bones in Nigeria illustrates how palaeontologists may be compelled to work within a tight, clearly-defined space, even when tackling the largest of creatures. The grid markers help the excavators to record the position of each part of the fossil.

Above: Excavation of a large dinosaur skeleton at Dinosaur Monument, Utah, Colorado, USA. As different sections of the specimen are uncovered, it is vital that the findings of each part are carefully recorded, to reconstruct accurately the creature's dimensions.

enough to warrant extra time and care? Perhaps there's another one nearby which is tougher and easier to remove. If not, then a weak or fragile specimen can be stabilized and protected in various ways, for example, by spray-on or brush-on adhesive or stabilizing compound, DIY spray-glue or purpose-made chemicals used by masonry restorers. This must be allowed to dry or set, so schedule time into the day to carry out other tasks during this period.

Jackets

Larger specimens that might crack or shatter can be protected and strengthened by jacketing. There are several common methods, usually involving plaster bandaging (plaster-of-Paris) or some type of glass-fibre resin or compound. One of the simplest ways is to use sheets of material or first aid bandages and ordinary plaster-of-Paris. An alternative is ready-made plaster-impregnated bandages as used to encase broken limbs, which simply need moistening. Wrap and smooth the jacket over the fossil and beyond, and allow plenty of time for it to set, before chipping the whole section free of the surroundings rock.

Wraps and containers

Each fossil should be put into a separate plastic bag – small transparent freezer-bags used for food are ideal. Tear off a piece of paper, write on the fossil's initial identification, as coded into your main notebook, and include this in the bag too. Smaller fossils can be put into rigid plastic boxes, but pad them to avoid rubbing and chipping. If there are no padding materials such as newspaper available, some dry vegetation like old leaves or grass stems will suffice.

Below: Uneven or largely-absent roads, and a shortage of road signs to indicate the direction of travel, are just two of the challenges that might confront a team of palaeontologists transporting fossils from remote locations.

CLEANING FOSSILS

Rarely, some fossils fall out of the rocks in almost perfect condition. All they need for display is buffing with a soft cloth, and a discreet label. But in most cases, specimens benefit from some judicious preparation and sympathetic cleaning.

Before rushing to clean and prepare a specimen, there are some questions to consider.

• Is it really worth a place in the displayed collection? What seemed like a fine example when you were removing it, out in the field some time ago, may not now seem quite so marvellous. It may have been eclipsed by specimens you found subsequently. On closer examination, it could have small flaws or chips. It might be very similar to a specimen you have already prepared or obtained. In these cases it might be worth saving for your general 'background' or reference collection, but without too much time spent on preparation since it will probably not go on display.

• How much should it be cleaned? Leaving some surrounding rock or matrix in place may add artistic merit and 'character' to a fossil. Take some time to look at real specimens in

Above: Some kind of magnification tool may be required in order to work out where the fossil ends and the matrix begins.

museums and exhibitions, and of photographs of specimens in books and on websites. See how sometimes only a portion has been exposed and cleaned up. The result can be more dramatic, as the fossil 'appears' mysteriously from its background, while at the same time providing enough scientific information for firm identification.

The work space

For cleaning and preparation, you need a clear working space with a hard non-slippery surface, such as wood, which does not matter if it chips or dents. Beware of fragments of rock flying away from the specimen as you work. Some preparators arrange series of long, low, upright panels around the work surface, like fencing, to stop this from happening.

Below: Items such as safety goggles and a face mask are a useful safeguard against dust thrown up when cleaning specimens. Before beginning to clean, wash your work space with a clean cloth or sponge, and keep a pair of protective gloves on hand, particularly if handling chemicals such as dilute acid.

Always do a 'test run'

Whichever technique you use to clean a fossil, try it first on an unwanted fragment of rock, or on one of the less important specimens, or on a less important surface of the main specimen which will not be visible on display. If things go wrong, you have not lost your most prized example. Or at least, the problem will be 'round the back' when the item is displayed.

Below: Dilute acid is carefully applied to a disposable area to see if the specimen contains certain reactive minerals, some of which may help to dissolve the matrix.

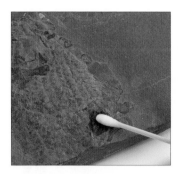

Above: For specimens without much adherent matrix, simple household items such as cotton buds (swabs) or small brushes can be useful when cleaning specimens. These can also be used to remove small patches of sediment once more rigorous methods have been tried.

Above: Similarly, a soft paintbrush can push away friable matrix in small amounts if used delicately – caution when applying strokes to the surface of the specimen is the main thing to remember. The brush can be washed and dried regularly to prevent clogging.

Above: A miniature sandblaster, powered by compressed air, helps to remove loose sediment without damaging the specimen.

Above: A vibrating pen, or 'vibrotool', is powered in a similar fashion, and can help to define the shape of a specimen.

Plenty of light from a couple of desk lamps, one on either side to minimize shadows, is important. Try not to place the light sources on the opposite side of the specimen from yourself, otherwise the areas you are working on will be shaded. Goggles for eye protection against flying shards are also strongly advised.

Experts usually clean smaller fossils while looking through a magnifier lens on a stand, or through a binocular (two-eye) microscope. This helps to protect your eyes and prevent eye strain as well as giving a closer view.

A fishing-tackle box or toolkit case, with small drawers and compartments, makes a good container for tools and equipment. Similar many-compartment cases intended for items such as screws and bolts, available from do-it-yourself

and hardware outlets, are very handy to store your specimens while they are being prepared.

It helps if you have a room or corner to leave this equipment laid out in place, rather than having to set it all out and then pack it away again after each session. If tools and specimens can be left out, covering them with a cloth or sheet will prevent dust gathering, which tends to dull the colour of fossils and obscure detail.

Cleaning with chemicals

Often a fossil is different in mineral composition from the matrix around it. If the fossil is much harder, it may be possible to brush away soft matrix, perhaps after softening or soaking it with water. You could test-soak unwanted pieces in water or perhaps

a dilute solution of vinegar, which may soften or dissolve calcium-rich matrix while leaving the fossil untouched. Fossils from the seashore may be soaked for a few hours in a watery, weak solution of bleach. This helps to remove the salt. Again, try these techniques on an unwanted piece first.

Another chemical method is acid etching. Kits of acid-etch equipment and solutions can be purchased from specialist fossil suppliers. This is a fairly complex, time-consuming technique and involves handling potentially harmful chemicals. Good ventilation is essential, and other safety precautions are also necessary. Sometimes local palaeontology club members band together to research, purchase and set up such equipment, so that it can be used during carefully monitored communal sessions.

Physical methods

When removing rock and matrix by physical means, it is advised to study the hidden shape and contours of the fossil, and where the matrix probably ends and the specimen begins. This can be done by consulting guide books and fossil identifiers. When chipping carefully with a lightweight hammer and narrow chisel, making sure the specimen is well supported so it cannot fly away or slide off the worktop. More delicate tools include awls, bradawls, dental picks and mounted needles for removing smaller and smaller particles. Even general household items such as cotton buds (swabs) and paintbrushes can be used.

Power tools

Powered engravers, drills or sanders can save much time. Dental drills and modelling power tools often have tiny circular-saw blades and fine file-like abraders for gradually and carefully removing adherent matrix. With all these methods, pause now and again to clear the dust. Take a wider view, from several angles, to check progress of the work. Power tools throw up a lot of dust and debris, so wear a face mask to filter the air, as well as the usual protective goggles.

IDENTIFYING AND STORING FOSSILS

After spending hours out in the field collecting fossils, and in the workroom cleaning them – what next?
Most collectors like to make a display to show off their prize specimens. But there is some forethought
and preparation to do first, such as setting the fossils in context.

Fossils can be admired for their simple shapes, colours and beauty. But this is like admiring a painting without the insight and knowledge of the painter, which period it dates from, the circumstances of the subject or scene, and how the work fits into the history of art. Likewise, identifying fossils and finding out which organisms left them – when and how and where – adds vastly to the interest and pleasure of owning and displaying them.

Identification

There are many ways to pin down the identity of a fossil. For some people a simple label such as 'ammonite' may suffice. But there are thousands of kinds of ammonites known from fossils, so it's worth delving more

Below: Identification guides, augmented by further information gleaned from the internet or museum displays, can help to pinpoint the origins of a fossil.

Above: Record as much information as possible about a specimen, though do keep to a consistent and acceptable labelling system for ease of reference.

Above: In addition to actually labelling the specimens, it is important to record corresponding information about your collection in a log book.

deeply into the science of taxonomy and the system of classifying living things. The traditional system starts with large groups, phyla, which are subdivided in turn into classes, orders, families, genera and species, as will be explained later. A name at the hierarchy level of family or genus is

usually sufficient for most amateur collectors, depending on the specimen's state of preservation and rarity. Identification is carried out by noting specific features, characteristics or traits in the specimen, as listed in classification keys, as well as by overall visual appearance, coupled with the age of the rocks and their general nature, such as sandstone or limestone, which indicates the original habitat of the organism.

Helpful aids to identification

• Pictures and notes in the later pages in this book.
• Similar pictures and lists of key features, in fossil guides and identification books.

Below: Specimens become dusty and details obscured if kept in open displays, so choose a suitable container for them.

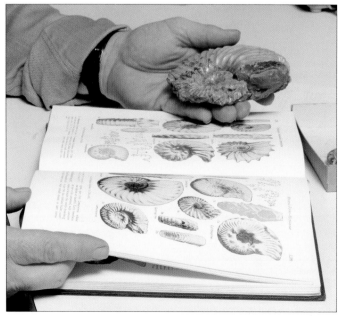

Left: Parts or fragments of one fossil item may be assembled like a jigsaw puzzle into the more complete version, simply by trial-and-error fitting.

• The same material from internet sites, which are a fast-growing resource for palaeontologists.
• Expert help and advice from knowledgeable people.
• Similar specimens in other collections, such as in museums or palaeontology societies.

Storage

Fossils that are not for display are best stored in rigid containers such as sets of drawers or compartments, which are dry and dark. Moisture and bright light can degrade several kinds of minerals. Purpose-made cupboards or chests of drawers, often with the classic shallow trays as used in museums, can be picked up at auctions, sales or house clearances. Or sets of wooden or plastic storage cases can be pressed into use. Open shelves are less useful, since dust accumulates and gradually dulls and obscures a fossil's detailed surface features. Remember that fossils are stone, and so heavy. Any storage system should be able to cope with the weight. The drawers, compartments or boxes should be clearly labelled with their contents, and arranged in some sort of logical order, for example, by time period or major groups of living things.

Below: Soft padding protects the fossils from scratches or cracks if the container is jolted. Do, however, avoid cotton wool or similar materials where fibres are likely to dislodge and cling to the specimen.

Labels, notes and indexing

Each fossil in a collection should be given a brief identification name and a unique code or log number. This keys into an index for the collection, which can be kept as cards in a box, in a loose-leaf folder or on computer disc. Information from the field notebook is transcribed onto a list for each specimen, along the lines of:
• Unique code, index or log number.
• Name, for example, to family, genus or even species level.
• Approximate date of preservation, from a period or era of geological time such as Carboniferous or Eocene, to much narrower or shorter units such

as ages or zones of time. This is linked to the type of rock in which the fossil was preserved, known as the lithological unit.
• Location and date of find, with map reference if possible.
• Nature of the matrix and features of surrounding rock.
• Special notes about the site, methods used for extraction or cleaning, glues and preservatives, and similar data.
• General information such as notes on palaeo-ecology (see next page), behaviour or lifestyle: 'active carnivore in shallow Silurian seas' or similar.
• To tie the fossil to its information, include a short label in its storage compartment. Or write the index code in indelible ink on an unimportant part of the fossil. Take fossils from their storage places one at a time, to avoid mixing and misplacing.

Below: Accessible museum displays may provide clues as to the identify of your fossils. Staff may allow you to handle them (always check), or the displays may be interactive, with information given at the touch of a button.

DISPLAYING FOSSILS

One of the greatest satisfactions of fossil-hunting is to build up a well-presented and informative display of the best specimens, so that other people can appreciate and understand these fascinating objects. This can be done by following a few very simple, practical tips.

Fossil displays can be a permanent installation, or 'collapsible' and brought out for special occasions. It's well worth putting some thought into what you would like to convey in showing a range of specimens together – the most interesting displays usually have some sort of linking theme or topic, for example:

• Varied fossils from the same locality at different times, illustrating the range of life which has populated the area through the ages.

• Fossils of the same geological age and site, revealing the variety of plants and creatures that lived together in the same place. This can allow reconstruction of a whole habitat and how the animals and plants lived together and interacted, an area of science known as palaeo-ecology.

• A group of organisms or similar fossils through time, such as sea-snails, petrified bark or fish teeth. These can be compared and contrasted to see how they evolved.

Below: Include notes on possible origins wherever you can. For example, it might be conjectured that the death of an entire shoal of fish (the species Gosiutichthys parvus, *shown below) was caused by poisonous gas in the water.*

A practical display

Almost any size of display can be made attractive and informative, from a shoebox to a huge wall cabinet or stand-alone glass case. Ensure the case or container is presentable, perhaps with a coat of paint or paper lining that contrasts with the samples. Choose only the best specimens available – do not 'dilute' them with poorly preserved or broken examples. As your collection builds, you can transplant new and better finds to replace older, less impressive ones. Position and support each specimen at its best angle to show off the most informative side or face.

Above: It makes sense to display fossils together which have similar origins. Notable differences between the members of a group may indicate stages in growth or evolution. Clockwise from top-left: seeds of the Carboniferous plant Trigonocarpus; *four echinoid, or sea urchin, specimens; the teeth of the huge shark* Carcharodon megalodon.

You may need to trim off unwanted edges to make a pleasing shape and set the fossil to its best advantage. Include neatly printed labels or cards, both for individual specimens and groups of them. Or label a diagram or photograph of the collection as a key.

Selection

If you have a container or case for a collection, try various options of fossils before deciding on the final selection. Move them about and group them in different ways, to show similarities or contrasts. It's not unlike trying furniture in different places in a room, before deciding on the best layout.

*Left: The cut of the matrix around this attractive Late Cretaceous fossil (*Ctenothrissa radians*) is perfectly suited to an eyecatching stand-alone display.*

Sections and infills

Sometimes the broken surface of a fossil can be used to advantage. It may be sawn or cut off flat and then sanded and polished to reveal the inner structure of the specimen. This may be very beautiful, with colourful swirls or patterns of mineral crystals adding to the effect. Another option is to 'fill in' the missing part, to make the specimen whole again. This is usually done with some type of plaster or resin, but in a colour that contrasts with the actual fossil. The size, shape and contours of the infill can be gleaned from pictures of whole specimens. Attempts to blend the infill portion so that it looks like the rest of the fossil need great skill, and usually end up detracting from the overall effect. A faintly tinted clear plastic resin is another option for infills. It is usually better, more honest, and also scientifically acceptable, to make the infill very obvious.

Varnish or not?

Some collectors like to varnish their specimens. This may help to seal and stabilize the minerals. It may also deepen hues and bring out textures and colours. However over the long term, certain varnishes can degrade the minerals of the fossils. Also a shiny varnish means light glints and reflects off the surface, which can be irritating and obscure detail. However, some fossils are made by a process called pyritization. The original material of the organism is replaced by mineral iron pyrites. In moist air this is unstable and gradually disintegrates. Such fossils are best dried thoroughly and varnished to seal them from moisture in the air.

Below: Following expert guidance, museum staff may decide to add certain finishing touches to enhance or protect the surface of the reconstructed skeleton.

Above: Casts made of glass reinforced plastic are laid out prior to the mounting of the dinosaur Baryonyx *on exhibition panelling.*

Preserving

Sometimes a broken fossil can be mended with clear glue. As already advised, try the glue on an unwanted piece or surface first, to check it adheres and does not discolour. Fossils that are weak or crumbly can be stabilized with chemicals called consolidants, hardeners or protective resins, specially made for the purpose. Again, try them on unimportant areas first, in case they cause discoloration or a chemical reaction which may degrade the minerals.

Below: The tail of this Diplodocus *replica at the Natural History Museum, London, was temporarily replaced with a cardboard one while the original was being reconstructed.*

RECONSTRUCTING FROM FOSSILS

For certain people, finely preserved and well-displayed fossils, with a wealth of information about their origins, is not quite the end of the process. Some collectors like to take the next step, of trying to reconstruct or 'rebuild' an extinct plant or creature as it would appear in life.

Lifelike reconstructions range from sketches on paper, to illustrations 'borrowed' from books or websites for display, to simple scale models or even complex and detailed full-sized renderings. Most of the fossils in the later pages of this book have illustrations showing the appearance of the living plant or animal, as it looked millions of years ago. How do we know it is accurate?

Above: This atmospheric diorama combines life-sized model dinosaurs with: their habitat; the fossil skeletons used as the basis of the reconstructions; and an informative text panel with illustrations.

Below: Artists' reconstructions of prehistoric creatures, such as Pteranodon shown here, may show them feeding, fighting, breeding or in the company of similar species. Concurrent flora and fauna should also be depicted.

Above: Examining the surface of fossilized body parts, such as limbs, for scars and indentations made by muscle and other body tissues helps with reconstruction. Both of the above specimens originate from dinosaurs of the Cretaceous. Top is a toe bone of the plant-eating Maiasaura. Below it is a hoof bone of the big-horned Styracosaurus albertensis.

Composites

As we have seen, many fossils are just pieces or fragments of whole living things. Not only this – the parts can be squashed and twisted out of shape. One way around the problem is to assemble a composite version, using pieces from another specimen identified as the same species. There are many limitations on this method of 'borrowing' from some fossils to fill in missing sections of others. But the composite can help to give an general view of shape, size and features.

What colour were they in real life?

This question often plagues those making reconstructions of fossilized animals and plants. The short answer is – no one knows. A glance through a selection of fossil books will probably show the same famous creature, such as the earliest known bird *Archaeopteryx*, in a startling variety of plumages. Fossils are not original copies of the once-living matter. They are mineral replacement versions made of rock or stone. So they are the colour and pattern of their constituent minerals. Was a long-extinct fish or shellfish dull green or brown for camouflage, or brightly striped with pink and yellow to advertize its venomous sting or bite? Take your pick. When scientists, artists and modelmakers reconstruct extinct organisms, they have to make intelligent guesses as to the patterns and hues visible on the outside. Their informed guesswork is often based on the features exhibited by similar organisms, or living relatives.

Above: A safe option is to reconstruct an image of Archaeopteryx using little colouring, or even in black and white.

Above: A more adventurous rendering paints Archaeopteryx in slate-blue shades. But even this might be a conservative treatment.

Comparisons

There are also comparisons with living organisms. The science of comparative anatomy has a long and honourable tradition in palaeontology. For example, molluscs such as ammonoids no longer exist. But their modern cousins do, including the cephalopod mollusc group such as octopus, squid and especially the deep-sea, curly-shelled nautilus. Comparisons of ammonoid fossils with the equivalent parts of these living relatives helps to reconstruct the ammonoid's soft parts. Similar principles are used for all manner of ancient life, from simple plants to sharks, reptiles and whales.

A note of caution involves the process called convergent evolution. Organisms of different kinds come to resemble each other, generally or in specific features, since they are adapted to the same mode of life. A simple example involves the body shapes of certain fish like sharks, the extinct swimming reptiles known as ichthyosaurs, and modern dolphins. They have all evolved a similar streamlined body shape, with fins and tail, as a result of adaptation to speedy swimming, rather than because of any shared ancestry.

Flesh on bones

Some animals and plants are defined in size, shape and external appearance by their strong outer casing, such as a tree's bark or a trilobite's shell. This helps greatly to recreate their appearance in life. However most vertebrate animals – those with backbones – have an inner skeleton which may fossilize, covered with muscles and other soft tissues which hardly ever do. How are these fibres reconstructed by scientists?

Soft tissues can be built up stage by stage. Many fossil bones show roughened areas on their surfaces called muscle scars. These are patches where muscles were attached to the bones, and they may have flanges, ridges or crests on the bone to secure their fixings. Often they correspond to the muscle anchorage sites in modern relatives of the creature. The size and extent of a muscle scar indicates the size and power of the muscle which anchored there. So a fossil skeleton can be partly clothed in muscles. In turn, the musculature often defines the shape and contours of the whole animal, since muscles are generally clothed only by skin.

Right: A museum reconstruction of a chalk sea floor of the Cretaceous Period.

Below: A fossil of a sea floor at Kings Canyon, Northern Territory, Australia. The ripples in the rock were created by water movement.

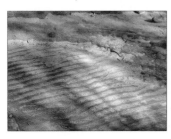

DATING FOSSILS

How old is a fossil? There are two main methods of dating or aging either the rocks themselves or their preserved remains, as used by geologists and palaeontologists. These are comparative or relative dating, and absolute or chronometric dating.

Palaeontologists often use comparative or relative dating, which deduces the age of a fossil by comparing it to the rock around it, especially the other fossils contained within this rock, and to the rocks and fossils in the layers above and below it. Because of the way sedimentary rocks form, the younger layers or strata usually overlie the older ones. So deeper fossil are older. Also the same sequence or series of sedimentary layers often crops up at many sites, with the same sequence of fossils within it. These sequences have been correlated and matched or combined to give an overall progression of rock types and fossils through the ages all around the world. This is known as general stratigraphic history. If a fossil comes from an isolated layer of rock, the features of this layer can be used to place it into the overall progression or stratigraphic history, and so the age is revealed.

Index fossils
Some types of organisms are very widespread as fossils, and they have also changed in a characteristic and

recognizable way through time. These evolutionary sequences are very useful for dating. The well-known fossils in them are known as index, marker or dating fossils. They help to pinpoint the time origin of more obscure fossils found with them. Common examples of index fossils include shelled marine animals, which formed plentiful remains in marine sediments and are often worldwide in distribution. (All are included on later pages in this book.) For instance:
• Trilobites are useful for dating Cambrian rocks.
• Graptolites are common and widespread index fossils for the Ordovician and Silurian Periods.
• Belemnites and ammonites show characteristic evolutionary sequences through the Jurassic and Cretaceous Periods.
• Foraminiferans, which are tiny and simple shelled organisms of the plankton, are used through the Tertiary Period.

Left: Successively aging rock strata are clearly visible in the steep walls of a canyon.

Above: A member of an excavation team from The Natural History Museum, London, uses a device known as a compass-clinometer. This measures the incline, or 'dip', of the bedding plane – the boundary separating one layer of rock from the layer above or below – at various magnetic compass orientations. Assessing the nature, formation and subsequent movement of each rock stratum will help the team to assess, from the position of the now-exposed fossil, its approximate age.

Absolute dating
Also known as chronometric dating, this method is based principally on the physical process called radioactive decay. Some minerals of the Earth's crust contain pure chemical elements that are radioactive (usually in a very minor, harmless way). Through time after their formation, these elements give off radiation energy (radioactivity), at a regular and constant rate. As they do so, they change from one form or isotope of a chemical element into another, or even from one element into another. Scientists can measure the relative proportions of different isotopes or elements in certain rocks, to deduce when the mineral formed.

Each isotope or element series has its own fixed rate of decay. Carbon is relatively fast, and is used in 'radio-carbon dating' for specimens up to about 70,000 years ago. Uranium decays very slowly and can date the oldest rocks, from billions of years ago. Potassium-argon decay is also widespread and commonly used for times spans greater than 100,000 years ago, mainly where there has been local volcanic activity and the rocks are rich in potassium. However, measuring radioactive decay involves complex and expensive scientific equipment such as mass spectrometers, which are beyond the finances of most amateurs!

In practice, absolute dating pinpoints the actual age in numbers of years, for a limited number of suitable rocks. There is usually a margin of error given. For example, rocks from the Cretaceous-Tertiary (Palaeogene) transition may be dated to 65.3 million years ago ± (+/- or plus-or-minus) 0.4 million years. The results from

Above: Samples containing fossil fungal spores being collected by scientists at Butterloch Canyon in Italy. The Permian-Triassic boundary between these rocks is visible as the dark sediment line running around the cliff area from upper left and to the right.

absolute dating are then fed across to comparative dating. Once certain fossils and their rocks are aged in this way, the dating can be used for similar specimens in other locations and for smaller timescales on a day-to-day basis.

Below: The limestone and shale cliffs at Gros Morne National Park, Newfoundland, Canada, define the boundary between the Cambrian and Ordovician Periods.

Above: Trilobite fossils, such as this specimen found in Montana, USA, are useful for dating the Cambrian rocks prominent in some of the geology of this state.

Palaeomagnetism

As some types of rocks formed, tiny iron-rich particles in their minerals were affected by the Earth's natural magnetic field. The field made the particles line up, like miniature compass needles. It is known that the planet's magnetic field has varied through time, both in strength and orientation, as the North and South Poles 'wandered' (and still do today). Sometimes the field even flipped or reversed as North became South and vice versa. All these changes are preserved in certain rocks, usually of volcanic origin. The sequences of changes are known, and fossils found in sedimentary rocks above or below the volcanic ones can be matched into the sequence. This gives another form of dating, known as palaeomagnetism.

Below: Iron ore displaying black areas of massive magnetite, and silvery quartz.

FOSSILS AND EVOLUTION

The general notion of evolution has been around for more than two thousand years. Fossils are one of the key areas of evidence supporting the theory of evolution, which is a cornerstone of the modern life sciences.

'The crust of the Earth with its imbedded remains must not be looked at as a well-filled museum, but as a poor collection made at hazard and at rare intervals.' Charles Darwin, Conclusion to *On The Origin of Species by Means of Natural Selection* (1859).

Aristotle (384–322 BC) of Ancient Greece vaguely mentioned what he called a hierarchy or ladder of life, with Man (humans) at the top. In these writings he perhaps foresaw some kind of evolutionary process. Many other natural philosophers mused on the idea of a time before humans, when different kinds of animals and plants lived. Some even suggested that kinds or species or living things were not fixed and unchanging – that is, they evolved. The notion gained ground in the early 1800s when experts such as Georges Cuvier began to accept that there had been previous extinctions. However at this time species were still

Above: German biologist Ernst Haeckel (1834–1919). Haeckel was greatly influenced by Darwin's work on evolution, although he remained suspicious about natural selection as a means of determining survival.

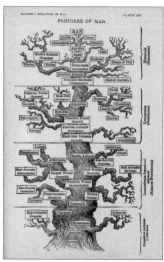

Above: An extract from Haeckel's work The Evolution of Man: a popular exposition of the principal points of human ontogeny and phylogeny, published in 1879. Haeckel believed in a link between phylogeny – the concurrent changes demonstrated by a group of organisms – and biological development. However, his geneaological trees, such as the one shown above, often represented older ideas about the 'scale of being'. The above illustration shows the evolution of the human species, the 'pedigree of man', with the trunk representing a complete and linear line of progress from higher to lower forms.

Below: Darwin's revolutionary theories about evolution were subject to both outrage and ridicule in certain quarters upon going into print. This cartoon shows a gorilla protesting of Darwin (shown right, holding his book On The Origin of Species): "That man wants to claim my pedigree. He says he is one of my descendants." Henry Bergh, co-founder of the Society for the Prevention of Cruelty to Animals (shown middle), replies: "Now, Mr Darwin, how could you insult him so?"

seen as never-changing between creation and extinction, according to teachings derived from the Bible.

The 'great book'
The idea of evolution smashed onto the scene in 1859 when English naturalist Charles Darwin published *On The Origin of Species by Means of Natural Selection*. Darwin argued that most living things produce too many offspring for all to survive the struggle for existence. Organisms struggle against the weather and physical conditions, against enemies and predators and similar problems, and against the limits of vital needs such as food, shelter or living space. The offspring which survive are those best suited or adapted to conditions of the time. This happens because not all offspring are identical. They naturally vary slightly. The variation usually

comes from genes, which are units of inheritance, like 'instructions' for how a living thing develops and functions. In sexual reproduction, genes from the parents are shuffled into different combinations for different offspring. Some of the offspring possess certain features or characters which other offspring lack.

Sexual reproduction and genetic variation provide the 'raw material' on which evolution acts. If a certain organism's features are an aid to survival, and are also inherited by its offspring, then the offspring are better adapted to the prevailing conditions. They have a better chance of survival. And so on, generation after generation.

Change with time

Darwin proposed that over very long time periods, as conditions and environments altered, certain kinds or species of living things gradually changed or evolved into different ones. Two chapters of *The Origin* dealt with fossils. Darwin realized that fossils represented excellent evidence for his ideas. They were remains of living things which had lost the struggle for survival. They died out as conditions changed, to be replaced by newer, better adapted forms. And this is a key point. Sooner or later, environmental conditions, such as the climate, begin to change. So living things are always playing 'catch-up' by evolving to fit the new conditions, even as that environment continues to alter.

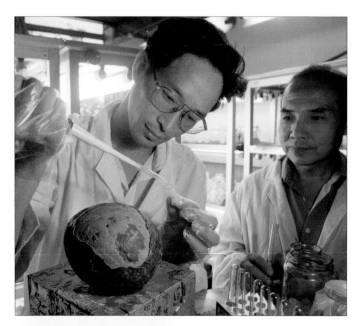

Above: Scientists at Beijing University attempt to extract fragments of DNA from a large fossilized dinosaur egg.

A long long time

In his great book, Darwin was cautious about time spans. Many people of his period believed the literal truth of the Bible, which led to the calculation that Earth was created in the year 4004 BC. Darwin saw that the formation of fossils according to the theory of evolution would need much longer. He estimated Earth's age at up to 400 million years. He was also extremely aware of the chance-ridden nature of fossilization, and the random nature and huge gaps in the fossil record. So he warned that fossils were unlikely to show complete and gradual evolutionary sequences – there would be many gaps and jumps.

Below: Charles Darwin (1809–1882).

Left: Organisms trapped in amber, like this spider (left), are helping palaeontologists in their endeavour to extend the DNA database from living to extinct organisms. The idea is that this will help them to clarify evolutionary relationships between genera and species.

In the early 1970s, Stephen Jay Gould (1941–2002) and Niles Eldridge (1943–) proposed a modified version of Darwin's original idea. Based on the fossil record, they suggested that many organisms go through long periods of stability or stasis, when conditions remain relatively constant. Then there is a brief period of change, when new species rapidly appear, before stability again. This twist on Darwinism is known as punctuated equilibrium, or 'evolution by jerks', in comparison to the traditional 'evolution by creeps'.

Acceptance

Many ordinary people were outraged by Darwin's ideas, which seemed to fly in the face of religious ethic. But most scientists quickly saw how his proposals fitted with many strands of evidence. These included the similarities between various groups of living things, leading to how they are grouped or classified, and the evidence of changing fossils through time. Since Darwin's day many more strands of evidence have supported the idea of evolution. They include the basic nature of genes, and the structure of the chemical DNA that forms them, which is shared by nearly all living things. Some genes that control basic biochemical pathways, such as breaking apart energy-rich food substances to obtain energy for life processes, are found in identical form throughout vast numbers of hugely varied organisms. This is powerful evidence for the evolutionary process and the relatedness of living things.

CLASSIFICATION OF FOSSILS

For a long time, naming and classifying living things, and their fossils, was based on a system devised in the mid-18th century. However recent years have seen the rise of a newer system, which its supporters contend is based more on logic and less on judgement, known as cladistical analysis.

Most fossil-hunters name their finds according to a system devised in 1758 by Swedish-born plant biologist Carolus Linnaeus (Carl von Linné, 1707–1778). In his vast work *Systema Naturae* Linnaeus proposed that each kind or species of living thing should have two names. The first was its genus name – a genus being a group of similar or closely related species. The second name was unique to the species. From about 1780 the Linnaean system was gradually applied to fossils as well as living or extant species. So one of the genus names for certain kinds of shellfish called brachiopods (lampshells) which are common as fossils is *Lingula*. Individual species include *Lingula gredneri, L. anatina, L. cornea*, and dozens of others. Genus and species names are usually printed in *italics*, while names of other groups, like classes or orders, are not.

The origins of names

Usually the scientific names for living things and fossils are derived from Latin or another ancient language. They are international and recognized

Below: Carolus Linnaeus (1707–1778), from a portrait completed after the death of the 'Founder of Taxonomy'.

Above: For many years experts have debated whether modern-day birds evolved from dinosaurs. In recent years the evidence has supported the answer 'Yes', and has also shown that feathers are not the unique possession of birds, as was once believed. Fossils of tyrannosaurs recently discovered in China show that these great predators had a partial covering of fine, downy feathers. A much smaller feathered dinosaur, Microraptor gui, is shown right.

by scientists all around the world, no matter what their own spoken or written languages. The meaning of a name may be based on a particular feature of the genus or species concerned, or perhaps where it is found, or who first discovered it.

Taxonomy

Linnaeus' binomial nomenclature (giving two names as a unique identification) has been extended and refined into a hierarchy of classification for all living things. The science of classifying organisms, living or extinct, is known as taxonomy, and its basic unit or 'building block' is the species. The species included in the same genus are selected by studying similarities and differences. The same is done with genera when they are grouped into a family, and so on, into larger groups. The biggest or topmost groups are kingdoms. Working from the top down:

- Kingdom
- Phylum (animals) / Division (plants)
- Class
- Order
- Family
- Genus
- Species

Levels of identification

The level of identification for a fossil, within the hierarchy of groups, varies hugely – according to practical considerations, amount of expertise, resources available, and scientific needs. Some amateur palaeontologists consider the label 'trilobite' is enough for a particular specimen. This is the everyday version of the scientific name for the class Trilobita. However other enthusiasts with more time and resources may wish to attempt a more accurate identification, perhaps even down to species level, such as:

Kingdom Animalia
Phylum Arthropoda
Class Trilobita
Order Phacopida
Family Calymenidae
Genus *Calymene*
Species *Calymene blumenbachii*

Below: The name of the trilobite Calymene blumenbachii may be rather a mouthful, so in England it has the nickname of the 'Dudley bug' after the Midlands region where this fossil species is especially common.

Left: Computers are massively powerful aids for comparing the features and relatedness of both living organisms and fossils, especially using the cladistic approach.

Traditional classification

Birds are a separate and higher rank (a Class) than dinosaurs (an Order).

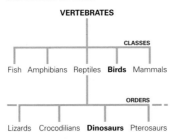

Above: Taking the classification of dinosaurs and birds as an example, we can see how the organization of animal groups differs radically in the traditional and cladistic methods. In the former, Birds are given the rank of class, equivalent to that of Reptiles. Dinosaurs are a subgroup of Reptiles, generally with the rank of order (Dinosauria). In cladistical analysis (shown right), Birds have a much lower rank than Dinosaurs, and are in fact part of the dinosaur group or clade.

Cladistics

From the 1960s, a different method of grouping living and extinct organisms has gradually been taking over from the traditional Linnaean version, especially among professional biologists, palaeontologists and life scientists. It is known as the cladistic method of phylogenetic systematics. It was devised by German biologist and expert on flies, Willi Hennig (1913–1976).

In the Linnaean system, the features or traits used to group organisms are often a matter of discussion or opinion. In cladistics, these features are specially identified as synapomorphies or 'unique derived characters'. Each unique derived character of feature arose only once. Descendants of the ancestor in which the character arose all share it. They, and only they, form a group known as a clade. This is an evolution-based group – all members of a clade are descended from the same common ancestor. As evolution continues, different derived characteristics evolve, so clades split

Cladistic view

Birds appear as a sub-group within the dinosaurs clade.

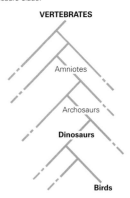

into subclades, and so on, and on. This creates the family tree type format shown above.

Cladograms

For example, assume that birds evolved from small, meat-eating dinosaurs. Then birds should be included within the dinosaur clade, as part of it. In the Linnaean system, birds are a separate and in fact larger group than dinosaurs. Birds are the class Aves, while dinosaurs are the order Dinosauria. Cladistics uses branching diagrams known as cladograms to show the evolutionary relationships between groups of organisms. The diagrams show branching points where new derived characteristics, and therefore new groupings, appear. This testable system is less prone to opinions and errors than the Linnaean version, and its administrative logic can be applied to other areas of life besides science. However for most practical and everyday purposes, the overall groupings of the Linnaean system are still in use.

Right: Limpets are included within the gastropod group, and given the genus name Patella, due to their similarity in shape to the human kneecap bone of this name.

FAMOUS FOSSILS

Fossils become famous for various reasons, such as scientific significance, scarcity or size. On the negative side, some specimens are more infamous or notorious, with links to tales of skulduggery, fossil-rustling and similar underhand tactics.

What makes a fossil famous? Usually, a mixture of reasons. The specimen might open up a whole new area of science, for example, by establishing a major and previously unsuspected group of extinct organisms. Its discovery could be a tale of romance and adventure, with fossil-hunters braving danger and taking risks to bring home their prize. The find might set a new record as the biggest, smallest or oldest of its kind. Or the fossil could turn up in a very unexpected place, chanced upon by a keen amateur who is suddenly catapulted into the media spotlight.

Conodonts

Tiny fossils commonly known as Conodonts or 'cone-teeth' resemble various tooth-like structures – long single fangs; many teeth in a line, like a crocodile's jaw; rows of spikes like teeth on a comb, either curved or straight; and other variations. Many are the size of sand grains and their wonderful shapes and arrangements can only be appreciated through a powerful hand lens or binocular microscope. These items are a common find in marine sediments worldwide during most of the Palaeozoic Era. They remained a mystery until the 1980s, when whole animals were

Below: The fossil Hallucigenia sparsa, *now held to have been a type of worm, found in The Burgess Shales, British Columbia.*

Above: Tooth-like conodont fossils from the Silurian Period, discovered in Russia. The real nature of these tiny yet intricate objects remained a mystery for centuries.

found which probably possessed them. A conodont creature resembled a long, slim fish or eel, roughly finger-sized or smaller, with two large eyes and blocks of muscles along the body. The conodont 'teeth' were arranged in the throat or neck region, but not in the jaws. Conodont creatures seem unrelated to any other groups of marine animals, living or extinct.

Hallucigenia

One of the best-known yet most puzzling creatures from the fossils in the 530 million-year-old Burgess Shales is *Hallucigenia*. It was described in 1977 as a surreal creature from a dreamworld – a long and vaguely worm-like body, blob-like head and narrow curved tail (or the reverse), seven pairs of stiff spines below for walking, and a row of about seven wavy tentacles above, each possibly tipped with a pincer-like 'mouth' for

feeding. However further finds shed more light on *Hallucigenia*. In 1991 a revised reconstruction showed the original version had been upside down. The twin rows of spines pointed upwards for protection. There were twin rows of tentacles too, not one. These pointed downwards and the 'mouths' were in fact feet used for walking. Hallucigenia may have been a very early type of onychophoran or velvet-worm, a group which includes *Peripatus* and still survives today, mainly in tropical rainforests.

Dimetrodon

Names are important for fossil-hunters. *Dimetrodon* was a three-metre-long predator from the Early Permian Period, some 280 million years ago. It had long fang-like teeth and a 'sail' of skin rising from its back, held up by long rods of bone. Its remains are plentiful in the fossil-rich 'Red Beds' of Texas, and have also been found in Oklahoma and in Europe. This powerful and impressive predator is often called a 'dinosaur'.

But it was not. It lived 50 million years before the first known dinosaurs. It belonged to a reptile group known as the pelycosaurs, which were the dominant large land animals of the time. The pelycosaurs were in turn part of the group known as synapsids or 'mammal-like reptiles'.

Mosasaurus

This fossil is mentioned several times in this book. It comprises parts of the skull, jaws and teeth of a large marine reptile. The remains were found in a chalk mine near Maastricht, Netherlands in 1770. In 1808 they were called *Mosasaurus* by Georges Cuvier, after the local region of the River Meuse. They led the renowned and influential Cuvier to a new proposal for the time, that many creatures had become extinct in previous catastrophes. Following many more similar finds, mosasaurs are now regarded as a group of large predatory sea reptiles from the Cretaceous Period. Some reached 15m/49ft in length. Their closest living relatives

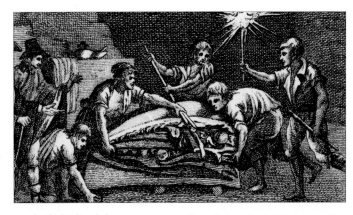

may be the big lizards known as monitors, such as the Nile monitor and Komodo dragon.

Forgeries

In 1912 remains of a human-like skull and ape-like jawbone were found at Piltdown, East Sussex, England. Experts hailed a marvellous new species of early human, *Eoanthropus dawsoni*. In 1953 careful scientific

Above: An engraving depicting the excavation of Mosasaurus *near Maastricht, published in a natural history study of the area in 1799.*

analysis revealed 'Piltdown Man' as a hoax. The 'fossils' were part of a amalgamation of a mediaeval human skull and an old orang-utan jawbone and chimpanzee tooth stained to match in colour. Piltdown still serves as a stark warning to over-zealous fossil sleuths everywhere.

Evidence of parental care

The parrot-beaked dinosaur *Psittacosaurus* from the Early Cretaceous Period is well known from many fossil finds in Asia. In 2004 a new discovery from Liaoning, China showed an adult *Psittacosaurus* surrounded by up to 34 part-grown youngsters. The amazing conclusion is that young from several parents formed a 'creche' that was looked after by one adult, perhaps while the others were feeding. These types of exciting discoveries allow us to reconstruct the behaviour of extinct animals with greater detail, showing that some dinosaurs were far from slow, stupid, simple beasts.

Below: Psittacosaurus *had a hooked beak for snipping off vegetation and rows of crushing cheek teeth.*

*Above and below: Two modern-day reptiles, the Nile monitor (*Varanus niloticus, *below left) and Komodo dragon (*Varanus komodoensis,

below right), may be closely related to prehistoric reptilian mosasaurs such as the species Platycarpus ictericus *(above).*

LIVING FOSSILS

Fossils cannot come to life, of course. But the close similarity of extant organisms to extinct ones has led to the concept of the 'living fossil'. This applies to plants and animals, but caution is needed when drawing conclusions from what may be misleading superficial comparisons.

The term 'living fossil' is something of a misnomer. Its usual implication is that exactly the same kind of plant or animal which was alive millions of years ago is still alive today. This is only partly true. Usually it is members of the same group which survive, such as a family or genus, rather than the actual species. However the survivors are largely unchanged from their cousins of millions of years ago.

Horsetails

The simple, flowerless plants called horsetails include the genus *Equisetum*, with about 20 species around the world. They are common 'weeds' of disturbed ground, each with a tall stem bearing whorls of

Left and below: Pictures from fossil horsetail specimens (left) display remarkable similarity with living species (below), even to the number of leaf-ribs in each whorl.

slim leaves like the ribs on an upside-down umbrella. Horsetails belong to the plant group called sphenopsids. They were far larger and more common in ancient times, with types such as *Equisetites*, *Asterophyllites* and *Calamites*. Their growths formed much of the vast Carboniferous forests and became preserved in coal.

Maidenhairs (ginkgos)

The maidenhair tree *Ginkgo biloba* is the only living species of a large group that flourished from the Early Permian through to the Tertiary Periods. Ginkgoes were especially common during the Jurassic, when giant dinosaurs walked among them and browsed their leaves. Today's maidenhair tree grows to 30m/130ft in height and has the characteristic fan-shaped leaves of its group. It was cultivated in the gardens of palaces and temples of Ancient China, its geographical home. In the early 18th century it was 'discovered' by European plant collectors and is now an ornamental park and street tree in many parts of the world.

Magnolias

The group known as angiosperms or flowering plants, which today includes familiar flowers, herbs, blossoms and broadleaved or deciduous trees, arose in the Cretaceous Period. Among the early types were magnolias, dating back more than 110 million years. Today's main ornamental types, with their large white and perhaps pink-tinged early blooms, are derived from Ancient Chinese species. Other flowers and trees which have changed little since Cretaceous times include waterlilies, planes and laurels.

Above: A reconstruction of a prehistoric brachiopod (of the Terebratula genus). Modern day relatives of these mollusc-like creatures look very similar to fossils (see opposite).

Lampshells (brachiopods)

From the outside, a lampshell or brachiopod ('arm-foot') looks similar to a bivalve mollusc such as a mussel, clam or oyster. However the two are very different. Lampshells have been

Above and below: Reconstructions of Cretaceous magnolias (below) show the same flower arrangement as the modern day Magnolia species, such as this Magnolia reliata (above).

*Above: This Jurassic brachiopod fossil (*Lingula beani*) exhibits a shiny lustre created by its mineral content (calcium phosphate). It has a characteristic lampshell shape.*

around since the Cambrian Period, more than 500 million years ago. Their two shells are usually very similar but one is larger than the other, and each shell is symmetrical from side to side (unlike most bivalves). More than 30,000 kinds of fossil lampshells are known. There are only 350 living species and most, such as *Lingula*, are filter-feeders in the deep sea.

Nautiluses

The few living species of pearly nautilus (including *Nautilus pompilius*) are the only remnants of a vast group of molluscs that were very common predators in Palaeozoic seas. Today's living nautiluses are large-eyed, curly-shelled, many-tentacled hunters of fish and other prey. They dwell in the deep sea. But there were more than 2,500 prehistoric types including straight-shelled nautiluses more than five metres long. Nautiloids are sometimes confused with ammonoids and belemnoids, which were also cephalopod molluscs and also extinct. Their living cousins are octopuses, squid and cuttlefish.

Tuataras

The tuatara resembles an iguana lizard. But it belongs to a very different group of reptiles called rhynchocephalians, which thrived at the time of the early dinosaurs, some 250–200 million years ago in the Triassic Period. Rhynchocephalians like *Scaphonyx* of the Middle Triassic were bulky plant-eaters almost two metres long, weighing nearly 100kg/220lb. Only two tuatara species now survive, on rocky islands off the coast of New Zealand.

They grow to about 60cm/24in long and come out of their burrows at night to feed on worms, insects and spiders.

Above and below: The 'relict reptile', the tuatara (Sphenodon, above), gives a rare and valuable insight into the evolution of its group, the rhynchocephalians (below) that were common during the Triassic Period.

Left: Millions of fossil nautiloid specimens (like the example left) confirm the close relationship with the living representatives of the deep sea, such as Nautilus pompilius (below).

An extinct species returns to life

The coelacanths are bony fish which have 'lobe-fins' (Osteichthyes) – a fleshy muscular base or stalk to each fin. They belong to the group Sarcopterygii, in contrast to the Actinopterygii or 'ray fins', the group that contains the vast majority of bony fish. Coelacanths first appeared way back in the Devonian Period. They reached 3m/10.5ft in length during the Early Cretaceous Period but faded away. Thought to be extinct from about 70 million years ago, a living coelacanth was caught off the coast of East Africa in 1938. Several specimens have been obtained since, and a second species, the Indonesian coelacanth, was discovered in the late 1990s. These fish grow to about 1.8m/6.5ft long, live in deep water, eat crabs and similar prey, and have a curious three-lobed tail.

Below: A reconstruction of an ancient (left) and modern day (right) coelacanth. These fish have many intriguing features, including a small tassel-like addition to the two main lobes of the caudal (tail) fin.

FOSSILS AND US

Since ancient times, people have speculated that we, as humans, evolved from some type of ape-like ancestors. The search for fossils of our ancestors and extinct cousins is one of the most exciting and controversial areas of palaeontology.

More than 2,000 years ago Aristotle of Ancient Greece wrote that 'some animals share the properties of Man and the quadrupeds, as the ape, the monkey and the baboon'. When Charles Darwin proposed the theory of evolution by natural selection in 1859, he was vilified for daring to suggest that our ancestors were some kinds of monkeys or apes. In fact, in *On The Origin of Species*, his only comment about human evolution was that 'Much light will be thrown on the origin of man and his history'.

The quest for 'missing links'
In 1856 some human-like bones were discovered by workmen mining limestone in a cave in the Neander Valley near Dusseldorf, Germany. The skull has a low brow, very thick bones and heavy jaw. Some experts dismissed it as 'an individual affected with idiocy and rickets'. But others began to think seriously that remains of ancient humans, including our ancestors, were preserved in rocks. The search for 'missing link' fossils had begun.

Below: Donald Johanson, discoverer of 'Lucy', with a plaster cast of her skull.

Above: Cast of an original skull of the 'Taung child', Australopithecus africanus, discovered by Raymond Dart in Taung, Cape Province, South Africa.

Gathering evidence
One of the first major discoveries was made by Dutch scientist Eugene Dubois near Trinil, Java in 1890–92. It consisted of part of an upper skull, a piece of jawbone with tooth, and a thigh bone (femur), and soon became known as 'Java Man'. Dubois named it *Pithecanthropus erectus*, and stated: 'I consider it a link connecting apes and men.' In 1927 a team led by Canadian anatomist Davidson Black excavated 'Dragon Bone Hill' at Zhoukoudian (Chou'kou'tien) near Beijing, China. They found many bones of another missing link which they named *Sinanthropus pekinensis*, 'Peking Man'. With continual revision of fossils and their names, both of these discoveries are now included within the species *Homo erectus*. Meanwhile in 1925 Australian anatomist Raymond Dart named a much more ape-like skull from Southern Africa, informally known as the 'Taung child', as *Australopithecus africanus*.

No longer missing
Gradually more fossils came to light of prehistoric humans. One of the most celebrated finds was 'Lucy' – the two-fifths complete skeleton of a species known as *Australopithecus afarensis*, found in Hadar, Ethiopia. It was

discovered in 1974 by Donald Johanson and represented a small 1m/3.5ft-tall ape-like creature from more than three million years ago, which could walk upright almost like us. Many experts now believe that 'Lucy' was in fact a male and have renamed him 'Lucifer'. Further finds in the 1990s and 2000s include even more ape-like creatures from even longer ago. They include *Ardipthecus ramidus* from Aramis, Ethiopia, whose fossils are almost four and a half million years old, and *Orrorin tugenensis*, a more controversial discovery from Kenya, which is some six million years old. Ethiopia was again the site of a remarkable discovery in September 2006: the skeleton of a 3 year-old child, more or less complete, was uncovered by scientists based at the Max Planck Institute for Evolutionary Anthropology, Leipzig, Germany. Although older than Lucy, the child was also a member of *A. afarensis*, and her lower limbs again suggested a

Below: Dr G.H.R. von Koenigswald examining the upper jaw of Pithecanthropus robustus, *once known as Java Man. This species was later assigned to the genus* Homo *as an example of* Homo erectus.

The 'hobbit humans'

In 2004 an astonishing find on the island of Flores, Indonesia, overturned many ideas about recent human evolution. It was believed that since the extinction of the last Neanderthal and *Homo erectus* people by 25,000 years ago, our own species *Homo sapiens* was the only hominid on the planet. However it seems that as recently as 13,000 years ago, diminutive humans lived on Flores. Only one metre tall, they are known as *Homo floresiensis*. The skulls of these mini-people are hardly the size of grapefruits.

Yet relatively sophisticated stone tools and the remains of charred animal bones have also been found at the site. This raises huge questions about brain size related to the intelligence needed for making tools and using fire. The size reduction of species when confined to an island habitat – a phenomenon known as 'island dwarfism' – appears many times in the fossil record, and can be seen in mammoths and elephants. However the conclusion that the Flores remains represent an entirely separate species of human is disputed until, as palaeontologists tend to say in furtherance of their profession, 'further evidence is forthcoming'.

Below: Debate surrounds the Flores hominids. Was the main species, reconstructed below, small but otherwise normal, or suffering from some kind of growth malformation?

Above: Our own species, Homo sapiens, *is thought to have appeared in East Africa less than 200,000 years ago (as shown by nucleus on map), and then spread mainly to the north and east (indicated by direction of arrows).*

capacity to walk upright. Her ape-like arms and shoulders, however, indicated that she may also have spent much of her life sheltering in trees.

'Found links'

Apart from fossils, the evidence of genes, DNA and other molecules within the bodies of ourselves and chimpanzees show that they are our closest living relatives. It is estimated that humans and chimps split from a common ancestor some seven or eight million years ago. Our 'branch' of the evolutionary tree makes up the family Hominidae. Some palaeontologists contend that it includes 20 or more species, many overlapping in time and place, especially in Africa. Others propose as few as eight species. It seems that the 'cradle of human evolution' was indeed Africa, that upright walking began several million years ago, that tool use dates back more than two million years ago, and that brain size has tended to increase through all this time.

DIRECTORY OF FOSSILS

No single bookbound collection of fossil images could ever incorporate every group and individual kind of organism that has left its record in the rocks. However, one can strive to create a soundly representative compilation of the common and recognizable forms – importantly, from different times and places around the world – plus a few glimpses of the most rare and precious of all fossils.

The following pages include many groups of organisms which are familiar to hordes of amateur fossil enthusiasts, such as ferns, corals, marine molluscs and echinoids (sea urchins), but which, nevertheless, retain their own beauty, fascination, and importance, especially in the context of a local collection. There are no apologies for including a few tantalizing examples of momentous finds that would make any palaeontologist gasp with awe and glow with a sense of achievement.

The directory is organized into three major traditional groupings: plants, invertebrates (mostly non-chordate) animals, and vertebrate (most chordate) animals. Each grouping is generally subdivided into the conventional taxonomic assemblages, such as, taking members of the phylum Mollusca as an example, the bivalves, gastropods, ammonites and others. However, as noted earlier in this book, there are disagreements among experts about the extent or separation of certain groups. And the ways in which these groups are ranked are being continually altered and refined with the aid of scientific scrutiny and the logical framework provided by the system of cladistical taxonomy (see Classification of Fossils in the previous chapter).

Left: The Dinosaur Provincial Park in Alberta, Canada, a designated World Heritage Site, demonstrates the 'pulling power' of important fossils.

HOW TO USE THE DIRECTORY

The information in the directory is easy to locate, thanks to its logical and consistent framework. The featured specimens range from fossils of simple organisms to the more complex and evolutionarily advanced, and are grouped as plants, invertebrate animals and vertebrate animals.

The following pages provide easily discerned and digested information on many hundreds of fossil specimens: through the use of photographs of the fossils themselves, often annotated to assist identification; through drawings, and of course through the arrangement of the accompanying text. The name of each specimen is usually given at the level of genus, or species 'group' – that is, above the rank of species and below the rank of family. Conventionally, the names of genera are italicized in the running text, but not always when standing alone, such as in headings.

Occasionally a full species is identified, which then has two Latin names, such as *Homo neanderthalensis*. This is the standard binomial method of classifiying and naming species. The first name is the genus; this always begins with an upper-case letter. The second name is for the species itself, and all letters here are lower-case.

Descriptions and terminology

The text attempts to describe each specimen in a straightforward way. However some technical terms are included as important 'shorthand',

especially for anatomical features used in identification. For a group of related organisms, these terms are usually explained in at least one of the specimen descriptions, but not all, to avoid unnecessary repetition. If you cannot immediately find the meaning of a term, it is worth checking adjacent specimen entries for explanations. There is an extensive glossary of terms near the end of the book. All of the individual specimen names, in their common and scientific forms, and key palaeontological terms, are included in an extensive index.

Main headings

These identify the major group of fossil organisms covered in that section (such as Molluscs) and, where applicable, subgroups (such as Ammonites). The major groups are often (but not always) equivalent to the classification levels known as divisions in plants and phyla in animals.

Introductory text

This introduces the group, with its main characteristics such as anatomical features and geological time span. Where a large group or even subgroup (such as Ammonites, shown here) extends over a number of pages, the continuation is indicated in the main heading.

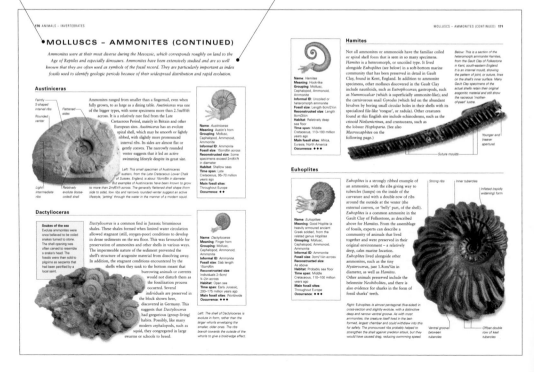

Scientific name
The internationally accepted scientific name for the organism is usually based on ancient Latin or Greek, or commemorates its finder or discovery site. Names are for genera, or species.

General description
The main text supplies useful information about the organism, such as its growth habits and ecology, its grouping and relationships, and methods of preservation where significant.

Factfile data
This panel summarizes the main categories of data for the specimen, as applicable and as available. It is shown below left in expanded form. (A? indicates uncertain data.)

Reconstruction
Illustrations recreate organisms as they may have appeared in life. However some fossils provide limited insight, so it should be borne in mind that reconstructions are conjectural.

Dactylioceras

Snakes of the sea
Evolute ammonites were once believed to be coiled snakes turned to stone. The shell opening was often carved to resemble a snake's head. The fossils were then sold to pilgrims as serpents that had been petrified by a local saint.

Dactylioceras is a common find in Jurassic bituminous shales. These shales formed when limited water circulation allowed stagnant (still, oxygen-poor) conditions to develop in dense sediments on the sea floor. This was favourable for preservation of ammonites and other shells in various ways. The impermeable nature of the sediment prevented the shell's structure of aragonite material from dissolving away. In addition, the stagnant conditions encountered by the shells when they sank to the bottom meant that burrowing animals or currents would not disturb them as the fossilization process occurred. Several individuals are preserved in the block shown here, discovered in Germany. This suggests that *Dactylioceras* had gregarious (group-living) habits. Possibly, like many modern cephalopods, such as squid, they congregated in large swarms or schools to breed.

Name: *Dactylioceras*
Meaning: Finger horn
Grouping: Mollusc, Cephalopod, Ammonoid, Ammonite
Informal ID: Ammonite
Fossil size: Slab length 15cm/6in
Reconstructed size: Individuals 2–5cm/ ¾–2in across
Habitat: Open sea
Time span: Early Jurassic, 200–175 million years ago
Main fossil sites: Worldwide
Occurrence: ◆ ◆ ◆

Left: The shell of Dactylioceras *is evolute in form, rather than the larger whorls enveloping the smaller, older ones. The ribs branch towards the outside of the whorls to give a braid-edge effect.*

Tinted panel
Occasional panels provide background or allied information, for example, about living relatives or about the period in which the specimen existed.

Specimen image
The photograph has been taken from a view that provides maximum visual detail. Many specimens include labels drawing out important features.

Caption
This text points out diagnostic or important features in the specimen image, and adds details that may not be visible in the view.

Geological time systems
There are several systems for organizing the Earth's history into time spans, though most have the same eras, periods and epochs or stages/ages.
• The terms Early, Middle (or Mid) and Late differ between schemes, with some periods lacking a Middle.
• Nomenclature may differ between regions. The Early Triassic period may consist of the Griesbachian, Dienerian, Smithian and Spathian, or (covering the same times) the Induan and Olenekian. Some regions term the latter two of these the Feixianguanian and Yongningzhenian, respectively.
• The Cenozoic Era may consist of the Palaeogene (65–23mya) and Neogene (23–1.8mya) Periods, and in some schemes the Quaternary Period (1.8mya to today).

Name
The specimen's scientific name, usually given at the genus level.

Grouping
The list of names descends through the taxa, that is, from larger to smaller groups.

Fossil size
Approximate dimensions of the specimen itself or the slab in which it is embedded.

Habitat
The broad habitat or environment of the organism when alive.

Main fossil sites
Broad geographical range of the sites of modern discoveries.

Name: *Dactylioceras*
Meaning: Finger horn
Grouping: Mollusc, Cephalopod, Ammonoid, Ammonite
Informal ID: Ammonite
Fossil size: Slab length 15cm/6in
Reconstructed size: Individuals 2–5cm/ ¾–2in across
Habitat: Open sea
Time span: Early Jurassic, 200–175 million years ago
Main fossil sites: Worldwide
Occurrence: ◆ ◆ ◆

Meaning
Most scientific names allude to features, people, places or events.

Informal ID
The casual or everyday name by which the specimen is known.

Reconstructed size
Dimensions of organism, within a range or up to a likely maximum.

Time period
Usually expressed in geological periods, with 'millions of years ago' to localize within that period.

Occurrence
A sliding scale, from ◆ for rare to ◆ ◆ ◆ ◆ for very common.

MICROFOSSILS

Many types of life have left microfossils – remains that are too small to see or identify individually with the naked eye. These include single-celled life-forms, such as bacteria, cyanobacteria or 'blue-green algae', protists or protoctists (protozoa and protophyta), and also micro-sized products of larger organisms, such as the spores of fungi, mosses and ferns, and the pollen grains of conifers and angiosperms.

Bacteria

Below: This computer-coloured SEM (scanning electron micrograph) shows fossilized bacteria as red sausage- or rod-like blobs. They are calcified on the sculptured shell surface of a single-celled life form called a foraminiferan. 'Forams' have beautifully geometric chambered shells, or tests, sometimes resembling large seashells, and are themselves preserved in vast numbers. Foram shells form an important component of chalk and many deep-sea muds and oozes.

Bacteria are generally regarded as being some of the earliest forms of life to have taken hold on the planet. They appeared in the 'primeval soup' of organic compounds in Earth's ancient seas more than 3,000 million years ago, and since then have been evolving, diversifying and dying out – just like bigger plants and animals, but in their trillions and in all habitats. Bacterial microfossils may be ball-shaped (cocci), rod-like (bacilli), corkscrew-shaped (spirilli) or take on many other forms. These early bacteria began to break apart the chemicals and minerals in the water in order to gain energy for life, growth and reproduction, and are known as chemosynthetic organisms. Some bacteria thrive in much the same way today in the mineral-rich, superheated water of deep-sea hot springs known as hydrothermal vents.

Name: Bacteria (various kinds)
Meaning: Little sticks
Grouping: Monerans (single-celled life forms having no proper nucleus or 'control centre' in the cell)
Informal ID: Bugs, bacteria, microbes, germs (if harmful)
Fossil size: Most types 0.2–20μm ($\frac{1}{6,000}$–$\frac{1}{60}$mm/ $\frac{1}{125,000}$–$\frac{1}{1,250}$in)
Reconstructed size: As above
Habitat: Warm, shallow seas at first, gradually spreading to every habitat on Earth
Time span: Early Precambrian (Archean), more than 3,000 million years ago, to today
Main fossil sites: Worldwide
Occurrence: ◆ ◆

Cyanobacteria

Below: This light micrograph shows fossilized Chlorellopsis, a freshwater cyanobacterium in Eocene rocks (55–33 million years ago) from Wyoming, USA. Each individual globular cell is about 100μm (0.1mm/$\frac{1}{250}$in) across. Cyanobacteria may be solitary or colonial, spherical, cylindrical or polygonal, and form clumped masses or long, hair-like filaments.

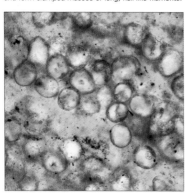

Cyanobacteria, like bacteria, are monerans – single cells lacking the membrane-contained nucleus, or 'control centre', found in cells of more complex organisms. Cyanobacteria are sometimes called blue-green algae. They are not true algae, but they are greenish, blue-green or red-brown and live by trapping light energy using photosynthesis. Cyanobacteria live in all aquatic habitats and are familiar as the 'scum' on ponds and also as 'toxic tides' when they bloom and release harmful byproducts. As they evolved and became more numerous, from about 3,000 million years ago, their photosynthetic activities produced oxygen, which accumulated in the water and then the atmosphere of the early Earth. The oxygen changed the previously poisonous air by, for example, screening out more of the sun's harmful ultraviolet rays, and such atmospheric changes allowed more complex oxygen-using life-forms to evolve.

Name: Cyanobacteria (various kinds)
Meaning: Blue little sticks (see Bacteria)
Grouping: Monerans (single-celled life forms having no proper nucleus or 'control centre' in the cell)
Informal ID: Blue-green algae, microbes
Fossil size: Most individuals 0.01–1mm/$\frac{1}{2,500}$–$\frac{1}{25}$in
Reconstructed size: As above
Habitat: Warm, shallow seas at first, gradually spreading to most aquatic habitats and damp land habitats
Time span: Early Precambrian (Archean), more than 3,000 million years ago, to today
Main fossil sites: Worldwide
Occurrence: ◆ ◆

Radiolarians

Name: Radiolarians
Meaning: Little radii (circular, wheel- or spoke-like patterns)
Grouping: Protists, Sarcodinans, Actinopods
Informal ID: Bugs, microbes, microplankton, zooplankton
Fossil size: Average 0.1–0.5mm/¹⁄₂₅₀–¹⁄₅₀in diameter, some species more than 1mm/¹⁄₂₅in
Reconstructed size: As above
Habitat: Warm shallow seas at first, gradually spreading to most marine habitats
Time span: Very Late Precambrian, about 550 million years ago, to today
Main fossil sites: Worldwide
Occurrence: ◆ ◆

Radiolarians are protists or protoctists – single-celled, animal-like life-forms, often called protozoa. Each individual 'body' is made of soft jelly similar to that of the well-known pond-mud protist amoeba. It is two-part, with the cell's main control centre, or nucleus, and inner jelly-like endoplasm within a porous container or shelly capsule, and more jelly-like ectoplasm, plus perhaps spines and long, thin filaments, around this. Characteristic of radiolarians after death are the beautiful and intricate 'skeletons', or shells, which are usually spherical, conical or cylindrical with many faces and pores (gaps or holes). They have been likened to chandeliers, and since in most radiolarians they are made from silicate (siliceous) minerals, which is the basic material of glass, these tiny organisms are said to live in 'glass houses'.

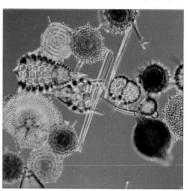

Below: Several different forms of fossilized radiolarians are shown in this light microscope photograph of material collected at Mount Hillaby, Barbados. Living radiolarians occur in marine plankton in countless trillions and are important constituents near the base of oceanic food chains.

Seeing microfossils

Palaeontologists will offer use the following when studying microscopic detail in fossils:
• A hand lens – single-lens magnifier or 'magnifying glass' – is always a useful tool for studying small details of bigger fossils as well as for examining large microfossils. The lens power is usually on the order of 5 to 20 times magnification.
• A stereo microscope on a stand, with plenty of bright light falling on the specimen, is useful for smaller items. Most stereo microscopes, which have two complete sets of lenses, work in a similar way to binoculars and have magnifying powers of up to 50. For the enthusiastic fossil-lover this is a worthwhile investment since it has many other 'close-up' uses.
• A standard light microscope (LM, transmission light microscope) can enlarge a few hundred times, with a practical limit in most models of 2,000. The specimen may be lit from below so this microscope is usually suited to very thin, ground-down sections of fossils, through which light can pass. There are monocular (one eyepiece lens) versions and, to avoid squinting, binocular, or 'two-eyed', versions. Unlike a stereo microscope, they do not give a three-dimensional image with 'depth'.
• When higher magnifications are called for, the equipment becomes far more specialized, and expensive. The main viewing tools are the scanning electron microscope (SEM) and scanning tunnelling electron microscope (STEM/STM), which give realistic three-dimensional images that are magnified hundreds to thousands of times.

Coccoliths

Coccoliths are microscopic scale-like plates of calcium-rich or calcite minerals that were once the outer 'skeletons' (shells or tests) of single-celled, plant-like algal organisms known as coccolithophores. Each of these organisms secreted a protective chamber around itself, the coccosphere, composed of perhaps 30 or more coccoliths. At death, the coccolith plates of the casing separate, sink to the sea bed mud and, being formed of calcium carbonate, may become fossilized in chalky or limestone deposits. Some coccolithophores continually shed plates when alive, as they grow and multiply. The plates occur in a bewildering diversity of shapes and sizes, from crystal-like rods and blocks to rings and 'hubcaps'.

Name: Coccoliths
Meaning: Berry stones
Grouping: Protoctists (Protists), Haptophytes
Informal ID: Plant microplankton, phytoplankton, calcareous nannoplankton
Fossil size: Individual plates vary but average 1–10µm (up to 0.01mm/¹⁄₂₅₀in), many at 2–4µm (¹⁄₅₀₀in)
Reconstructed size: Individual whole organism 10–50µm (¹⁄₂,₅₀₀–¹⁄₅₀₀in)
Habitat: Marine
Time span: Triassic, about 225 million years ago, to today
Main fossil sites: Worldwide
Occurrence: ◆ ◆

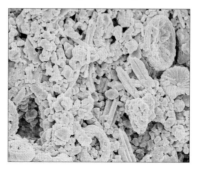

Left: This SEM (scanning electron micrograph) reveals a diversity of coccoliths from the famous Cretaceous chalk 'White Cliffs of Dover' near Folkestone, south-east England. Names such as 'calcareous nannoplankton' and 'calcareous microplankton' are used for coccoliths and similar fossils.

PLANTS

 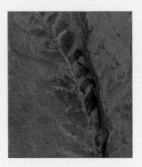 

Most biologists offer the defining feature of the kingdom Plantae as

photoautotrophism, or making one's own food with light – absorbing

minerals and other raw materials from the surroundings, and using

captured sunlight energy to convert these to sugars and new tissues.

Fossils cannot show any of this directly. But the anatomy of fossil plants

is often immediately comparable to their living cousins. This section aims

to trace the appearance of the main plant groups through time, charting

increasingly complex structures such as roots, stems thickened with

woody fibres, and fronds or leaves. Much of the classification is based on

modes of reproduction, from spores in the earlier groups, such as mosses

and ferns, to the cones of gymnosperms. The angiosperms, broadly

meaning 'enclosed seeds' or 'seeds in receptacles', were the last major

plant group to appear, in the Cretaceous. They now dominate as flowers,

herbs and broad-leaved, deciduous bushes and trees.

Above from left: Fern imprint, Archaeopteris *(the world's first tree), Sassafras.*

Right: The Triassic 'petrified forests' of Arizona, USA, are literally trees turned to stone. Woody tissues reinforced by lignin are more resistant to decay, and specimens of the extinct conifer Araucarioxylon arizonicum *were buried by stream sediments or volcanic ash before they could rot away, then mineralized as quartz.*

EARLY PLANTS

The very first life on Earth was mainly microscopic. The first multicelled plants appeared in the sea, perhaps around one billion years ago. They are usually known as algae – the simplest category of plants, lacking true roots and leaves and reproducing by simple spores instead of flowers and seed-containing fruits. Well-known algae today include sea-lettuces, wracks, kelps, oarweeds and dulses.

Mixed algal–Chaetetes deposit

Below: This specimen, which incorporates algae and Chaetetes depressus, *is from varied Late Carboniferous limestones that were found on inland cliff deposits exposed at the River Avon Gorge in Clifton, Bristol, south-west England.*

Chaetetes has long been something of a mystery. It has been interpreted as a coral of the tabulate (flat-topped or table-like) group, or an encrusting sponge (poriferan) of the coralline demosponge type. Specimens are often combined with encrusting algae rich in the mineral calcium carbonate, making varied forms of limestone. Similar fossil structures have been called stromatoporoids, or 'layered pores', and these, in turn, show similarities to a relatively newly identified group of living sponges – the encrusting sclerosponges. So Chaetetes may well have been a sponge rather than a coral. However, in fossils it is often difficult to differentiate between the algal, poriferan and coral elements. Similar algal–Chaetetes carbonate accumulations from the Ely Basin, dating to the Mid to Late Carboniferous, are found along the western edge of North America. 'Chaetetes Bands' are also common in northern England and several European regions, including Germany and Poland.

Name: Algal–Chaetetes limestone
Meaning: —
Grouping: Encrusting alga (plants) and *Chaetetes* (probably poriferan or sponge)
Informal ID: Algal-sponge-coral accumulation, 'sea floor stone'
Fossil size: Specimen 6cm/2½in across
Reconstructed size: Some formations cover many square kilometres
Habitat: Warm, shallow seas
Time span: Mainly Mesozoic, 250–65 million years ago
Main fossil sites: Europe, North America
Occurrence: ◆ ◆

Carboniferous algal deposit

Below: This Carboniferous structure may be a cyst – a tough-walled container enclosing the thallus, or main body, of the alga, possibly a frond. What looks like the 'leaf' of a seaweed-type alga is known as the frond, the 'stem' is termed the stipe, and some types have 'root'-like structures, known as holdfasts, to anchor them to rocks.

Like many simple plants, some types of algae do not contain hard materials, such as lignin (as in wood), nor do they produce tough, resistant structures, such as nuts or pollen grains. Usually they are preserved in detail only if they incorporate some type of resistant mineral, such as silica or chalk/limestone (calcium carbonate or calcareous minerals, see opposite) into their bodies, or thalli. In some examples, the encysted form shows a tough wall developed to resist drying or similar adverse conditions (see left). However, algal fossils have an immense time span extending back to the Precambrian Period, more than 540 million years ago, and have been used as index or indicator fossils to date marine deposits, especially in the search for petroleum oil.

Name: Carboniferous algal deposit
Meaning: —
Grouping: Alga, Cyanophyte
Informal ID: Seaweed
Fossil size: 5cm/2in across
Reconstructed size: Whole plant up to 1m/3¼ft
Habitat: Warm seashores and shallow seas
Time span: Precambrian, before 540 million years ago, to today
Main fossil sites: Worldwide
Occurrence: ◆ ◆

Coelosphaeridium

Name: Coelosphaeridium
Meaning: Little hollow spheres
Grouping: Alga, green alga
Informal ID: Ball-shaped stony seaweed
Fossil size: Individual specimen 7cm/2¾in across
Reconstructed size: As above, forming large beds of many square metres
Habitat: Warm seashores and shallow seas
Time period: Mainly Palaeozoic, 540–250 million years ago
Main fossil sites: Northern Europe
Occurrence: ◆ ◆

Calcareous alga such as *Coelosphaeridium* lay down deposits of chalky or limestone minerals (calcium carbonate) and jelly-like substances within and sometimes around their tissues. This gives the plant a stiff, stony feel and aids preservation. *Coelosphaeridium* is common in certain parts of northern Europe, especially Scandinavia. It forms mixed beds along with other algae, such as *Mastopora* and *Cyclocrinus* (named from its original identification as a sea-lily or crinoid, a member of the echinoderm group, but now regarded by some authorities as a siphonean alga), and with various encrusting animal invertebrates, such as sponges and corals.

Below: These fossilized remains of the algal 'cells' of Coelosphaeridium are from Ringsaker, Norway, where they occur in large accumulations. They date back to the Ordovician Period, about 450 million years ago. The outer wall resembles bark with a pattern of radiating spoke-like elements enclosing a central chamber, where the radial structure is less defined.

— Outer wall

— Radiating spokes

Central chamber

Algal stromatolitic limestone (mixed composition)

Name: Algal stromatolitic limestone
Meaning: Stromatolite = 'layer stone'
Grouping: Algae
Informal ID: As above, 'seaweed rock'
Fossil size: Specimen 19cm/7½in across
Reconstructed size: Large deposits can extend for kilometres
Habitat: Warm seashores and shallow seas
Time period: Precambrian, before 540 million years ago, to today
Main fossil sites: Worldwide
Occurrence: ◆ ◆

Fossilized stromatolites, or 'layered stones', were once thought to be produced by tiny animals known as protozoans, or by inorganic (non-living) processes of mineral deposition. However, comparison with rocky deposits found along many warm seashores today, famously Shark Bay in Western Australia, reveal that these humped or mound-like structures, generally varying in size from that of a tennis ball up to that of a family car, usually have an organic origin. Tiny threads of green algae and blue-green 'algae' (see Cyanobacteria, discussed earlier) thrive in tangled, low mats, covering themselves with slime and jelly for protection. These growths trap sand, silt and other sediments, as well as fragments of shell and other organic matter. New algal mats grow on top as the ones below harden, and slowly the mound builds up as a multi-layered stromatolite. In calm waters, the stromatolite shape is often rounded, resembling a burger bun, while strong currents cause them to elongate, like French baguettes (sticks), lying parallel to the current's direction.

Below: This specimen dates from the Late Carboniferous Period and is from Blaenavon, in Monmouth, Wales. The laminated, or layered, structure is typical of stromatolitic formations.

— Laminated structure

— Limestone

EARLY LAND PLANTS

Before the evolution of primitive land plants, some 440 million years ago, the land was rocky and barren except for mats of algae and mosses along the edge of the water. By about 400 million years ago vascular plants, such as the Rhyniales and Zosterophyllales, began to spread. These early plants reproduced by unleashing clouds of spores, in the manner of simpler plants, such as mosses and ferns, today.

Cooksonia

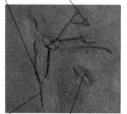

Y-shaped branching point | Terminal spore capsule

Stem | Eurypterid

Above: The presence of a eurypterid (sea-scorpion) in this sample, from the Upper Olney Limestone of Onondaga County, New York, USA, suggests that the rock was formed on the sea bed. So the plant had been transported and washed out to sea, perhaps by heavy rains.

One of the earliest and best-known vascular land plants appeared late in the Silurian Period. *Cooksonia* was a small and simple plant, yet it achieved worldwide distribution – although it is dominantly known from Eurasia and, especially, Great Britain. Its success may be largely due to its vascular system (see *Rhynia*, overleaf), which allowed water, minerals and sugars to be distributed throughout its entire body. *Cooksonia* had no leaves like modern plants, but it was probably green and photosynthesized (captured the sun's light energy) over its whole stem surface. It is recognizable by its characteristic smooth, Y-branching stems that end in spore capsules shaped like kidney beans.

Right: Features of Cooksonia *include the Y-shaped branching stem and the spore capsules (sporangia) borne singly at the end of each stem. Some specimens have just one branch forming a Y; others have five or more levels. The stems are smooth, rarely carrying surface features.*

Name: *Cooksonia*
Meaning: Named for Australian palaeobotanist Isabel Cookson
Grouping: Rhyniale, Rhyniacean
Informal ID: Simple vascular plant, early land plant
Fossil size: Smaller slab 4cm/1½in across
Reconstructed size: Entire height usually less than 10cm/4in
Habitat: Shores near rivers, lakes
Time period: Late Silurian to Devonian, 410–380 million years ago
Main fossil sites: Worldwide, especially Eurasia and Britain
Occurrence: ◆ ◆

Zosterophyllum

Branching point | Laterally clustered sporangia

A late Silurian vascular plant, like *Cooksonia* (above), *Zosterophyllum* is distinguished by having Y-like and also H-shaped branches, where each branch is divided into two equal stems. Each stem was smooth, and the spore capsules were clustered in the manner of a 'flower spike' towards the end of the stem but on the sides, rarely the tip. The capsules split along the sides, unfurling like a fern to release their spores. Nutrients were shared between stems by a network of underground root-like rhizomes. Plants such as *Zosterophyllum* were probably ancestral to the giant lycopods, or clubmosses, that dominated the coal swamps of the Carboniferous Period.

Left: Zosterophyllum *had its oval- or kidney-shaped sporangia (spore capsules) on short stalks, clustered in long arrays along the sides of the terminal stem, rather than at its end (as in Cooksonia).*

Name: *Zosterophyllum*
Meaning: Girded leaf
Grouping: Zosterophyllale, Zosterophyllacean
Informal ID: Simple vascular plant, early land plant
Fossil size: Specimen length (height) 4.5cm/1¾in
Reconstructed size: Entire height 25–30cm/10–12in
Habitat: Edges of lakes, slow rivers
Time period: Late Silurian to Middle Devonian, 410–370 million years ago
Main fossil sites: Worldwide
Occurrence: ◆ ◆

Gosslingia

Name: *Gosslingia*
Meaning: For Gosling
Grouping: Zosterophyllale, Gosslingian
Informal ID: Simple vascular plant, early land plant
Fossil size: Slab 4cm/1½in across
Reconstructed size: Height up to 50cm/20in
Habitat: Edges of lakes
Time period: Early Devonian, 400 million years ago
Main fossil sites: Throughout Europe
Occurrence: ◆ ◆

This fossilized remains of this early land plant show it to be smooth-stemmed with a distinguishing Y-shaped branching pattern. The sporangia (spore capsules) are scattered along the length of the stem on small side branches, rather than clustered at or near the end. In addition, some stem tips are coiled, much like those of a modern fern, in a form known as circinate. Many of these plants were washed downstream by floods and deposited in oxygen-deficient mud. These anaerobic conditions prevented decay and allowed the plants to fossilize as pyrite, or 'fool's gold' (known as pyritization), preserving in microscopic detail the cellular structure of the original plant as it was in life.

Below: Gosslingia *shows the typical Y-shaped branching pattern of many early plants. However, in this specimen, small lateral or side branches are also evident, some bearing sporangia.*

Sporangia (spore capsules)

Main stem

Lateral branch

Compsocradus
This genus of plant forms part of a group known as the iridopteridaleans, from the Mid to Late Devonian Period in Venezuela and the Carboniferous of China. The branches are whorled (grouped like the ribs of an umbrella) and vascularized for photosynthesis. Some of the uppermost branches divide up to six times before ending in curled tips, while others have paired spore capsules at their tips.

Right: Laterally compressed (squashed flat from side to side), this fossilized specimen of Sawdonia shows its spiny nature. In life, the stems may have bunched together, possibly to form a prickly thicket that gave mutual support and protection and allowed the plants to reach greater heights.

Sawdonia

Sawdonia is distinctly different from other early land plants in being covered with saw-toothed, spiny or scale-like flaps of tissue along its stems. However, these flaps of tissue were not vascularized – in other words, did not have fluid-transporting pipe-like vessels – and therefore cannot be considered as true leaves. Their function is not clear. They may have been spiky defences against early insect-like land animals. The presence on the flaps of stomata – tiny holes allowing the exchange of gases and water vapour between the inside of the plant and the surrounding air – suggests that they increased the photosynthetic surface area of the plant for greater capture of light energy. The sporangia of *Sawdonia* are found laterally (along the sides) and the branch tips are circinate, uncoiling like the head of a fern.

Name: *Sawdonia*
Meaning: Saw-tooth
Grouping: Zosterophyllale, Sawdonian
Informal ID: Simple vascular plant, early land plant
Fossil size: 23cm/9in
Reconstructed size: Height up to 30cm/12in
Habitat: Shores
Time period: Early Devonian, 400 million years ago
Main fossil sites: Worldwide
Occurrence: ◆ ◆

Stem branching

Saw-toothed tissue

RHYNIOPHYTES, HORSETAILS

A great advance in plants was vascularization, which consists of networks of tiny vessels – pipes or tubes – within the plant. There are two main types: xylem vessels transport water and minerals; phloem carry sugar-rich sap around the plant as its 'energy food'. Xylem vessels, in particular, became stronger and stiffer in early plants. This gave rigidity to the stem, enabling these plants to grow taller and stronger.

Rhynia

One of the most famous early plants, *Rhynia* is named after the village of Rhynie in Aberdeenshire, Scotland. This area was once marshy or boggy, probably with hot springs that gushed water rich in silica minerals. These conditions have preserved various organisms, including *Rhynia* and the insect-like creature *Rhyniella*, in amazing detail in rocks known as Rhynie cherts. *Rhynia* had horizontal growths, or rhizomal axes, bearing hair-like fringes, which probably had stabilizing and water-absorbing functions, but were not true roots. The horizontal growths bent to form upright, gradually tapering leafless stems, or aerial axes. These branched successively in a V-like pattern, each with a spore capsule at its tip. In the vascular system, each 'micro-pipe' is made from a series of individual tube-shaped cells attached end to end, with their adjoining walls degenerated to leave a gap – like a jointed series of short lengths of hosepipe. In *Rhynia* the xylem vessels were clustered in the centre with phloem vessels around, forming a vascular bundle. Similar arrangements are seen in vascular bundles in many other plants, including flowers and trees living today. The vascular bundles branch out of the stem and into the leaves, forming the thickened leaf 'veins'.

Below: This much enlarged view (25-30 times life size) shows complete soft-tissue preservation, down to the level of individual cells. The view is a transverse section through the stem of a plant – much as a tree trunk could be sliced across in order to reveal its growth rings (see panel below). The bundles of tiny tubes or vessels, phloem and xylem, are the key feature of vascular plants. Xylem vessels conduct water and minerals, which are usually absorbed from the ground, to the leaves of the plant to sustain their growth, while phloem vessels transport energy-rich sap, the product of photosynthesis, away from the leaves and around the rest of the plant.

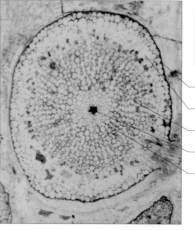

Cuticle (outer 'skin')

Outer cortex

Inner cortex

Xylem vessels

Phloem vessels

Name: *Rhynia*
Meaning: After the location, Rhynie (see text)
Grouping: Vascular plant, Rhyniophyte
Informal ID: Early land plant
Fossil size: Stem actual size 2–3mm/¹⁄₁₆–⅛in across
Reconstructed size: Whole plant height up to 20cm/8in, rarely 40cm/16in
Habitat: Various, from sandy to marshy
Time period: Early Devonian, 400 million years ago
Main fossil sites: Europe (Scotland)
Occurrence: ◆

Stronger stems

As plants became taller, in the evolutionary race to outshade their competitors and receive their full quota of sunlight, their stems not only needed greater width but also increased stiffness or rigidity. This is achieved by laying down woody fibres, usually of the substance lignin, as seen in today's bushes, shrubs and trees. In a cut tree trunk or large branch, the annual growth rings show where each season's set of new vessels develops. As more rings are added on the outside, the inner ones become more fibrous and stiff, as sapwood. The oldest rings towards the centre of the trunk, forming the heartwood, play almost no role in transporting water, minerals or sap.

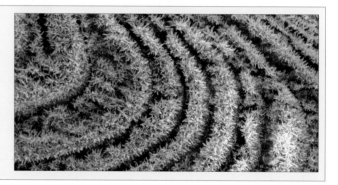

Calamites (Annularia, Asterophyllites)

Name: *Calamites*
Meaning: Reed
Grouping: Sphenopsid, Equisetale
Informal ID: Giant horsetail
Fossil size: Stem length 30cm/12in, *Annularia* slab 15cm/6in across
Reconstructed size: Height up to 30m/100ft
Habitat: Shifting sands by rivers and lakes
Time period: Carboniferous, 300 million years ago
Main fossil sites: Worldwide
Occurrence: ◆ ◆ ◆

Below: Asterophyllites *leaves were rigid and sword-like, arching away from their node (the point where they grew from the stem) to touch the whorl growing above them. In some types of plant, the stems branched off the main trunk in pairs and the reproductive spore cones grew at their tips.*

During the Carboniferous Period, some 300 million years ago, vast forests of giant tree-like plants thrived in the warm, damp swamps and marshes that covered much of the land at this time. One of these early giants was *Calamites*, which could grow to reach heights of 30m/100ft. It was a member of the group called horsetails, scouring rushes, sphenopsids or sphenophytes. These are still seen today, although they are much smaller in stature – such as *Equisetum*, the common horsetail, which springs up from freshly disturbed soil, such as a dug garden. The general form of horsetails is a stiff central stem or trunk with whorls of upswept leaves (like inverted umbrellas) at regular intervals. *Calamites* was successful worldwide, particularly along the banks of rivers, where it was often buried by the shifting sands even as it continued to grow. This adaptation to its environment actually helped to support the plant, preventing it from falling over during times of local flooding. *Calamites* formed spore cones and, much like the earliest plants, released spores from these as its method of reproduction. In addition, it also had an underground system of runner-like rhizomes that could produce new individuals asexually (as in ferns, such as bracken, today), to colonize new environments rapidly. The names *Annularia* and *Asterophyllites* are both applied to the leaves of *Calamites* and similar sphenopsids.

Stem

Above: Annularia *is the name that is given to certain types of leaves from* Calamites-*type sphenopsids or, in some cases, to the whole plant itself. The leaves were softish and lance- or blade-like in shape, and they were arranged in whorls, or rings (annuli), looking like the spokes of an umbrella.*

Whorl of leaves

Main stem

Branch

Transverse bands showing old whorl leaf segments

Fine vertical ribbing

Left: The term Calamites *was originally applied only to the stem of this tree-sized horsetail plant, recognizable by its distinctive vertical ribbed pattern. After burial, probably by the banks of a river or the shores of a lake, the plant's thick trunk – up to 30cm/12in in diameter – rotted away. The resulting cavity was quickly filled by sediment creating a cast of the inner pith cavity, as in this specimen, which was flattened during preservation.*

Living representatives

The main extant horsetail genus *Equisetum* is represented by about three dozen species and hybrids, found in most corners of the world. The water or swamp horsetail *E. fluviatile* (here shown with a few leaves of marsh yellowcress, *Rorippa palustris*) grows rapidly in shallow water and can be a troublesome aquatic weed. The hollow stem is rich in silica minerals, which give a gritty or abrasive texture – hence the old-time uses of these plants as abraders and polishers, with the common name of scouring rushes.

HORSETAILS (CONTINUED), LIVERWORTS AND FERNS

Liverworts are non-vascular plants usually with a low, lobe-like body, or thallus. They grow mainly in damp places such as near streams. Ferns, or monilophytes (pteridophytes), are common today and were especially so throughout prehistory, some growing as large as trees and known appropriately as tree-ferns.

Sphenophyllum

Below: The whorled leaves of many specimens are larger at the bottom than farther up. This suggests some sort of light-partitioning system to ensure maximum productivity, allowing lower whorls to receive light energy that bypassed the upper ones.

A creeping or climbing plant with an exceptionally long time range, *Sphenophyllum* appeared in the Devonian and survived into the Triassic. Like many of its modern horsetail relatives, it favoured damp conditions, growing on floodplains or along the banks of rivers and lakes. It may have formed a tangled understorey in lycopod (clubmoss) forests, draping itself over the large trunks in the manner of vines and creepers in rainforests today. The stems were long and thin, and branches rare. The slightly fan-like leaves were distinctive, forming whorls in threes or multiples of three. Another distinctive feature of the plant was that its vascular system comprised three bundles of vessels arranged in a triangular shape. Fertile (reproductive) branches can be recognized by the spore cones they carry.

Name: *Sphenophyllum*
Meaning: Wedge leaf
Grouping: Sphenopsid
Informal ID: Climbing horsetail
Fossil size: Slab size 12cm/4¾in across
Reconstructed size: Trailing stems for many metres, height depending on available support
Habitat: Damp places, floodplains, around the edges of streams and lakes
Time span: Carboniferous to Early Triassic, 350–240 million years ago
Main fossil sites: Worldwide
Occurrence: ◆ ◆

Hepaticites

Below: Hepaticites (including some species formerly classified as Pallavicinites) was one of the first liverworts, from Late Devonian times, and survived through to the Carboniferous Period, and beyond in some regions. Its fossils are known from most continents; this specimen is from Jurassic rocks in Yorkshire, northern England. Thallose liverworts have lobed or ribbon-like branching bodies with ribs that resemble the veins of true leaves, but which lack conducting vessels inside.

A member of the liverwort group, *Hepaticites* was low growing, fleshy and non-vascular – it lacked the network of water- and sap-carrying tubes found in most plants. The liverworts, or hepatophytes (Hepaticae or Hepatopsida, with more than 8,000 living species), along with the mosses (Musci), make up the major plant group known as the Bryophyta. They have no proper roots, stems, leaves or flowers. The main part of the plant is known as the thallus, and while there may be root-like rhizoids, these are only for anchorage. The thallus absorbs moisture directly from its surroundings, which is why many bryophytes were and are confined to damp, shady places. Bryophytes appeared early in the fossil record, but their soft tissues, without woody parts, mean they were rarely preserved. The common name 'liverwort' refers to the often fleshy shape, which is reminiscent of an animal's liver.

Name: *Hepaticites*
Meaning: Of the liver, liver-like
Grouping: Bryophyte, Hepaticean, Metzgerialean
Informal ID: Liverwort
Fossil size: 4.1cm/1¾in
Reconstructed size: As above
Habitat: Damp places, floodplains, around the edges of streams and lakes
Time span: Late Devonian to Cretaceous, 360–100 million years ago
Main fossil sites: Northern Hemisphere
Occurrence: ◆

Phlebopteris

Name: *Phlebopteris*
Meaning: Fleshy wing
Grouping: Monilophyte, Matoniale
Informal ID: Fern
Fossil size: Slab 10cm/ 4in across
Reconstructed size: Height 1–2m/3¼–6½ft
Habitat: Marsh edges, levees and flood plains
Time span: Triassic to Early Cretaceous, 230–120 million years ago
Main fossil sites: North America, Europe
Occurrence: ◆ ◆ ◆

This genus of fern first appeared during the Early Triassic Period and persisted at least into the early part of the Cretaceous – an immense time span of more than 100 million years. The leaves, or fronds, followed one of the typical fern patterns of paired, branching leaflets. However, the leaves appear to have formed a radial pattern, something like the spokes of a wheel, around the terminal part of the stalk or stem – the remainder of which was bare. Like most later ferns (and many ferns living today) *Phlebopteris* grew in drier areas, such as those around the edges of marshes and swamps, and on top of river levees (banks). This specimen is of the species *Phlebopteris smithii* from the Triassic deposits known as the Chinle Formation, in New Mexico, USA. They are also found in the nearby famous Petrified Forest National Park of Arizona.

Above: The main frond had up to 14 pinnae, or leaflets, and these divide into oblong, narrow pinnules or subleaflets with rounded ends (for a definition of this terminology see the following page). Each pinnule bears a strong central ridge, the main vein or midrib, which extends along most of its length and then divides into several smaller veins that run to the edge.

Cladophlebis

Name: *Cladophlebis*
Meaning: Branching flesh
Grouping: Monilophyte, Filicale
Informal ID: Fern
Fossil size: Slab 10cm/ 4in long
Reconstructed size: Whole leaf frond 60cm/24in long
Habitat: Marsh edges, levees and floodplains
Time span: Triassic to Cretaceous, 230–120 million years ago
Main fossil sites: North America
Occurrence: ◆ ◆ ◆

This Mesozoic fern, like *Phlebopteris* above, also survived from the Triassic Period through to the Cretaceous Period. It is one of the most common fern-like leaves found in the famed location of the Petrified Forest National Park, Arizona, USA. The pinnules, or subleaflets, were small – just a couple of millimetres wide and twice that in length. Each pinnule bears a midrib (the central main vein), from which thinner side, or lateral, veins branch in an alternating pattern. The pinnae, or leaflets, branch off in pairs from the main stem. Some species of *Cladophlebis* have small, saw-like serrations on the margins of their leaflets. This is not, however, a distinctive character as other *Cladophlebis* species lack them.

Ferns and coal

Fern fossils and impressions are common in lumps of coal formed during the Carboniferous (Mississippian-Pennsylvanian) Period, when great 'coal measure' steaming tropical swamps covered much of the Earth's land. Sometimes, a piece of coal splits, or cleaves, easily along its natural bedding plane to reveal beautiful fern shapes. These may be indistinct in colour due to the coal's blackness. But in soft coals they can, with care, be turned into dark, rubbed images on white or pale paper, in the way that brass rubbings are created.

Terminal edge

Central stem or rachis

Broad, angular leaflets

Above: The pairs of broad, angular leaflets are preserved in this fossil along with the depression of the central stem. The frond was probably longer than that shown here, and it is the missing part that would have attached to the main stem.

FERNS (CONTINUED), SEED FERNS

There are more than 11,000 species of fern today, making them the largest main group of plants after the flowering plants, or angiosperms. Like many other types of simpler plants, they reproduce by spores. Ferns first appeared in the Devonian, thrived through the Carboniferous, became less common during the Late Permian and the Middle Cretaceous, but underwent a resurgence during the Tertiary.

Psaronius, Pecopteris

Fern sporangia

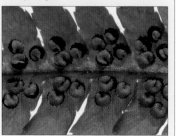

A fern's spore containers, or capsules, known as sporangia, sometimes look like rows of 'buttons' or 'kidneys' along the underside of the fern frond. These are the sporangia of the extant male fern *Dryopteris filix-mas*, a common woodland species. The protective scale which forms the outside of each sporangium is known as the indusium. This becomes grey as the spores ripen ready for release into the wind.

Main leaflet (pinna) composed of paired subleaflets (pinnules)

Fragmented leaflets

Central stem or rachis

The identification and grouping of fern fossils is a very tricky subject, as exemplified by the preserved remains of fronds called *Pecopteris*. It was eventually discovered that these grew on tree ferns that had already received their own names, such as *Psaronius*, from the fossils of their strong, thick trunks. In addition, other parts of these plants, such as the rhizomes ('roots'), have also received yet more names. (The same problems have also arisen with seed ferns, see overleaf.) *Psaronius* was one of the most common tree ferns of Late Carboniferous and Early Permian times. It would have superficially resembled a modern palm tree, growing with a tall, straight, unbranched trunk and an umbrella-like crown of fronds. Small roots branching from the lower main stem, called adventitious roots, caused thickening of the lower trunk, which was known as the root mantle. This arrangement helped to stabilize the whole tree fern. *Psaronius* is thought to have grown on elevated and drier areas around the swamplands. Its dominance towards the end of the Carboniferous Period is associated with climate warming and the disappearance of flooded wetlands. It faded later in the Permian, when the climate became drier and hotter. To add to the confusion, some specimens of *Pecopteris* have been reassigned to the genus *Lobatopteris*, which is not a true fern but a member of a different plant group – the seed ferns (see opposite and overleaf).

Left: The genus Pecopteris *is plentiful and widespread in the fossil record. Some specimens are in excellent condition, but others are only fragments, making identification difficult. This has caused considerable confusion with several hundred species assigned to the genus in some listings. In most specimens, the leaflets had two or three subdivisions (see opposite) and were shaped like rectangles with rounded ends. The central vein, or midrib, gave off smaller side veins at right angles.*

Name: *Psaronius*
Meaning: Of grey, in grey
Grouping: Monilophyte, Marattiale
Informal ID: Tree fern
Fossil size: —
Reconstructed size: Height up to 10m/33ft
Habitat: Elevated, drier areas of swampland
Time span: Late Carboniferous to Mid Permian, 310–270 million years ago
Main fossil sites: Worldwide
Occurrence: ◆ ◆ ◆

Name: *Pecopteris*
Meaning: Comb wing
Grouping: Monilophyte, Marattiale
Informal ID: Frond of tree fern such as *Psaronius*
Fossil size: Slab 10cm/4in long
Reconstructed size: Frond length to 1.5m/5ft
Habitat: See *Psaronius*
Time span: See *Psaronius*
Main fossil sites: Worldwide
Occurrence: ◆ ◆ ◆

Lobatopteris

Name: *Lobatopteris*
Meaning: Lobed wing
Grouping: Pteridosperm
Informal ID: Tree-like
seed fern
Fossil size: Slab 10cm/
4in long
Reconstructed size: Height
5m/16½ft
Habitat: Drier parts of
swampland
Time span: Carboniferous to
Permian, 320–270 million
years ago
Main fossil sites:
Northern Hemisphere
Occurrence: ◆ ◆

Part of the famous Mazon Creek fossils of central North America, *Lobatopteris* is an example of a common problem that occurs in palaeontology. Often, a genus name has to be changed at some later date, because new discoveries about its true nature and classification come to light as further finds are made. As a result, some species of *Pecopteris*, from the true ferns (see opposite), have now been renamed in the genus *Lobatopteris*, and reclassified as seed ferns, or pteridosperms (see overleaf). The whole plant would have resembled a sizable tree, growing several metres in height, and living in the drier, probably more elevated areas around the swamplands. Pteridosperms mostly had fern-like foliage, but they produce real seeds, as opposed to spores as in true ferns.

Right: This fossilized imprint shows a typical fern-like leaf, or frond, preserving the individual leaflets in detail. The central stem, or rachis, while not visible, is represented by a depression running along the middle.

Subleaflets

Leaflet

Central stem
depression

Ferns, fronds, leaves and leaflets

The parts of a typical fern commonly called leaves are also known as fronds. These may be smooth-edged and undivided, as in today's hart's-tongue fern. Alternatively, they may be deeply divided, or 'dissected', into many smaller sections, which are themselves subdivided, and so on, with a repeating pattern. The terminology associated with all these parts is complex, but in general:

• The frond is comparable to the whole leaf with its stalk, which grows up from the root area.
• The stalk of the frond is called the stipe.
• The rachis is the main stalk, or stem, that runs along the middle of the frond, from which the other parts branch to each side, often in simultaneous pairs or alternately.

Below: The unfurling frond or 'fiddlehead' of a male fern.

• The pinna, or leaflet, is one of these branches from the main stalk, or rachis, of the frond.
• Pinnules, or subleaflets, may branch from the stalk of the pinna. This is called a twice-divided, or twice-cut, frond.
• A pinnule may, in turn, have a lobed structure, giving a thrice-divided, or thrice-cut, frond.
• When the fronds are young, they are curled up in a spiral form and as they unfurl they are known as the fiddle-head.

With their changing shapes and detailed structures, ferns are often important as index, or marker fossils, helping to date the rock layers in which they are found.

Below: Oak ferns jostle for space with a familiar angiosperm, the violet (the genus Viola*).*

SEED FERNS (CONTINUED)

The seed ferns or pteridosperms were once grouped with the true ferns. However, discoveries during the last century showed that these plants reproduced by seeds, which form when female and male structures come together at fertilization, as in the conifers and flowering plants on later pages. This was an advance on more primitive spore-bearing and other methods used by horsetails, ferns and other simpler plants.

Neuropteris, Alethopteris, Medullosa

The confusion that has arisen over the years from giving different names to the different parts of the same plant, such as the tree ferns on the previous pages, is all too familiar when we come to the seed ferns. Examples of this include the leafy foliage known as *Alethopteris*, *Neuropteris* and *Macroneuropteris* (see opposite), which are regarded by many experts as being borne on smaller branch-like leaf stalks, or petioles, known as *Myeloxodon*, which in turn grow from a large, thick, trunk-like main stem known as *Medullosa*. The whole formed a tree-like plant that grew up to about 5m/17ft tall, which is sometimes also known by the name *Medullosa*, and generally classified as a seed fern. To add to the confusion, its seeds are given yet another name, *Trigonocarpus* (see overleaf). However, this is a generalization, and not all species of the above-mentioned genera may have been part of the same plant in this way. In addition, some authorities continue to use names such as *Neuropteris* or *Trigonocarpus* when referring to the whole plant. Researchers continue to discover new associations as they investigate fossil specimens and work out the relationships between them.

Above: The leaves of the genus Alethopteris *were highly variable in shape. Some specimens show that mature leaves, or fronds, sprout subdivisions, pinnae (leaflets) and pinnules (subleaflets, see previous page), only after reaching a certain size. In some cases, division continues to produce ever-increasing multi-leaflet fronds. In other forms, the pinnae were smooth-edged. Fossil slab 21cm/8¼in across.*

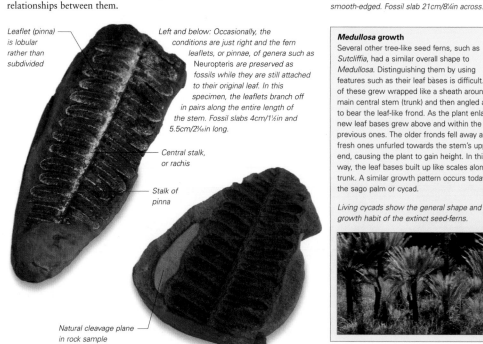

Leaflet (pinna) is lobular rather than subdivided

Left and below: Occasionally, the conditions are just right and the fern leaflets, or pinnae, of genera such as Neuropteris *are preserved as fossils while they are still attached to their original leaf. In this specimen, the leaflets branch off in pairs along the entire length of the stem. Fossil slabs 4cm/1½in and 5.5cm/2³⁄₁₆in long.*

Central stalk, or rachis

Stalk of pinna

Natural cleavage plane in rock sample

Medullosa growth

Several other tree-like seed ferns, such as *Sutcliffia*, had a similar overall shape to *Medullosa*. Distinguishing them by using features such as their leaf bases is difficult. Each of these grew wrapped like a sheath around the main central stem (trunk) and then angled away to bear the leaf-like frond. As the plant enlarged, new leaf bases grew above and within the previous ones. The older fronds fell away as the fresh ones unfurled towards the stem's upper end, causing the plant to gain height. In this way, the leaf bases built up like scales along the trunk. A similar growth pattern occurs today in the sago palm or cycad.

Living cycads show the general shape and growth habit of the extinct seed-ferns.

Name:
Medullosa (used for main trunk and also whole plant); *Alethopteris* (foliage), *Neuropteris* (foliage)
Meaning: Marrow, inner layer (*Medullosa*); lacy wing (*Neuropteris*)
Grouping: Pteridosperm, Medullosale
Informal ID: Tree-like seed fern
Fossil size: Slab length 10cm/4in
Reconstructed size: Height of whole plant up to 5m/16½ft
Habitat: Swamps, damp regions
Time span: Late Carboniferous to Early Permian, 310–270 million years ago
Main fossil sites: Worldwide
Occurrence: ◆ ◆

The detailed study of leaves such as *Neuropteris* and *Alethopteris* has shown that adaptations have occurred that are normally associated with low light levels, especially in the former. This is evidence to suggest that the Carboniferous forest canopy was layered, and that these tree-like seed ferns may have been found in the understorey where light would have been restricted. In addition to the foliage shown here (right), other fern-type leaves that are often assigned to *Medullosa* or related tree ferns include *Odontopteris*, *Callipteridium* and *Mixoneura*.

Right: This is one of the detached leaves of a seed fern that has been assigned to the genus Neuropteris. *The specimen of the rock type, called siderite concretion, is from Braidwood, Mazon Creek, Illinois, USA. Fossil slab size is 10cm/4in long.*

Lacy pattern
In the *Neuropteris* and *Macroneuropteris* series of seed fern foliage, the thickened vein-like areas branch in a curved pattern from the central stem to produce a lacy, fan-like, filamentous effect, reminiscent of the branching nerve system within the human body. A similar effect is seen in the wings of the predatory insect called the lacewing, in the group Neuroptera.

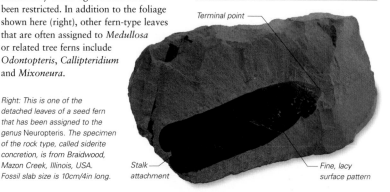

Terminal point

Stalk attachment

Fine, lacy surface pattern

Macroneuropteris

Name: *Macroneuropteris*
Meaning: Big lacy wing
Grouping: Pteridosperm, Medullosale
Informal ID: Leaf of tree fern eaten by insect
Fossil size: Slab width 4cm/1½in
Reconstructed size: See *Medullosa*, opposite
Habitat: Floodplain deposits
Time span: Late Carboniferous, 300 million years ago
Main fossil sites: Worldwide
Occurrence: ◆

Macroneuropteris follows the typical fern growth pattern of having individual leaflets (or pinnae) branching alternately from either side of a single stem. The leaflets in this fern are characteristically long and fat with rounded tips. This type of leaf was born on the tree-like seed fern plant that is sometimes referred to as *Medullosa*, as described opposite. Arthropod predation of early plants – such as spore-eating as well as the piercing and sucking of fluid from the stems and leaves of plants – probably originated as far back as the Devonian Period, some 400–360 million years ago, when land animals made their first appearance. Direct evidence for leaf grazing, as in the example shown here (right), becomes common during the Carboniferous, due to a number of factors, including the increasing volume of plant growth and the rapidly diversifying insect groups. It is the generally good state of fossil preservation from the Carboniferous period that allows us to study the evidence.

Leaflet

Central stalk left uneaten

Grazing trace

Grazed area

Grazed area

Above: The distinctive semicircular grazing patterns that are evident on certain fossil leaves give a direct insight into the feeding behaviour of herbivorous arthropods that lived millions of years ago. The consumer of this specimen has nibbled away successive arcs of leaf flesh, in a way similar to today's caterpillars.

SEED FERNS (CONTINUED)

The leaves, or fronds, of seed ferns are commonly found in 'Coal Age' Carboniferous deposits, mainly across the Northern Hemisphere. As explained on previous pages, the different parts of what is now known to be a single plant have often received different names. Seed ferns combined features of true ferns with characteristics of the more advanced trees known as cycads.

Trigonocarpus

The seeds of tree ferns are known as *Trigonocarpus* or, sometimes, *Pachytesta*, depending on the way they have been preserved. Such seeds may represent one of the first steps in animal–plant relationships – animal dispersal of seeds. The seeds themselves are large, up to 6cm/2⅓in long, avocado-like and with a fleshy layer beneath a tough outer coat. This size alone would have made these wingless seeds difficult to transport far from the parent plant unless they were first eaten by animals and then transported to new growing sites.

Below: Isolated seeds such as these Trigonocarpus, *each embedded in a rocky nodule, come from seed ferns. Although commonly found, they are very rarely preserved in situ, attached to the parent plant. Each seed is strongly ribbed and divided into three equal sections, with several longitudinal fibrous bands acting to toughen the seed wall.*

— *Fleshy layer*

— *Tough outer coat (test)*

— *Stone-like seed*

Fossil counterpart of specimen on left

Name: *Trigonocarpus*
Meaning: Three ribbed cup
Grouping: Pteridosperm, Medullosale
Informal ID: Ancient seed of seed fern
Fossil size: Seed length 1–1.5cm/⅜–½in
Reconstructed size: Seed length varies from 5mm–6cm/³⁄₁₆–2⅓in
Habitat: Floodplains, swamps, marshy ground
Time span: Mostly Late Carboniferous, 300 million years ago
Main fossils sites: Worldwide
Occurrence: ◆ ◆

Mariopteris

Smaller, younger leaflets

Central stem

The presence of 'climbing hooks' suggests that this seed fern may have been a climbing, trailing or scrambling plant, similar to a modern vine, in swampy or waterlogged habitats. The plant itself may have grown up to heights of around 5m/16½ft. However, it is the leaflets that best identify this genus. Unlike many other seed ferns, the leaflets of this plant all have the same shape, with stems originating alternately from a central branch, and decreasing in size with growth. The distinctive four-pronged shape of the leaflet is most obvious towards the base of the stem. It becomes sharper and more shovel-like towards the terminal edge of the branch.

Left: A late Cretaceous swamp plant, the seed fern Mariopteris had a distinctive leaf, or frond, shape, where each leaflet was part of a four-pronged frond. These leaflets had a central vein or midrib from which secondary veins sprouted. The specimen shows part of one frond, from the Late Carboniferous layers of Caerphilly, Wales.

Older, larger leaflets at base

Lateral stem

Name: *Mariopteris*
Meaning: Sea wing
Grouping: Pteridosperm, Medullosale
Informal ID: Trailing seed fern
Fossil size: Slab 10cm/4in across
Reconstructed size: Up to 5m/16½ft
Habitat: Swamps
Time span: Late Carboniferous to Early Permian, 310–270 million years ago
Main fossil sites: Worldwide
Occurrence: ◆ ◆ ◆

Glossopteris

Name: *Glossopteris*
Meaning: Tongue wing
Grouping: Pteridosperm, Glossopteridale
Informal ID: Gondwana tree, tree-like seed fern
Fossil size: Leaf length could exceed 10cm/4in
Reconstructed size: Whole plant height 6m/19½ft, rarely 8m/26¼ft
Habitat: Warm, damp lowlands
Time span: Permian to Triassic, 270–210 million years ago
Main fossil sites: Southern Hemisphere
Occurrence: ◆ ◆ ◆

This is one of the largest and best known of the seed ferns, and it has given its name to its own subgroup – the Glossopteridales. Although a large plant, managing to reach heights of up to 8m/26ft, precisely what it looked like in life is still much discussed. For many years it was reconstructed as a bush or shrub, but it is now thought to have been more tree-like in appearance, with one main stem or trunk. *Glossopteris* originated in the great southern supercontinent of Gondwana during the Permian Period and rapidly spread across the rest of the Southern Hemisphere. The plant was unusual in many respects. Its leaves, or fronds, were narrow in shape and elongated, in some cases lanceolate – shaped like the head of a lance or spear. The roots of the plant had a characteristic pattern of regularly spaced partitions, giving it the appearance of a vertebrate backbone (like our own spinal column) and earning isolated specimens of it a separate name, *Vertebraria*. Lobed wood is also present at the centre of these roots, with internal spaces between the lobes. The seeds appear to have developed on the undersides of the leaves, while the pollen was produced in anther structures found elsewhere on the plant. The rise and spread of *Glossopteris*, as shown by its fossil distribution, have both helped to map the drifting continents and the extent of Gondwana. At the end of the Permian this seed fern's domination, combined with the characteristic vegetation of the region, is known as the '*Glossopteris* fauna' and the plant itself has the informal name of the 'Gondwana tree'.

Below: Some mature leaves of Glossopteris grew in excess of 10cm/4in in length, as shown by this Triassic specimen from the Upper Karroo region of South Africa. The well-developed central vein was actually configured from many small veins. Minor veins branched from this and spread to form a characteristic network enclosing small polygonal flatter regions, looking like tiny crazy-paving.

Above: Many fossils of Glossopteris show large numbers of leaves preserved together. This suggests a seasonal shedding each year, as with most modern deciduous trees. This specimen is Permian and from Mount Sirius in the Central Transantarctic Mountains of Antarctica. It bears different-shaped leaves from two species, Glossopteris indica and G. browniana.

Central vein

Numerous lateral veins

Polygonal 'crazy paving' network effect

The Gondwana Tree

During the Permian Period the world's land masses were linked into the greatest supercontinent, Pangaea. The masses were subgrouped into northern and southern clusters. From the Triassic and through the Jurassic, these would pull apart as northern Laurasia and southern Gondwana (Gondwanaland). Fossils of *Glossopteris* have been found in swathes of sites that cut across South America, Africa, Madagascar, India, Antarctica and Australia. This provides major evidence for the arrangement of these land masses at the time. Since Permian times India has drifted far northwards and collided with southern Asia, while the other continents have moved apart but mainly stayed in the Southern Hemisphere. In late 1912 Antarctic explorers found *Glossopteris* among the specimens collected on Captain Robert Scott's ill-fated trip to the South Pole earlier the same year. In 1915 Alfred Wegener proposed early ideas about continental drift, using *Glossopteris* to suggest the existence of Pangaea.

Laurasia

Gondwana

CLUBMOSSES (LYCOPODS)

The swamps of the Carboniferous represented perhaps the greatest accumulation of biomass (living matter) ever. We exploit these fossilized remains when burning coal and natural gas. Much of this wetland vegetation consisted of plants called lycopods (lycopsids), or clubmosses – some as tall as 50m/165ft. Clubmosses were not closely related to true mosses (Bryophytes, Musci) or to early ferns and seed ferns.

Baragwanathia

Name: *Baragwanathia*
Meaning: After Australian geologist William Baragwanath
Grouping: Lycopod, Baragwanathiale
Informal ID: Clubmoss
Fossil size: Slab height 10cm/4in
Reconstructed size: Plant height up to 25cm/10in
Habitat: Damp lowland areas, floodplains
Time span: Late Silurian to Early Devonian, 420–400 million years ago
Main fossil sites: Australia
Occurrence: ◆

This curious and controversial plant is named in honour of William Baragwanath, who was the Director of the Geological Survey in the southern state of Victoria, Australia, from 1922 to 1943. William Baragwanath was born in the gold-mining town of Ballarat in 1878, the son of Cornish immigrants from the west of Britain lured to Australia in the hope of striking it rich in the booming gold fields of the time. The plant that bears his name is regarded by many experts as being a clubmoss, but from a very early time, more than 400 million years ago. This was when very few other land plants are known, and those that were present – such as *Cooksonia* (detailed earlier) – were much more primitive. In this context, 'primitive' means that it had fewer specialized features. *Baragwanathia* was first identified as imprints in rocks from the well-known Yea site in Victoria, Australia, and has since been discovered in other Australian localities. Dating methods put the remains at the Ludlovian Age of the Late Silurian Period, some 420 million years ago. The dating uses the fossils of graptolites, which are commonly found in sediments deposited in deep-water settings, and has been challenged by some authorities. However, it is possible that those plants of the great southern supercontinent of Gondwana were more advanced than their northern contemporaries.

Living clubmosses

There are more than 1,000 species of extant (still living) clubmosses on the planet today. However, these are mostly smallish, low-growing, creeping plants, generally simple in form, and are most often to be found growing in the undergrowth, and they are merely a shadowy relict of their former glory in the Carboniferous Period when they could attain heights of up to 50m/165ft. Today's clubmosses resemble tough, tall mosses, but they possess the distinguishing feature of having a simple yet definite vascular system of vessels (tubes) to distribute water and nutrients around the plant. The spores are shed from spore-bearing leaves known as sporophylls. The species shown below is *Lycopodium annotinum*, commonly known as the 'stiff clubmoss'. It has narrow shoots comprised of tightly overlapping pointed leaves. When mature, it may grow to 30cm/1ft in height. Its favoured habitat is moist forest and thickets, and this species is particularly common in the foothills of Alberta, Canada.

Central stem

Clothing strip-like leaves give 'brush' effect

Leaves were borne at upright angle

Left: The stems of Baragwanathia *were clothed in what are regarded as true leaves – which resembled small strips, narrow ribbons or spines – each up to 1cm/⅜in in length. The growth habit included branching horizontal stems, which also branched to give upright stems, growing to 10–25cm/4–10in in height. There were spore capsules in the axils – where the leaves joined the stem.*

Drepanophycus

Name: *Drepanophycus*
Meaning: Sickle plant
Grouping: Lycopod, Baragwanathiale
Informal ID: Clubmoss
Fossil size: Fossil slab 14cm/5½in long
Reconstructed size: Height 50cm/20in, rarely 1–2m/3¼–6½ft
Habitat: Moist settings, river and lake banks
Time span: Early Devonian to Carboniferous, 390–300 million years ago
Main fossil sites: Eurasia
Occurrence: ◆ ◆

The clubmoss *Drepanophycus* had a lowish 'creeping' form, evolved sometime in the Early Devonian Period and persisted through most of the Carboniferous, although as a genus it appears to have been restricted to the Northern Hemisphere. Some of these plants could attain several metres in height, although 50cm/20in was more usual. Each upright stem forked into two at an acute angle, perhaps more than once. The stem was covered with spiny, thorny or scale-like leaves, probably as a means of defence against insect predation. The leaves arose from the stem in a spiral pattern, although this was variable and at times they could appear whorled (emerging like the spokes of a wheel).

Right: The fossil shows the impression of Drepanophycus *along with its spiny leaves. A characteristic feature of the genus is its thickened stem, which can reach several centimetres in diameter. This specimen is from the Devonian Old Red Sandstone of Rhineland, Germany.*

Spiny leaves

Side fork

Thickened stem

Sigillaria

Name: *Sigillaria*
Meaning: Seal-like
Grouping: Lycopod, Lepidodendrale
Informal ID: Tree-like clubmoss
Fossil size: Slab size could not be confirmed
Reconstructed size: Height 20m/66ft, rarely 30m/100ft plus
Habitat: Moist settings, marshy forests
Time span: Early Carboniferous to Permian, 340–260 million years ago
Main fossil sites: North America, Europe
Occurrence: ◆ ◆

Sigillaria is a large, well-known clubmoss, known mainly from the Late Carboniferous Period. The genus varies in form, but most types were fairly tall, standing around 20m/66ft in height, yet also very sturdy – as much as 2m/6½ft across at the base. The main trunk tapered slowly with height and did not divide profusely, with many specimens sending out only a few arm-like side branches. The upper regions of the plant were covered with long, slim leaves, resembling blades of freshly growing grass, that grew directly from the main stem and fell away to leave behind characteristic leaf scars between the strengthening vertical ribs. The leaves were long and narrow – up to 1m/3¼ft long and only about 1cm/⅓in across. Some of the fossils known as *Stigmaria* may be preserved roots of *Sigillaria*.

Right: This section of Sigillaria trunk bears the distinctive 'seal'- or 'crab'-like leaf scars, from where the leaves grew straight out. Older leaves fell from the main trunk as the plant gained height, so most foliage was found in the upper region. Some types of Sigillaria are thought to have reached heights of 35m/115ft. This specimen comes from Carboniferous rocks near Barnsley, England.

Strengthening vertical ribs

Leaf scars

CLUBMOSSES (CONTINUED)

Clubmosses are one of the earliest major plant groups. Their history stretches back to the Late Silurian, more than 400 million years ago, and there are about 700 species still living today – including Lycopodium, Phylloglossum and Selaginella. Most are smallish plants creeping on the ground or up larger plants, such as trees. They are small shadows of their Carboniferous cousins, such as Lepidodendron.

Lepidodendron

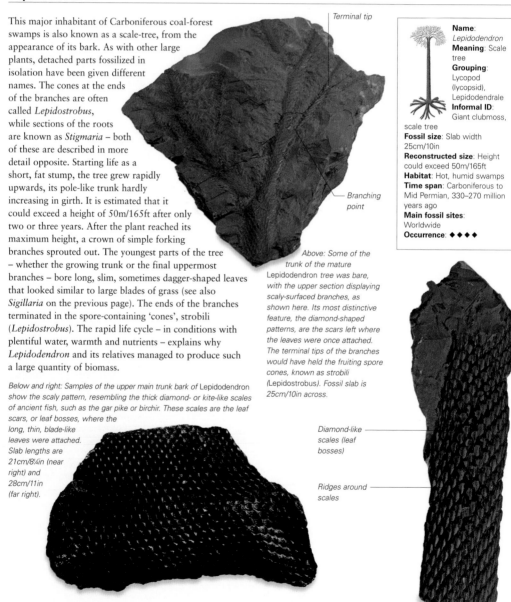

This major inhabitant of Carboniferous coal-forest swamps is also known as a scale-tree, from the appearance of its bark. As with other large plants, detached parts fossilized in isolation have been given different names. The cones at the ends of the branches are often called *Lepidostrobus*, while sections of the roots are known as *Stigmaria* – both of these are described in more detail opposite. Starting life as a short, fat stump, the tree grew rapidly upwards, its pole-like trunk hardly increasing in girth. It is estimated that it could exceed a height of 50m/165ft after only two or three years. After the plant reached its maximum height, a crown of simple forking branches sprouted out. The youngest parts of the tree – whether the growing trunk or the final uppermost branches – bore long, slim, sometimes dagger-shaped leaves that looked similar to large blades of grass (see also *Sigillaria* on the previous page). The ends of the branches terminated in the spore-containing 'cones', strobili (*Lepidostrobus*). The rapid life cycle – in conditions with plentiful water, warmth and nutrients – explains why *Lepidodendron* and its relatives managed to produce such a large quantity of biomass.

Terminal tip

Branching point

Below and right: Samples of the upper main trunk bark of Lepidodendron *show the scaly pattern, resembling the thick diamond- or kite-like scales of ancient fish, such as the gar pike or birchir. These scales are the leaf scars, or leaf bosses, where the long, thin, blade-like leaves were attached. Slab lengths are 21cm/8¼in (near right) and 28cm/11in (far right).*

Above: Some of the trunk of the mature Lepidodendron *tree was bare, with the upper section displaying scaly-surfaced branches, as shown here. Its most distinctive feature, the diamond-shaped patterns, are the scars left where the leaves were once attached. The terminal tips of the branches would have held the fruiting spore cones, known as strobili (*Lepidostrobus*). Fossil slab is 25cm/10in across.*

Name: *Lepidodendron*
Meaning: Scale tree
Grouping: Lycopod (lycopsid), Lepidodendrale
Informal ID: Giant clubmoss, scale tree
Fossil size: Slab width 25cm/10in
Reconstructed size: Height could exceed 50m/165ft
Habitat: Hot, humid swamps
Time span: Carboniferous to Mid Permian, 330–270 million years ago
Main fossil sites: Worldwide
Occurrence: ◆ ◆ ◆ ◆

Diamond-like scales (leaf bosses)

Ridges around scales

Lepidostrobus

The genus name *Lepidostrobus* is assigned to the reproductive parts – variously called fruiting bodies, cones, spore capsules, sporangia or strobili – of the huge, tree-like clubmoss *Lepidodendron* (opposite). Some specimens of *Lepidostrobus* are smallish, only about finger-size, while others are considerably larger and can exceed 30cm/12in in length. Most of them were elongated in shape, resembling cigars, cylinders, eggs or pears in outline. These spore-bearing cones were made up of sporophylls with sporangia on the upper surface of the base. The cones are always found intact as fossils, proving that they were integrated structures rather than aggregate clumps of sporangia. On the living tree they would be sited at the ends of the branches at the top of the plant.

Left: The fruiting body, or spore-bearing cone, of the Lepidodendron *tree is known by the name* Lepidostrobus. *These structures housed the spores, which were tiny (microsporous, male), large (megasporous, female) or both, depending on the species, and there are an estimated 100-plus species in the genus. This is* Lepidostrobus variabilis *from Carboniferous rocks in Staffordshire, England.*

Name: *Lepidostrobus*
Meaning: Twisted scale
Grouping: Lycopsid, Lepidodendrale
Informal ID: Spore cone or fruiting body of *Lepidodendron* and similar giant clubmosses
Fossil size: Length 8cm/3¼in
Reconstructed size: As above (can be up to 30cm/12in)
Habitat: As *Lepidodendron*, see opposite
Time span: As *Lepidodendron*, see opposite
Main fossil sites: As *Lepidodendron*, see opposite
Occurrence: ◆ ◆

Stigmaria

Name: *Stigmaria*
Meaning: Holed, pricked, marked
Grouping: Lycopsid, Lepidodendrale
Informal ID: Root system, or rhizome, of *Lepidodendron* and similar giant clubmosses
Fossil size: See captions for slab widths of both specimens
Reconstructed size: Length up to 5m/16½ft
Habitat: As *Lepidodendron*, see opposite
Time span: As *Lepidodendron*, see opposite
Main fossil sites: As *Lepidodendron*, see opposite
Occurrence: ◆ ◆

Stigmaria is the genus name for the detached rhizomes, or root structures, of large tree-like lycopods, such as *Lepidodendron* (opposite) and *Sigillaria* (previous pages). These strong, woody, branching rootstock systems had a number of functions, such as stabilizing the tall, slender tree-like structure above, in the manner of prop roots, and taking up nutrients from the watery sediment. A typical *Stigmaria* branched into two stems close to the base of the tree, and these stems tended to run almost horizontally within the sediment or soil for as far as several metres. Along this length, branches, variously called rootlets or 'giant root hairs', emerged at right angles, helping with anchorage and absorbing water and nutrients.

Below: In this impression of a Stigmaria *root, the texturing of circular scars preserved along the length of the fossil represents the scars where fine rootlets once attached to the main root during life. Fossil slab 25cm/10in across.*

Circular scars
Rootlets ('giant root hairs')
Main root
Rootlets branch at right angles

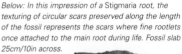

Right: The straight depressions running away from the main root represent the areas where the branching rootlets once existed. These often resemble black ribbons in the grey shale rocks. Fossil slab 36cm/14in across.

EARLY TREES – CYCADS

Plants can be divided into two groups. Sporophytes reproduce by spores (simple cells with no food store or protective coat). In spermatophytes, male and female cells come together and the resulting fertilized cells develop into seeds. Spermatophyes are divided into gymnosperms ('naked seeds') – including cycads, cycadeoids or bennettitales, cordaitales, ginkgos and conifers – and the flowering plants.

Williamsonia

Below: The fronds of Williamsonia are characteristically slender. Like all cycadeoids (the group Bennettitales), they have many small leaflets, or pinnae, alternating on either side of the main stem, or midrib. This pattern is known as the Ptilophyllum type, and differs from cycadales in which the pinnae usually occur in opposite pairs.

Cycads were among the dominant large plants found in the Mesozoic Era. The cycadales include both fossil and living forms, with about a hundred extant species in Mexico, the West Indies, Australia and South Africa, while the cycadeoids (bennettitales) are all extinct. *Williamsonia* is the best-known cycadeoid. The trunk was long and slender (although it could be short and bulbous in other cycadeoids), and the leaves narrow and frond-like. Fossil cycadeoids and cycadales can be distinguished if the leaf cuticle is exceptionally well preserved and cell walls can be seen under the microscope. They are quite different in their reproductive structures. Cycadales (including all living species) produce conifer-like cones, while cycadeoids had flower-like structures that suggest they could have played a part in the origin of true flowering plants, the angiosperms.

Name: *Williamsonia*
Meaning: Honouring W C Williamson (1816–95), surgeon and naturalist
Grouping: Gymnosperm, Cycadophyte, Cycadeoid
Informal ID: Gymnosperm, cycad, cycadeoid
Fossil size: Slab 29cm/11½in across
Reconstructed size: Frond width 6–7cm/2½–2¾in; height of whole plant 2m/6½ft
Habitat: Dry uplands
Time span: Early Triassic to Cretaceous, 245–120 million years ago
Main fossil sites: Western Europe, Asia (India)
Occurrence: ◆ ◆

Cycadeoidea

Below: This section of fossilized Cycadeoidea trunk distinctly shows the reproductive structures (or 'buds') embedded just under the surface. These were originally thought to have been precursors to true flower structures, but they are now known to have remained closed in life and so were probably self-pollinated.

Cycadeoidea was one of the most common North American cycadeoids. Its fossils are usually of the short, almost spherical or barrel-shaped trunk that was topped by a crown of fronds. When these trunks are well preserved, several 'buds' can be seen embedded just below the surface. These buds bear many small ovules (containing egg cells) in a central structure, surrounded by filaments bearing pollen sacs with the male cells. It was thought that these buds would later emerge as flower-like structures, but they are now known to have remained closed, and were probably self-pollinated. *Cycadeoidea* was a very common plant in the Cretaceous Period of North America, but it is rarely found elsewhere. The leaf bases are usually preserved covering the trunk, making many of the fossils resemble petrified pineapples.

Name: *Cycadeoidea*
Meaning: Cycad-like
Grouping: Gymnosperm, Cycad, Cycadeoid
Informal ID: Cycadeoid, bennettitale
Fossil size: Slab 15cm/6in high
Reconstructed size: Whole plant height up to 1m/3¼ft
Habitat: Dry uplands
Time span: Jurassic to Cretaceous, 170–110 million years ago
Main fossil sites: North America, Asia (India)
Occurrence: ◆ ◆ ◆ (North America only)

Cycadites

Name: *Cycadites*
Meaning: Related to cycads
Grouping: Gymnosperm,
Cycad, possibly Cycadale
Informal ID: Cycad
Fossil size: Slab 8cm/3⅛in
wide
Reconstructed size: Whole
fronds may exceed 20cm/8in
in length
Habitat: Moist to dry forests
Time span: Jurassic to
Cretaceous, 180–100 million
years ago
Main fossil sites:
Worldwide
Occurrence: ◆ ◆ ◆

The fossil leaf *Cycadites* is found in many parts of the
world, from the Indian subcontinent through to
Scandinavia. Despite its abundance, however, comparatively
little is known of *Cycadites* in life. This is because well-
preserved fossils of the whole plant are exceptionally rare.
The plant seems to be more closely related to the cycadales
than to the cycadeoids (bennettitales), as evidenced by the
leaflets (pinnae) emerging in opposing pairs from the
frond's main stem, or midrib. *Cycadites* is an example
of a form-genus – a scientific name that is assigned to
a certain part of a plant. As with examples such as
Psaronius and *Medullosa*, which have been detailed
on previous pages, this has resulted in numerous
difficulties for researchers and scientists in
identifying and naming specimens. Other cycad
fragments similar to *Cycadites* include
Pagiophyllum and *Otozamites* (*Otopteris*).

Right: This fragment of Cycadites *frond has been
preserved in red (oxidized) mudstone. The fragment
is approximately 12cm/4¾in long. Note the leaflets
(pinnae) in opposite pairs. Some species of*
Cycadites *are known from Permian times, but most
thrived during the Jurassic and Cretaceous Periods.*

Midrib | Pinnae

Zamites

Name: *Zamites*
Meaning: From Zamia
Grouping: Gymnosperm,
Cycad, Cycadale
Informal ID: Cycad
Fossil size: Fronds up to
20cm/8in across
Reconstructed size: Height
up to 3m/10ft
Habitat: Wide range of
terrestrial habitats
Time span: Tertiary, less than
65 million years ago
Main fossil sites: Worldwide
Occurrence: ◆ ◆ ◆

Right: Here a fragment of
Zamites *leaf, or frond, has
been preserved in red (oxidized)
mudstone. The species is*
Zamites buchianus *from the
Fairlight Clays of Sussex,
England. The living* Zamia *has a
short, wide, pithy stem topped
by leathery fronds.*

Zamites is, like *Cycadites* (above), a form-genus – and its fossil leaf is extremely similar in
form to the living cycad genus *Zamia*. Today, *Zamia* is found exclusively in the Americas, its
habitat ranging from Georgia, USA, south to Bolivia. *Zamites* and similar forms have been
found in places as far apart as France, Alaska and Australia, a pattern which suggests that
Zamia, or its ancestors, had a much wider geographic distribution in the past. This makes
Zamites very interesting from the point of view of biogeography, which
is the study of the distribution of animals and plants across the
planet. The oldest cycad fossils are from the Early Permian of
China, some 280 million years ago, and show that cycads have
remained virtually unchanged through their long history. In
general, a typical cycad looks outwardly like a palm tree or
tree fern, with a trunk-like stem that can be either short
and bulbous (resembling a pine cone or pineapple) or
tall and columnar, crowned by an 'umbrella' of arching
evergreen fronds. Cycads have ranged widely in size:
some ground-hugging at just 10cm/4in tall; others
more tree-like at almost 20m/66ft. Their
average height, however, is about 2m/6½ft.
Some types are informally called
sago palms, although they are not
true palms (which are flowering
plants, Angiosperma).

Strap-like leathery fronds

Central frond stalk (midrib)

EARLY TREES – PROGYMNOSPERMS, GINKGOS

The first woody trees appeared around Middle Devonian times, about 375 million years ago. These trees were progymnosperms such as Archaeopteris. *They shared many features with gymnosperms, such as leaves, trunks and cones, but they shed their spores into the air, like ferns. In contrast, gymnosperms such as the ginkgos retain their large female spores on the plant and these become seeds when fertilized.*

Archaeopteris (includes Callixylon)

Archaeopteris, from the Late Devonian Period, has been called the 'world's first tree' and formed the Earth's early forests, becoming the dominant land plant worldwide. *Archaeopteris* was originally named from its leaf impressions. In the 1960s, palaeontologist Charles Beck showed that *Callixylon*, a fossil known only as mineralized tree trunks, and *Archaeopteris* were actually different parts of the same plant. *Archaeopteris* is an important fossil in that it combines spore-releasing reproductive organs similar to ferns with an anatomy, particularly in its wood structure, that resembles the conifers. Some experts believe that *Archaeopteris* is an evolutionary link between the two groups.

Left: This frond, or leaf, of Archaeopteris hibernica is from the Old Red Sandstone (approximately 375 million years old) Devonian rocks of Ireland. The leaflets, or pinnules, overlap one another and within the genus the leaflet shape ranges from almost circular to nearly triangular, rhomboid or wedge-shaped. Fertile branches had spore capsules rather than leaves.

Name: *Archaeopteris*
Meaning: Ancient leaf
Grouping: Progymnosperm, Archaeopteridale
Informal ID: *Archaeopteris*, 'world's first tree'
Fossil size: Slab 20cm/8in long
Reconstructed size: Whole plant height 10m/33ft
Habitat: Seasonal floodplains
Time span: Late Devonian to Early Carboniferous, 370–350 million years ago
Main fossil sites: Worldwide
Occurrence: ◆ ◆

Cordaites

Below: This leaf fragment from a Cordaites tree shows the distinctive parallel vein pattern known as linear venation. The great size of what would be a whole leaf is evident when compared with the Archaeopteris fronds (see above) preserved alongside it.

Part of Cordaites leaf | Parallel veins

With fossil trunks measuring up to 1m/3¼ft in diameter and 30m/100ft in height, the long-extinct cordaitales were some of the tallest trees growing in the Carboniferous Period. Their large strap-shaped leaves were similar in shape to the living kauri pines, *Agathis*, of the Chilean pine, or monkey-puzzle, group, and were arranged in a spiralling fashion along slender, long branches. The veining pattern is distinctive, with long parallel veins but no midrib in most species. The root system was extensive, often consisting of lateral (side) roots forming arch-like clusters on only one side of the main root. In living trees, this pattern is typical of species with 'stilt roots' inhabiting mangrove swamps, which might provide a clue to the environment in which *Cordaites* grew. From the structure of the loosely clumped cones and other reproductive parts, the cordaitales are considered to be ancestors of the true conifers, Coniferales.

Archaeopteris *fronds*

Name: *Cordaites*
Meaning: Heart-like
Grouping: Gymnosperm, Cordaitale
Informal ID: *Cordaites*, Conifer ancestor
Fossil size: Leaf length up to 1m/3¼ft; width up to 15cm/6in
Reconstructed size: Whole tree height 10–15m/33–50ft; some forms up to 30m/100ft
Habitat: Swamps
Time span: Early Carboniferous to Permian, 340–260 million years ago
Main fossil sites: Worldwide
Occurrence: ◆ ◆

Ginkgo

Name: *Ginkgo*
Meaning: Traditional name for the tree (see panel below)
Grouping: Gymnosperm, Ginkgophyte
Informal ID: Ginkgo, maidenhair tree
Fossil size: Leaf widths 5cm/2in, 8cm/3¼in
Reconstructed size: Living tree height up to 40m/130ft
Habitat: Wide-ranging
Time span: Early Jurassic, 180 million years ago to today
Main fossil sites: Worldwide
Occurrence: ◆ ◆

The living maidenhair, or ginkgo tree, *Ginkgo biloba*, is a popular ornamental plant grown today, and is often seen in city parks and avenues in temperate regions. The fact that *Ginkgo* is a common sight belies its unique status as one of the plant world's genuine 'living fossils'. Fossilized preserved remains virtually identical to the living species are known from the Early Jurassic Period, about 180 million years ago. As a group, the ginkgophytes had their heyday between the Triassic and Cretaceous Periods, a span of about 165 million years – the 'Age of Dinosaurs' – when they extended their range throughout Laurasia (the Mesozoic northern supercontinent that included Europe, North America and most of Asia) and diversified into at least 16 genera. The end of the Cretaceous Period saw all but one of these genera, *Ginkgo* itself, become extinct. Although *Ginkgo* managed to retain a wide geographical range during most of the Cenozoic Era, reaching as far north as Scotland, by about 2 million years ago, it had disappeared from the fossil record virtually everywhere in the world apart from a small area of China. It was from this relict population (a species surviving as a remnant) that Chinese people first took seeds for cultivation in the eleventh century. *Ginkgo* became a traditional feature of temple gardens, and spread along with Buddhism to Japan and Korea. From there it was taken around the world by European traders. It is somewhat ironic that this ancient Mesozoic survivor is one of today's most urban-tolerant trees, growing in conditions that are too harsh for many other species to survive.

Right and below: These two Ginkgo *leaves (species* G. adiantoides*) are from the Palaeocene Epoch, about 60–55 million years ago, and were found in the Fort Union Formation of Mandan, North Dakota, USA. The pattern of the veins in the leaves is characteristically open and dichotomous (divides repeatedly into two branches). Gingko leaves, symbols of long life, are commonly fan-shaped and usually are partially split into two lobes. However, there is considerable variation in the degree of lobing and splitting displayed, even among the leaves from a single tree.*

Leaf stalk

Fan-like margin | | Branching veins

Lone survivor

The extant ginkgo tree grows in a relatively upright habit when young, but branches out in the upper regions with age. Some specimens reach 30m/100ft in height and 30m/100ft across the broadest part of the crown. The leaves are bright green but not always obviously bilobed, since the central division halfway along the 'fan' may be almost non-existent, or it may be accompanied by other subdivisions in each of the halves. Fossil specimens show similar variation. The name 'ginkgo' is apparently derived from the Chinese term *yin kuo*, which refers to the silvery fruits. The hard fruit kernels can be roasted as a hangover cure.

CONIFERS (GYMNOSPERMS)

The conifers, Coniferales (Coniferophytes), are gymnosperms ('naked-seed' plants) that include forest trees like pines, firs, cedars and redwoods. They also include yews and monkey-puzzle trees (araucarians). Most bear woody cones in which the seeds ripen. Although a few conifers are medium-sized shrubs, the majority are tall with straight trunks and represent the highest and most massive trees on Earth.

Araucaria

Araucaria cones
Araucarias are dioecious – that is, they produce male (pollen) cones and female (seed) cones on separate trees. When the smaller male cones are mature, the woody scales open to allow the tiny pollen to blow away and reach the female cones. Later, the female cones open to let their ripe seeds disperse in the wind. These fossil cones of the species *Pararaucaria patagonia* are from the Cerro Cuadrado region of Argentina.

Mature (open) male cone

Immature (closed) male cone

A 'living fossil', remains of *Araucaria* date back to the Triassic, about 230 million years ago. Today it survives in the wild in isolated areas of the Southern Hemisphere, although it formerly had a worldwide distribution. However, it is widely planted as the ornamental species *Araucaria araucana*, or the monkey-puzzle tree. Tall and elegant, it bears arc-like horizontal branches covered in small, tough, spiny, scale-like leaves.

Needle-like leaves on twig

Separated leaves

Right: These fossil twigs of Araucaria sternbergii from the Eocene rocks of Germany (55 million years ago) are very similar to the living forms, and show the characteristic covering of small, sharp leaves.

Name: *Araucaria*
Meaning: After the Arauco Indians, Chile
Grouping: Gymnosperm, Coniferale
Informal ID: Monkey-puzzle tree, Chile pine
Fossil size: Twig length 5cm/2in
Reconstructed size: Tree height typically 30m/100ft plus
Habitat: Subtropical forests
Time span: Triassic, 230 million years ago, to today
Main fossil sites: Worldwide
Occurrence: ◆ ◆ ◆

Taxodites

This 20-million-year-old fossil is of a twig bearing very small lanceolate (spear-point shaped) leaves, similar to leaves seen today in living cypresses, such as the swamp cypresses (*Taxodium*) and the Chinese swamp cypress (*Glyptostrobus*). However, because there is insufficient detail that can be seen – the specimen lacks clearly visible reproductive features – it cannot confidently be assigned to either group. The main difference between the groups is the shape of the seeds – winged in *Glyptostrobus* and not in *Taxodium*. Because, as their common names imply, both groups favour a swampy habitat, *Taxodites* is a good indicator fossil for its environmental conditions.

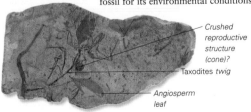

Crushed reproductive structure (cone)?

Taxodites twig

Angiosperm leaf

Name: *Taxodites*
Meaning: Related to *Taxus* (yew)
Grouping: Gymnosperm, Coniferale
Informal ID: Cypress-type twig
Fossil size: Twig diameter less than 1cm/⅜in
Reconstructed size: Whole tree height up to 30m/100ft
Habitat: Swampy forests
Time span: Miocene, 20–10 million years ago
Main fossil sites: Worldwide
Occurrence: ◆ ◆ ◆

Left: In this Miocene specimen from Germany, the smaller twigs are Taxodites while the larger leaves belong to an angiosperm (flowering plant). The rounded shape in the centre may be the reproductive structure, or cone, of Taxodites, but it is too damaged for identification.

Sequoia, Metasequoia

Name:
Sequoia,
Metasequoia
Meaning:
After Sequo-
yah, a native
American
(Cherokee)
from the
early 19th
century
Grouping:
Gymnosperm, Coniferale
Informal ID: Sequoia,
redwood
Fossil size: See text
Reconstructed size: Whole
tree height up to 70m/230ft
Habitat: Damp
mountain slopes
Time span: *Sequoia* –
Jurassic, 200 million years
ago, to today; *Metasequoia* –
Cretaceous, 110 million years
ago, to today
Main fossil sites: *Sequoia*,
Worldwide; *Metasequoia*,
Northern Hemisphere
Occurrence: ◆ ◆

The sequoias, or redwoods, are conifers that include the largest organisms ever to have lived on the planet. Members of the cypress family Taxodiaceae (see opposite), they were an important part of the extensive Mesozoic forests that were roamed by the dinosaurs, although today their distribution in the wild is much restricted. In fact, *Metasequoia*, the dawn redwood or 'water fir', was known as Mesozoic fossils from China, until a small stand of living trees was discovered in an isolated valley in Szechwan province, China, in 1941. For fossil plant experts at the time, it was like discovering a living dinosaur! The cones are small and ball-like. During the past two centuries, American sequoias have been planted in parks and gardens around the world.

Rght: The three or so living species of sequoias are the coastal redwood (S. sempervirens, see below), the dawn redwood (Metasequoia glyptostroboides) and the giant or Sierra redwood, or 'big tree' (Sequoiadendron giganteum), shown here. It can grow to almost 100m/330ft in height and can live for several thousand years.

Conifer wood

Conifer wood lacks hard fibres and is composed almost exclusively (about 90 per cent) of types of tube-like cells called tracheids. These are elongated woody cells that transport water (containing dissolved minerals) around the tree. As a result, this made the wood permeable, allowing a fossilization process by which waterlogged wood was replaced with minerals dissolved in the water, called permineralization. This occurs when water-borne minerals deposit around the structure of the wood itself, and this happened more frequently in areas that were prone to seasonal flooding. The famous 'petrified forest' of Arizona, USA is made up of permineralized conifers.

Left: This Sequoia affinis twig is from Miocene rocks associated with the Florissant Beds of Colorado, USA. Today, the genus Sequoia in North America is restricted to Sequoia sempervirens, the coast redwood, which grows wild only in damp mountain forests along the western coastline. Slab 7cm/2¾in across.

Collections of small, flattened, scale-like needles (leaves)

Main twig

Right: This open Metasequoia cone, typically globular, is from the famous Hell Creek Formation of Late Cretaceous rocks in South Dakota, USA. Today, the genus Metasequoia grows wild only in isolated valleys of China. Cone about 2cm/¾in across.

Seed recess

Scales of cone

FLOWERING PLANTS (ANGIOSPERMS)

The angiosperms include most flowers, herbs, shrubs, vines, grasses and blossom-producing broadleaved trees. The presence of flowers, and seeds enclosed in fruits (angiosperm means 'seed in receptacle'), differentiate them from gymnosperms, such as conifers. There are two great groups of angiosperms: monocotyledons and dicotyledons. 'Monocot' seeds have one cotyledon, or seed-leaf, in the seed.

Phragmites (reed)

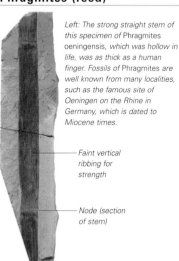

Left: The strong straight stem of this specimen of Phragmites oeningensis, *which was hollow in life, was as thick as a human finger. Fossils of* Phragmites *are well known from many localities, such as the famous site of Oeningen on the Rhine in Germany, which is dated to Miocene times.*

Faint vertical ribbing for strength

Node (section of stem)

The genus *Phragmites* is well known today around the world as the common reed or marsh grass *P. australis*. Tall and tough, in some regions it grows higher than 5m/16½ft and its dense, tangled rootstock spreads rapidly. *Phragmites* fringes not only lakes and slow rivers but also brackish water, and is regarded in many areas as an invasive pest. It has stout unbranched stems and long, slim leaves with bases that sheath the stem as it grows. The soft, feathery flower-heads are a shiny purple-brown colour. The dried stems are cut for many purposes, including roof thatching. *Phragmites* fossils are among the most common plant remains in some localities, especially from the Miocene Epoch to recent times. Reeds, grasses and rushes are placed in the large monocotyledon family Gramineae.

Name: *Phragmites*
Meaning: Fence-like growth
Grouping: Angiosperm, Monocotyledon, Graminean
Informal ID: Reed
Fossil size: Specimen height 18cm/7in
Reconstructed size: Plant height 4m/13ft or more
Habitat: Fringing bodies of fresh and brackish water
Time span: Mostly Tertiary, 60 million years ago, to today
Main fossil sites: Worldwide
Occurrence: ◆ ◆

Sabal (palm)

Below: This specimen of a fan-like leaf pattern from Aix-en-Provence, France, dates to the Eocene Epoch. Palm leaves are generally tough and durable (as known from their uses today, such as thatching, wrapping and cooking). They have thickened veins that run side by side, known as parallel venation, which is characteristic of all monocotyledons.

Palm trees (family Palmae or Arecaceae) are familiar in many warmer regions, and are grown for their wood, frond-like leaves and nut-like or juicy seeds that produce oil, starch and other useful materials, as well as providing edible dates and coconuts. A typical palm has an unbranched, almost straight trunk covered with ring-, arc- or scale-like scars where leaf bases were once attached. The trunk cannot grow thicker like most other trees but remains almost the same diameter to the crown of frond-like leaves, which may be fan-like, feathery or fern-like. Palm fossils of genera such as *Sabal* and *Palmoxylon* are known from the Late Cretaceous Period, 80-plus million years ago. By the Early Tertiary Period, 60 million years ago, they were evolving fast, and living genera such as *Phoenix* (date palms) and *Nypa* (mangrove palms) had appeared. There are hundreds of extinct species and more than 2,700 living ones.

Name: *Sabal*
Meaning: Food
Grouping: Angiosperm, Monocotyledon, Palmaean
Informal ID: Palm tree
Fossil size: Specimen length 32cm/12½in
Reconstructed size: Tree height 20–30m/66–100ft
Habitat: Tropics
Time span: Eocene, 50 million years ago
Main fossil sites: Worldwide
Occurrence: ◆ ◆

Bevhalstia

Name: *Bevhalstia*
Meaning: For palaeontologist
L Beverly Halstead
Grouping: Angiosperm
Informal ID: 'Wealden weed'
Fossil size: Stems and
shoots up to 15cm/6in;
flower-like structure 5mm/³⁄₁₆in
across
Reconstructed size: Whole
plant height up to 25cm/10in
Habitat: Freshwater swamps
Time span: Early Cretaceous,
130–125 million years ago
Main fossil sites: Europe
(Southern England)
Occurrence: ◆ ◆

Bevhalstia was possibly one of the first flowering plants to have appeared on the Earth and it dates back to the Early Cretaceous Period, some 130–125 million years ago. The plant had an enigmatic combination of features, with leaves that had a vascular system (tube-like network) similar to those of ferns and mosses, together with angiosperm-like buds and flower-like features. *Bevhalstia* was likely to have been a delicate herbaceous (non-woody) plant. Despite its fragile nature, however, it has been found in abundance in the fossil record, suggesting that it grew very near to its burial sites, which were possibly quiet lakes or swamp bottoms. If this is accurate, then *Bevhalstia* probably had an aquatic way of life, perhaps similar to today's *Cabomba* or fanwort pond and aquarium plants. Some of the first specimens of *Bevhalstia* were collected in the 1990s as part of the studies of the fish-eating dinosaur *Baryonyx* being carried out at London's Natural History Museum.

Above: In this fragment of Bevhalstia the delicate nature of the stem is a clue to the plant's probable way of life, part-submerged in the manner of modern pondweeds.

Right: The flower-like structure of Bevhalstia *is one of the first to appear in the fossil record, in the Early Cretaceous, and it already shows what could be interpreted as 'petals'.*

Pabiana

Name: *Pabiana*
Meaning: After Pabian
(see text)
Grouping: Angiosperm,
Dicotyledon, Magnoliacean
Informal ID: Magnolia leaf
Fossil size: Leaf length
5–7cm/2–2¾in
Reconstructed size: Tree
height 10m/33ft plus
Habitat: Warmer forests
Time span: Middle
Cretaceous, 100 million
years ago
Main fossil sites:
North America
Occurrence: ◆ ◆

Pabiana is usually regarded as a Cretaceous member of the magnolias, family Magnoliaceae. These were among the first flowering trees to evolve, in the Early to Middle Cretaceous Period. The group still has about 80–120 living species, mostly distributed in warmer parts of the Americas and Asia. Although many similar flowers are usually associated with pollination by bees, magnolias evolved their large blossoms well before the appearance of bees, and instead they are pollinated by beetles. Because of this, the bloom is quite tough and fossilizes fairly well – that is, compared with other flowers. A primitive aspect of magnolias is their lack of – or combination of, depending on the point of view – distinct petals or sepals. The name 'tepal' has been coined to describe these intermediate structures in magnolias, which look like the petals of other flowers. The original specimens of *Pabiana* were discovered at the Rose Creek Quarry near Fairbury, Nebraska, USA, in 1968 by a team including American palaeontologist Roger K Pabian, who was actually searching for fossil invertebrates. The genus was named after him in 1990.

Right: Leaves of Pabiana *were lanceolate (lance-shaped) and were very similar to those of living magnolias. This specimen is from Middle Cretaceous rocks found in Nebraska, USA.*

FLOWERING PLANTS (CONTINUED)

Most of the 250,000 living angiosperm, or flowering plant, species are 'dicots' – their seeds have two cotyledons, or seed-leaves. An enormous area of interest in both gymnosperms and angiosperms centres around the study of pollen. Pollen grains are tough, resistant, incredibly numerous and mostly microscopic. Their preserved remains give vast amounts of data on the origins and ranges of plant species.

Typha

Below: Bulrush leaves are long and strap- or blade-like, with virtually parallel sides and prominent, almost parallel veins, held nearly upright on the unbranched stem. In some species of Typha, *the leaves are more than 50cm/20in in length. This species is* Typha latissima *from Oligocene rocks of the Isle of Wight, southern England.*

The monocotyledonous genus *Typha* is known to some people as bulrushes and to others as reedmace. The confusion is usually traced back to a painting of the Bible's account of Moses in the Bulrushes, *Finding Moses*, in 1904 by Sir Lawrence Alma-Tadema. He substituted the more impressive plant with the then-common name of reedmace for the plant that was then known as bulrush, which has much more delicate, branching flower spikes. Other common names for *Typha* include false-bulrush, cattail and cat's-tail. The scientific name *Typha* cannot be confused, however. Its brown, sausage-shaped female flower head is closely packed with many tiny flowers. The fluffy, feathery male flower head is on the same stem above the female one. For almost 100 million years bulrushes (reedmace) have had thick underwater roots and been invasive, quickly choking waterways such as brooks and streams, and diminishing the open water of lakes and slow rivers.

Name: *Typha*
Meaning: Bog, marsh
Grouping: Angiosperm, Monocotyledon, Typhacean
Informal ID: Reedmace, bulrush
Fossil size: Slab 13cm/5in across
Reconstructed size: Plant height 2m/6½ft or more
Habitat: Margins of still or slow fresh water
Time span: Middle Cretaceous, 100 million years ago, to today
Main fossil sites: Northern Hemisphere
Occurrence: ◆ ◆

Populus

The poplars, members of the willow group, are well known for their long-stalked 'trembling' leaves, large and colourful hanging catkins, and rapid growth, which makes them useful as seasonal windbreaks. The genus *Populus* includes aspens and cottonwoods and consists of more than 30 living species, mainly in the Northern Hemisphere. These are grouped as balsams, white poplars, aspens and black poplars. *Populus* is well known from several Eocene Epoch sites, such as the Florissant Fossil Beds National Monument in Colorado, USA, where they thrived in the dampness along stream banks and adjacent to lakes. Leaf shape generally varies from rounded to heart-like, with smooth or slightly toothed edges. Some species have conspicuous glands on the upper side of the leaf where it joins its stalk.

Name: *Populus*
Meaning: People, crowd
Grouping: Angiosperm, Dicotyledon, Salicacean
Informal ID: Poplar tree
Fossil size: Leaf width 8cm/3in
Reconstructed size: Tree height 30m/100ft
Habitat: Temperate mixed woodland
Time span: Eocene, 50 million years ago, to today
Main fossil sites: Northern Hemisphere
Occurrence: ◆

Left: Many species of Populus *have the characteristically long leaf stalk, or petiole, which, combined with the alternate and well-spaced pattern of leaves along the twig, allows them to rustle in the breeze.* Populus glandulifera *may be the ancestor of today's black poplar group. This specimen is of Miocene origins from Oeningen, Baden, Germany.*

Fruits, nuts and seeds

The terminology of plant reproductive structures is famously complex. In general, a fruit is the ripe or mature ovary or seed-container of a plant, together with its contents. In fruits such as apples (known technically as pomes) the fruit is strictly only the apple core, while the fleshy part is derived from structures around the ovary – in this case the floral receptacle. Usually only hard fruits, such as nuts, form fossils. The kernels, or 'nuts', themselves are the seeds, while the surrounding container (pericarp, exo/endocarp and/or cupule) is known as a shell or husk, especially when it is dry and fibrous.

Walnuts are fruits known botanically as drupes, with an outer fleshy exocarp, a hard endocarp (shell) and the woody, wrinkled nuts within.

Carya

The genus *Carya* includes about 22 species of living trees, known variously as hickories and walnuts, that are mainly native to North America. They are usually placed in the walnut family, known as the juglands group. Hickory wood, being straight-grained and strong yet elastic, is often compared with ash, and it is used to make tool handles, oars, wheel spokes and similar items where shock absorbency is important. The tough-walled nuts fossilize well and can usually be distinguished by their similarity to a walnut with one end more pointed, generally flat and angular sides, and four lengthwise grooves or narrow, wing-like extensions.

Right: This preserved seed of Carya ventricosa from Hungary is dated within the Eocene Epoch, some 45 million years ago. Inside the tough husk the seeds would have been pale and edible.

Name: *Carya*
Meaning: From the Greek *karya*, walnut (formerly applied to many similar nuts)
Grouping: Angiosperm, Dicotyledon, Juglandacean
Informal ID: Hickory tree
Fossil size: Seed length 4cm/1½in
Reconstructed size: Tree height 20–30m/65–100ft
Habitat: Temperate mixed woodland
Time span: Palaeocene, 60 million years ago, to today
Main fossil sites: Chiefly Northern Hemisphere
Occurrence: ◆ ◆

— Nut

Fagus/Berryophyllum

Name: *Berryophyllum*
Meaning: Fagus – beech; Berryophyllum – berry leaf, rounded leaf
Grouping: Angiosperm, Dicotyledon, Fagacean
Informal ID: Beech tree
Fossil size: Leaf length 9cm/3½in
Reconstructed size: Tree height 20–30m/65–100ft
Habitat: Temperate woodland regions
Time span: Eocene, 45 million years ago
Main fossil sites: North America
Occurrence: ◆

Beech trees, genus *Fagus*, are familiar plants growing in northern temperate countries today. One species is found in North America and one grows in Europe, with another 10 or so species native to East Asia (principally China). With colloquial identities such as 'Queen of the Forest' these stately, massive trees provide homes and food for myriad wildlife. In addition, they produce vivid autumn leaf colours, small nuts called beechmast in spiny or prickly husks (cupules) and valuable timber for a variety of uses. The fossil history of *Fagus* is complex and has been much discussed. The genus may date back to Palaeocene times and was far more widespread than it is today, growing in huge areas around almost all of the Northern Hemisphere. The preserved three-angled nuts and paired husks, either together or separated, have been given various names. So have the preserved fossils of the characteristically smooth bark and also isolated leaves, which are alternate on the stem, typically ovate to lanceolate in shape with a range of tooth- or saw-like serrated edges. Since the leaves, husks and nuts of living beech are variable, not only within one species but even on the same tree, the fossil record of the genus will take much unravelling.

Below: Mystery surrounds the leaves known as Berryophyllum. They may come from an early type of beech tree. The central vein, or midrib, is prominent, as are the parallel lateral or secondary veins. Similar leaves are known as Castenophyllum. This specimen comes from the Eocene of Tennessee, USA, and is associated with 'frilly' beech-like husks.

FLOWERING PLANTS (CONTINUED)

The earliest angiosperm fossils are generally Early Cretaceous, about 130 million years ago – so in terms of plant evolution they are relative latecomers. They could, however, have evolved much earlier in dry uplands where fossilization was unlikely. Or their evolution could have been triggered by interaction with animal groups such as browsing dinosaurs or possibly new types of pollinating insects.

Castanea

Below: Sweet chestnut leaves are simple (that is, they are not divided into lobes or leaflets), and are usually arranged alternately along the twig. Their shape is long or lanceolate and with serrations, crenations, or fine teeth, although some species are smoother-edged. This specimen from southern Germany, dated to the Eocene Epoch, shows the typical parallel lateral veins branching from the main vein, or midrib.

Midrib —   Fine serrations

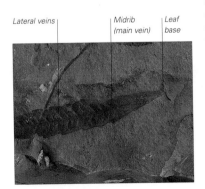

Sweet chestnut trees and chinkapins, with about eight living species in the genus *Castanea*, are members of the beech and oak family, Fagaceae. (They should not be confused with horse chestnuts or buckeyes, *Aesculus*, which form their own family, Hippocastanaceae.) Sweet chestnuts, including the Spanish and American types, are known for their highly edible fruits, which are sweet-tasting, smooth-surfaced nuts, usually two or three together in a fleshy, prickly or thorny husk. The Spanish chestnut bark is also characteristic when fossilized, being smooth in younger trees but developing a pattern of heavy, hard ridges arranged in a right-handed spiral pattern up the main trunk as the tree ages.

Name: *Castanea*
Meaning: From the Greek *kastanon*, chestnut
Grouping: Angiosperm, Dicotyledon, Fagacean
Informal ID: Sweet chestnut tree
Fossil size: Leaf width 3cm/1in
Reconstructed size: Tree height 30m/100ft or more
Habitat: Mixed warm-temperate woodland
Time span: Late Cretaceous, 70 million years ago, to today
Main fossil sites: Worldwide
Occurrence: ◆ ◆

Myrica

Below: Most Myrica leaves are simple in outline with a tough, shiny surface in life, and possibly with finely toothed or crinkled edges. The leaves are arranged spirally along the stem and their shape is known as oblanceolate (tapered to a point at both ends but broader towards the tip). Lateral veins branch off the midrib in a 'herringbone' pattern.

Lateral veins | Midrib   Leaf
(main vein)   base

A genus of the beech and oak order, Fagales, *Myrica* (or myrtles) includes between 35 and 50 species of plants living today, varying from small-growing bushes or shrubs to tall trees reaching up to about 20m/66ft in height. They are mostly evergreen plants and are widely distributed throughout the African, Asian, North American, South American and European continents – the only exception being Australasia. Some species are well known in ornamental woods, parks and gardens, and are planted for their aromatic qualities. They include bayberry, sweet gale or bog myrtle, candleberry and wax-myrtle. The flowers are arranged as catkins, and the berry-type fruits (known as drupes) often have a thick, waxy coating. At one time, this wax was collected for making into candles, leading to such common names as candleberry, wax-myrtle and tallow-myrtle.

Name: *Myrica*
Meaning: Myrtle
Grouping: Angiosperm, Dicotyledon, Myricacean
Informal ID: Myrtle
Fossil size: Leaf length 7cm/2¾in (incomplete)
Reconstructed size: Shrub height 10m/33ft
Habitat: Warm temperate woods, including peat bogs
Time span: Oligocene, 30 million years ago, to today
Main fossil sites: Northern Hemisphere
Occurrence: ◆

Zelkova

Name: *Zelkova*
Meaning: From the local Caucasian name
Grouping: Angiosperm, Dicotyledon, Ulmacean
Informal ID: Zelkova, Asian elm, Japanese elm and others (see text)
Fossil size: Leaf length 4cm/1½in
Reconstructed size: Tree height up to 35m/115ft
Habitat: Mixed temperate woodland
Time span: Palaeocene, 55 million years ago, to today
Main fossil sites: Europe, Asia
Occurrence: ◆

There are about six species in the genus *Zelkova* (*Zelcova*) living today, varying from small shrubs to tall trees. In the wild, they are found in Southern Europe (on the Mediterranean islands of Crete and Sicily) and they are also native to Central to East Asia. The genus is classified within the elm family but it is separate from the true elms. This has led to confusion with common names such as Caucasian elm and Japanese elm being applied to the Caucasian zelkova *Z. caprinifolia* and the Japanese zelkova or keaki *Z. serrata*, which is commonly planted as a street tree in North America; it not only produces good shade and attractive autumn colour, but is also tolerant of wind, heat, drought and the pollution associated with urban conditions. Evidence suggests that the genus may have arisen in Palaeocene times, more than 50 million years ago, possibly in the lands around the North Pacific – there are fossils both from Asia and from North America to support this, as in the specimen here, which is from the Eocene Epoch in Utah, USA. Various forms of *Zelkova* continued to thrive throughout North America and Northern Europe, but these disappeared with the Pleistocene glaciations. Fossils from Europe, dated to the Miocene and Pliocene Epochs, resemble the modern *Z. carpinifolia* and *Z. serrata*, as mentioned above.

Above: Most Zelkova leaves have saw- or tooth-like edges, with the size of the teeth varying from fine to coarse, and their tips ranging from almost blunt to very finely sharp-pointed. The overall leaf shape of early Tertiary types is long and narrow, as here, with some modern species being more rounded or oval. This specimen is part of the same item as Cardiospermum *(see following pages).*

Sassafras

Name: *Sassafras*
Meaning: From Native American 'green stick'
Grouping: Angiosperm, Dicotyledon, Lauracean
Informal ID: Sassafras tree
Fossil size: Leaf width 8cm/3⅛in
Reconstructed size: Tree height 20–30m/66–100ft
Habitat: Temperate mixed woodland
Time span: Middle Cretaceous, 100 million years ago, to today
Main fossil sites: Scattered, mainly North America
Occurrence: ◆

Sassafras – which is both its scientific and its common name – is familiar in some parts of the world as a tree planted for the aromatic qualities of its oil, bark and roots. In some areas it is also planted in order to help repel mosquitoes and other insects. Also called the root beer tree, ague tree and saloo, its root essences were used as a central flavouring in root beers and teas, and are also incorporated into cosmetics, ice-creams, salads, soups, jellies, perfumes and many other food and drink items. There are three living species of *Sassafras*, the chief one known in the wild from eastern North America. The genus is classified as part of the laurel family, and is closely related to the 'true' laurels. The whole tree is roughly cone-shaped and is admired for its blazing red and gold autumn leaf colours. The leaves, both fossilized and from living specimens, are famous for their heterophylly, or variation in shape – they range from roughly oval (unlobed), bilobate (mitten shaped) and trilobate (three pronged), even on the same branch of the same tree.

Below: The leaves of Sassafras are commonly three-lobed, or trilobate, with three equal lobes. However, they may also be trilobate with a larger central lobe, or two-lobed (bilobate) with equal or unequal lobes, or even elliptical with almost no lobing at all. Each lobe has a central midrib with branching lateral veins. This specimen is from the Dakota Group of Central Kansas, USA.

Regular three-lobed form

Tripartite vein branching

Leaf stalk (petiole)

FLOWERING PLANTS (CONTINUED)

*Angiosperms, or flowering plants, range from delicate flowers and soft herbs to shrubs, bushes and trees.
Fossilized remains of tender, soon-shrivelled parts, such as flower petals, are rare. Most specimens are
of bark, woody stems, roots, hard seeds such as nuts, and leaves which have fallen into mud
or similar sediments with good preserving qualities.*

Liquidambar

Below: Liquidambar *leaves are typically palmate with three (rarely), five (more commonly) or seven (rarely) sharply pointed lobes. The leaves resemble those of Platanus (see below) in shape, and are borne alternately, spiralling along the stem. This specimen of* Liquidambar europaeum *is from the Miocene Epoch of Germany.*

Trees of the genus *Liquidambar* are known commonly as sweetgums. The gum, sometimes called storax or styrex, is used in herbal medicine and the fruits are burr-like capsules ('gumballs'). Formerly, *Liquidambar* was included in the family Hamamelidaceae, the witch-hazels. Newer schemes place it in the family Altingiaceae, along with the altingia trees of South-east Asia. There are about six living species of *Liquidambar*, most in East Asia, with the American sweetgum in eastern North America down to northern Central America. The genus is a relict, being much more widespread in the Middle Tertiary Period. The numerous fossil species include *Liquidambar europaeum*, shown here. However, the European representatives disappeared during the recent ice ages, and climate changes caused it to fade also in western North America.

Name: *Liquidambar*
Meaning: From the runny gold-coloured gum
Grouping: Angiosperm, Dicotyledon, Altingiacean
Informal ID: Sweetgum tree
Fossil size: Leaf width 9cm/3½in
Reconstructed size: Tree height to 30m/100ft
Habitat: Mixed woodland
Time span: Eocene, 40 million years ago, to today
Main fossil sites: Worldwide
Occurrence: ◆

Platanus

Below: This Eocene specimen of the species Platanus wyomingensis *is from Utah, USA. The fine, well-spaced points, or 'teeth', sometimes termed multi-serrate or multi-denticulate, are visible chiefly on the three central lobes.*

Main vein per lobe | Deep lobes | Small tooth-like edging

Palmate central area | Leaf stalk (petiole)

Considerable confusion surrounds the common names of species in the genus *Platanus*. In general, they are known as planes in areas such as Great Britain, but sycamores in North America. (The sycamore in Britain is a member of the genus *Acer*, otherwise called the sycamore maple.) The American sycamore is also called the buttonwood tree, and the London plane is hardy and resistant to air pollution. Plane leaves can be mistaken for those of the maples, with their palmate form (lobes coming from a central area, like the fingers of a palm), and often deep and sharp-pointed lobes, sometimes bearing toothed edges. However, *Platanus* leaves are arranged alternately along the twig, while *Acer* leaves grow in opposite pairs. The group has one of the longest fossil records of any well-known tree, and the six living species of *Platanus* are all found in the Northern Hemisphere.

Name: *Platanus*
Meaning: Broad, flat
Grouping: Angiosperm, Dicotyledon, Platanacean
Informal ID: Plane or sycamore tree
Fossil size: Leaf width 19cm/7½in
Reconstructed size: Tree height up to 40m/130ft
Habitat: Mixed woodland
Time span: Early to Middle Cretaceous, 115 million years ago, to today
Main fossil sites: Northern Hemisphere
Occurrence: ◆ ◆

Acer

Name: *Acer*
Meaning: Maple
Grouping: Angiosperm, Dicotyledon, Aceracean
Informal ID: Maple tree
Fossil size: Leaf width 4cm/1½in
Reconstructed size: Tree height 20–35m/66–115ft
Habitat: Temperate mixed woodland
Time span: Oligocene, 30 million years ago, to today
Main fossil sites: Mainly Northern Hemisphere
Occurrence: ◆ ◆

The maple family, Aceraceae, includes about 150 living species of maples and sycamores, and possibly as many fossil species. The species living today include both trees and shrubs and are renowned for their often spectacular autumn colour. One of their most characteristic features is the seeds, each with a single membraneous 'wing' that causes the seed to twirl around like a mini-helicopter as it is shed from the parent tree. The seeds are borne in pairs, with the angle between the pair varying from almost a straight line to a very sharp V, according to the species. These seeds are fairly hardy and make easily identifiable fossils. The leaves are usually long-stalked and distinctively three-lobed, with each lobe toothed to a varying degree, again depending on the species concerned. The sugar maple is the state tree of both New York and West Virginia, USA. Most maples, both living and fossilized, are from the Northern Hemisphere, with the majority in East Asia.

Above: The three-lobed maple leaf is an internationally recognized symbol of the North America region, especially of the latitudes around the border between Canada and the USA, and it is also the central motif of the Canadian flag. This French specimen in loosely cemented limestone from Quaternary rocks has minimal toothing – that is, it has a rounded outline.

Cardiospermum

Name: *Cardiospermum*
Meaning: Heart seed
Grouping: Angiosperm, Dicotyledon, Sapindacean
Informal ID: Balloon vine (also see text)
Fossil size: Leaf length 5cm/2in
Reconstructed size: Height to 3–4m/10–13ft
Habitat: Mixed temperate woodland
Time span: Eocene, 40 million years ago
Main fossil sites: North America
Occurrence: ◆ ◆

The genus *Cardiospermum* includes living woody vines and shrubby plants with a trailing tendency, mostly from the tropical Americas. It is part of the Sapindaceae, or soapberry, family with more than 1,300 species worldwide, many of which are toxic. A well-known living species is *Cardiospermum halicacabum*, the balloon vine, which has been commonly planted and in some areas has escaped to become a problem weed. The flowers are small and white, but the plant is known for its fruits, which are pale, inflated-looking, membraneous 'balloons', each about 3cm/1¼in across, containing three black seeds. Each seed has a white heart-shaped scar – hence the genus name, which means 'heart seed'. Another common name for this species is love-in-a-puff, which belies its status as a noxious weed and plant pest in some regions. The species *Cardiospermum coloradensis* is well known from the Eocene Epoch rocks of the Green River Formation, Utah, USA, where its leaves form some of the most distinctive fossils. This extinct species appears to have been more of a shrub than a trailing vine.

Above: The leaves of the Colorado balloon vine, Cardiospermum coloradensis, are typically trilobate, although some specimens show four or five rounded lobes. The leaf stalk, or petiole, can be considerably longer than that seen on this specimen.

Below: The balloon vine, originally from Central and South America, is now a weed in North America, Australia, South Africa and other regions.

ANIMALS – INVERTEBRATES

Vertebrae are commonly known as backbones – we have them in our own

'backbone' or spinal column. This feature is often used to divide the

kingdom Animalia into two great groups – those with vertebrae and those

without. (The accurate biological situation is slightly more complicated, as

explained on the opening pages of the next chapter, Animals – Vertebrates).

Invertebrate or 'spineless' animals range from the simplest sponges, the

poriferans, which are devoid of nerves or muscles or brains, to complex

and highly developed cephalopod molluscs such as the octopus and squid,

with sophisticated and intelligent behaviour. The molluscs are one of the

best-represented invertebrate groups in the fossil record, since their hard

shells end up in the high-probability preservation conditions of the sea bed.

One of the largest invertebrate groups is the arthropods or 'joint-legs'.

It takes in the extinct trilobites, myriad crustaceans such as barnacles and

crabs, and the land-dwelling insects and arachnids.

Above from left: the coral Meandrina, *trilobite* Trinucleus *and mollusc* Dactylioceras.

Right: Ammonites are one of the most recognizable and evocative symbols of the prehistoric world. This huge group of molluscs came to prominence in the Devonian Period and faded during the Cretaceous, along with the dinosaurs. These specimens are Promicoceras planicosta *from the Jurassic Period.*

EARLY INVERTEBRATES

The most ancient animal fossils, such as those from Precambrian Ediacara in Australia or the Middle Cambrian Burgess Shale in North America, have received varying interpretations over the years. Some of those life-forms were so different from any others, living or extinct, that the term 'Problematica' is used when precise taxonomic position is uncertain.

Mawsonites

Hand-sized *Mawsonites* are one of the most difficult of the Ediacaran life-forms to interpret with any degree of certainty. With its multi-lobed, expanding radial symmetry – that is, a wheel- or petal-like structure – it has been called almost everything from a flower to an aberrant sea lily (crinoid). However, it comes from a time well before flowering plants had yet evolved. One of the more established theories regarding its origins is that it was some kind of scyphozoan – that is, a jellyfish from the cnidarian group. Its unique features, however, make it difficult to assign to any

of the known jellyfish groupings, either those living or extinct. In addition, its surface topography, which has some fairly sharp and well-defined ridges, is not reminiscent of a floppy, jelly-like organism. Another possibility regarding its origins is that the fossils are the remains of a radial burrow system made by some type of creature, perhaps a worm, tunnelling and looking for food in the sandy, silty sea bed of the seas and oceans of the time. This would mean it is a trace fossil – traces left by an organism, rather than preserved parts of the actual organism itself.

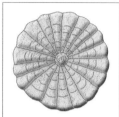

Name: *Mawsonites*
Meaning: Mawson's animal (after Australian Antarctic explorer Sir Douglas Mawson)
Grouping: Animal, Cnidarian, Scyphozoan?
Informal ID: Ediacara 'jellyfish' or trace fossil
Fossil size: Overall width 12–14cm/4¾–5½in
Reconstructed size: Unknown
Habitat: Sea bed
Time span: Precambrian, about 570 million years ago
Main fossil sites: Australia
Occurrence: ◆

— Central disc

— Innermost set of concentric rings

— Outermost lobes

— Outer margin

Left: Resembling multiple, expanding whorls of flower petals, the reddish sandstone impression known as Mawsonites *has an overall circular outline composed of curved lobes. The central disc is well defined, with concentric sets of roughly circular raised 'rings' that become more straight-sided towards the outer margin.*

Naraoia

This thumb-size arthropod was at first believed to be some kind of branchiopod crustacean (a cousin of today's water-flea, *Daphnia*). The shiny, two-part covering 'shield', or carapace, bears a central groove from head to tail and a division from side to side into two valves, front and rear. Around the edge of the carapace is a fringe of limb and appendage endings. Dissection into the thickness of the fossil, down through the carapace, has revealed the limbs and appendages in more detail, showing how and where they join to the main body underneath. The results indicated, very unexpectedly, that *Naraoia* was some type of trilobite. However it is not tri-lobed, with left, middle and right sections to the carapace, but rather bi-lobed, with just left and right. Similarly, it has not three divisions from head to tail, but two.

Below: Preservation of Burgess Shale trilobites is exceptional, as some of these are entire animals rather than just shed body casings. Naraoia is an early and unusual trilobite, with front and rear sections to the carapace and one central furrow from head to tail. Comparison of specimens shows that Naraoia may have retained immature features into mature adulthood, a phenomenon known as neoteny.

Name: *Naraoia*
Meaning: From the nearby locally named Narao lakes
Grouping: Arthropod, Trilobite
Informal ID: Early trilobite
Fossil size: Carapace front–rear about 3cm/1¼in
Reconstructed size: Width 2.5cm/1in, including limbs
Habitat: Sea bed
Time span: Middle Cambrian, 530 million years ago
Main fossil sites: North America
Occurrence: ◆

Burgessia

Named after the shale rocks of its Burgess Pass discovery region in Canada, *Burgessia* was probably some type of bottom-dwelling arthropod. The creature is known from thousands of specimens discovered at the locality. *Burgessia* probably walked, burrowed or swam weakly across the sea floor, and fed mainly by filtering tiny edible particles of food from the general ooze on the ocean floor. Its protective, convex (domed) shield-like carapace was about the size of a fingernail and it covered the softer, vulnerable parts beneath, so that only the ends of the limbs, two antennae-like feelers, which were directed forwards, and the long tail spine were visible from above. In the carapace was a branching set of canals, or grooves, which may have been part of the digestive system. In some specimens the tail spine is twice as long as the body.

> **Hurdia**
> The Burgess fossils show the first large-scale evolution of a mineralized, or chitinous, exoskeleton – a hard outer casing, usually found over the top of the body and used for protection as well as muscle anchorage. *Hurdia* has been included in the group known as anomalocarids. Its mouthparts may have had an extra set of teeth within, forming a so-called 'pharyngeal mill' that would be able to grind up other harder-bodied victims – showing that predators were already adapting to well-protected prey.

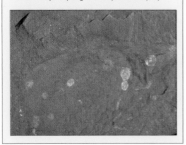

Name: *Burgessia*
Meaning: Of Burgess
Grouping: Arthropod, otherwise uncertain
Informal ID: Burgess arthropod
Fossil size: 1cm/⅜in across
Reconstructed size: Head–tail length 2.5cm/1in
Habitat: Sea bed
Time span: Middle Cambrian, 530 million years ago
Main fossil sites: North America
Occurrence: ◆

Tail section · Main carapace
Tail spine · Head end

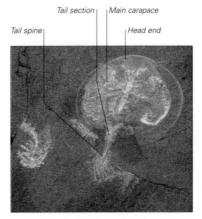

Left: Detailed study of Burgessia reveals that the body has a cephalic (head) region, about nine main body sections or segments, a telson (tail section) and a long spiny tail. The two antennae were directed so that they pointed forwards. Piecing together the remains of many specimens shows that the creature's 9 or 10 pairs of legs were uniramous (unbranched) and probably bore gills for obtaining oxygen from the water.

SPONGES

The sponges, phylum Porifera, are strange animals that live permanently rooted to the rocks or mud of the sea bed. They flush water through their porous bodies and filter out tiny food particles. Sponges have an extremely simple anatomy, lacking specialized organs, nerves and muscles and possessing only a few basic cell types. From Cambrian times, most sponges have left plentiful fossils of their mineralized bodies.

Doryderma

Name: *Doryderma*
Meaning: Porous-skinned
Grouping: Poriferan, Demosponge, Lithistid, Megamorinan, Dorydermatid
Informal ID: Doryderma sponge
Fossil size: Specimen 7cm/2¾in high
Reconstructed size: 50cm/20in plus
Habitat: Sea floor
Time span: Carboniferous to Late Cretaceous, 350–85 million years ago
Main fossil sites: Throughout Europe
Occurrence: ◆ ◆

Doryderma is an example of the Demospongea class of sponges – a group that is distinguished by building their skeletons out of both silica spicules and/or a network of tough, cartilage-like fibres of the substance spongin, which is a nitrogenous, hornlike material. Where spicules are present in this class, they are typically both highly complex in shape and capable of meshing together to form a network of significant strength – the skeletons of living demosponges have been observed to hold together long after the death of the animal itself. *Doryderma* is a reasonably common fossil in European marine rocks. However, the atypical branching form that makes it so attractive also makes it prone to damage and fragmentation.

Exhalant openings (oscula)

Branching points

Left: The Cretaceous genus Doryderma has an unusual branching form. The ends of the branches bear multiple openings that are exhalant: that is, from which water would have been expelled from them after having been filtered for food inside the main body cavity.

Sponge shapes and anatomy

There are something in the region of 10,000 species of sponges living in the world today, and many thousands of them are also known from the fossil record. They have existed since Cambrian times, more than 500 million years ago, and the abundance of individual specimens as well as the number of different species provide useful marker, or index, fossils for dating rocks. Common sponge shapes include vases, tubes, mushrooms and funnels. Some types of sponge branch either regularly (as illustrated here) or follow a more random pattern, but they all share the same major feature – a cavity inside where the water is sieved and the food removed. In addition, a growing sponge may be constrained by its locality, such as a cleft in the sea bed rock, or be nibbled by predators, and both of these factors can have an effect on its overall form and size. The three main types of sponge are calcareous (calcisponges) with spicules (small, pointed structures) of hard, calcium-containing minerals; siliceous sponges, in which the spicules are based on the mineral silica and have a glass-like quality; and horny sponges, in which the skeleton is composed of protein-based or similar substances such as spongin.

Spongia

Name: *Spongia*
Meaning: Sponge
Classification: Poriferan, Demosponge, Keratosid, Spongiid
Informal ID: Bath sponge
Fossil size: 8cm/3in across
Reconstructed size: Up to 20cm/8in across
Habitat: Sea floor
Time span: Carboniferous, 350 million years ago, to today
Main fossil sites: Worldwide
Occurrence: ◆ ◆

The Spongiidae family includes excellent examples of demosponges, which possess a skeleton composed entirely of branching and interwoven fibres made of spongin. This makes it highly flexible even when dry. The much harder, mineralized, spicule-type elements of the skeleton are almost completely absent. Modern forms of the genus *Spongia* are probably most familiar as the traditional 'bath sponges' of recent years – which are actually the dried corpses of this most 'spongy' of sponges, used for their mild exfoliating properties and ability to absorb water. The fossil record of the Spongiidae shows that these sponges have been a feature of the sea floor at varied depths since the beginnings of the Carboniferous Period.

Right: Spongia *is a fossil from the same group as the modern 'bath sponge'. It possessed a soft, highly flexible skeleton – a feature that often resulted in poor preservation as a fossil. The example shown here is from the Cretaceous Red Chalk of Hunstanton in Norfolk, England.*

Verruculina

Verruculina is a genus of demosponge that lived from the Mid Cretaceous to the Tertiary, chiefly in Europe. The genus possessed a network of spongin reinforced by small, simple spicules embedded in the elastic material (in a similar manner to fibreglass). This gave the whole sponge a skeleton midway in rigidity between those of *Doryderma* and *Spongia*. *Verruculina* did not have an almost fully enclosed central space in the manner of most sponges – with many small, inhalant pores for drawing in water, and one large exhalant pore (the osculum) for pushing the water out. Instead, it possessed a broad, squat body that unfolded at the top, resembling a sprouting leaf or a bracket fungus.

Below: Verruculina *was a distinctive demosponge and it resembles the bracket fungus, which grows on tree trunks. It was once common in the Cretaceous seas that covered Europe – this specimen is Late Cretaceous chalk – but it steadily declined during the Tertiary Period before its eventual extinction.*

Name: *Verruculina*
Meaning: Wart-like
Grouping: Poriferan, Demonsponge, Lithistid, Leiodorellid
Informal ID: Bracket-fungus sponge
Fossil size: 7cm/2¾in across
Reconstructed size: Typically 10cm/4in diameter
Habitat: Sea floor
Time span: Middle Cretaceous to Tertiary, 110–2 million years ago
Main fossil sites: Throughout Europe
Occurrence: ◆ ◆ ◆

SPONGES (CONTINUED)

Most sponges, past and present, lived in the seas, and typically had a hollow, porous body attached to the sea bed at one end. Water is drawn through the body wall, where feeding cells lining the interior extract food particles. The internal skeleton can consist of horny material; hard, mineralized shards or spicules; or both horny and mineralized elements, embedded in the body wall.

Porosphaera

Porosphaera is an example of the calcarean sponges, or calcisponges. This is a group that builds skeletons made entirely of spicules made from calcite, with no spongy material or silica. Each of the hundreds of tiny spicules that form the skeleton often resembles a Y or tuning fork in shape, allowing them to mesh together and form a strong, rigid network that is often easily fossilized. Porosphaera possessed a roughly grape-size, spherical body, made rigid by interlocking spicules and also covered in tiny spines, presumably for defence against predators. These could range from fish to starfish and sea urchins. It is a relatively common fossil from the Cretaceous marine rocks of Europe, particularly chalk deposits.

Below: Tiny Porosphaera *was a Cretaceous calcisponge that was relatively common in European rocks, especially – as with this specimen – from the Upper Chalk beds of Sussex, England. This view shows the large exhalant opening, or osculum, from which water left the chamber within, and which probably faced directly upwards in life.*

— Globular body

— Exhalant opening (osculum)

Name: *Porosphaera*
Meaning: Porous sphere
Grouping: Poriferan, Calcarean, Pharetronid, Porosphaeridan
Informal ID: Spiny globe sponge
Fossil size: Generally less than 1cm/⅜in but some specimens over 2cm/¾in
Reconstructed size: As above
Habitat: Sea floor
Time span: Mainly Cretaceous, 145–65 million years ago
Main fossil sites: Throughout Europe
Occurrence: ◆ ◆ ◆

Raphidonema

The calcisponge *Raphidonema* was basically elongated and cup-shaped, but individuals grew in a great many variations on this simple theme. The thick walls tapered downward from a broad exhalant opening at the top, often giving a form similar to a vase or funnel. The walls themselves were well perforated with small canals, and the outer surface was frequently covered by knobbly or nodular protrusions characteristic of this genus, while the inner walls lining the interior chamber were much smoother. *Raphidonema* was widespread in the warm, shallow seas of the Cretaceous Period.

Name: *Raphidonema*
Meaning: Seamed one
Grouping: Poriferan, Calcarean, Pharentronid, Lelapiid
Informal ID: English vase sponge or vase 'coral'
Fossil size: 7cm/2¾in
Reconstructed size: Variable, height typically up to 10cm/4in
Habitat: Sea floor
Time span: Triassic to Cretaceous, 250–65 million years ago
Main fossil sites: Throughout Europe
Occurrence: ◆ ◆ ◆

Left: Fossils of Raphidonema *are famously common in the Farringdon Sponge Gravels of Oxfordshire, England, where colonies of individuals formed enormous, coral-like structures known as sponge-beds.*

Above: Raphidonema, *a vase-shaped Cretaceous sponge, can be easily recognized by the lumpy, nodule-like ornamentation on the outside surface. In contrast, the interior of the sponge is smooth. The simple vase- or cup-like shape was often bent, curved, squashed and distorted during preservation.*

Ventriculites

Ventriculites belongs to the Hexactinellidae, which is a class of sponges that form skeletons of glassy mineralized silica spicules only, without networks of the more flexible spongin material. Hexactinellid spicules occur in both small and large forms, a novel feature that allows them to interlock more tightly and so form a strong skeleton.

This sponge was an important element of the Santonian Micraster Chalk Communities found on the coast of Kent, in the south of England. (*Micraster* was an echinoid, or sea urchin, and appears later in this chapter.) These sea-bed assemblages of urchins, starfish and other echinoderms, plus molluscan shellfish, probably relied on the large sponges for shelter, both from currents and predators – a role more usually held by corals. Remains of *Ventriculites* are often found in association with the fossils of huge, coiled-shelled ammonoids, up to 2m/6½ft across. It is possible that the sponges provided shelter and protection for the young of these predatory molluscs.

Left: The attractive Ventriculites *from the Cretaceous Period of Europe grew in a funnel shape, tapering from a very broad exhalant opening at the summit to a surprisingly narrow base, which was anchored to the shallow sea bed.*

Name: *Ventriculites*
Meaning: Stomach stone
Grouping: Poriferan, Hexactinellid, Lychniscosan, Ventriculitid
Informal ID: Funnel sponge, funnel 'coral'
Fossil size: Height 15cm/6in
Reconstructed size: Height up to 30cm/12in
Habitat: Sea floor
Time span: Middle to Late Cretaceous, 110–65 million years ago
Main fossil sites: Throughout Europe
Occurrence: ◆ ◆

Archaeocyatha

Name: *Archaeocyatha*
Meaning: Ancient cup
Grouping: Uncertain – classified on their own or within the phylum Porifera
Informal ID: Cambrian cup 'sponge'
Fossil size: Longest side 10cm/4in
Reconstructed size: Height up to 25cm/10in
Habitat: Sea floor
Time span: Cambrian, 550–500 million years ago
Main fossil sites: Worldwide
Occurrence: ◆ ◆

The archaeocyathans (archaeocyathids) are a very ancient 'anomaly' from the Cambrian Period. They have many similarities to sponges and also to certain corals. Some experts consider them to be sponges, others as allied to corals, and still others as not closely related to sponges or corals at all. They are sometimes called the 'first reef-builders', but their actual importance in the earliest reefs is not certain. Archaeocyathans were solitary organisms, each inhabiting a double-walled, porous skeletal structure that resembled a tall cup – their name is derived from the old Greek for 'ancient cup'. The cup was attached to the sea floor by thick roots, but the form and lifestyle of the animal that lived within remains a mystery. The strange structure and lack of soft tissue anatomy has frustrated attempts to define their relationships to other groups of sponges and similar simple creatures.

Below: The mysterious archaeocyathans are sometimes found in great concentrations that resemble primitive reefs. This assemblage is from Cambrian rocks of the Flinders Ranges, Australia. In some Cambrian rocks found in Russia, the fossils are numerous enough to be used as indicator or marker fossils for dating layers.

CNIDARIANS – JELLYFISH, CORALS AND RELATIVES

Cnidarians are often regarded as the most basic forms of true animals. The soft, sac-like body has a single opening, which doubles as both mouth and anus. The life cycle of most cnidarians includes a free-swimming, jellyfish-like stage, or medusa, and an anemone-like stage, or polyp, attached to the sea bed.

Essexella

Jellyfish, known as scyphozoans, spend most of their lives as large, free swimming medusae. Their soft bodies have bequeathed them a generally poor fossil record, restricted to areas where an unlikely combination of circumstances have combined to preserve exceptionally detailed fossils. *Essexella*, from the Upper Carboniferous rocks of North America, is one of the better-known fossil jellyfish, due to mass discoveries of them in several quarries within the state of Illinois, USA. The fine preservation shows an unusual anatomy with a large, mushroom-like body, the bell, trailing an apron- or sheet-like membrane rather than the usual dangling mass of tentacles. This strange feature has earned it, and similar forms, the nickname 'hooded jellyfish'.

Below: This specimen of Essexella had its umbrella-like body preserved in semi-3D, as part and counterpart in two halves of a split rock. The sheet-like membrane hangs below the bell, which may have pulsated gently as the jellyfish drifted with the currents.

Bell

'Hood' (apron-like sheet)

Name: *Essexella*
Meaning: From the estuarine Essex fauna of Mazon Creek
Grouping: Cnidarian, Scyphozoan, Rhizostoman
Informal ID: Hooded jellyfish
Fossil size: Bell 5cm/2in across
Reconstructed size: Bell width up to 10cm/4in
Habitat: Open sea
Time span: Late Carboniferous, 300 million years ago
Main fossil sites: North America
Occurrence: ◆ ◆

Ediacaran medusoid

Above and right: Ediacaran medusoids are a well-known form among the rare and beautiful fossils of that time. Despite their name, however, it is likely that they are unrelated to modern jellyfish, and were probably incapable of swimming. The fossilized ripple effect shows that the creature was preserved on the sea bed.

The incredible fossils of Ediacara offer a rare glimpse into the long-vanished world of the Precambrian Era, some 570 million years ago. They are the faint, compressed outlines of strange, soft-bodied animals that bathed in shallow seas about 50 million years before the dawn of the Cambrian 'explosion' of more modern life-forms. Some experts contend that they were a 'failed experiment' – long-vanished organisms that came and went, were fundamentally different to all modern creatures, and left no descendants. Some are termed vendobionts, or 'gas creatures', because of their inflated, sac-like bodies.

Name: Ediacaran medusoid
Meaning: Jellyfish-like creature from Ediacara
Grouping: Unknown
Informal ID: Ediacaran 'jellyfish'
Fossil size: Up to 10cm/4in across
Reconstructed size: As above
Habitat: Sea floor
Time span: Late Precambrian, 570 million years ago
Main fossil sites: Australia
Occurrence: ◆

Zaphrentoides

Zaphrentoides was a solitary form of rugose coral from the Early or Lower Carboniferous Period (for general information on corals, see next page). It had a form typical of the solitary rugose corals – a curved, horn-shaped structure subdivided by many radiating internal ribs, known as septa. Rugose corals have long disappeared, seemingly wiped out in the truly catastrophic series of extinctions that marked the end of the Permian Period, 250 million years ago. Unlike their tabulate and scleractinian cousins, the solitary rugose corals did not solidly attach themselves to the seabed, and probably did not form a large part of Palaeozoic reef communities. *Zaphrentoides* is one of the less common forms. Known informally as a horn coral, *Zaphrentoides* would have lived half-buried in the soft mud. Being overturned was a common danger, as many fossil specimens are found on their sides or even upside down.

Below: The horn-like structure of Zaphrentoides *is shown cut through to reveal the flanges, or ribs, arranged in a radiating pattern, like the spokes of a wheel. This specimen is from County Fermanagh, in Northern Ireland.*

— Septa

— Horn-like body shape

— Narrow end of horn

Name: *Zaphrentoides*
Meaning: Tube connections
Grouping: Cnidarian, Anthozoan, Rugosan, Hapsiphyllid
Informal ID: Horn coral
Fossil size: Width 2cm/¾in
Reconstructed size: Typical width 2cm/¾in, height 10cm/4in
Habitat: Sea floor
Time span: Early Carboniferous, 350 million years ago
Main fossil sites: Europe, North America
Occurrence: ◆ ◆

Lithostrotion

Name: *Lithostrotion*
Meaning: Star stone, tread rock
Grouping: Cnidarian, Anthozoan, Rugosan, Lithostrotionid
Informal ID: Spaghetti rock
Fossil size: Individual 'threads' 1cm/⅜in thick
Reconstructed size: Colonies commonly 10m/33ft across
Habitat: Sea floor
Time span: Early to Middle Carboniferous, 350–320 million years ago
Main fossil sites: Worldwide, especially Central Europe and Asia
Occurrence: ◆ ◆ ◆

A colonial (group-living) form of rugose coral, *Lithostrotion* remains are usually composed of thousands of individual polyp skeletons consolidated into a single, tight-knit structure. (For general information on corals, see next page.) It occurs in Early Carboniferous rocks on all continents, and especially in Middle Carboniferous limestone rocks in Central Europe and Asia. In some localities in Scotland, deposits are so common that blocks measuring metres across are nearly entirely composed of these fossils. *Lithostrotion* forms a major part of the Carboniferous 'coral-calcarenite' fossil assemblages, such as those commonly found in limestones of northern England dated to Asbian (Visean) times, 340 million years ago. These fossilized sea-bed communities of corals, brachiopods and brittlestars were an important haven for marine life in the Mid-Palaeozoic seas.

Right: Lithostrotion, *a colonial rugose coral, can be recognized by its structure of thick, thread-like strands, which to some people resemble over-cooked pasta. This has earned it the nickname 'spaghetti rock'.*

CORALS

Corals (zoantharia) are cnidarians that have discarded the free-swimming stage and live as attached polyps, either singly or in colonies. They are common fossils due to their mineralized, often elaborate skeletons, which generally resemble a cup surrounding the anemone-like creature. Coral reefs have occurred for much of the last 500 million years and are useful indicators or markers for dating rocks.

Favosites

Below: Favosites *is recognized by its characteristic hexagonal column structures, which have earned it the nickname 'honeycomb coral'.*

The tabulate coral *Favosites* was one of the longest-surviving members of this now-extinct group. Tabulates are named for the plate-like structures, tabulae, that divide them horizontally, so that each individual when cross-sectioned resembles a packet of sweets (candies) cut lengthways. *Favosites* colonies formed medium-size, dome-like structures that were an important element of the tabulate reef communities during the Silurian and the Devonian Periods, around 400 million years ago. The remains of *Favosites* are often found in association with fellow reef-builders *Heliolites* and *Halysites*. After their heyday, which was from the Ordovician to the Devonian Periods, they became less common, although in some areas they are known to have persisted until the Permian Period.

Name: *Favosites*
Meaning: Favoured form (used in ancient Greece for a hexagon)
Grouping: Cnidarian, Anthozoan, Tabulatan, Favositinan
Informal ID: Honeycomb coral
Fossil size: 5cm/2in across
Reconstructed size: Variable, up to 40cm/16in
Habitat: Sea floor
Time span: Ordovician to Permian, 500–250 million years ago, gradually becoming less common
Main fossil sites: Worldwide
Occurrence: ◆ ◆ ◆

Heliolites

Close examination of the remarkable *Heliolites*, or 'sun stone' fossil, shows that it appears to be covered with circles surrounded by radiating lines, bearing a striking resemblance to tiny, rayed suns. In this genus of extinct tabulate corals (see *Favosites* above), the tiny 'suns' are, in fact, formed by the skeletal ribs, or septa, in the chambers inhabited by the polyps that built the coral skeleton. *Heliolites* formed a major part of Mid-Palaeozoic tabulate reef communities, and it is often found in association with *Favosites* and *Halysites*.

Right: Heliolites *formed large, pillow-like structures that contributed greatly to the reefs that existed 400 million years ago. These would have provided shelter for a variety of different primitive fish, molluscs such as ammonoids, and other creatures, as well as food, as predators tried to nibble the soft-bodied coral polyps from their stony chambers.*

Tiny rayed 'suns' dot the surface

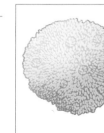

Name: *Heliolites*
Meaning: Sun stonel
Grouping: Cnidarian, Anthozoan, Tabulatan, Heliolitid
Informal ID: Sun coral
Fossil size: 7cm/2¾in across
Reconstructed size: Colonies 1m/3¼ft or more across
Habitat: Sea floor
Time span: Late Silurian to Middle Devonian, 415–380 million years ago
Main fossil sites: Worldwide
Occurrence: ◆ ◆ ◆

Halysites

Halysites, a colonial tabulate coral (see *Favosites*), is relatively common in Silurian rocks. It can be recognized by the distinctive pattern of winding, beaded lines covering its surface, rather like a conglomeration of pearl necklaces. This feature has earned it the informal name of 'chain coral'. Like the other specimens on these two pages, *Halysites* was an important Mid-Palaeozoic reef builder. It formed large, upright colonies that resembled a curved or folded sheet. Its remains are often found in association with those of *Heliolites* and *Favosites*.

Above: The skeletons of colonial Halysites *polyps linked together laterally (that is, side to side), as can be seen in this three-quarter view. In this way, their fossils formed sheet-like folds of mineralized material.*

Left: When viewed from above, Halysites *has a distinctive beaded, winding pattern, earning it the name 'chain coral'.*

Name: *Halysites*
Meaning: River stone
Grouping: Cnidarian, Anthozoan, Zoantharian, Tabulatan, Halysitid
Informal ID: Chain coral
Fossil size: 5cm/2in
Reconstructed size: Typically 10–20cm/4–8in across
Habitat: Sea floor
Time span: Ordovician to Silurian, 500–410 million years ago
Main fossil sites: Worldwide
Occurrence: ◆ ◆ ◆

Syringopora

Name: *Syringopora*
Meaning: Porous tube
Grouping: Cnidarian, Anthozoan, Zoantharian, Tabulatan, Auloporid
Informal ID: Organ pipe coral
Fossil size: 6cm/2¼in across at top
Reconstructed size: Average colony 5–10cm/2–4in; columns about 5mm/⅕in across
Habitat: Sea floor
Time span: Silurian to Late Carboniferous, 440–310 million years ago
Main fossil sites: Most continents
Occurrence: ◆ ◆

Right: Syringopora *colonies were bundles of loosely interconnected tubes, often called organ-pipe coral from their resemblance to the stack of pipes of a large concert organ.*

Syringopora is a relatively common Mid to Late Palaeozoic genus of colonial tabulate coral (see *Favosites*). It is often found in association with the rugose colonial coral *Lithostrotion* as part of the Carboniferous 'coral-calcarenite' fossil assemblages, where the smaller *Syringopora* probably grew in the shelter provided by the larger corals. *Syringopora* consists of a loose fabric of tubes, which can be distinguished from similar corals by the presence of cross-links joining together neighbouring columns. It displays a very similar shape to the unrelated modern genus *Tubipora*, suggesting that it occupied a similar ecological role in Palaeozoic seas. *Syringopora* is a relatively common fossil in marine rocks from the Silurian Period.

CORALS (CONTINUED)

The tabulate and rugose ('wrinkly') corals shown on the previous pages did not survive the major end-of-Permian mass extinction event. All post-Triassic corals, such as those shown on these two pages, and including living types, are known as scleractinians. They superficially resemble rugose corals, but they can be distinguished by their internal ribs, or septa, which are always arranged in multiples of six.

Montlivaltia

This solitary scleractinian coral, squat and cup-shaped, colonized 'hardground' areas of the sea floor during much of the Mesozoic Era. These were areas where the sediment had become saturated with minerals produced by the decomposition of shelly material, resulting in a solid, concrete-like seabed. *Montlivaltia* probably established itself in such an environment by inhabiting holes eroded by current- or wave-borne pebbles or abandoned mollusc borings. It is a moderately common fossil of Triassic and Cretaceous rocks, and it is found on all continents. Like all coral polyps, it would extend its stinging tentacles from its surrounding skeleton.

Left: Montlivaltia was a small, solitary form, and one of the few corals capable of colonizing hardened areas of sea floor. This specimen is from the Lower Lias of Walterston, near Cardiff, Wales.

Name: *Montlivaltia*
Meaning: From a French site
Grouping: Cnidarian, Anthozoan, Zoantharian, Scleractinian, Montlivaltid
Informal ID: Hardground cup coral
Fossil size: Slab 6cm/2½in across
Reconstructed size: Individuals 1–5cm/½–2in across
Habitat: Sea floor
Time span: Middle Triassic to Late Cretaceous, 240–70 million years ago
Main fossil sites: Worldwide
Occurrence: ◆ ◆

Thamnasteria

This Middle Mesozoic genus is an example of a colonial scleractinian coral – the group that forms the largest and most elaborate colonies known. *Thamnasteria* formed medium-size, domed colonies, and is a relatively common fossil in marine deposits. As a colonial coral, it is more colonial than most. In fact, *Thamnasteria* is the model genus for a type of structural organization among corals known as 'thamnasteroid'. In this growth pattern, the skeletons of individual polyps overlap and merge to form a cohesive whole. This further blurs the boundaries between individuals of the colony, making it hard to distinguish where one polyp ends and another begins.

Individual polyp chambers

Adjoining wall

Right: Thamnasteria inhabited Mesozoic environments known as 'patch reefs'. These were discontinuous reefs formed in warm, shallow waters, where large corals provided habitats for a diverse range of molluscs, crustaceans and fish. This is a Jurassic specimen.

Radiating ribs, or septa

Name: *Thamnasteria*
Meaning: Bushy star
Grouping: Cnidarian, Anthozoan, Zoantharian, Scleractinian, Thamnasteriid
Informal ID: Colonial scleractinian coral with polygonal cups
Fossil size: 7cm/2¾in across
Reconstructed size: Individuals 5–10mm/⅛–½in across
Habitat: Sea floor
Time span: Middle Triassic to Mid Cretaceous, 240–100 million years ago
Main fossils sites: Most continents
Occurrence: ◆ ◆ ◆

Meandrina

This genus takes its name from the meandering, wandering ridges and furrows that cover its surface. It is an excellent example of the so-called 'brain corals', an informal term that refers to a variety of colonial scleractinian corals that are not closely related. In the brain corals, the skeletons form bulbous domes covered in convoluted, lobe-like folds, the whole structure bearing an uncanny resemblance to the human brain. Modern *Meandrina* corals form large groups of colonies in the Atlantic coastal waters of southern North America, Brazil, the West Indies and Europe. Fossil forms can be found from about 55 million years ago, especially in Europe, the West Indies and in Brazil.

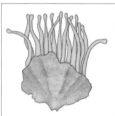

Left: Meandrina, *a brain or maze coral, gets its latter name from the maze-like surface network of grooves. Discoveries of fossil* Meandrina *show that this coral has been an important part of Atlantic sea-bed communities for nearly 55 million years. This specimen from Florida, USA, is about 5 million years old (Late Miocene to Early Pliocene).*

Name: *Meandrina*
Meaning: Meandering coral
Grouping: Cnidarian, Anthozoan, Zoantharian, Scleractinian, Meandrinid
Informal ID: Maze coral, brain coral
Fossil size: Length 8cm/3in
Reconstructed size: Up to 30cm/12in
Habitat: Sea floor
Time span: Eocene, 55 million years ago, to today
Main fossil sites: North and South America, Europe
Occurrence: ◆ ◆ ◆

Flabellum

A genus of solitary scleractinian coral, *Flabellum* is today commonly found living attached to boulders and other hard substrates, in the seas around Hawaii and the Azores islands. The coral can be readily recognized by its fan-shaped body, which is typically a flattened circle in cross section and gives *Flabellum* a superficial resemblance to solitary forms of the extinct rugose corals. *Flabellum* fossils are found in deposits from the Eocene Epoch to the present day in rocks all around the world, although it is particularly abundant in Middle Tertiary rocks of the Apennine Mountains in Italy.

Oppelismilia
The solitary scleractinian coral *Oppelismilia*, up to 5cm/2in across, is a relatively rare fossil from rocks of Upper Triassic to Jurassic times in the Americas and Eurasia. This small, conical coral grew in soft, muddy conditions that resulted in frequent uprooting. Thus, it was never able to establish firm anchorage and develop substantial reef communities.

Above: The fan coral Flabellum *is today known to survive at spectacular depths – the deepest recorded colonies are more than 3,000m/9,840ft below the surface. Fossil finds show that this coral has been present in sea-bed communities since the Early Eocene Epoch. The flange-like septa within the outer wall and the elliptical cross-sectional shape are clearly visible.*

Name: *Flabellum*
Meaning: Fan-shaped
Grouping: Cnidarian, Anthozoan, Zoantharian, Scleractinian, Flabellid
Informal ID: Fan coral
Fossil size: Individual structures 1.2–1.5cm/ ½–⅝in wide
Reconstructed size: Height up to 10cm/4in
Habitat: Sea floor
Time span: Eocene, 55 million years ago, to today
Main fossil sites: Most continents
Occurrence: ◆ ◆ ◆

WORMS

Worms are entirely soft-bodied animals, which means they are rarely found as fossils except where there is an exceptional level of preservation. Worms are found in the Burgess Shale Formations of North America preserved as carbon films, and in the Chengjiang Formations of China, where they have been mineralized with pyrites. Their trace fossils, such as furrows and burrows, are found worldwide.

Ottoia

A common marine worm from the Burgess Shale fossils of British Columbia, Canada, *Ottoia* is from the worm group known as priapulids or proboscis worms, which appeared in Cambrian times, some 530 million years ago, but which has only about 10 living species. *Ottoia* was about 8cm/3in long with a spiny, bulbous, moveable 'snout', or proboscis. The spines on the proboscis were probably used like stabbing teeth to capture prey. How *Ottoia* lived is uncertain, but it may have been an active tunneller living in a U-shaped burrow, in the manner of today's lugworm. At Burgess, its fossils have been found with soft tissue preserved showing both muscle and gut material. Analysis of the gut contents shows a diet of mainly molluscs – although there is also evidence of cannibalism.

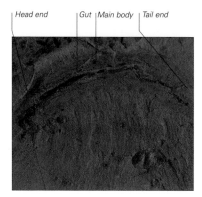

Below: Ottoia *is commonly found in the Cambrian Burgess Shale. Its fossils are most often preserved as a thin film on the fine-grained shale. This specimen has its gut preserved.*

| Head end | Gut | Main body | Tail end |

Name: *Ottoia*
Meaning: Of Otto
Grouping: Priapulid
Informal ID: Priapulid worm, proboscis worm
Fossil size: Length 7cm/2¾in
Reconstructed size: Length 8cm/3in
Habitat: Shallow sea floor
Time span: Cambrian, 530 million years ago
Main fossil sites: North America
Occurrence: ◆ ◆

Serpulid worm casts

Below: These serpulid worm casts are preserved in chalk from the Late Cretaceous rocks of Suffolk, England. They are not equivalent to the squiggly 'worm casts' familiar on lawns, which are the eaten and excreted soil of earthworms. They are calcareous tubes that the serpulid worms constructed and inhabited. These remains show the irregular spiralled shape typical of the casts.

Serpulid worms are members of the Annelida or segmented worms. It is the most familiar worm group known today and it includes both earthworms and seashore ragworms. Modern serpulids, also called tubeworms or plume worms, each live in a calcareous tube that they construct around themselves. This is attached to a hard surface, such as a seashore rock, mussel or crab shell. Serpulids have structures called radioles, made of rows of micro-hairs called cilia, which are used for respiration and feeding. Modern serpulid worms are very diverse, but their fossil record is limited. The main evidence for them includes trails, burrows and casts – their stony living tubes – but these cannot be linked with a specific species. The earliest serpulid worm tubes date from the Silurian Period, although serpulids become abundant only from the Jurassic onwards.

Name: Serpulid worm
Meaning: Spiral
Grouping: Annelid, Polychaete, Serpulid
Informal ID: Tube worm or plume worm
Fossil size: Each coiled tube 2cm/¾in across
Reconstructed size: Length up to 10cm/4in
Habitat: Wide range of marine environments
Time span: Arose in the Silurian, 420 million years ago, but common from the Jurassic, to today
Main fossil sites: Worldwide
Occurrence: ◆ ◆

Nereites

Nereites is a fossilized trace or trail, probably left by a wandering annelid worm, consisting of a middle furrow with tightly spaced lobes on either side. *Nereites* facies (a group of rocks with this trace fossil as the common element) are used to represent deep ocean environments that are subjected to turbidity currents. This means that *Nereites* can be used as a palaeo-environmental and palaeodepth indicator – that is, it lived in the very deep sea and so, therefore, did other creatures whose fossils are found associated with it. Geologist Roderick Murchison named this particular trace fossil *Nereites cambrensis* in 1839 – the species name of *cambrensis* for its discovery site of Wales. It is the holotype – the specimen used for the original description of the species, and with which all subsequently discovered specimens are then compared.

Name: *Nereites*
Meaning: From Nereus, the all-wise son of Gaia, a Roman sea god
Grouping: Annelid, Pascichnian
Informal ID: Worm feeding or grazing trail
Fossil size: Slab width 5cm/2¾in; length 6cm/2½in
Reconstructed size: Worms reached tens of centimetres in length
Habit: Deep sea bed
Time span: Specimen is from the Silurian Period (about 430 million years ago)
Main fossil sites: Worldwide
Occurrence: ◆ ◆

Left: The trace represents the feeding trail made by the worm as it meandered across the sea-bed sediment looking for food. The lobed depressions may have been left by the parapodia – oar-like flaps along the sides of the worm's body, which are used for 'walking' and swimming, as in the modern ragworm.

Spirorbis worm casts

Name: *Spirorbis*
Meaning: Spiralled coil
Grouping: Annelid, Polychaete, Sabellid
Informal ID: Coiled tubeworm
Fossil size: Individual coils less than 1cm/⅜in across
Reconstructed size: Range from a few millimetres across the coil to 2cm/¾in
Habitat: Varied marine environments
Time span: Late Ordovician (450 million years ago), to today
Main fossil sites: Worldwide
Occurrence: ◆ ◆

Spirorbis worms are related to serpulid worms (see opposite) and are commonly known as coiled tubeworms. Like the serpulids, *Spirorbis* builds itself a white calcareous tube in which to live. It pokes a 'plume' of tiny greenish tentacles from the tube's open end in order to catch any floating particles of food or micro-organisms from the plankton. Today's *Spirorbis* tubes are a common sight on seaside rocks, large seaweeds, such as kelps, and also shellfish. Each coil is just a few millimetres in diameter and resembles a miniature white snail. Fossils show that *Spirorbis* lived like this in the past, too, attaching itself to hard surfaces such as the shells of other organisms, including ammonites and crabs.

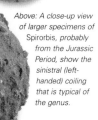

Right: Spirorbis worm casts are the living tubes of tiny worms related to fanworms and other tubeworms. In this specimen, the tubes have a loosely spiralled form and are preserved in sandstone.

Above: A close-up view of larger specimens of Spirorbis, probably from the Jurassic Period, show the sinistral (left-handed) coiling that is typical of the genus.

BRYOZOANS

Bryozoans are groups or colonies of zooids, which superficially resemble miniature sea anemones. They construct calcareous cups, tubes, bowls, boxes or other containers around themselves, known as zooecia. As they multiply, the colony grows in a certain pattern according to the genus, from an encrusting 'carpet' over the rocks, to upright delicate fan-, lace- or bush-like structures. Today there are about 4,300 species.

Fenestella

A marine bryozoan, *Fenestella* was particularly common during the Early Carboniferous Period (350–320 million years ago), but it became extinct at the end of the Permian. Sometimes called a 'lace-coral', it is not a colony of coral polyps, but tiny bryozoan zooids as explained above. Its network of interconnected branches often preserve in a pale colour compared with the substrate, making its fossils look like pieces of delicately woven lacework. *Fenestella* colonies fed by producing water currents that flowed through holes in the colony, where the feeding zooids filtered out suspended food particles.

Left: *This example of*
Fenestella plebia *from a road cutting in Oklahoma, USA clearly shows the lace-like branching structure typical of the genus. The net-like colony would have been erect or vertical in life. The crosswise connecting bars, called dissepiments, lacked the tiny zooid creatures, while the upright branches each had a double row of zooids.*

Name: *Fenestella*
Meaning: Small window
Grouping: Bryozoan, Fenestellid, Fenestratan
Informal ID: Lace 'coral'
Fossil size: Slab width 5cm/2in
Reconstructed size: Colonies range in size from less than 1cm/⅖in to 50cm/20in across
Habitat: Hard substrate on the sea floor
Time span: Silurian to Early Permian, 420–280 million years ago
Main fossil sites: Worldwide
Occurrence: ◆ (◆◆ in the Early Carboniferous)

Archimedes

Archimedes is an extinct bryozoan that had a central 'screw' structure to support the colony. Often the branches and the tubes secreted by the zooids are not preserved, since they are very delicate, so all that remains is the more robust central support. The individual zooids had a flat, table-like shape. *Archimedes* is most commonly found in fine-grained sediments laid down in calmer areas of the sea, such as sheltered bays. New colonies formed by branching off a parent colony before growing a new screw. In some instances, thousands of colonies can be traced back to a single parent branch.

Below: *Four specimens of* Archimedes *show the central 'screw'. The outer edges of each show traces of the branching structure of the bryozoan animals themselves, which attached to this central support structure.*

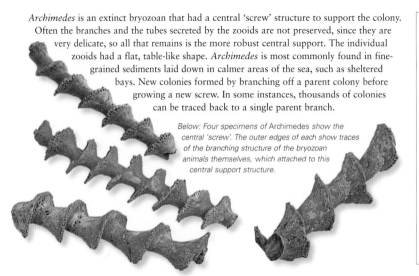

Name: *Archimedes*
Meaning: After Archimedes, inventor of the screw device for lifting water
Grouping: Bryozoan, Fenestrid, Fenestellid
Informal ID: Archimedes screw, screw bryozoan
Fossil size: Specimens about 3cm/1in long
Reconstructed size: Length up to 50cm/20in
Habitat: Calm, sheltered marine environments
Time span: Carboniferous to Permian, 350–270 million years ago
Main fossil sites: Worldwide
Occurrence: ◆◆

Chasmatopora

One of the bryozoans that formed colonies in curtain-like curved sheets, *Chasmatopora* (sometimes known as *Subretepora*) formed its fronds by branching off the main stems from the narrow base or 'root' anchored to the substrate. Each of the stems or strips is about six zooecia wide – that is, formed from six rows of tiny zooid animals in their box-like containers. These sets of parallel rows of tiny containers, known as zooecia, branched and then joined to form an enlarging net riddled with a regular pattern of holes. More than a dozen species of *Chasmatopora* have been identified, most from Eastern Europe (Estonia, Russia) and China, with a few from North America.

Right: This Chasmatopora *specimen is dated to the Middle Ordovician Period, about 465 million years ago, and comes from Kuckersits, Estonia. The original wavy curtain-shaped colony probably broke into several pieces due to a storm that caused an underwater sediment slump.*

Name: *Chasmatopora*
Meaning: Ravine or gorge holes
Grouping: Bryozoan, Fenestrid, Phylloporinin
Informal ID: Sea fan, lacy sea mat
Fossil size: Colonies about 10cm/4in across
Reconstructed size: As above
Habitat: Sea floor
Time span: Ordovician to Silurian, 480–420 million years ago
Main fossil sites: Europe, Asia, North America
Occurrence: ◆ ◆

Ptilodyctia

In this bryozoan, the colony grows in a slightly curved or an almost straight, single-branch structure. It consists of a middle wall with rows of box-shaped zooecia (containers) along either side, like tiny shoe boxes arranged in a row. In each zooecium lived a zooid, which typically had a pear- or stalk-like body and a crown of tentacles (the lophophore), for catching tiny particles of suspended food and also for obtaining

oxygen. However, in some bryozoan colonies different types of zooids specialized in feeding, respiration, protection, cleaning or reproduction – which was by asexual 'budding', where a new individual grew as a plant-like bud from an older one. Just above the example shown below is a fossil brachiopod, or lampshell (see next page). The brachiopods are considered to be the bryozoans' closest relatives.

Name: *Ptilodyctia*
Meaning: Soft or downy finger
Grouping: Bryozoan, Cryptostomatid, Ptilodyctyid
Informal ID: Bryozoan, sea-comb
Fossil size: Length 23cm/9in
Reconstructed size: Length up to 30cm/12in
Habitat: Sea floor
Time span: Ordovician to Devonian, 450–370 million years ago
Main fossil sites: Worldwide
Occurrence: ◆

Left: From the Silurian Wenlock Limestones of Dudley in the English West Midlands, this specimen of Ptilodyctia *would have been attached to the sea bed at its narrow end. This had a rounded or cone-shaped end that fitted into a similar-shaped depression in the base, which was attached to the sea bed.*

BRACHIOPODS

Brachiopods, or lampshells, are soft-bodied marine creatures that live in a shell consisting of two parts called valves. Superficially they look like bivalve molluscs, such as oysters and mussels, but brachiopods form a separate main grouping, or phylum. One of the key differences between the shells of brachiopods and bivalves concerns the line of symmetry. Brachiopods often have different-sized valves and are symmetrical along the midline, whereas the valves of bivalves are the same size: that is, the symmetry runs between the two valves. Brachiopods originated in the Cambrian and became very common and useful as indicator fossils, but their diversity was much reduced by the end-of-Permian mass extinction event.

Orthid brachiopod

Name: Orthid brachiopod
Meaning: Straight arm-foot
Grouping: Brachiopod, Orthid
Informal ID: Brachiopod, lampshell
Fossil size: Slab length 10cm/4in
Reconstructed size: Individuals 2cm/¾in wide (grew up to 5cm/2in)
Habitat: Sea floor
Time span: Cambrian to Permian, 500–250 million years ago
Main fossil sites: Worldwide
Occurrence: ◆ ◆ ◆

The orthids were an early and important group of articulate brachiopods (see later in this chapter). They first appeared in the Early Cambrian Period and were extremely diverse by the Ordovician Period, some 450 million years ago. The brachiopods in this group are sub-circular to elliptical in form, with generally biconvex (or outward-bulging) valves, although one valve is flatter and so bulges less than the other. The hinge line of this brachiopod is normally strophic, or straight, giving rise to the name 'orthid'. Other common features of this brachiopod group include ribs radiating outwards in the shape of a fan from the area of the hinge, and the presence of a concave sulcus (a depression or groove) on one valve and a corresponding fold in the opposite valve.

Plectothyris
Plectothyris is a brachiopod from the Jurassic Period. It is biconvex (both valves bulge outwards) with a non-strophic, or curved, hinge line. It has no sulcus, or fold. The line along which the two valves meet, called the commissure, is zigzagged, with the zigzag becoming more defined towards the midline. Each valve is ribbed towards the edge. Also growth lines are visible towards the centre of the valve. They formed as the valves became bigger, probably due to seasonal growth, similar to the growth rings of a tree trunk. Details such as these help to distinguish many hundreds of types of brachiopod. Their sea-bed habitat and their very hard and resistant shells mean that brachiopods were preserved in huge numbers and are very useful for dating rock layers.

Left: A mass accumulation is a large number of the same organisms found preserved in one place. Such accumulations usually form under extreme conditions – for example, a large influx of sediment causing the organisms to be rapidly buried, or a similar sudden change to a hostile environment. These particular orthids may have been buried by an underwater avalanche of mud or silt.

Pedicle area

Convex pedicle valve

Radiating ribs on shell

Brachial valve (non-pedicle 'shell')

Strophomenid brachiopod

Name: Strophomenid brachiopod
Meaning: Twisted or malformed arm-foot
Grouping: Brachiopod, Strophomenid
Informal ID: Brachiopod, lampshell
Fossil size: 4.5cm/1¾in wide along the hinge line
Reconstructed size: As above
Habitat: Sea floor
Time span: Ordovician to Triassic, 450–210 million years ago
Main fossil sites: Worldwide
Occurrence: ◆ ◆

Strophomenid brachiopods are more diverse in form than any other brachiopod group. They are normally plano-convex, which means that one valve is convex (bulging out), while the other is flat; or concavo-convex, meaning that one valve bulges out, while the other curves inwards. In addition, strophomenids have no pedicle opening – the pedicle is a muscular structure, like a stalk or the 'foot' of a mollusc, that secures the brachiopod to a hard surface. So strophomenids probably remained unattached on the sea floor. The subgroup known as true strophomenids were wider than they were long, and had a very small body cavity between the valves. They were important in Early Palaeozoic times, but faded by the Jurassic Period. Other groups of strophomenids became abundant during the Late Palaeozoic.

Valve margin
Hinge line
Second brachiopod impression

Above right: This view shows the valve of a strophomenid brachiopod. The valves are very unornamented and there is a long strophic (straight) hinge line. This specimen has an impression of another brachiopod near its hinge line.

Pentamerus

Name: *Pentamerus*
Meaning: Five parts or portions
Grouping: Brachiopod, Pentamerid
Informal ID: Brachiopod, lampshell
Fossil size: 5cm/2in wide
Reconstructed size: As above
Habitat: Sea floor
Time span: Late Cambrian to Devonian, 500–365 million years ago
Main fossil sites: Worldwide
Occurrence: ◆ ◆

Pentamerus is an articulate brachiopod, explained in more detail on the next page, but differs from other articulate brachiopods in that it has a spoon-shaped structure, the spondylium, on the rear portion of the pedicle valve, which is the valve bearing the muscular stalk-like pedicle that usually faced downwards. The hinge line is short and non-strophic (not straight). In addition, the fold and sulcus (depression) are opposite to those found on most brachiopods, with the fold on the pedicle valve. *Pentamerus* arose in Mid-Cambrian times and became very common in the Ordovician Period. During the Silurian Period, it lived in colonies with its pedicle buried in the sea floor. In some species within the genus, there was no pedicle and the colony was self-supporting. When displayed in museums the colonies are often exhibited upside down! The name comes from its five-fold symmetry, which, when the fossil is seen in section, can often resemble an arrow head.

Brachial valve
Pedicle foramen
Hinge line
Pedicle valve
Vaguely five-sided valve margin
Radiating ribs

Right: Both valves in this species of Pentamerus *are ribbed in shape. The downwards-facing pedicle valve is larger than the opposing valve, known as the brachial valve, which usually faced upwards. The shell looks roughly five-sided, or pentagonal, in outline – hence its name.*

BRACHIOPODS (CONTINUED)

Most brachiopods were connected to a hard surface by a pedicle – a muscular stalk-like structure. They were filter-feeders, using a structure called a lophophore to extract food from the water. The two main groups are the Articulata, which has a socket that hinges the two valves, and the hingeless Inarticulata. More than 3,000 fossil genera are known, but only 350 species survive today – all in the sea.

Spirifer

Spiriferids made up a diverse group of brachiopods that had an enormous range of shell shapes. *Spirifer* had a spiralled brachidium – the support arrangement for the feeding structure, or lophophore, within the shell. Some experts regard this as a uniting feature of the spiriferids, although others disagree. The valves are biconvex (both bulge outwards), usually with a long, straight hinge line, and typically with ribs. Some species are 'winged', but these wings are often missing in the fossil record.

Below: External (top) and internal (bottom) views of Spirifer. *The internal view shows the spiral brachidium after which the genus is named.*

Name: *Spirifer*
Meaning: Bearing or carrying a spiral (from the spiralled brachidium)
Grouping: Brachiopod, Spiriferid
Informal ID: Brachiopod, lampshell
Fossil size: Width 3cm/1⅛in
Reconstructed size: Less than 10cm/4in
Habitat: Sea floor
Time span: Ordovician to Permian, 480–250 million years ago
Main fossil sites: Worldwide
Occurrence: ◆ ◆

Below: Internal view of one valve of Spirifer, *which is broad, ribbed and has a strophic (straight) hinge line.*

Brachidial region

Torquirhynchia

Torquirhynchia is an exception to the rule that states brachiopods are bilaterally symmetrical. Its shell is fairly large and has the outline of a wide triangle. It is also ornamented with thick ribs, and the two valves are slightly out of line with each other. The hinge line is non-strophic (not straight) and the commissure – the line along which the two valves meet – is jagged or zigzagged.

Below: Two specimens of Torquirhynchia, *both showing strong ribbing, the non-strophic hinge line and the 'nut shape' that is typical of its subgroup, called the rhynchonellids. In these examples, the two valves are slightly opened.*

Name: *Torquirhynchia*
Meaning: Twisted beak, twisted nose
Grouping: Brachiopod, Rhynchonellid
Informal ID: Brachiopod, lampshell
Fossil size: Width 3cm/1⅛in
Reconstructed size: As above
Habitat: Sea floor
Time span: Late Jurassic, 150 million years ago
Main fossil sites: Throughout Europe
Occurrence: ◆ ◆

Zigzagged commissure

Non-strophic hinge line

Strong ribbing

Lingulid brachiopod

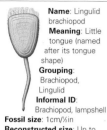

Name: Lingulid brachiopod
Meaning: Little tongue (named after its tongue shape)
Grouping: Brachiopod, Lingulid
Informal ID: Brachiopod, lampshell
Fossil size: 1cm/⅜in
Reconstructed size: Up to a few cm/about 1in
Habitat: Inter-tidal zones
Time span: Cambrian, more than 500 million years ago, to the present
Main fossil sites: Worldwide
Occurrence: ◆ ◆ ◆

Lingulid brachiopods have an extremely long fossil record, which stretches back into the Cambrian Period, more than 500 million ago, and belong to one of the oldest families of multi-cellular animals known to science. Since their origins, these creatures have remained fairly unchanged, and they still survive today in the deep sea, earning them the nickname 'living fossils'. Lingulids became fairly diverse during the Cambrian Period but went into decline during the following Ordovician Period and have never since been a varied group. *Lingula* itself is a relatively small inarticulate brachiopod (one that lacks a hinge to hold the two valves together). Its valves are thin, biconvex (both bulge outwards) and tongue-shaped in outline, lacking strong ornamentation. Today's *Lingula* lives buried in sediments along the shore's inter-tidal zone, and is eaten as a delicacy in some parts of South East Asia. The lingulid shell is made of protein, chitin and calcium phosphate.

Umbo · · · Calcium phosphate shell

Above: This fossilized specimen of a lingulid brachiopod shows the typical tongue shape that gives the genus its name. The specimen also shows the characteristic lack of ornamentation, although some growth lines are visible.

Actinoconchus

Name: *Actinoconchus*
Meaning: Rayed shell
Grouping: Brachiopod, Spiriferid
Informal ID: Brachiopod, lampshell
Fossil size: Length 2.5cm/1in
Reconstructed size: Length up to 4.5cm/1¾in
Habitat: Sea floor
Time span: Carboniferous, 300 million years ago
Main fossil sites: Worldwide
Occurrence: ◆ ◆

In this distinctively shaped brachiopod, both of the valves are very convex in outline and are almost the same overall size, thus creating a nearly circular outline. Thin but broad expansions of the shell can be seen along the ridged growth lines. The valves are finely ribbed, with the ribs diverging towards the front. Living during the Carboniferous Period, *Actinoconchus* attached itself by a short, stalk-like pedicle to hard surfaces. The shape of the brachial (upper) valve is similar to that of the hard surface to which the brachiopod was attached.

Below: Seen upside down here, this pedicle (lower) valve of Actinoconchus *shows the expansions along the growth lines, but the fine ribbing is not clearly visible in this specimen. These layered expansions helped to prevent* Actinoconchus *sinking into the muddy sea floor it inhabited, and also acted as camouflage, protecting it from the attentions of predators. These creatures fed by filtering out tiny particles of food from the surrounding water.*

Umbo

Expanded shell along growth lines

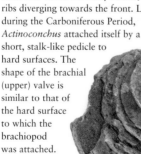

ARTHROPODS – TRILOBITES

Arthropods include millions of species that are alive today: insects, arachnids or spiders and scorpions, millipedes or diplopodans, centipedes or chilopodans, and crabs, shrimps and other crustaceans. These are covered in the following pages, starting with the long-extinct trilobites. The uniting feature of arthropods is their hard outer casing and usually numerous jointed limbs. The name means 'joint-foot'.

Anomalocaris

Most creatures of Cambrian times, as revealed by Burgess Shale fossils, were small – generally one to a few centimetres. The arthropods known as anomalocarids, however, commonly grew to 50cm/20in, and some reached almost 2m/6½ft. They were the largest animals of their time. *Anomalocaris* had a disc-like mouth that was originally interpreted as being a separate jellyfish-like animal, known as *Peytoia*. It also had large, strong, forward-facing appendages, which in some species bore sharp spines. These powerful spiked 'limbs', along with large eyes and strong swimming lobes, like paddles along the sides of the body, suggest that *Anomalocaris* was the top predator of its age. It probably fed on soft-bodied animals, such as worms, and perhaps even on trilobites. The relationship of anomalocarids to other arthropods is not yet fully understood (see also *Hurdia*).

Below: This lateral (side) view shows one of the two multi-segmented frontal appendages. Such specimens were originally interpreted as separate shrimp-like creatures, until experts eventually realized that they were detached parts of a larger animal. The small spines on each segment may have assisted in capturing their prey.

Name: *Anomalocaris*
Meaning: Anomalous shrimp
Grouping: Arthropod, Anomalocarid
Informal ID: Anomalocarid, Burgess 'supershrimp'
Fossil size: 7.5cm/3in
Reconstructed size: Total length, including front appendages, 60cm/24in
Habitat: Shallow seas
Time span: Cambrian, 530 million years ago
Main fossil sites: North America (Burgess), Asia (China)
Occurrence: ◆

Cruziana

The name *Cruziana* is used for a trackway, or 'footprints', made by an arthropod filter-feeding in the muddy sea bed. The chevron-like indentations were created as the animal used its limbs to plough into the ooze, stirring the sediment into suspension (floating in the water). While moving the sediment towards its rear end, the animal could filter out edible particles and move them forward towards its mouth. As a trace fossil, or ichnogenus, *Cruziana* refers to a particular type of behaviour and the evidence that results, but not the type of animal that created it. However, it is commonly assumed that some types of trilobites were responsible. In some examples, specimens of *Calymene* (see opposite) have been found at the end of the trackway. But any arthropod feeding or moving in this manner could conceivably be the trackmaker.

Left: It is most likely that the trace fossils known as Cruziana were made by trilobite-like creatures. The trackmaker's direction of travel is towards the open end of the V-shapes, left by appendage movement.

Name: *Cruziana*
Meaning: Of Cruz (in honour of General Santa Cruz of Bolivia)
Grouping: Arthropod, trilobite
Informal ID: Cruziana, trilobite trackway
Fossil size: Track width 3cm/1in
Reconstructed size: As above
Habitat: Muddy sea floor
Time span: Cambrian to Permian, 540–250 million years ago
Main fossil sites: Europe, North America, South America, Australia
Occurrence: ◆ ◆ ◆

Calymene

Name: *Calymene*
Meaning: Stony crescent
Grouping: Arthropod,
Trilobite, Phacopid
Informal ID: Trilobite
Fossil size: 3.2cm/1¼in
Reconstructed size: Unrolled
head–tail length 4cm/1½in
Habitat: Shallow seas
Time span: Silurian to
Devonian, 430–360 million
years ago
Main fossil sites: Europe,
North America
Occurrence: ◆ ◆ ◆ ◆

Calymene was a medium-size trilobite. It was probably a predator and was found in shallow Silurian seas, usually in lagoons or reefs. It had a semicircular-shaped cephalon (head shield) with three or four distinct 'lobes' that ran laterally along its central head section, known as the glabella. The glabella itself was bell-shaped, containing small eyes. There was a variable number of segments (or tergites) in the middle region, the thorax, depending on the species concerned – British specimens, for example, may have up to 19 segments, while those from North American species have only 13. Its tough exoskeleton, like that found on many post-Cambrian trilobites, was a good defence against predation and also increased its own chances of being preserved in the fossil record. This has helped to make *Calymene* one of the most commonly found trilobite genera from the Middle Ordovician Period.

Above: Viewed from above,
Calymene *shows its segmented main body structure and its almost non-existent pygidium, or tail.*

Right: This is a three-quarter front view of a partially enrolled Calymene. *The ability of many trilobites to roll up is thought to be a defence against predators attacking the unprotected underside.*

Right: In front view, the cephalon of Calymene blumenbachii *was more triangular, compared with the rounded cephalon of most other trilobite groups.*

Diacalymene

Name: *Diacalymene*
Meaning: Through Calymene
Grouping: Arthropod,
Trilobite, Phacopid
Informal ID: Trilobite
Fossil size: Head–tail
length 5cm/2in
Reconstructed size:
As above
Habitat: Shallow seas
Time span: Silurian to
Devonian, 430–360 million
years ago
Main fossil sites: Europe,
North America
Occurrence: ◆ ◆ ◆ ◆

Diacalymene is closely related to *Calymene*, to the point where some palaeontologists have suggested that they should be regarded as the same genus. However, there are some differences between the two. For a start, *Diacalymene* has a distinct ridge along the anterior of the cephalon, as well as a narrower glabella (central head region) than *Calymene*. In addition, *Diacalymene* also has a slightly more triangular-shaped cephalon (head shield), and it also tended to live in muddier sediments than did *Calymene*. Like *Calymene*, however, *Diacalymene* could roll up tightly for protection against threats, such as predators and storms.

Right: This large and complete fossilized specimen of Diacalymene *was discovered in a trilobite-rich formation in an area known as the Laurence Uplift, Oklahoma, USA.*

ARTHROPODS – TRILOBITES (CONTINUED)

Almost all trilobites had a similar body: a cephalon (head end), thorax (middle section) and pygidium (tail). However, there were exceptions (see Naraoia). Note that the name 'trilobite' does not come from this three-section head-to-tail structure. It is derived from the three lobes seen from side to side, being the left, central and right lobes, which were formed by two furrows or divisions running from head to tail.

Ogygopsis

Ogygopsis was a medium-size trilobite, and was more highly evolved than its early Cambrian ancestors. The body was fairly wide, and although the cephalon (head end) lacked the complexity or ornamentation of other forms, Ogygopsis did have long genal spines projecting from the 'cheeks' or edges of its cephalon. These genal spines reached to about the middle of the thorax. The tail, or pygidium, was larger than in most other Cambrian trilobites, consisting of multiple thoracic segments fused together to form a single large plate. When the pygidium is almost as large as the cephalon, such as in Ogygopsis, this is known as an isopygous type of trilobite. However, loss of segments to the tail meant that there were only eight segments in the thorax.

Left: The lack of side-cheeks on the cephalon (head region) of this specimen indicates that this is a moulted or cast-off body casing, which happened as the animal grew (as in crabs and insects today), rather than a whole dead animal.

Name: *Ogygopsis*
Meaning: Eye of the ancient King Ogyges
Grouping: Arthropod, Trilobite, Corynexochid
Informal ID: Trilobite
Fossil size: Head–tail length 4cm/1½in
Reconstructed size: As above
Habitat: Muddy sea floor
Time span: Middle Cambrian to Early Ordovician, 520–470 million years ago
Main fossil sites: Worldwide
Occurrence: ◆ ◆ ◆

Phacops

Phacops was a medium-to-large trilobite that lived in shallow water. The creature had 11 segments in its thorax section, and the pygidium (tail unit) was small and semi-circular. Like other trilobites, Phacops was capable of rolling itself into a tight ball when under threat of predation. The distinctly round glabella ('forehead') expands forward and is covered in rounded lumps, known as tubercles. Another distinctive feature of Phacops was its eyes, which were schizochroal, or multi-faceted. This means that each eye had many discrete, individual lenses, each with its own covering, or cornea, and separated from neighbouring lens units by areas called sclerae.

Below: A view from above shows the large eyes on either side of the head region, or cephalon.

These large eyes could swivel, and would have allowed an almost all-round field of vision. This indicates that Phacops was most likely a predator, perhaps hunting in low light levels.

Left: This specimen shows how tightly enrolled Phacops could become. All the antennae and appendages would have been protected within this tight exoskeletal (outer-cased) ball.

Name: *Phacops*
Meaning: Shiny eye
Grouping: Arthropod, Trilobite, Phacopid
Informal ID: Trilobite
Fossil size: Head–tail length 4cm/1½in
Reconstructed size: As above
Habitat: Muddy sea floor
Time span: Silurian to Devonian, 430–360 million years ago
Main fossil sites: North America, Europe
Occurrence: ◆ ◆ ◆ ◆

Encrinurus

Name: *Encrinurus*
Meaning: In hair
Grouping: Arthropod, Trilobite, Phacopid
Informal ID: Strawberry-headed trilobite, stalk-eyed trilobite
Fossil size: Head–tail length 2.5cm/1in
Reconstructed size: Head–tail length 4.5cm/1¾in
Habitat: Shallow sea floor
Time span: Middle Ordovician to Silurian, 470–410 million years ago
Main fossil sites: Worldwide
Occurrence: ◆ ◆ ◆

Encrinurus was a large type of trilobite with a forward-facing, rounded glabella (or forehead), and pimple-like lumps, known as tubercles, all over its cephalon (head). These distinctive characterisitics have led to the creature's informal name of the 'strawberry-headed trilobite'. Leading away from the outer corners, or cheeks, of the cephalon were short genal spines. The thorax had 11 or 12 segments. *Encrinurus*'s pygiduim was fairly long and unusual in construction in that there were many more segments in the central, or axial, portion than on the two lateral portions, called pleural ribs. These pleural ribs curved towards the rear. However the most unusual feature was the stalked eyes prominently protruding from the side-cheeks, which accounts for its other informal name of the 'stalk-eyed trilobite'.

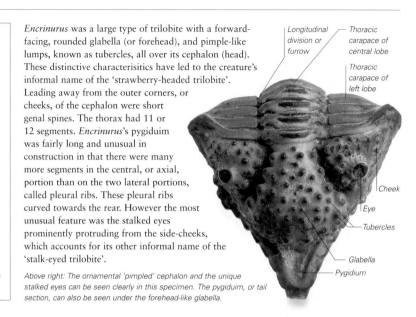

Longitudinal division or furrow
Thoracic carapace of central lobe
Thoracic carapace of left lobe
Cheek
Eye
Tubercles
Glabella
Pygidium

Above right: The ornamental 'pimpled' cephalon and the unique stalked eyes can be seen clearly in this specimen. The pygiduim, or tail section, can also be seen under the forehead-like glabella.

Acaste

Name: *Acaste*
Meaning: After the mythical Greek goddess
Grouping: Arthropod, Trilobite, Phacopid
Informal ID: Trilobite
Fossil size: Head–tail length 2cm/¾in
Reconstructed size: As above
Habitat: Shallow sea bed
Time span: Silurian to Early Devonian, 430–390 million years ago
Main fossil sites: Worldwide
Occurrence: ◆ ◆

Acaste is a medium-size trilobite with large, schizochroal (multi-lens) eyes, a round, forward-facing glabella (central head section), and a small, tapered pygidium (tail section). Although its overall shape and body plan is very similar to that of *Phacops* (opposite), these two genera belong to different trilobite families, and were not directly related. The physical likeness between the two was achieved through convergent evolution, which means that both groups evolved similar features separately, probably due to living in a similar environment and following a similar lifestyle. In both types of creature, natural selection favoured certain adaptations, such as schizochroal eyes to see well, and so the two types end up looking very similar. Indeed, it has been suggested that its visual acuity was more than the creature actually required. The two differ in some features, however, including ornamentation at the head end.

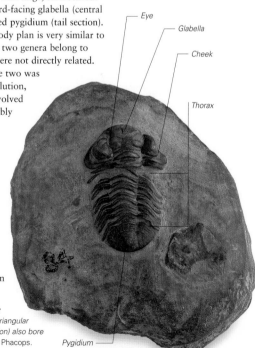

Eye
Glabella
Cheek
Thorax
Pygidium

Right: Acaste had a more tapered body shape than Phacops, and also a more triangular pygidium (tail). Its head section (cephalon) also bore more complex ridges and furrows than Phacops.

ARTHROPODS – TRILOBITES (CONTINUED)

Trilobites appeared in Cambrian times as some of the earliest of the complex, hard-cased creatures. They were adapted to a wide range of habitats, from shallow reefs to deep ocean floors. More than 5,000 genera and 15,000 species have been identified, with more discovered every year. Their abundance and distinctive features, which changed through time, make them useful indicator fossils for dating rock layers.

Ogygiocaris

Name: *Ogygiocaris*
Meaning: Shrimp of the ancient King Ogyges
Grouping: Arthropod, Trilobite, Asaphid
Informal ID: Trilobite
Fossil size: 20cm/8in
Reconstructed size: Head–tail length 13cm/5in
Habitat: Deep ocean floor
Time span: Early to Middle Ordovician, 490–470 million years ago
Main fossil sites: Worldwide
Occurrence: ◆ ◆

Ogygiocaris was a large, wide trilobite with a flattened body margin (edge) that probably helped it stay on top of the muddy sea floor rather than sinking in. Its cephalon (head section) was round and had short genal spines leading away from the corners. The pygidium, or tail, was also round and was about the same size as the head. As the tail was so large, there are a reduced number of segments in the thorax – only eight. The multiple rear-facing lateral (side) segments of the tail, known as pleural spines, are also a distinct feature.

Right: This specimen of Ogygiocaris *became disarticulated (its main sections came apart) at some point prior to fossilization. However, the large cephalon (head shield) and pygidium (tail), with its curved pleural spines, can be clearly seen.*

Ogyginus
Similar and closely related to *Ogygiocaris*, *Ogyginus* had small genal spines on the corners of its cephalon. Like *Ogygiocaris*, it probably lived in muddy marine environments, feeding on small edible particles swept up from the substrate with its appendages. Note the smaller juvenile forms near the larger adult.

Agnostus

Agnostus was a blind, simply shaped trilobite reaching the size of a little fingernail. The cephalon, or head end, lacked the usual grooves or sutures that separate its central glabella from the side-cheeks. The pygidium, or tail, was rounded and smooth. In addition, *Agnostus* had only two segments in its thorax. This was the result of a pattern of thoracic segment reduction that began in the Early Cambrian and reached its peak at the end of that period. *Agnostus* probably lived on the deep ocean floor, using its short antennae to sweep up food particles from the sediment.

Name: Agnostus
Meaning: Ignorant, not known
Grouping: Arthropod, Trilobite, Agnostid
Informal ID: Trilobite
Fossil size: Slab length 12cm/4¾in
Reconstructed size: Individual head–tail length 1cm/⅜in
Habitat: Deep sea floor
Time span: Late Cambrian, 510–500 million years ago
Main fossil sites: Europe, North America, East Asia, Australia
Occurrence: ◆ ◆ ◆

Left: The presence of different types of agnostid trilobites – seen here in a specimen from Sweden – is used to help demarcate rocks of specific dates within the Cambrian Period.

Above: In this close-up view of the specimen seen on the left, the isopygous pygidium (which means it was about the same size as the head, or cephalon) and the fact that the two are plain and very similar in outline, make it difficult to tell the head of Agnostus from its tail.

Ellipsocephalus

Name: *Ellipsocephalus*
Meaning: Ellipse
(oval) head
Grouping: Arthropod,
Trilobite, Ptychopariidid (?)
Informal ID: Blind trilobite
Fossil size: Fossil slab
length 18cm/7in
Reconstructed size:
Head–tail length 2cm/¾in
Habitat: Muddy sea floor
Time span: Middle
Cambrian, 520–510 million
years ago
Main fossil sites: Worldwide
Occurrence: ◆ ◆

This small, eyeless trilobite was micropygous: that is, it had a very small pygidium, or tail section. This allowed it to tuck not only its pygidium but also some thoracic segments under the front edge of its cephalon (head shield) when enrolled. *Ellipsocephalus* lacked any complex features on its cephalon and a suggested reason for this is that, because it could not see, it did not select a mate of its own kind based on visual features that distinguished it from other trilobite types. The lack of eyes is a secondary condition, since from their beginning most trilobites were sighted – in fact, they were the first creatures known to have large, complex eyes. The ancestors of *Ellipsocephalus* had them, but as part of its evolution when living in the dark depths, the eyes gradually became reduced as they were no longer necessary, and eventually sealed over.

Below: The fossilized remains of Ellipsocephalus are often found crowded together, either as moulted, or cast-off, body casings, or as whole-animal death assemblages, as is the case in the specimen seen here. Some experts consider that this is evidence for some form of social behavior among trilobites. They may, for example, have come together in sizeable groups when migrating or mating.

Trinucleus

Trinucleus was a small, blind trilobite with several unique and distinguishing features. The glabella, or forehead, and side-cheeks on the cephalon, or head shield, form raised elevations, giving *Trinucleus* its name, which means 'three centres'. The cephalon is also very large in comparison with the rest of the body, accounting for almost half the animal's total length. Projecting from either edge of the cephalon were genal spines that were longer than the body itself. In addition, along the anterior margin, or front edge, of the cephalon was a fringe that contained rows of small pits. This wide fringe, combined with the long genal spines, may have helped *Trinucleus* to stay on top of the muddy substrate it lived in without sinking down, working in a similar way as a snowshoe to spread the animal's weight. There was a reduced number of thoracic segments, and the pygidium, or tail section, was also very short and circular.

Right: The long genal spines sticking out from the head end, which would face the rear along the sides of the body, are missing from this specimen. However, the unique cephalic fringe is clearly visible.

Name: *Trinucleus*
Meaning: Three nuclei,
three centres
Grouping: Arthropod,
Trilobite
Informal ID: Trilobite
Fossil size: Head–tail length
2cm/¾in
Reconstructed size:
As above
Habitat: Muddy deep-
sea floor
Time span: Middle to Late
Ordovician, 470–440 million
years ago
Main fossil sites: Western
Europe, North Africa
Occurrence: ◆

ARTHROPODS – CRUSTACEANS

Crustaceans are the largest group of sea-dwelling arthropods, occupying a vast variety of environments and with more than 40,000 living species, including some in freshwater and on land. They include crabs, lobsters, shrimps, prawns and the shrimp-like krill in the seas, as well as pillbugs and woodlice on land, water-fleas in ponds, and barnacles along seashores.

Beaconites

Regular infills (menisci)

Usually straight burrow

Branching points are less common

Beaconites is the name given to the trace fossils of burrow or tunnel networks that were first seen in the Cambrian Period more than 500 million years ago. These burrows tend to be small in scale, cylindrical and unbranched, and they may have been constructed either in a straight line or in a more curving, sinuous shape. The burrows often display regularly organized infill layers, called menisci, that were produced behind the animal as it moved forward. The burrows themselves typically have rounded ends. Beaconites is often found in sediment that has been heavily disrupted by various different feeding and burrowing organisms, known as bioturbation. As is the case with most ichnogenera, it is difficult to specify precisely which type of animal left these traces behind. A variety of arthropods, including crustaceans, may have been responsible for making them.

Name: *Beaconites*
Meaning: From the Beacon Heights Mountain, Antarctica
Grouping: Probably Arthropod, possibly Crustacean
Informal ID: Fossilized dwelling/feeding tunnel system
Fossil size: Slab length 50cm/20in
Reconstructed size: Burrow width rarely up to 20cm/8in
Habitat: Shallow seas and lakes
Time span: Cambrian, 540 million years ago, to today
Main fossil sites: Antarctica, Europe, North America
Occurrence: ◆ ◆ ◆

Left: The direction of travel of the animal that made this burrow – most likely an arthropod of some description – was opposite to the concave (dished) infillings within the burrow itself. This specimen is from the Wealden Lower Cretaceous beds in Surrey, England.

Barnacles

Also known as cirripedes, barnacles are ancient creatures. They are found way back in the fossil record, some 540 million years ago, yet they still exist in huge numbers in the seas and oceans of today. Although they are sometimes confused with molluscs, barnacles are in fact a distinct group of crustaceans that have lost most of their crustacean features, as these are unnecessary in their sessile (meaning settled or stationary) lifestyle. Some types of barnacle live in the deep oceans, but many more thrive on the narrow intertidal band of rocky shores, where they have evolved special adaptations to surviving periods of low tide when the water retreats and they are exposed to the air. At this time, the biggest threat to the creatures' survival is water loss, so barnacles have special plates that seal them within their own calcareous 'shell' until the tide rises once more. There are two main groups of barnacle. Acorn barnacles cement their cone- or volcano-like shells directly to an object, while goose barnacles attach with a long stalk.

Six sections or plates form a cone-like mound

Opening sealed with plates while exposed to air

Hard surface

Balanus

Name: *Balanus*
Meaning: Acorn
Grouping: Arthropod,
Crustacean, Cirriped
Informal ID: Acorn barnacle
Fossil size: Each individual
3.2cm/1¼in high
Reconstructed size: Height
4cm/1½in, including
feathery limbs
Habitat: Intertidal rocks or
shallow sea floor
Time span: Middle
Cretaceous, 125–100 million
years ago, to today
Main fossil sites: Worldwide
Occurrence: ◆ ◆ ◆ ◆

Balanus is a common and widespread genus of medium-to-large barnacles, some growing to a sizeable 10cm/4in across. Today they are found living on most rocky shorelines and they are extremely abundant worldwide. *Balanus*, like most other crustaceans, begins life as a tiny planktonic larva (young form). However, during this juvenile period, it loses most of its typical crustacean features, such as a long body with numerous walking limbs. The larva spends a month or more floating through the ocean, moulting several times before settling onto a firm base. Here, it secretes six calcareous plates that eventually grow to form a cone-like shell. Four further plates seal the opening of the shell, except when the barnacle extends its feather-like limbs. These curl through the water, like a grasping hand, in order to catch any passing planktonic food.

Below: The thick, calcareous shell of Balanus is robust, meaning that it is more likely to be preserved in the fossil record than many other thinner-shelled crustaceans. This view, which was taken from above, shows four individuals that have settled and grown together.

Cretiscalpellum

Cretiscalpellum is an extinct member of a group of barnacles known as goose or gooseneck barnacles, many of which still thrive today. The name derives from the long, flexible, extendable muscular stalk, like a goose's neck, that attaches to the substrate. Five bivalve-like calcareous plates protect the soft body. Goose barnacles live in groups attached to a variety of both floating and stationary objects, from pieces of driftwood and great whales to solid rocks, molluscs and other barnacles. As in acorn barnacles, the large, feathery limbs, or cirri, extend through the opened shell to filter small, floating edible particles from the water.

Below left: Cretiscalpellum is the most abundant type of barnacle found in British Chalk beds. Pictured here are parts of the outer casing or shell, which, in life, resembled the covering of a mussel. Cretiscalpellum beds coincided with a period of worldwide chalk deposition that occurred during the Late Cretaceous Period, around 100 million years ago.

Name: *Cretiscalpellum*
Meaning: Small sharp chalk
Grouping: Arthropod,
Crustacean, Cirriped
Informal ID: Goose or
gooseneck barnacle
Fossil size: Plates 1.2cm/
½in long
Reconstructed size: Main
body 4.5cm/1¾in long, plus
length of stalk
Habitat: Warm seas
Time span: Middle
Cretaceous, 125–100 million
years ago, to today
Main fossil sites: Worldwide
Occurrence: ◆ ◆ ◆ ◆

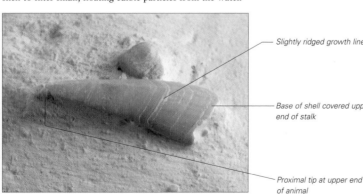

— Slightly ridged growth lines

— Base of shell covered upper end of stalk

— Proximal tip at upper end of animal

ARTHROPODS – CRUSTACEANS (CONTINUED)

Crustaceans are found in the fossil record from as early as the Cambrian Period. But apart from barnacles, with their strong calcareous plates, they are generally rare due to their lack of truly hard body parts. It was not until the appearance of decapods, or 'ten-limbs' – crabs, lobsters, crayfish, shrimps and prawns – with their thick exoskeletons, that crustaceans began to fossilize with some regularity.

Cyamocypris

Countless tiny crustacean 'shellfish' crop up in the fossil record – then, as now, vital links in the food chain for larger creatures. One group is the ostracods, also called mussel-shrimps or seed-shrimps. They look superficially like very small bivalve shellfish, but they are not molluscs or shrimps – they form their own major group, Ostracoda, within the Crustacea. Mostly smaller than a fingernail, their two-part body casings, or carapaces, are familiar components of mud and ooze in today's oceans, lakes and ponds, and also in preserved sediments from these habitats. Ostracods have thrived since Ordovician times, almost 500 million years ago, at first in the sea, and then from the Carboniferous Period in fresh waters, with genera such as *Darwinula*.

Below: The Jurassic freshwater Cyamocypris *was approximately the size of a large grain of rice. As with many ostracods, the left and right parts of the valves of its carapace had a rounded outline, with a small pointed 'beak' on the underside. The left valve was larger than the right and overlapped it.*

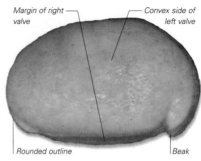
Margin of right valve — / — Convex side of left valve
Rounded outline / Beak

Name: *Cyamocypris*
Meaning: Bone shrimp
Grouping: Arthropod, Crustacean, Ostracod, Podocopid
Informal ID: Ostracod, 'tiny shellfish'
Fossil size: Length 5mm/³⁄₁₆in
Reconstructed size: As above
Habitat: Fresh water
Time span: Early Cretaceous, 100 million years ago
Main fossil sites: Europe
Occurrence: ◆ ◆

Palaeastacus

Below: Although one of the more common crustaceans from the Late Cretaceous Period, whole Palaeastacus *specimens are rarely found intact. The enlarged first appendages with pincer ends, known as chelae, are the most common parts found fossilized. The exoskeleton (outer casing) of these appendages was thicker and stronger than in other areas of the body, and so was more likely to remain intact after death.* Palaeastacus *may have lurked in a crevice or burrow, emerging only to grab victims or scavenge.*

Astacus is one of the main genera of today's crayfish. *Palaeastacus* is its fossil equivalent as a lobster, most commonly found in the Late Cretaceous Chalk rocks of England and Germany. Its features are very similar to those of modern lobsters and crayfish. The long, thin exoskeletal covering over most of the head and thorax is known as a carapace. There are also large, powerful chelae or pincers at the front and an elongated abdomen at the rear containing powerful swimming muscles. At the end of the abdomen was a flattened, fan-like tail, the telson, used to propel *Palaeastacus* rapidly backwards, away from advancing predators.

Main body of chela —
Joint with body —
— Tips of chela (claw or pincer)
— Hinge area of chela

Name: *Palaeastacus*
Meaning: Ancient lobster/crayfish
Grouping: Arthropod, Crustacean, Decapod
Informal ID: Lobster/crayfish
Fossil size: Whole specimen length 19cm/7½in
Reconstructed size: Pincer–tail length 35cm/14in
Habitat: Shallow seas
Time span: Early Jurassic to Late Cretaceous, 190–65 million years ago
Main fossil sites: Europe, North America, Australia, Antarctica
Occurrence: ◆ ◆

Enoploclytia

Name: Enoploclytia
Meaning: Loosely folded
Grouping: Arthropod, Crustacean, Decapod
Informal ID: Lobster
Fossil size: Pincer-appendage length 12cm/4¾in
Reconstructed size: Pincer–tail length 32cm/12½in
Habitat: Shallow seas
Time span: Late Cretaceous to Palaeocene, 95–55 million years ago
Main fossil sites: Throughout Europe
Occurrence: ◆

Enoploclytia was a type of lobster found in Upper Cretaceous Chalk beds, very much like *Palaeastacus* (opposite, below). It displayed the characteristic section of exoskeleton, known as the carapace, that covered both the creature's head and thorax, with an extended abdomen containing powerful swimming muscles. Species of this creature tend to have robust exoskeletons (outer casings) with coarse nodes or spines. *Enoploclytia* is generally rare in the fossil record, and is usually found only in Cretaceous beds. Some species, however, have been found in rocks dating to the Palaeocene. This means that it managed to survive the catastrophic end-of-Cretaceous, or K/T, extinction that occurred 65 million years ago. This wiped out a large proportion of the world's marine and terrestrial life and brought about the end of the dinosaurs.

Below: Like modern lobsters, Enoploclytia had a pair of large pincers. These looked similar to a pair of needle-nose pliers, being thinner and more elongated than those of Palaeastacus. They were perhaps used for probing into crevices to search for food rather than for simple crushing.

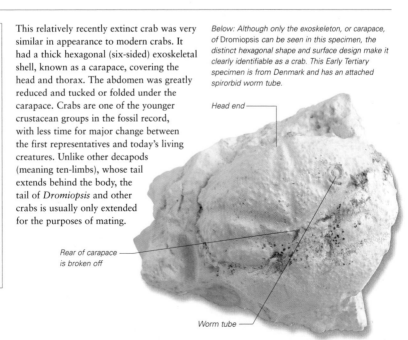

Joint with body

Hinged tip of chela

Main body of left chela (claw or pincer)

Fixed tip of chela

Dromiopsis

Name: Dromiopsis
Meaning: Running face
Grouping: Arthropod, Crustacean, Decapod
Informal ID: Crab
Fossil size: Carapace width 2cm/¾in
Reconstructed size: Width across legs 4cm/1¼in
Habitat: Shallow marine environments
Time span: Late Cretaceous and Early Tertiary, 95–55 million years ago
Main fossil sites: Throughout Europe
Occurrence: ◆

This relatively recently extinct crab was very similar in appearance to modern crabs. It had a thick hexagonal (six-sided) exoskeletal shell, known as a carapace, covering the head and thorax. The abdomen was greatly reduced and tucked or folded under the carapace. Crabs are one of the younger crustacean groups in the fossil record, with less time for major change between the first representatives and today's living creatures. Unlike other decapods (meaning ten-limbs), whose tail extends behind the body, the tail of *Dromiopsis* and other crabs is usually only extended for the purposes of mating.

Below: Although only the exoskeleton, or carapace, of Dromiopsis can be seen in this specimen, the distinct hexagonal shape and surface design make it clearly identifiable as a crab. This Early Tertiary specimen is from Denmark and has an attached spirorbid worm tube.

Head end

Rear of carapace is broken off

Worm tube

ARTHROPODS – CRUSTACEANS (CONTINUED)

The group of crustaceans we are most familiar with is the decapods. This term refers to the 'ten feet' or, rather, limbs of these types of crustacean, being the two front pincers and usually four pairs of walking legs. Decapods include more than 20,000 living species, which encompass shrimps and prawns – two common names that have no strict scientific basis – along with all types of crayfish, lobsters and crabs, as also shown on the previous pages.

Eryma

Appearing in the Jurassic Period, *Eryma* represents the oldest known 'true' lobster. *Eryma* is characterized by having typical decapod-like features, which include multiple pairs of appendages, such as antennae and mouthparts, as well as the ten main limbs. In addition, it had an elongated, segmented body, tough exoskeletal armour (carapace) that covers the thorax and head, and a fan-like tail, or telson. Like modern lobsters, *Eryma* most likely swam backwards, using its large tail muscles to flick its telson down and forwards and so propel itself quickly backwards, away from any predators. The pair of long pincers (chelae) could also be used for defence as well as for feeding. Compared with thicker-shelled crabs, however, *Eryma* and other lobsters and shrimp have a relatively thin carapace. This means that only rarely is the entire body preserved completely intact, usually in cases of Konservat-Lagerstätten – a German term for a site of 'exceptional preservation'.

Name: *Eryma*
Meaning: Fence, barrier or guard
Grouping: Arthropod, Crustacean, Decapod
Informal ID: Lobster
Fossil size: Large slab length 8cm/3in
Reconstructed size: Pincer–tail length up to 9cm/3½in
Habitat: Shallow seas
Time span: Late Jurassic, 150–140 million years ago
Main fossil sites: Throughout Europe
Occurrence: ◆

Left: The Late Jurassic Solnhofen Limestones of Bavaria, southern Germany, where this specimen originates, constitute a site of exceptional preservation. The limestones were deposited in the calm marine environment between a reef and land. A wide variety of animals, including small dinosaurs and the earliest-known bird, Archaeopteryx, became preserved after their bodies were quickly buried in the hypersaline (extra-salty) bottom waters.

Right: More than 600 fossil species have been preserved in the Solnhofen Limestones in Germany. Among the crustaceans found here, decapods are the most abundant group. Soft-tissue preservation is so good in some specimens that even the eyes may remain intact. This individual is about 3.5cm/1⅜in long from its claw-tips to the end of its tail.

Below: Modern lobsters like Homarus *have one larger, more robust claw or chela for crushing, and one narrower, slimmer claw for cutting and picking.*

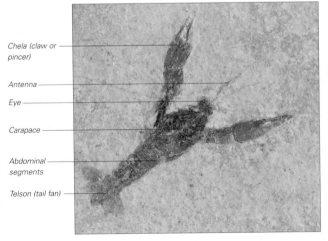

Chela (claw or pincer)

Antenna

Eye

Carapace

Abdominal segments

Telson (tail fan)

Thalassinoides

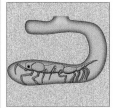

Name: *Thalassinoides*
Meaning: Of the sea
Grouping: Arthropod,
Crustacean, probably
Decapod
Informal ID: Fossilized
feeding tunnel system
Fossil size: Entire specimen
25cm/10in across
Reconstructed size: Burrow
width average 4–5cm/1½–2in
Habitat: Fairly calm deeper
sea floor
Time span: Jurassic, 190
million years ago
Main fossil sites:
Worldwide
Occurrence: ◆ ◆ ◆

Thalassinoides is a trace fossil tunnel system most likely made by a decapod crustacean, such as a shrimp, while feeding. The tunnels range from between 2 and 6cm/¾ and 2⅓in in diameter and are usually found in rocks that were deposited in calm waters, below the turbulent waves and currents of the tidal zone. Because wave and current action were not dominant here (unlike the settings for *Ophiomorpha*, see below), animals tended to feed closer to the substrate. This often resulted in branching Y- or T-shaped tunnel networks, as with *Thalassinoides*. Again, unlike *Ophiomorpha*, the tunnels are usually smooth-sided. *Thalassinoides* burrows were often infilled by sediment after the inhabitant had vacated them. Following erosion, the network may have become separated from the original substrate, transported and then reburied in younger sediments. This makes it unusual, being one of the few trace fossils that may not have been made at its discovery site.

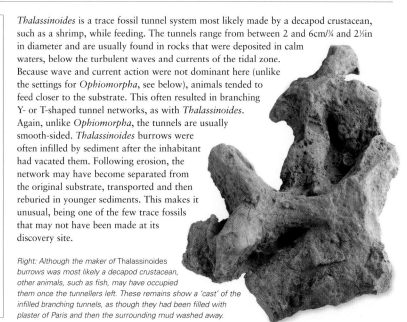

Right: Although the maker of Thalassinoides *burrows was most likely a decapod crustacean, other animals, such as fish, may have occupied them once the tunnellers left. These remains show a 'cast' of the infilled branching tunnels, as though they had been filled with plaster of Paris and then the surrounding mud washed away.*

Ophiomorpha

Ophiomorpha, like *Thalassinoides* above, is a trace fossil tunnel network most likely made by a decapod crustacean, such as a shrimp. It is usually found in rocks deposited under shallow, high-energy settings where wave action and tidal currents are present. In this type of environment, the majority of organisms live within the sediment (known as infaunal). *Ophiomorpha* tends to be more vertically orientated, as these tunnels were probably a dwelling, rather than just a feeding burrow. This can be deduced from the pellet-like ornamentations along the tunnel walls, which may have been faecal material (droppings) from the animal living there, or possibly lumps of sand grains. Often *Ophiomorpha* tunnels become infilled and eroded, as described above for *Thalassinoides*. This would result in an isolated 'cast' of the tunnel network that could be transported and redeposited somewhere else.

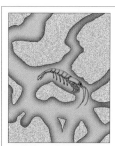

Left: These fossilized infilled specimens of Ophiomorpha *were discovered in Eocene rocks in Berkshire, southern England. They were eroded out of the sediment where they were originally dug in the Jurassic Period, most likely by a decapod crustacean, revealing the internal shape of the construction. The burrow system, which may have been used as a dwelling by the tunneller, was lined with nodules of sand.*

Name: *Ophiomorpha*
Meaning: Serpent shape
Grouping: Arthropod,
Crustacean, probably
Decapod
Informal ID: Fossilized
dwelling tunnel system
Fossil size: Longest item
9cm/3½in
Reconstructed size:
Burrow width average
1.5–2cm/½–¾in
Habitat: Shallow sea floor
Time span: Permian to Late
Tertiary, 270–3 million
years ago
Main fossil sites: Worldwide
Occurrence: ◆ ◆ ◆ ◆

ARTHROPODS – EURYPTERIDS, XIPHOSURANS

The eurypterids were predatory arthropods that appeared in the Ordovician Period. Also called 'sea scorpions', some ventured into fresh water, and a few could survive on land for a time. They were chelicerates, the same group as spiders and scorpions, with large claw-like front limbs, or chelicerae.

Erieopterus

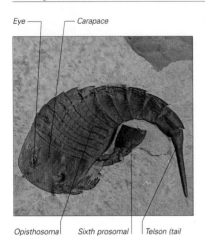

Eye — Carapace

Opisthosoma (abdomen) | Sixth prosomal appendage, or 'swimming paddle' | Telson (tail spine)

Erieopterus was one of the most widespread genera of eurypterids. Unlike some of its group – who could walk on land for short periods of time – it was fully aquatic. It possessed a pair of well-developed, paddle-like sixth appendages, behind feeding claws and four pairs of walking limbs. This characteristic of eurypterids gave them their name, from the Greek for 'broad wing'. These rearmost legs were used as oars for swimming. The relatively small eyes and leg spines of *Erieopterus* suggest that, unlike many others in its group, it was not a top predator of its shallow seas, rivers and estuaries. Instead, it was probably an unspecified feeder, taking primarily small invertebrates.

Above left: Erieopterus would have used its paddle-like sixth limbs to swim actively over the sand and mud of both salty and fresh water, looking for small invertebrate prey, such as worms and molluscs.

Name: *Erieopterus*
Meaning: Erie wing (from the North American Great Lake)
Grouping: Arthropod, Chelicerate, Eurypterid
Informal ID: Sea scorpion
Fossil size: Head–tail length 13cm/5in
Reconstructed size: Whole specimens reached 20cm/8in in length; fragmentary remains suggest much larger individuals
Habitat: Inshore sea coasts, tidal estuaries
Time span: Silurian to Devonian, 410–370 million years ago
Main fossil sites: North America
Occurrence: ◆ ◆

Eurypterus

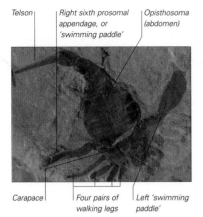

Telson | Right sixth prosomal appendage, or 'swimming paddle' | Opisthosoma (abdomen)

Carapace | Four pairs of walking legs | Left 'swimming paddle'

Above: This Silurian specimen from New York State shows the different specializations of Eurypterus's appendages. The relative positions of the left and right 'swimming paddles' highlight their wide range of movements.

The genus that gave the eurypterid group its name was relatively small and unspecialized. (Its close cousin, the Devonian *Pterygotus*, was one of the largest arthropods of all time at 2.5m/8¼ft long.) However, *Eurypterus* was relatively widespread and common, considering the eurypterids' overall rarity. Its fossils are usually found in fine-grained dolostone (waterlime) containing 'salt hopper' structures, which indicate hypersaline (extra-salty) conditions. However, the fossils seem to have been transported to the area before burial. Many specimens are incomplete and most are the remains not of the animals, but of moulted, or cast-off, body casings. Many individuals of *Eurypterus* seem to have congregated in the area to moult and mate – giving them safety in numbers and from the high salinity of the water, which would deter other creatures – before dispersing.

Name: *Eurypterus*
Meaning: Broad wing
Grouping: Arthropod, Chelicerate, Eurypterid
Informal ID: Sea scorpion
Fossil size: Head–tail length 8cm/3in
Reconstructed size: Total length up to 40cm/16in
Habitat: Shallow coasts, hypersaline lagoons
Time span: Silurian, 430–410 million years ago
Main Fossil Sites: North America
Occurrence: ◆ ◆

Belinurus

Name: *Belinurus*
Meaning: Dart or needle tail
Grouping: Arthropod, Chelicerate, Xiphosuran, Limulid
Informal ID: Extinct horseshoe crab
Fossil size: Length, including tail, 5cm/2in
Reconstructed size: As above
Habitat: Freshwater and brackish (part-salty) swamps
Time span: Devonian to Late Carboniferous, 360–300 million years ago
Main fossil sites: Throughout Europe
Occurrence: ◆

Belinurus was another aquatic chelicerate. It was not a eurypterid, but a member of the group called xiphosurans ('sword tails'), which includes the horseshoe or king crabs of today. (These are not true crabs from the crustacean group, but are more closely related to scorpions and spiders.) *Belinurus* is one of the first known xiphosurans and already possessed the large spine- or dagger-like telson, or tail. Other features that are characteristic of the group include the large, hoof-shaped prosoma, or head, bearing the mouth, eyes and legs, and a shorter abdomen. The abdomen was still segmented in *Belinurus*. Unlike its living marine relatives, *Belinurus* was a freshwater, swamp-dwelling animal. However, it probably fed in a similar fashion, by walking over soft mud or sand as it searched for worms and other small invertebrate creatures to eat.

Below: Belinurus *remains are mostly found associated with plants of the Carboniferous 'Coal Forests', which grew mainly in warm, tropical freshwater to brackish swamps.*

Mesolimulus

Mesolimulus was almost identical to today's horseshoe crab, *Limulus*, which is why the latter is often dubbed a 'living fossil'. *Mesolimulus* probably had a similar lifestyle, crawling on the soft bottom of shallow coastal marine waters, feeding on small invertebrates and perhaps scavenging dead fish. Its fossils are famously known from the German Solnhofen Limestones. Some specimens are found at the centre of spiraling 'death march' tracks, left as the dying animal was succumbing to the toxic waters at the bottom of the lagoon. Paradoxically, this suggests that *Mesolimulus* could tolerate a wide range of conditions – most other Solnhofen creatures were already dead by the time they settled on the bottom. Other preserved tracks show that *Mesolimulus* probably swam like the modern *Limulus* – upside down. The traces show evidence of the animal turning itself over after 'touchdown' from swimming, before walking off.

Name: *Mesolimulus*
Meaning: Mesozoic (Middle Life) equivalent of *Limulus* (horseshoe crab)
Grouping: Arthropod, Chelicerate, Xiphosuran, Limulid
Informal ID: Extinct horseshoe crab
Fossil size: Specimen head–tail length 9cm/3½in
Reconstructed size: Average head–tail length 12cm/4¾in (however, most specimens are interpreted as being juveniles)
Habitat: Warm, shallow coastal waters, brackish estuaries
Time span: Jurassic to Cretaceous, 170–100 million years ago
Main Fossil Sites: Europe, Middle East
Occurrence: ◆ ◆

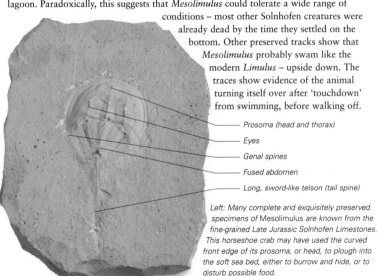

— Prosoma (head and thorax)
— Eyes
— Genal spines
— Fused abdomen
— Long, sword-like telson (tail spine)

Left: Many complete and exquisitely preserved specimens of Mesolimulus *are known from the fine-grained Late Jurassic Solnhofen Limestones. This horseshoe crab may have used the curved front edge of its prosoma, or head, to plough into the soft sea bed, either to burrow and hide, or to disturb possible food.*

ARTHROPODS – SPIDERS, SCORPIONS

The arthropods include several kinds of chelicerates – spiders, scorpions, xiphosurans (horseshoe crabs) and eurypterids (sea scorpions). These all possess chelicerae, powerful front appendages variously modified as pincers, claws or fangs. Scorpions and spiders are known as arachnids, characterized by four pairs of walking limbs. Scorpions were among the first wave of land animals more than 380 million years ago.

Leptotarbus

Head end   Mouthparts   Abdomen

Above: This Late Carboniferous specimen of Leptotarbus *lacks its walking legs, but illustrates the wide 'waist' and overall oval shape typical of a phalangiotarbid or living harvestman.*

Leptotarbus belongs to an obscure group of arachnids, the Phalangiotarbida. It resembled a spider, having four pairs of walking legs, multiple pairs of eyes (*Leptotarbus* had three, contrasting with the four pairs of most modern spiders), a combined head and middle body section, the cephalothorax or prosoma, and a large abdomen. Overall it resembles the living long-legged arachnids called harvestmen, such as the modern genus *Phalangio*, which are not classed as true spiders. The body is flattened and oval in shape, with a wide connection between prosoma and abdomen, instead of the narrow 'wasp waist' of true spiders. It is difficult to interpret their lifestyles, considering their extinction and the rarity and poor condition of their fossils. Their air-breathing organs suggest they were terrestrial, and their mouthparts were weak.

Name: *Leptotarbus*
Meaning: Slender terror
Grouping: Arthropod, Chelicerate, Arachnid, Phalangiotarbid
Informal ID: Extinct spider-like arachnid or harvestman
Fossil size: Head–body length 1.5cm/½in
Reconstructed size: Total width across legs 4cm/1½in
Habitat: Unknown, possibly dense undergrowth
Time span: Carboniferous, 300 million years ago
Main Fossil Sites: Throughout Europe
Occurrence: ◆

Maiocercus

Maiocercus was a relatively large spider for its group, the Trigonotarbida, and lived in the humid, tropical forests that covered Europe in the Carboniferous Period. Although superficially similar to the 'true' spiders, or araneans, *Maiocercus* lacked the 'wasp waist' and perhaps also silk glands. It possessed a thick, plated, chitinous outer body casing, or exoskeleton. However, it was a close relative of araneans and probably had a similar lifestyle to today's wolf-spiders, hunting smaller invertebrates by ambushing them in thick forest undergrowth or by chasing or cornering them. This interpretation is strengthened by the discovery of certain specimens with four pairs of strong walking legs. Trigonotarbid spiders represent the oldest known land arachnids, appearing in the Late Silurian Period. They became most diverse in the Late Carboniferous, and had faded by the early Permian Period.

Below: This Maiocercus *abdomen was recovered in coal from the Rhondda region of South Wales. It represents the holotype of the genus – the one that is used for the original description, and against which all subsequent specimens are compared, to identify them as* Maiocercus.

Name: *Maiocercus*
Meaning: Mother (original) cercus (tail-like appendage)
Grouping: Arthropod, Chelicerate, Arachnid, Trigonotarbid
Informal ID: Spider
Fossil size: 1–2cm/⅖–¾in
Reconstructed size: Head–body length 2–3cm/¾–1in
Habitat: Warm, dense, humid forest
Time span: Carboniferous, 310 million years ago
Main fossil sites: Throughout Europe
Occurrence: ◆

Fossil scorpions

Name: Scorpions
Meaning: From *skorpios* (Greek)
Grouping: Arthropod, Chelicerate, Arachnid, Scorpion
Informal ID: Scorpions
Fossil size: More complete specimen (far right), head–tail length 1.4cm/⅝in
Reconstructed size: The group varies from head–tail length less than 1cm/⅜in to almost 1m/3¼ft – larger forms were aquatic
Habitats: Variable, generally warm, including deserts, forests, grasslands, marine intertidal; many Palaeozoic types were aquatic
Time span: Middle Silurian, 420 million years ago, to today
Main fossil sites: Worldwide
Occurrence: ◆

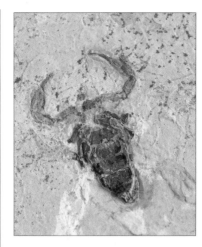

Above: Protoischnurus, *from Brazil's Crato Formation, lacks its walking legs and tail. However, its remains show well-developed pincers.*

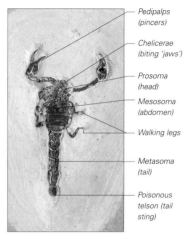

Pedipalps (pincers)

Chelicerae (biting 'jaws')

Prosoma (head)

Mesosoma (abdomen)

Walking legs

Metasoma (tail)

Poisonous telson (tail sting)

Above: This scorpion was also found in the Crato Formation of north-east Brazil – a location known for the remarkable level of detail preserved in its fossils.

True scorpions appeared in the Middle Silurian Period, some 420 million years ago, and most early types were, in fact, aquatic creatures. Land-living (or terrestrial) forms of scorpions are known from the fossil record of the Early Devonian Period, while the last aquatic types survived into the Jurassic Period. They are thought to be cousins or descendants of eurypterids (sea scorpions), from which they inherited their overall body plan. This comprised a large mesosoma (or abdomen) of seven segments, and an elongated metasoma (tail section) of five slender segments, ending with a telson or tail spine. The telson of true scorpions is a poisonous sting.

Origins of spiders

The true spiders, Araneae, have an obscure ancestry. Specimens are known throughout the Late Palaeozoic Era, especially from the Carboniferous Period. A few have been found from the Mesozoic Era, and many more from the Tertiary, often preserved in amber. Many of the living types of spider can be traced back to the Mesozoic Era. For example, a tarantula relative is known from Late Triassic rocks (dating back 210 million years) in France, and relatives of web-spinning species are known from the Jurassic Period. In particular, a Lower Cretaceous specimen from Spain shows three claws on the end of each leg, which modern spiders use for walking on their webs. Defining characteristics of spiders include the appendages known as chelicerae modified into poisonous fangs, a thin 'waist', and a system of glands and appendages (spinnerets) that produces silk. The example here is one of the Saticidae (jumping spiders), entombed in Baltic amber dating back to the Late Eocene, some 40 million years ago. Typical victims of the sticky tree sap before it fossilized include midges, cockroaches, nymphs and ants, as well as jumping spiders.

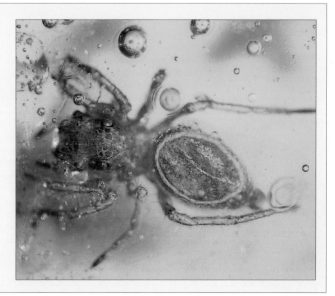

ARTHROPODS – INSECTS

In the fossil record, the vast arthropod or 'jointed-leg' group is dominated by aquatics, such as the still-thriving crustaceans and long-gone trilobites. In comparison, there are few remains of the main arthropod group we encounter nearly every day – insects. This is because most were (and are) small, relatively fragile and often consumed by predators. If not, they died in places such as moist forests, where decay was swift.

Proeuthemis

The very first insects were tiny and wingless, and were among the early land animals of the Devonian Period. By the next period, the Carboniferous, they had evolved into several groups and greatly increased in size – and some had developed wings to become the first creatures to take to the air. Indeed, the steamy swamps of the Late Carboniferous, 300 million years ago, saw the ancestors of dragonflies, known as protodonatans, which were the largest flying insects ever. The famed protodonatan 'dragonfly' *Meganeura* had wings spanning 70cm/28in. The true dragonflies and their smaller cousins, damselflies, in the group Odonata, follow their ancestors' lifestyle as fast, darting aerial predators. (See also *Libellula*, below.)

Main vein
Root of wing
Subsidiary vein
Wing tip

Above: This Proeuthemis wing shows the dragonfly pattern of veins. In life they were tubes taking blood to the wing membrane and also helping to stiffen the wing. Dragonflies and their ancestors are four-winged insects.

Name: *Proeuthemis*
Meaning: Before *Euthemis* (a similar dragonfly genus)
Grouping: Arthropod, Insect, Odonatan
Informal ID: Dragonfly
Fossil size: Wing length 2.5cm/1in
Reconstructed size: Wingspan 5cm/2in
Habitat: Swamps, moist woodlands
Time span: Early Cretaceous, 120 million years ago
Main fossil sites: Throughout Europe
Occurrence: ◆

Libellula

Below: Identified as Libellula ceres, this Miocene specimen, possibly showing segments of the abdomen, is from Rott, near Siegburg, in the Rhine-Sieg region of Germany. Rott is known for its brown coal or lignite formations, which have also preserved bees, flies and mites.

Dragonflies and damselflies (Odonata), like mayflies (Ephemoptera), have the primitive winged-insect feature known as palaeopteran – they cannot fold their wings back to lie along the body. Instead they project sideways at rest. With about 5,000 living species, the dragonflies and damselflies are relatively well represented as fossils. They occur in rocks that were originally formed in swamp and marsh habitats – where dragonflies pursue small flying insects, such as midges, gnats and moths, to eat. Libellulids survive today as the dragonflies known as darters or skimmers, most of which have a broad body flattened from top to bottom. Their typical behaviour is to rest on a waterside perch, watch for victims with their domed eyes – their vision is among the sharpest in the insect world – and then dart out to catch the prey in a 'basket' formed by their six dangling legs.

Name: *Libellula*
Meaning: Leaflet, booklet
Grouping: Arthropod, Insect, Odonatan
Informal ID: Darter dragonfly
Fossil size: Fossil slab 6cm/2½in across
Reconstructed size: Wingspan up to 15cm/6in
Habitat: Marshes, bogs
Time span: Late Miocene, 8 million years ago
Main fossil sites: Northern Hemisphere
Occurrence: ◆

Palaeodictyopteran

Below: A typical palaeodictyopteran had not only two pairs of dragonfly-like wings, but also a smaller pair of 'winglets' in front of the foremost main wings. It also had a beak-like mouth for tearing and sucking. In some types, the bold-patterned markings on the wings are clearly visible in the fossil.

'Dictyopteran' was an older name for a main group, or order, of insects that has now, in most modern classifications, been split into two orders: the cockroaches, Blattodea, and the mantids (preying mantises), Mantodea. The palaeodictyopterans, all extinct since the Palaeozoic Era, were medium-to-large insects with an outward similarity to odonatans, such as dragonflies (opposite). They had a palaeopterous wing structure, which did not allow the wings to be folded back along the body, but only held out to the sides or above. The two pairs of wings were similar in size and shape. Palaeodictyopterans are not now regarded as being one evolutionary group with a single ancestor, but an assemblage of primitive insect groups. They lived from the Middle Carboniferous to the Late Permian, about 320 to 255 million years ago. In some evolutionary schemes, certain of the Palaeodictyoptera are regarded as ancestors of the Protodonata (see *Proeuthemis*, opposite).

Name: Palaeodictyopteran
Meaning: Ancient net wing
Grouping: Arthropod, Insect, Palaeodictyopteran
Informal ID: Palaeodictyopteran, extinct dragonfly cousin
Fossil size: Wingspan 7cm/2¾in
Reconstructed size: Wingspan of some types exceeded 50cm/20in
Habitat: Forests
Time span: Most types Late Carboniferous to Late Permian, 320–255 million years ago
Main fossil sites: Europe, Asia
Occurrence: ◆ ◆

Blattodean (cockroach)

Name: Blattodean
Meaning: From Greek *blatta* for cockroach
Grouping: Arthropod, Insect, Blattodean
Informal ID: Cockroach
Fossil size: Overall length 2.5cm/1in
Reconstructed size: As above
Habitat: Damp places, leaf litter, forests
Time span: Carboniferous, 340 million years ago, to today
Main fossil sites: Worldwide
Occurrence: ◆ ◆ ◆

Cockroaches are infamous as hardy survivors in almost every habitat, including urban settings where they infest houses, food stores and other buildings. However fewer than 25 of the 4,000 or so living species are serious pests. These flattened, tough-bodied, fast-scuttling lovers of dark, damp warmth are also well known as some of the earliest insects, dating from Carboniferous times. Their remains are common from the Coal Forest swamps, where they lived among damp vegetation and were readily buried by mud and preserved. Most had generalized mouthparts and were omnivores, eating a wide range of foods. Their body shape and design has changed little since, with a low profile that allows them to hide in cracks and crevices. Some types of cockroach have large wings extending over the abdomen, while others have much reduced or even absent wings.

Above: A cockroach has the usual three insect body parts of head, thorax and abdomen. However the head may be obscured by a shield-like pronotum, and the tough wings lie over the abdomen. These Late Carboniferous specimens are from the Coal Measure rocks of Avon, southwest England.

ARTHROPODS – INSECTS (CONTINUED)

A typical insect has three principal body parts. These are the head, usually bearing antennae or feelers, eyes and mouthparts; the thorax, carrying the wings and legs; and the abdomen, containing the insect's digestive, waste-removal and reproductive organs. Typically, an adult insect has six legs and four wings, although true flies (Diptera) have just one pair of wings.

Cratoelcana

Below: Amazing detail can be seen in this Mesozoic cricket, which is some 120 million years old – yet its features are very similar to living types. The rear leaping legs are almost fully extended, as they would be in life as the animal jumped. The wings are folded back in the resting position. They could also be extended as the animal leaped, to allow a fluttering flight, usually to escape from predators.

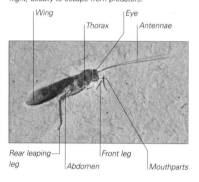

Wing | Eye

Thorax | Antennae

Rear leaping leg | Front leg | Mouthparts

Abdomen

The famed Early Cretaceous rocks of the Crato Formation, in the northeast region of Brazil, have yielded many amazingly detailed fossils, ranging from small scorpions through to huge pterosaurs, which were the first vertebrate animals to evolve true flight, and fish such as *Dastilbe*. Among the most represented insect groups found at the site are the orthopterans, which today include more than 20,000 living species of grasshoppers, crickets and katydids. *Cratoelcana* is a type of ensiferan – the subgroup including bush crickets, which are sometimes called long-horned grasshoppers, also field and cave crickets, and katydids. The very long 'horns' referred to are, in fact, antennae or feelers. The genus name refers to the Crato Formation and also to the primitive cricket family Elcanidae, which is now extinct.

Name: *Cratoelcana*
Meaning: Elcanid of Crato
Grouping: Insect, Orthopteran, Ensiferan
Informal ID: Cricket
Fossil size: Total length including antennae 5cm/2in
Reconstructed size: As above
Habitat: Woods, forests, shores
Time period: Early Cretaceous, 120 million years ago
Main fossil sites: South America
Occurrence: ◆ ◆

Panorpidium

A member of the Ensifera, or long-horned grasshoppers and bush crickets (see *Cratoelcana*, above), *Panorpidium* dates from the Late Cretaceous Period, between 80 and 65 million years ago. Orthopterans as a group are far older, stretching back to the Triassic Period more than 220 million years ago. However, there could be no 'grasshoppers' at that time, since grasses would not evolve for almost another 200 million years. The early orthopterans presumably lived among the conifers, cycads and similar dominant plants of the time. The rear pair of orthopteran wings are enlarged for flight. The front pair, if present, are small and hardened flaps that help to protect the rear pair. The antennae vary from short to very long, depending on the species involved, and the hind legs are enlarged and especially modified for jumping.

Below: The rear wing of this Panorpidium *has an area of damage towards the lower tip that could have been an injury in life. The box-like network of main longitudinal veins and cross-connecting transverse veins typical of the orthopterans is clearly visible. The specimen is from the Late Cretaceous Wealden Formation of Surrey, southern England.*

Area of damage | Veined network | Wing root (joins to body)

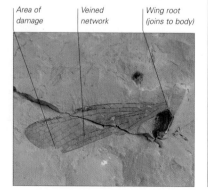

Name: *Panorpidium*
Meaning: Not known
Grouping: Insect, Orthopteran, Ensiferan
Informal ID: Bush cricket
Fossil size: Wing length 1.5cm/⅝in
Reconstructed size: Total length (excluding antennae) 2cm/¾in
Habitat: Undergrowth
Time period: Late Cretaceous, 80–65 million years ago
Main fossil sites: Europe
Occurrence: ◆

Trichopterans (caddisflies)

Caddisflies are not true flies (which belong to the insect group Diptera), but form their own group, Trichoptera. This has more than 8,000 living species and is most closely related to butterflies and moths (Lepidoptera). Fossils from before the Mesozoic Era show that caddisflies have been following a similar way of life for more than 250 million years. The soft-bodied larvae dwell in fresh water and most build tube-like homes from sand, pebbles, leaf fragments or pieces of twig, depending on the species and material available. They emerge from the water and moult into the adults, which vaguely resemble a combination of moth and lacewing, with two pairs of long wings, long, slim legs and long antennae.

Right: These specimens are from the Yixian Formation near Beipiao, northern China. They are similar in many details to today's caddisflies. The Early Cretaceous Yixian rocks are perhaps more famous for amazingly preserved dinosaurs, many with feathery or filamentous coverings. Specimen total length 1.2cm/½in (right) and 2.5cm/1in (far right).

Above: This Tertiary larval case was fashioned from tiny shards of rock and shells, similar to the 'homes' built today by Mystacides, the genus whose adults are known by freshwater anglers as the 'silverhorn' caddis. Each time the larva shed its soft skin, it would construct a new, larger case. The length of this example is 2cm/¾in.

Name: Trichopteran
Meaning: Hairy wing
Grouping: Arthropod, Insect, Trichopteran
Informal ID: Caddisfly
Fossil sizes: See text
Reconstructed size: Most types 1–5cm/ ½–2in long
Habitat: All habitats in or close to fresh water
Time period: From Late Permian, 250 million years ago, to today
Main fossil sites: Worldwide
Occurrence: ◆

Trapped in amber
Small insects and other arthropods were often trapped in the resin oozing from pines and other conifers, which hardened over millions of years into amber. Some amber is so transparent that every detail can be seen of the creature within. These specimens are two dipterans, or true flies, one resembling a gnat (below left), the other a midge (below right), along with a small moth or lepidopteran (bottom). They are all dated to the Late Eocene Epoch, about 35 million years ago.

Cupedid (reticulated) beetle

Beetles, Coleoptera, are the largest subgroup of insects, with more than 370,000 living species. One of their distinguishing features is that the front of the two pairs of wings has usually thickened and hardened into a pair of wing cases called elytra. In flight, the elytra pivot to the side and upwards, and the main flying wings unfold. The family Cupedidae is widely known from the Mesozoic Era, and in some regions forms almost a third of all beetle fossils during the Late Triassic Period. But their numbers fell away drastically by the Early Cretaceous. Today, they are regarded as a primitive and relict family (showing ancient features), being much less common than previously.

Name: Cupedid beetle
Meaning: Cup, dome, turret
Grouping: Arthropod, Insect, Coleopteran
Informal ID: Beetle
Fossil size: Total length 1.5cm/½in
Reconstructed size: As above
Habitat: Varied
Time period: From Early Permian, 280 million years ago, to today
Main fossil sites: Northern Hemisphere
Occurrence: ◆ ◆

Left: Cupedid beetles are also called reticulated or net beetles due to the pattern on the elytra, which variously resembles a chessboard, net or rows of small depressions. This specimen is from China and is about 125 million years old.

ARTHROPODS – INSECTS (CONTINUED), MYRIAPODS

Myriapods, 'myraid legs', is a general name used for the arthropods most people know as centipedes and millipedes, with the scientific names Chilopoda and Diplopoda, respectively. Millipede-like creatures were among the earliest-known land animals in Silurian times.

Trematothorax

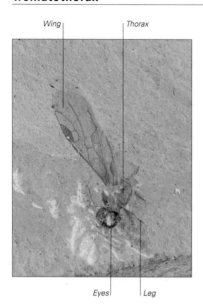

Wing | Thorax

Eyes | Leg

The Hymenoptera group of insects includes some 200,000 living species of bees, wasps, ants and sawflies. Like many major insect groups, it appeared in the Permian–Triassic Periods, some 250 million years ago, and then diversified rapidly with the spread of flowering plants (angiosperms) from the Early Cretaceous. Most types of bee and wasp have two pairs of fairly long, narrow wings. The front and rear wings on each side are joined by tiny hooks so that they effectively beat as one. Another feature of modern hymenopterans is the 'wasp waist', the narrow constriction between the thorax and abdomen. The egg-laying tube at the rear of the abdomen is modified into a sting.

Left: Trematothorax is a genus of the sepulcid group, which in turn is more closely related to the sawflies called stem sawflies than to typical wasps. Sawflies are more primitive, have wider 'waists' and do not sting. The eyes, thorax, legs and wings, with the characteristic pattern of veins, are clearly seen here.

Name: *Trematothorax*
Meaning: Three-clubbed or three-rod chest
Grouping: Arthropod, Insect, Hymenopteran, Sepulcid
Informal ID: Wasp, sawfly
Fossil size: Total length 1cm/⅖in
Reconstructed size: As above
Habitat: Woods, scrubland
Time span: (*Hymenoptera* genus) Triassic, 220 million years ago, to today
Main fossil sites: Worldwide
Occurrence: ◆ ◆

Tiphid ant

Below: This specimen shows the characteristic ant features – long, powerful running legs, fairly large eyes and crooked, or 'elbowed', antennae (feelers). The fossil comes from the famous Crato Formation of Brazil (see Cratoelcana), and shows the amazing detail of preservation in these rocks, known as Lagerstatten. It is dated to the Early Cretaceous, about 125–120 million years ago.

Ants, which belong to the subgroup of Hymenoptera known as formicids, have about 9,000 species alive today. The other major subgroups are apids (including honey bees and bumblebees) and vespids (including hornets and wasps). Most ants are less than 1cm/⅖in long. The tiphid ants still thrive in warmer parts of the world, such as the genus *Thipia* in the Caribbean region. They are active creatures during the summer months and are predators of ground beetle larvae, or 'grubs'. Some female tiphids dig into the soil to look for the larvae. For many years ants were thought to have appeared in the Tertiary Period, dating from about 45 million years ago. However, more recent discoveries have pushed back their origins to Cretaceous times, some 125 million years ago.

Name: Tiphid ant
Meaning: Swamp/marsh ant
Grouping: Arthropod, Insect, Hymenopteran, Formicid
Informal ID: Ant
Fossil size: Total length 1cm/⅖in
Reconstructed size: As above
Habitat: Woods, forests
Time span: From Early Cretaceous, 125 million years ago, to today
Main fossil sites: Worldwide
Occurrence: ◆ ◆

Diplopodan (millipede)

Name: *Diplopodan*
Meaning: Double footed
Grouping: Arthropod, Diplopodan
Informal ID: Millipede ('thousand feet')
Fossil size: 7.3cm/3in
Reconstructed size: This specimen (unstraightened) 6.3cm/2½in; largest species exceeded 2m/6ft in length
Habitat: Moist forest floor
Time span: Ordovician, over 435 million years ago, to today
Main fossil sites: Worldwide
Occurrence: ◆

Preserved remains of millipedes date back to the Silurian Period, and some of their tracks or traces may be even earlier (see panel below). This suggests that they originated in aquatic habitats but soon moved onto land. Millipedes are also known as diplopodans, reflecting the feature of two pairs of legs per body section or segment (centipedes have one pair). Most of the 10,000 living species chew vegetable matter, from juicy leaves to dead wood. The first millipedes probably led a similar lifestyle. They were among the first of all land creatures, perhaps capitalizing on the largely uncontested decaying remains of early terrestrial plants. *Arthropleura*, a millipede of the Late Carboniferous, possibly exceeded 2m/6ft in length, making it the biggest known land invertebrate of all time.

Above: An unidentified diplopodan preserved as part and counterpart in a Carboniferous siltstone nodule of Yorkshire, north-east England. Most millipedes have always lived in damp habitats, such as forest floors, and their exoskeletons are not mineralized, making their fossils scarce.

Chilopodan (centipede)

A centipede has one pair of legs per body section, or segment (millipedes have two pairs, see above), and usually more than 15 segments. Most of the 3,000 living species are predators of small worms, insects and similar creatures. What is effectively the first pair of walking legs has become a pair of curved, fang-like claws called forcipules. These seize prey and inject poison. Like millipedes, most centipedes frequent moist places, such as woods and leaf litter, where they would soon rot after death, and so their fossils are scarce. Centipedes also often consume their own shed body casings as they grow and moult and, presuming ancient centipedes did the same, this would further reduce the material available for fossilization. The fossil record for centipedes may stretch back to the Devonian or even Late Silurian, with relatively plentiful numbers from the Carboniferous, but finds from the Mesozoic Era are rare.

Name: Chilopodan
Meaning: Poison feet
Grouping: Arthropod, Chilopodan
Informal ID: Centipede
Fossil size: Centipede length 14mm/⅛in
Reconstructed size: Large species up to 30cm/12in
Habitat: Moist forests
Time span: This specimen, Late Eocene, 40–35 million years ago
Main fossil sites: Worldwide
Occurrence: ◆

Millipede trace fossils

These tracks (footprints) were probably made by a millipede-like creature scurrying across a silty underwater surface. As the water current pushed it one way, the animal placed its legs out to one side in order to stay balanced, to keep itself in touch with the substrate and to keep itself going in the desired direction. Its feet slid sideways in the soft silt, leaving slim furrows. The fossil is Devonian, from the Old Red Sandstone near Brecon, Wales.

Right: In this piece of Baltic amber, dating from the Late Eocene Epoch, about 40–35 million years ago, the trapped centipede is in the centre. Its long horn-like antennae protrude at the head (left) with the first few pairs of walking legs just visible as the body curves away, terminating in the tail (upper-right). Some small flies and other insects were also entrapped.

Head

Tail

MOLLUSCS

The phylum (major animal group) Mollusca is one of the largest in the animal kingdom, with more than 100,000 living species. They range from gastropods – slugs, sea slugs (nudibranchs), land snails and sea snails, such as whelks and limpets – and bivalves, which are shellfish with a two-part shell, such as oysters, clams and mussels, to the many-tentacled cephalopods – octopus, squid and cuttlefish. The ancient representatives of creatures such as these, as well as many thousands of their long-extinct molluscan cousins, such as the ammonites and belemnites, form a significant portion of the fossil record. The various subgroups of the Mollusca are covered on the pages that follow.

Dentalium

Scaphopods are distinctive molluscs with a long, slim, tapering, tubular shell that is open at both ends. Its resemblance to an elephant's tusk has earned the group the common name of 'tusk shells'. In the living animal, the fleshy, finger-like 'foot' and head extend from the wider, lower end for feeding. Water is drawn into the narrow upper end for obtaining oxygen. Unlike most molluscs, scaphopods lack gills and, instead, absorb oxygen over the folded fleshy surfaces within the shell. Scaphopods live part-buried in mud or similar sediments on the sea floor and use the foot to construct a feeding cavity. Most types consume microorganisms, such as foraminifera. One subgroup, the dentaliids, have rigid sets of teeth, which they use to grind small prey. In another subgroup, the gadilids, the teeth are more flexible and function to chop and crush. Scaphopods occur in the fossil record from the Ordovician Period, more than 450 million years ago. They are extremely common in certain places and their preserved shells range in size from larger than a forefinger to as small as a matchstick.

Below: Dentalium striatum *is named after the striations, or stripes, along its length, which show patterns of growth rings (like a tree) as the shell lengthens with age. This specimen, from the Late Eocene Epoch, is from the Barton Beds of Hampshire, England.*

Name: *Dentalium*
Meaning: Small tooth
Grouping: Mollusc, Scaphopod
Informal ID: Tusk shell
Fossil size: *D. striatum* shell length 4.5cm/1¾in
Reconstructed size: Most specimens 1–10cm/⅜–4in
Habitat: Sea floor
Time span: Ordovician, over 450 million years ago, to today
Main fossil sites: Worldwide
Occurrence: ◆ ◆ ◆

Bands of striations

Faint longitudinal faces give hexagonal cross-section

Narrow upper (posterior) opening for respiratory water current

Wide lower (anterior) opening where main body protruded in life

Left: Scaphopods show little variety of form, most having the curved, tapering shape of an elephant's tusk. The shell surface ornamentation is either absent or comprised of raised ridges or ribs, as here in Dentalium neohexagonum, *which is from the Pleistocene Palos Verdes Sand of San Pedro, Los Angeles, California, USA.*

Helminthochiton

Name: *Helminthochiton*
Meaning: Leaf shield
Grouping: Mollusc,
Polyplacophoran
Informal ID: Chiton,
coat-of-mail shell
Fossil size: Total length
8cm/3⅛in
Reconstructed size: Total
length 10cm/4in
Habitat: Sea floor
Time span: Ordovician to
Carboniferous, 500–300
million years ago
Main fossil sites: North
America, Europe
Occurrence: ◆

Chitons are known scientifically as polyplacophorans, and informally as coat-of-mail shells. A chiton has a slug-like body shielded beneath eight jointed plates or valves, and flanked by an oval spiny girdle. When threatened, the chiton can roll up for protection in the manner of a woodlouse. Unlike most molluscs, chitons possess multiple pairs of gills for obtaining oxygen from water. Some scientists interpret this as a primitive feature inherited from a segmented ancestor, but others view it as an evolutionary adaptation for better respiration. Chitons are common today in rocky marine environments where they cling limpet-like to hard surfaces. Most are fingernail-sized but the giant chiton is as large as a shoe. However, they are scarce in the fossil record, usually occurring as isolated valves from the Cambrian Period, more than 500 million years ago.

Below: A chiton's valves usually separate soon after death to form isolated fossils. This specimen has been reconstructed with all its main valves articulated (positioned as in life), although the flange-like girdle, which would have joined to their edge all around, like a 'skirt', is missing.

Second valve *Head end*

Eighth valve (tail end)

Proplina

Name: *Proplina*
Meaning: Early pot
Grouping: Mollusc,
Monoplacophoran
Informal ID:
Monoplacophoran
Fossil size: 3cm/1in
Reconstructed size:
As above
Habitat: Sea floor
Time span: Late Cambrian to
Early Ordovician, 510–470
million years ago
Main fossil sites: North
America, Northeast Asia
Occurrence: ◆ ◆

Monoplacophoran molluscs are termed 'living fossils'. These primitive marine molluscs were presumed extinct from the Devonian Period, more than 300 million years ago, until live specimens were collected in 1952 from the Pacific deep-sea floor. They are considered similar in form to the ancestral or 'original' mollusc, comprising a simple conical shell and a fleshy foot for locomotion. They also possess multiple gills, like the chitons. Superficially they resemble limpets, but the latter belong in a different group, the gastropods or snails, due to the internal twisting of the body. Monoplacophorans appeared during the Cambrian Period and they were common in the shallow seas of the Early Palaeozoic Era.

Margin (lower edge) of shell   *Apex (upper tip) of shell pitched forward over anterior (head) end*

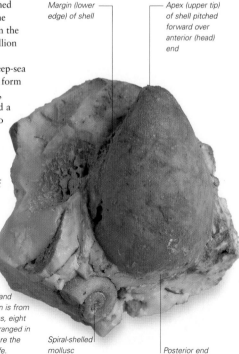

Right: The spoon-shaped monoplacophoran Proplina *is found in various rocks, such as cherts from eastern and southeastern North America. This specimen is from Missouri, USA. In well-preserved specimens, eight muscle 'scars' can be seen on the shell, arranged in a horseshoe pattern. These 'scars' are where the foot-retracting muscles were anchored in life.*

Spiral-shelled mollusc   *Posterior end*

MOLLUSCS – BIVALVES

In general the mollusc group have left plentiful fossils and they are especially common in rocks from the Cambrian Period onwards. The bivalves are perhaps the most familiar molluscs and include the clams, oysters, cockles, scallops and mussels. The shell has two parts or valves. The group seems to have appeared in the Cambrian Period and become well established by the Ordovician.

Inoceramus

The hard parts of a bivalve consist of a pair of calcareous valves. Broadly speaking, the two valves of a bivalve are mirror images of each other, which distinguishes them from the brachiopods. The valves close to protect the soft parts, with an articulation or hinge composed of teeth and sockets. Ligaments on one side of the hinge-line hold the valves open, while powerful muscles, called adductors, pull the valves tightly shut. Typically, each bivalve has a pair of adductor muscles that attach to the inside of the valves, leaving distinctive impressions called muscle scars. The exact structure of the hinge area and the arrangement of the muscle scars are key features when it comes to distinguishing the various bivalve groups.

Left: The two valves of this specimen of Inoceramus lamarckii, *a type of mussel (see* Sphenoceramus, *below), have been preserved together, still articulated. The decaying fleshy remains within the shell acted as a site for silica precipitation within the sediment, and the valves are now partially engulfed within a flint (silica) concretion.*

Name: *Inoceramus*
Meaning: Strong pot
Grouping: Mollusc, Bivalve
Informal ID: Mussel
Fossil size: 10cm/4in
Reconstructed size: Most specimens up to 20cm/8in
Habitat: Sea floor
Time span: Late Cretaceous, 90 million years ago
Main fossil sites: Worldwide
Occurrence: ◆ ◆ ◆

Sphenoceramus

Right: This elaborate specimen of Sphenoceramus, *from the Late Cretaceous Chalks of Sussex, England, has sets of radiating ridges arranged in growth arcs, leading to its species name of S. pinniformis (meaning 'in the form of a leaf').*

Pseudomytiloides
Freak currents have swept these shells along the sea floor and banked them against a log of driftwood. During the fossilization process the shells have incorporated the iron mineral pyrite, or 'fool's gold', giving them an unusual and attractive golden coloration.

Sphenoceramus and *Inoceramus* (above) belong to a group known as the inoceramids. They were particularly successful during the Late Cretaceous, where many grew to a great size – individuals more than 1m/3¼ft in length were not uncommon. Most lived reclining on the sea floor and acted as oases of hard substrate for small communities of oysters, sponges, corals, barnacles, brachiopods, worms and bryozoans. Some shells contain the remains of schools of fish, which apparently lived within them and were trapped when the shell died and clamped shut.

Name: *Sphenoceramus*
Meaning: Wedge pot
Grouping: Mollusc, Bivalve
Informal ID: Mussel
Fossil size: 17cm/6¾in in length
Reconstructed size: Some individuals more than 1m/3¼ft in length
Habitat: Sea floor
Time span: Late Cretaceous Period, 85 million years ago
Main fossil sites: Worldwide
Occurrence: ◆ ◆ ◆

Spondylus

Name: *Spondylus*
Meaning: Vertebra (backbone)
Grouping: Mollusc, Bivalve
Informal ID: Thorny or spiny oyster
Fossil size: 4cm/1½in
Reconstructed size: Up to 15cm/6in across, including the spines
Habitat: Sea floor
Time span: Jurassic, 190 million years ago, to today
Main fossil sites: Worldwide
Occurrence: ◆ ◆ ◆

Right: The upper valve is largely free of spines, while the lower valve is densely armoured. Only the spine bases have been retained in this specimen.

Some bivalves have shells ornamented with tall, sharp ridges, and there are even spines protruding from along the edge or margin of one or both valves. These ribs and spines can provide strength, protection and stability, as well as encouraging other organisms, such as algae (seaweeds), to grow on top to act as camouflage. Modern forms of *Spondylus* are called spiny or thorny oysters, although they are not actually true oysters. In many, the lower valve becomes encrusted to a hard substrate, such as a rock. The Cretaceous species *S. spinosus* was not encrusted but free-living. In life, it possessed a dense array of particularly elongated and slender spines projecting from around the valve edge, which possibly prevented the animal from sinking into soft sediment.

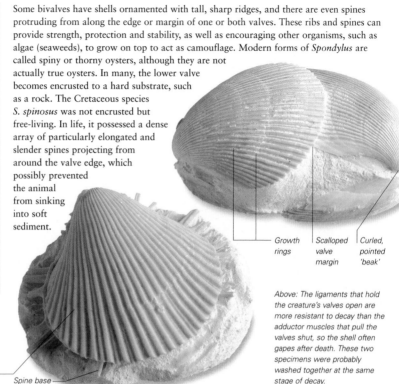

Growth rings | Scalloped valve margin | Curled, pointed 'beak'

Radial ridges — Spine base —

Above: The ligaments that hold the creature's valves open are more resistant to decay than the adductor muscles that pull the valves shut, so the shell often gapes after death. These two specimens were probably washed together at the same stage of decay.

Neithea

Name: *Neithea*
Meaning: Reliquary, strongbox
Grouping: Mollusc, Bivalve
Informal ID: Clam, scallop
Fossil size: 3cm/1in across
Reconstructed size: Up to 10cm/4in across
Habitat: Sea floor
Time span: Cretaceous, 130–70 million years ago
Main fossil sites: Worldwide
Occurrence: ◆ ◆ ◆

Neithea was a scallop-like bivalve in the group called pectens (see following page), with one flat valve and one convex (outward-bulging) valve. Presumably it lived reclined on the surface of the sea floor with the convex valve lowermost. Like all bivalves, it lacked a defined 'head'. Instead, the shell gaped slightly so that water could pass over the sheet-like gills hanging within the body cavity, moving as a current generated by the gill lining of microscopic, whip-like structures known as cilia. In addition to taking in oxygen, the gills act as sieves, straining the water for tiny food particles, typically microscopic organisms of the plankton. These are gathered in sticky mucus (slime) and passed to the mouth.

Right: Neithea *had about five large radiating ridges or ribs interspersed with groups of four or so narrower, lower ribs. This design, like the wavy corrugations in metal sheet, provided strength and stiffness for minimum material usage and weight.*

Convex valve | Overhanging 'beak' of hinge region

Main ribs | Secondary ribs | Flattened valve

MOLLUSCS – BIVALVES (CONTINUED)

During the Early Palaeozoic, bivalves were successful in aquatic environments where the water was shallow and salty – conditions shunned by their main rivals, the brachiopods (lampshells). Through the Devonian and Carboniferous, bivalves became more common in lagoons, estuaries and fresh water. Today, bivalves dominate many shallow marine habitats while brachiopods have become relatively scarce.

Aviculopecten

Below: Aviculopecten had the typical scallop, fan-like structure of ribs and furrows radiating out to the valve margins (edges). The 'ears' on either side of the hinge area are asymmetrical. The front, or anterior, ear has an in-curved notch (more pronounced in the right valve).

The typical behaviour of the scallops, or pecten bivalves, is to rest on the sea floor. Some types anchor themselves to a hard substrate, such as rock, by tough stringy structures called byssus threads (see opposite), in the manner of mussels. Others are able to 'swim', as described below, but take flight only when they are threatened by predators or when the environmental conditions become unfavourable for some reason. *Aviculopecten* was probably anchored by threads to a hard surface and so could not swim freely. Bivalves are often brightly coloured in life, but colour pigments quickly break down after death and are preserved in fossils only in exceptional circumstances. The specimen shown here has retained its striking pattern of zigzag banding, but the original colours have been lost.

Name: *Aviculopecten*
Meaning: Bird/winged comb
Grouping: Mollusc, Bivalve
Informal ID: Scallop
Fossil size: 3cm/1in
Reconstructed size: Most specimens less than 10cm/4in
Habitat: Sea floor
Time span: Devonian to Permian, 360–260 million years ago
Main fossil sites: Worldwide
Occurrence: ◆ ◆ ◆

Streblopteria

Scallops include forms with the ability, unique among bivalves, to 'swim'. This is achieved by repeated powerful contractions of the adductor muscles, which cause the valves to 'clap'. Jets of water are expelled through openings either side of the hinge area and thus propel the animal across the sea bed and even up into mid water. In life, scallops possess a feature unique to bivalves – rows of tiny iridescent light sensors, or 'eyes', fringing the opening of the shell. These are relatively simple, but are able to sense light and movement and can be regrown if damaged or lost. The development of sight among scallops complements their swimming ability, and allows them to orientate themselves and swim purposefully in a particular direction.

Left: The preservation of fossil patternation is generally very rare. It is well known in bivalves from the Carboniferous limestones of Castleton in Derbyshire, England, however, where this specimen and Aviculopecten *(above) were found. The direction of patternation follows, but does not coincide exactly with, the radiating ribs that strengthen the valves.*

Name: *Streblopteria*
Meaning: Twisted/rolled wing
Grouping: Mollusc, Bivalve
Informal ID: Scallop
Fossil size: 3cm/1in
Reconstructed size: As above
Habitat: Sea floor
Time span: Carboniferous to Permian, 350–260 million years ago
Main fossil sites: Worldwide
Occurrence: ◆ ◆ ◆

Plagiostoma

Name: Plagiostoma
Meaning: Slanting mouth, sideways opening
Grouping: Mollusc, Bivalve
Informal ID: Clam
Fossil size: 10cm/4in
Reconstructed size: As above, reaching 20cm/8in
Habitat: Sea floor
Time span: Triassic to Cretaceous, 230–65 million years ago
Main fossil sites: Worldwide
Occurrence: ◆ ◆ ◆

Extinct bivalves such as *Plagiostoma* probably produced a unique substance known as byssus, as used by many types of living bivalve today. Byssus is a form of fine thread that the animal uses to attach and anchor itself to hard substrates, such as rocks. (The common mussel, for example, attaches itself to rocks and breakwaters using byssal threads.) Byssus is produced by the bivalve's foot as a fluid that solidifies once it is in contact with water. The foot draws the material out into threads that it then attaches to the substrate. It is not necessarily a permanent connection, and it is possible for the animal to break free if threatened or if it needs to relocate. (Fabric made from byssus was prized in ancient times and referred to as sea-silk. The fabled Golden Fleece of ancient myth was perhaps made of bivalve byssus.)

Right: Plagiostoma *is believed to have attached itself to rocks or large pieces of driftwood using byssal threads. This species, P. giganteum, is a common fossil from the Liassic rocks of the Jurassic Period. It grew to a large size and can be found preserved in the position it would have adopted in life, orientated vertically.*

Myophorella

Myophorella belongs to a group of bivalves known as trigoniids – types of clam characterized partly by hinge structure. The right valve part of the hinge has two broad, ribbed teeth forming a V shape. The teeth fit into corresponding indentations in the left valve. The thick shell of *Myophorella* is partly covered by curving lines of knobs or tubercles, which would have aided its passage through and purchase within the sediment when burrowing. The area lacking tubercles would have projected above the sediment, with the line where the ornamentation is lost marking the surface of the sediment. Trigoniids often occur in dense associations within Mesozoic marine limestones, but they are rare today.

Name: Myophorella
Meaning: Little muscle bearer
Grouping: Mollusc, Bivalve
Informal ID: Clam, brooch clam
Fossil size: 5cm/2in across
Reconstructed size: As above
Habitat: Sea floor
Time span: Early Jurassic to Early Cretaceous, 190–130 million years ago
Main fossil sites: Worldwide
Occurrence: ◆ ◆ ◆

Laevitrigonia

If the shell of a fossil such as a bivalve decays, it leaves an internal mould shape in the rock, as shown here. This is referred to by the German word *steinkern*, meaning 'stone seed'. The steinkerns of *Laevitrigonia* are referred to in folklore as 'osses 'eds'. When viewed from a certain angle, their shape can be likened to the head of a horse. The shell itself, before it decayed to leave the mould, was quite similar in general form to that of *Myophorella* (see right).

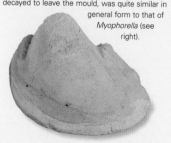

Below: Myophorella *has an almost half-circle shell shape partially ornamented by rows of low bumps or pimples termed tubercles. The rear, or posterior, part of each valve is plain and would have projected above the sediment in life. Fossils associated with this bivalve suggest that it lived in deep-sea sands, muds and similar types of sediment.*

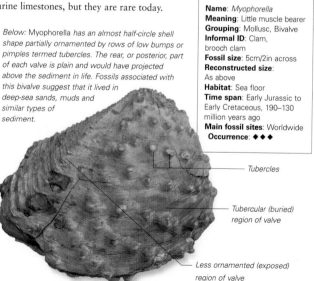

Tubercles

Tubercular (buried) region of valve

Less ornamented (exposed) region of valve

MOLLUSCS – BIVALVES (CONTINUED)

The bivalve molluscs known as oysters are characterized by their tendency to encrust rocks and other shells. Oysters are useful 'way-up' indicators. This is because they lie encrusted on one valve, so the other exposed, upward-facing valve acts as a hard surface for its own smaller encrustations such as barnacles. This indicates which way up the oyster – and often fossils associated with it – were in life.

Lopha

The lifestyle and habitat of ancient bivalves are usually derived from analogy to their living relations. The shell shape and form of oysters such as *Lopha*, *Ostrea* and *Rastellum* are often highly irregular and reflect the shape of the surface on which that particular individual grew. In many cases the external features of oyster shells are so variable that recognizing the various species is very difficult, especially among mixed assemblages. As a general rule, internal features, such as muscle scars, are more reliable for identification. Oysters possess only one adductor muscle, which produces large and distinct muscle scars where it attaches to the inside of the valves. A much smaller pair of muscles, the Quenstedt muscles, attach to the gills and leave small muscle scars.

Above: Jurassic Lopha marshi *(Ostrea marshii) grew in a variety of shapes, partly determined by the room available. The curled shape and prominent V-like ridges have led to the common name of coxcomb oyster.*

Left: Lopha marshi *often lived among hardground communities where ageing, lithified sediments were exposed on the sea floor, giving a weathered, cement-like substrate.*

Name: *Lopha*
Meaning: Crested, peaked
Grouping: Mollusc, Bivalve
Informal ID: Oyster, coxcomb (cock's comb) oyster
Fossil size: 6–7cm/2½in
Reconstructed size: Less than 10cm/4in
Habitat: Shallow sea floor
Time span: Late Jurassic to Late Cretaceous, 160–70 million years ago
Main fossil sites: Europe, Asia
Occurrence: ◆ ◆

Gryphaeostrea

Below: The flattened attachment surface present on one of these oysters suggests that they were attached to a large aragonite bivalve, which has not been preserved.

Attachment ——
surface

Most mollusc shells are calcareous, which means that they are built from calcium carbonate minerals. There are two main forms of calcium carbonate: calcite and aragonite. Aragonite is less robust than calcite, and often dissolves away during fossilization. Oysters form their shells from calcite, but many of the groups that they encrust, such as cephalopods, gastropods and other bivalves, have shells formed of aragonite. The result is that fossil oysters are often found apparently unattached, because the shells they were encrusting have not been preserved. However, the encrusting surface of the oyster represents a very faithful mould showing the shape of the surface it was once attached to – often sufficiently detailed for the former host to be identified.

Name: *Gryphaeostrea*
Meaning: Grabber oyster
Grouping: Mollusc, Bivalve
Informal ID: Oyster
Fossil size: 4cm/1½in
Reconstructed size: Up to 10cm/4in
Habitat: Hard objects, such as shell or bone, found on the sea floor
Time span: Cretaceous to Miocene, 115–10 million years ago
Main fossil sites: Worldwide
Occurrence: ◆ ◆ ◆

Gryphea

Name: Gryphea
Meaning: Grabber
Grouping: Mollusc, Bivalve
Informal ID: Oyster, 'devil's toenails'
Fossil size: Specimen lengths 7–10cm/2¾–4in
Reconstructed size: As above
Habitat: Sea floor
Time span: Late Triassic to Late Jurassic, 220–140 million years ago
Main fossil sites: Worldwide
Occurrence: ◆ ◆ ◆ ◆

Various forms of *Gryphea* were among the first true oysters, appearing in the Triassic Period. The tiny free-moving larva, or 'spat', attached to a small particle (rather than a large rock) as its initial hard substrate. It soon outgrew this, however, and became essentially free-living, reclined on the sea floor. Like other bivalves, the valves of the oyster shell are on either side of the animal (even though one usually faces up and the other down) and can be referred to as the left and right valves. For true oysters which encrust, the left valve attaches to the hard substrate. In the free-living adult *Gryphea* the left valve is large and coiled while the right valve is more like a small cap. In life, the animal would have rested on the left valve with the right valve facing upwards. The thick plug of calcite around the umbo (the original, first-formed, beak-like part) of the left valve acted as a counterbalance to keep the opening between the valves raised above the sediment. Many types of *Gryphea* were very successful through the Mesozoic Era.

Pearls
Oysters are famed for containing pearls. These are generated as a defensive substance to 'wall off' particles that enter the shell and irritate the animal. This process can be simulated artificially by inserting shell fragments into farmed oysters. Pearls are sometimes found preserved in fossil oysters. However, the usual mineral replacement, which is part of fossilization, has taken place, and so the pearly lustrous appearance has long been lost.

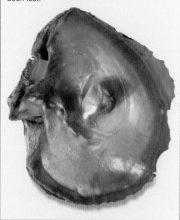

Left: Gryphea oysters usually show pronounced growth ridges, as the valves of the shell grew seasonally at their widening edges, or margins. Fossils of these early oysters are common enough finds to have entered into folklore – their talon-like shape has earned them the nickname of 'devil's toenails'.

Thick inrolled umbo (first-formed part of valve), acting as a counterbalance

Cap-like right valve

Large coiled left valve

Growth ridges

Umbo

Area of cap valve

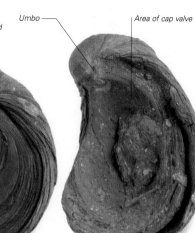

Right: Gryphea of the Early Jurassic display changes in time whereby the left, or coiled, valve becomes broader and more flattened, while the right, or cap, valve becomes larger and more concave. This gave the animals an overall bowl-like appearance, perhaps representing an adaptation to the sediment on which they were living.

MOLLUSCS – BIVALVES (CONTINUED)

The morphology (shape and form) of a bivalve shell can say a lot about the owner's mode of life, its orientation within the sediment, depth of burial, the strength of the currents and the layout of the soft body parts within. Many burrowing bivalves have a well-developed, muscular foot. It can extend between the valves, expand at the tip to anchor itself, and then shorten to pull the valves towards it.

Tellina

Tellins are mostly smallish bivalves with a thin-walled, symmetrical, plain shell. They live along sandy and muddy coasts and estuaries today. Many tellins are brightly coloured, although this characteristic is seldom seen in life since they remain buried just under the surface. Like other burrowing bivalves, such as cockles and clams, the tellin extends two muscular tubes, called siphons, which project just above the surface. One takes in water, which is filtered for food and from which oxygen is absorbed. The water then exits through the other siphon. Tellins are sometimes found packed in dense groups with many hundreds in one square metre/yard.

Name: *Tellina*
Meaning: Of the earth
Grouping: Mollusc, Bivalve
Informal ID: Freshwater tellin
Fossil size: 4cm/1½in
Reconstructed size: As above
Habitat: Rivers, lakes
Time span: Mainly Early Tertiary, 50 million years ago, to today
Main fossil sites: Worldwide
Occurrence: ◆ ◆

Left: This specimen of freshwater tellin, Tellina aquitanica, is from Pliocene rocks of Asti, Italy. It shows the growth rings typical of many bivalves. These reflect different rates of shell enlargement through the seasons, with cold weather slowing growth. Tellin valves typically have smooth, 'clean' lines, with little ornamentation. However, their thin and relatively delicate shell structure means that they are among the less common bivalves found as complete fossils.

Modiolus

Life within sediments, such as sand, silt and mud, is known as infaunal. Members of the genus *Modiolus*, which still thrive along shorelines today, are known as horse mussels. When alive, they tend to lie part-buried in the sediment with their generally oblong, slightly lop-sided valves lying parallel to the sediment surface, and with their byssal threads (see *Plagiostoma*) attached to the relatively firm substrate. *Modiolus* tends to grow larger than common mussels (*Mytilus*) and has a thicker, tougher shell. This forms a hard surface for small encrusting organisms such as barnacles and tubeworms, which are themselves sometimes preserved on the mussel.

Name: *Modiolus*
Meaning: Washer, collar
Grouping: Mollusc, Bivalve
Informal ID: Horse mussel
Fossil size: 7cm/2¾in
Reconstructed size: As above, but some specimens grow to 20cm/8in or more
Habitat: Sea floor
Time span: Devonian, 400 million years ago, to today
Main fossil sites: Worldwide
Occurrence: ◆ ◆ ◆

Left: Modiolus, the horse mussel, has altered very little in the course of its evolutionary history. Its slipper-shaped valves show growth lines and are unornamented, except for very fine ribs in some specimens that spread out like the ribs of a fan. The overall shell shape is bulging or swollen, mainly in the central region, known technically as a tumid form.

Growth rings

Long hinge line

Tumid central region

Pholadomya

Name: *Pholadomya*
Meaning: Piddock clam
Grouping: Mollusca, Bivalve
Informal ID: Gaper,
gaper clam
Fossil size: 5cm/2in
Reconstructed size: Up
to 10cm/4in
Habitat: Sea floor
Time span: Triassic,
220 million years
ago, to today
Main fossil sites: Worldwide
Occurrence: ◆ ◆ ◆

Pholadomya belonged to a group of bivalves called gapers, gaper clams or soft-shelled clams, which still thrive on the sea floor today. They burrow deep into the sediment in order to gain protection and to avoid unfavourable conditions, such as a withdrawing tide. Their shell does not fully close and so is of lesser protective importance. This allows for greatly enlarged siphons. The siphons are paired and part-fused tubes that extend to the surface of the sediment, draw in particles of food and water, and expel the water, after absorbing oxygen, along with any wastes. A large gap between the 'closed' valves shows this deep-burrowing mode of life, and can be seen in fossils. A broad but shallow furrow on the inner surface of the shell, known as the pallial sinus, is also a sign of the enlarged siphons, which, when fully extended, could be up to twice the length of the shell.

Below: The posterior of
Pholadomya's *shell is drawn out and expanded so that it can accommodate the greatly enlarged siphons. In life, this end would have been orientated upwards, towards the surface of the sediment, several centimetres above.*

Umbo (original growing point of shell)

Collar-like gap for siphons

Growth lines

Posterior (rear) of shell

Teredo

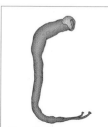

Name: *Teredo*
Meaning: Grub
Grouping: Mollusc, Bivalve
Informal ID: Shipworm
Fossil size: Wood specimen
length 12cm/4¾in
Reconstructed size: Shells
about 1cm/⅜in across; whole
animal may be 50cm/20in
plus in length
Habitat: Driftwood
Time span: Eocene, 50
million years ago, to today
Main fossil sites: Worldwide
Occurrence: ◆ ◆

Many bivalves have developed the capacity to bore into hard substrates, such as wood or rock, where they are largely protected from predators as well as any hostile elements. The bivalves can employ both physical and chemical means to achieve this goal. The piddock, which is familiar from most rocky shores, rotates its abrasive shell to bore into stone. *Teredo*, erroneously known as the 'shipworm', is a bivalve mollusc that has greatly modified its body for a life within driftwood. Its trace fossils of burrows are familiar in preserved wood. The shell has been reduced to two small rasping plates that abrade the tunnel, and the worm-like body then fills the tube and lines it with calcareous cement. The entrance to the tube has two small trapdoors, termed pallets, that can close to seal off completely the outside world. The shipworm siphons water containing suspended nutrients into its burrow, and it is also able to digest the wood as it bores.

Below: This piece of fossilized conifer driftwood has been water-worn to expose the Teredo *tubes within, lined with stony calcium-rich minerals. This example is from the Eocene deposits of the Isle of Sheppey, in south-east England, where such specimens are commonly found.*

Teredo *tunnels*

MOLLUSCS – GASTROPODS

Gastropods include very familiar creatures, such as garden snails and slugs, along with pond and water snails, a huge variety of marine shelled forms, such as seashore winkles, periwinkles, whelks, limpets and abalones, and the sea-slugs. The name 'gastropod' means 'stomach-foot', and comes from the early observation that these animals seem to slide along on their bellies. The group first appeared in the seas towards the end of the Cambrian Period, more than 500 million years ago. Since then, they have spread to freshwater and terrestrial habitats. Their shells are not especially tough but have left huge numbers of fossils, mainly during the Cenozoic Era (from 65 million years ago to the present). For details of the gastropod shell and body, and gastropod classifications, see the following pages.

Athleta

Typically, it is only the shell of a gastropod that is preserved and comes to us in the form of a fossil. The shell is constructed mainly from a calcareous mineral called aragonite, which is unstable over geological time, and is often either replaced by calcite or dissolved away, leaving a void in which a mould fossil may form. *Athleta* was similar in overall shape to the living oyster-drill or sting-winkle, *Ocenebra*. This creature preys on living bivalve molluscs, such as oysters and mussels, scraping out the soft flesh from within. *Athleta* may have had a broad foot, which it used to pull apart the two valves and so gain access to its food.

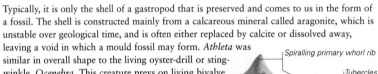

Spiralling primary whorl rib

Tubercles

Apex

Secondary axial ribs

Aperture

Outer lip

Right: This specimen of Athleta *dates from the Eocene and came from eastern North America. The shell was ornate, with ribbed whorls bearing small tubercles (lumps) at regular intervals, and had an elongated aperture.*

Name: *Athleta*
Meaning: Contestant, athlete
Grouping: Mollusc, Gastropod, Prosobranch, Neogastropod
Informal ID: Sea snail
Fossil size: Shell length 5cm/2in
Reconstructed size: Shell length up to 12cm/4¾in
Habitat: Marine
Time span: Mainly Late Palaeocene and Early Eocene, 55–45 million years ago
Main fossil sites: North America, Europe
Occurrence: ◆ ◆

Potamaclis

Below: In this accumulation, the orientation of tiny Potamaclis *specimens records the direction in which the water was flowing at the time of deposition – the tips of the spires point downstream.*

Gastropods which have shells with tightly formed whorls that progress rapidly along the main lengthways axis as they grow are known by the common names of spireshells or turretshells. Many types live in estuarine mudflats today. Several species of *Potamaclis* inhabited freshwater environments with flowing water, such as rivers and streams. Their remains are particularly common in Oligocene rocks from the Isle of Wight and Hampshire, southern England. The most prevalent form is known as *Potamaclis turritissima*.

Name: *Potamaclis*
Meaning: Closed/shut river
Grouping: Mollusc, Gastropod, Prosobranch, Mesogastropod
Informal ID: River spireshell, turretshell
Fossil size: Slab width 16cm/6¼in
Reconstructed size: Individual shell length up to 3cm/1in
Habitat: Flowing fresh water
Time span: Mainly Oligocene, 30–25 million years ago
Main fossil sites: Europe
Occurrence: ◆ ◆

Viviparus (including Paludina)

The common freshwater river snail *Viviparus* of today has changed little throughout its long fossil record. It has a thin-walled shell, which is quite brittle, and rounded, bulging whorls with shallow sutures giving a relatively smooth outline when viewed laterally. The shell surface is also smooth, with little in the way of spines or other ornamentation, although in life the young snail has small hair-like processes in bands around each whorl. The aperture shape is almost oval or perhaps slightly heart-like, and the aperture is at right angles to the main axis along which the shell lengthens. The operculum, or closure plate, for the aperture is horny and so rarely forms a fossil. These snails cannot tolerate much in the way of salty (saline) water and so their fossil presence indicates that a body of water was fresh rather than brackish or saline. Like many gastropods, *Viviparus* is mainly a herbivore, grazing on small plants. Most specimens previously identified as *Paludina* are usually now referred to as *Viviparus*: for example, *P. lenta* is synonymous with *V. lentus*, and *P. angulosa* with *V. angulosus*. (See also *Lymnaea* on the following pages, which is another common freshwater snail, usually called the pond snail.)

Apex — — Suture
— Main whorl

Above: Within the genus Viviparus *are numerous species, each with a modification on the basic river snail shape. This specimen is the species* Viviparus lentus, *and it comes from Oligocene deposits on the Isle of Wight, southern England.*

Right: This accumulation of Viviparus *may have been picked up by a flush of river water and deposited as the current slackened at the river estuary, where salty water would kill the snails.*

Name: *Viviparus*
Meaning: Bearing live young
Grouping: Mollusc, Gastropod, Prosobranch, Mesogastropod
Informal ID: River snail, pond snail, live-bearing snail
Fossil size: 2.5cm/1in
Reconstructed size: Shell length usually up to 7cm/2¾in
Habitat: Fresh water including ponds, lakes, slow rivers
Time span: Jurassic, 200 million years ago, to today
Main fossil sites: Worldwide
Occurrence: ◆ ◆

Fossil operculum

Some gastropods in the prosobranch group have an operculum. This is a hard door-like flap or fingernail, which is used for defence after the animal has withdrawn its soft parts into the shell. In some kinds of gastropod, the operculum fits neatly into the aperture itself; in others, it is considerably smaller than the aperture and is drawn part way into the first whorl. When the gastropod emerges from its shell, the operculum usually lies out of the way on the upper surface of the rear foot. The operculum is horny or calcareous. Horny types soon decay leaving no trace, but the calcareous forms may be tougher than the shell and are often preserved as fossils, having characteristic shapes that allow identification.

Right: This turban or wavytop snail Lithopoma undosum *has withdrawn most of its body (partly visible upper right) into the shell. The door-like operculum is the central dark-edged surface with three pale curves; as the snail continues withdrawal, the operculum will fit snugly within the shell.*

MOLLUSCS – GASTROPODS (CONTINUED)

Gastropods are by far the most successful mollusc group, with perhaps 75,000 species alive today, and upwards of 15,000 types known from fossils. The body is soft, covered by a sheet- or cloak-like mantle, with a well-developed head bearing eyed tentacles and a mouth equipped with a file-like radula 'tongue' for rasping food. Characteristic of the group is a twisted body inside a spiral or helical shell.
The twisting, which happens early in development, is known as torsion. It means the mantle cavity and gills (for aquatic gastropods) are positioned above the head rather than behind, as in most other molluscs.

Neptunea

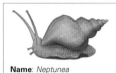

Below: The rounded whorls of Neptunea *are indented by deeper sutures to give a 'stepped spire' appearance. The final whorl where the animal lives, known as the body whorl, is typically convex, or dish-shaped. There are also visible transverse growth lines, usually caused by the seasonal speeding up and then slowing down of the rate at which material was added to the shell opening.*

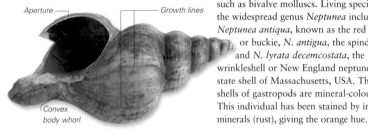

Aperture — | — Growth lines

Convex body whorl

The typical 'sea-shell' we pick up on the beach and hold to our ear, to listen to the sounds of the waves, is likely to be a whelk, or buccinid. This gastropod group includes mainly carnivorous sea snails that scrape up flesh, either scavenging on carcasses of dead crabs and fish or actively preying on victims such as bivalve molluscs. Living species of the widespread genus *Neptunea* include *Neptunea antiqua*, known as the red whelk or buckie, *N. antiqua*, the spindleshell, and *N. lyrata decemcostata*, the wrinkleshell or New England neptune – the state shell of Massachusetts, USA. The fossil shells of gastropods are mineral-coloured. This individual has been stained by iron minerals (rust), giving the orange hue.

Name: *Neptunea*
Meaning: From the Greek god of the sea
Grouping: Mollusc, Gastropod, Prosobranch, Neogastropod
Informal ID: Whelk, sea snail
Fossil size: Shell length 7cm/2¾in
Reconstructed size: Shell length up to 10cm/4in
Habitat: Marine
Time span: Eocene, about 40 million years ago, to today
Main fossil sites: Worldwide
Occurrence: ◆ ◆

Vermetus

The vermetids were, and are, gastropods with a misleading appearance. They resemble the spiral tubes built on rocks and other hard surfaces by true worms (annelids), such as the spirorbid and serpulid worms, known as coiled tubeworms. In *Vermetus*, the whorls separate with growth, so that the inner surface of the later whorl does not contact the outer surface of the preceding one. In some species, the shell lies flat on the substrate; in others, it lengthens as it grows, producing a shape like an enlarging corkscrew. Most living vermetids occupy tropical waters, are cemented to a hard substrate, and secrete mucus that traps food items.

Name: *Vermetus*
Meaning: Worm-like
Grouping: Mollusc, Gastropod, Prosobranch, Mesogastropod
Informal ID: Worm-shell, worm-snail
Fossil size: Slab width 4cm/1½in
Reconstructed size: Shell length up to 10cm/4in
Habitat: Marine, mainly tropical and subtropical seas
Time span: Early Tertiary, about 60 million years ago, to today
Main fossil sites: Worldwide
Occurrence: ◆ ◆

Below: This Vermetus *worm-shell specimen is from the Atherfield Clays at Atherfield Point, Isle of Wight, southern England. The typical vermetid shell gradually coils wider and straighter with age. Also its growth becomes more irregular, leading to many differently shaped individuals.*

Parts of the gastropod shell
Typically, the gastropod shell is twisted, either in one plane, as a spiral (like a hosepipe coiled on the ground), or as a widening helix, as in the familiar snail. The turns of the shell are called whorls, and the junction lines between them are known as sutures. The open end is the aperture, and the pointed end is the apex. In many types of gastropod, the whorls form a lengthening spire as they grow. The animal grows from the apex by adding more shell material to the aperture, which is formed by two lips – the outer or free lip and the inner lip based on the previous whorl.

Lymnaea (Limnaea)

Name: *Lymnaea*
Meaning: Of the marsh
Grouping: Mollusc, Gastropod, Pulmonate
Informal ID: Pond snail, great pond snail
Fossil size: Specimen shell lengths 2–3cm/¾–1in
Reconstructed size: Shell length in some species up to 6cm/2⅜in
Habitat: Fresh water, usually still or slow flowing
Time span: Late Palaeocene, 55 million years ago, to today
Main fossil sites: Mainly Northern Hemisphere
Occurrence: ◆ ◆

The great pond snail *Lymnaea stagnalis* is a well-known inhabitant of still fresh waters and grows as big as a thumb. Its thin-walled shell is longer and more spire-like than that of *Viviparus*, which is another freshwater gastropod with the common name of pond or river snail (see previous pages). In particular, the apex of *Lymnaea* is relatively pointed or 'sharp'. This snail is a pulmonate gastropod, having adapted to life on land with a lung-like organ instead of gills, but then returning to the water. Its aperture is flared, especially in older specimens, which often exhibit growth lines. The last, or body, whorl of *Lymnaea* tends to look out of proportion and larger than it should, relative to the size increase of the other whorls.

Below: The genus Lymnaea *has a long fossil record, stretching back to the Palaeocene Epoch, and has been very widespread across northern continents. In these Oligocene specimens the apex characteristically narrows to a sharp point.*

Gastropod classification

For many years, gastropods have been classified according to the following categories:

Prosobranchia, with three main orders:
• Archaeogastropoda: these are sea-living forms such as limpets, abalones and ormers. The twisting is not clear in the adult form, which has a cone-like shape.
• Mesogastropoda: these mostly marine animals include towershells, worm-shells and periwinkles.
• Neogastropoda: this order includes predatory forms, such as whelks and coneshells, as well as tritons. Most fossils fall into the prosobranch group.

Opisthobranchia, the sea-slugs or nudibranchs, which are usually shell-less, soft-bodied and brightly coloured.

Pulmonata, familiar snails and slugs of the garden, which are mostly terrestrial with the gills modified as air-breathing lungs. Some pulmonates have gone back to fresh water and the lung has been further modified for breathing under the surface of the water.

Recent studies have shown that the above groupings do not reflect the evolution and true relationships of the gastropods. A newer cladistic system is being developed based around groups including the Orthogastropoda and Eogastropoda. Most modern systems of biological classification are now based on cladistic analysis. This system (as explained earlier in the book) uses evolutionary relationships and the possession of what are known as derived features, inherited from a common ancestor and which no other organisms possess, to form groups into units known as clades.

Planorbis

Several genera of freshwater snails are known as ram's-horns or ramshorns, from the flattened spiral shell shape that resembles the curled horns of a male sheep when viewed from the side. These genera include *Planorbis*, *Planorbarius* (*Planorbarius corneus* is known as the great ram's-horn), *Gyraulus* and *Anisus*. Today, these snails live mainly in shallow, weedy waters. Like *Lymnaea* (above), the ram's-horns are air-breathing pulmonates. At the surface, they take a bubble of air into the body cavity, which lasts a considerable time when submerged. Some species have sharp ridges or keels around the widest part of the whorl and transverse growth lines are often prominent.

Name: *Planorbis*
Meaning: Flat spiral or circle
Grouping: Mollusc, Gastropod, Pulmonate
Informal ID: Ram's-horn snail
Fossil size: Shell diameter 2–4cm/¾–1½in
Reconstructed size: Shell diameter in some species up to 8cm/3⅛in
Habitat: Fresh water, usually still or slow flowing
Time span: Late Palaeocene, 55 million years ago, to today
Main fossil sites: Worldwide
Occurrence: ◆ ◆

Right: This species is identified as Planorbis euomphalus, *from Oligocene deposits on the Isle of Wight, southern England. It has a relatively square whorl cross-section showing little curvature on each side, with transverse growth ridges and grooves.*

Mineralized banding

Mould surface

Body whorl

MOLLUSCS – GONIATITES, CERATITES

The Ammonoidea were a huge group of molluscs, mostly with coiled shells, that lived in the seas and oceans. They started to establish themselves in the Early to Mid Devonian Period, from about 400–390 million years ago. Different subgroups came and went, some becoming incredibly numerous and widespread, until the end of the Cretaceous Period, some 330 million years later. Ammonoid subgroups included goniatites and ceratites shown here, and the ammonites. Together with belemnoids and nautiloids, as well as squid, octopuses and cuttlefish, the ammonoids are included in the major cephalopod, or 'head-foot', group of molluscs (see following pages).

Goniatites

The goniatite subgroup of ammonoids takes its name from the genus *Goniatites*, meaning 'angle stones'. This refers to the angled zig-zags in the sutures – the lines showing clearly at intervals on the outside of the shell. Sutures mark the sites where the coiled part of the shell is joined internally to a series of thin, dividing cross-wall partitions, known as septa. These septa separate the inside of the shell into a succession of compartments, which become larger as the animal grows. The creature itself lived in the last, latest compartment. The septa were rarely simple, flat cross-walls. They often had complex wave-like angles and undulations, like large pieces of paper pushed into the shell's interior, where they folded and crumpled as they became wedged in. The pattern of septal folding can be discerned in fossils broken open and its edging shows on the outside as the suture. This pattern is the same for all the septa within an individual shell and for all members of a species, but it differs between species and genera. So the patterns of both sutures and septa can be used to distinguish the thousands of ammonoid species.

The goniatite group, which were among the first ammonoids to appear, were present in the seas for 170 million years. However, they suffered a major decrease in numbers at the end of the Permian Period, 250 million years ago, with just a few types surviving through to the following Triassic Period. The specimen shown here, like many in the genus *Goniatites*, has a relatively wide shell when looked at 'end-on' – that is, directly into the opening (at right angles to the view in this photograph). This wide, fat shell suggests that the animal was a poor swimmer. Faster, more manoeuvrable ammonoids had a narrow shell when viewed end-on. *Goniatites* probably lived in groups or swarms on midwater reefs.

Name: *Goniatites*
Meaning: Angle stone
Grouping: Mollusc, Cephalopod, Ammonoid, Goniatite
Informal ID: Goniatite
Fossil size: 4.5cm/1¾in across
Reconstructed size: Some species up to 15cm/6in across
Habitat: Seas, probably reefs
Time span: Early Carboniferous, 355–325 million years ago
Main fossil sites: Worldwide, mainly Northern Hemisphere
Occurrence: ◆ ◆ ◆

Below: This specimen of Goniatites crenistria *is from the Carboniferous Poyll Vaaish Limestones on the shores of the Isle of Man in the Irish Sea. It has the typical thin shell, curving lobes and sharp-angled saddles of the genus* Goniatites. *The umbilicus, the first-made portion of the shell at the centre, is narrow and deep. The shell is tightly coiled, or involute.*

— Suture lines

— Umbilicus

— Curved lobe

— Sharp-angled saddle

— Living compartment

The importance of sutures

Ammonoids are immensely important as marker or index fossils for dating Late Palaeozoic and Mesozoic rocks and characterizing various kinds of marine communities. Much of their identification relies on the patterns of sutures – the wavy or angled lines on the shell. For how these relate to the inner dividing walls, or septa, see the main text for *Goniatites*.

• The parts of the suture curving or angled towards the open, head end are known as lobes.
• Those directed towards the shell's diminishing centre or umbilicus are called saddles.
• The contours of the suture reflect the folding, waving and crumpling of the edges of the septum, the dividing partition within the shell.
• Goniatites, in general, were early ammonoids with relatively direct sutures, which consisted of curves and sharp angles, but neither lobes nor saddles were subdivided.
• Ceratites were slightly later and had subdivided lobes, but undivided saddles.
• Ammonites were the third major ammonoid group to appear. Their sutures are overall more complex, with both lobes and saddles subdivided in an enormous variety of patterns.

Cheiloceras

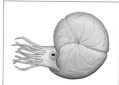

Name: *Cheiloceras*
Meaning: Lip horn
Grouping: Mollusc,
Cephalopod, Ammonoid,
Goniatite
Informal ID: Goniatite
Fossil size: 1.5cm/⅝in across
Reconstructed size: As
above, some specimens
3–4cm/1–1½in across
Habitat: Seas
Time span: Late Devonian,
375–360 million years ago
Main fossil sites: Worldwide
Occurrence: ◆ ◆ ◆

*Below: These specimens of
Cheiloceras were preserved in iron
pyrite. They are small – each would fit
on a thumbnail – and show the widely
spaced sutures characteristic of
several species in the genus. They are
from Famennian Age deposits near
Gladbach, along the River Mulde in the
Sachsen region of eastern Germany.*

This well-known, small, geometrically shaped,
involute (tightly coiled), distinctive goniatite – one of the
earlier types in the group – has been found at several
locations, including Europe (Iberian Peninsula, France
and Germany), North Africa (Morocco), East Asia
(China) and Australia (Western Australia, New South
Wales). It is a useful marker or index fossil and lends its
name to the Cheiloceras beds or deposits typical of the
time span known as the Famennian Age of the Late
Devonian Period, which is dated to approximately
375–360 million years ago. In some localities it has
been suggested that *Cheiloceras* is also found in the
Late Frasian Age, the time span before the
Famennian. Cross-matching *Cheiloceras*
and other fossils
found with it
in these layers
has allowed
the detailed
correlation
of rocks
from around
the world.

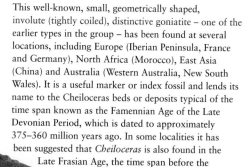

Ceratites

The ceratites, the second main group of
ammonoids to evolve, appeared during the
Mississippian – the first phase of the
Carboniferous Period – about 350 million years
ago. They became much more numerous and
diverse during the Early Triassic, after the
goniatites had faded, but then went extinct
themselves by the end of that period.

*Hollandites was a Mid Triassic ceratite. This
specimen hails from the McLearn Toad
Formation along the Tetsa
River of northern British
Columbia, Canada.
Note the subdivided
lobes – the curved
parts of the sutures
facing towards the
main opening.
Specimen measures
3cm/1in across.*

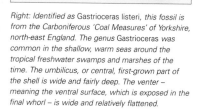

Right: Identified as Gastrioceras listeri, *this fossil is
from the Carboniferous 'Coal Measures' of Yorkshire,
north-east England. The genus* Gastrioceras *was
common in the shallow, warm seas around the
tropical freshwater swamps and marshes of the
time. The umbilicus, or central, first-grown part of
the shell is wide and fairly deep. The venter –
meaning the ventral surface, which is exposed in the
final whorl – is wide and relatively flattened.*

Gastrioceras

This Carboniferous goniatite shows the
beginnings of shell ornamentation that
would become more complex among the
ceratites and reach elaborate forms in
the ammonites of the Mesozoic Era. The
main ornamentation of *Gastrioceras* consists
of lumps, or tubercles, on the side flanks,
towards the dorsal surface – the inward- or
centre-facing surface of an outer whorl (turn
of the shell), where it is fused to the ventral,
or outward-facing, surface of the whorl
within it. In some specimens, the tubercles
narrowed to form ribs
that passed around
the curve of the
shell to the
tubercles
situated
on the
opposite
side.

Name: *Gastrioceras*
Meaning: Stomach horn
Grouping: Mollusc,
Cephalopod, Ammonoid,
Goniatite
Informal ID: Goniatite
Fossil size: 3cm/1in across
Reconstructed size: Up to
6cm/2⅜in across
Habitat: Seas
Time span: Carboniferous,
340–295 million years ago
Main fossil sites: Worldwide,
mainly Northern Hemisphere
Occurrence: ◆ ◆ ◆

— Venter

— Umbilicus

Tubercles |

MOLLUSCS – AMMONITES

The ammonites' name comes from the shell's resemblance to a coiled ram's horn (the ram being the symbol of the Egyptian god Ammon). Like the extinct belemnites and the living nautiloids, octopuses, squid and cuttlefish, they belonged to the mollusc group known as the cephalopods. This name comes from the Greek 'kephale' (head) and 'podia' (foot), referring to the tentacles they have in the head region.

'Ammonite jaws'

Palaeontologists do not agree on the true function of these common wing-shaped fossils, also known as aptychi (singular aptychus). They are usually interpreted as being part of the 'jaw'-like mouthparts of ammonites, other ammonoids and nautiloids. Aptychi are abundant and often well preserved as fossils. But they are usually found separated from the main shells of their owners. For this reason, only rarely can palaeontologists match the aptychus with the ammonite species to which it belonged. Other theories regarding their identity have suggested that they were the preserved shells of creatures in their own right, perhaps the valves of bivalve molluscs, such as clams and oysters, or the operculum, or 'door', that closed the shell opening in many other kinds of molluscs, such as gastropods.

Above: These 'ammonite jaws', or aptychi, date from the Late Jurassic Period. An aptychus is only rarely found alongside the ammonite of which it was part, and to which it can be attributed, so most specimens are usually given their own scientific names. This is Laevaptychus – the 'smooth aptychus'.

Name: *Laevaptychus*
Meaning: Smooth fold
Grouping: Mollusc, probably Cephalopod, Ammonoid, Ammonite
Informal ID: Ammonite jaws
Fossil size: Each item 3cm/1in across
Reconstructed size: Unknown
Habitat: Sea
Time span: Mainly Mesozoic, 250–65 million years ago
Main fossil sites: Worldwide
Occurrence: ◆ ◆ ◆ ◆

Phylloceras

Phylloceras is one of the earlier ammonites and is moderately commonly found in Northern Hemisphere deposits dating from the Early Jurassic Period, some 185–180 million years ago. *Phylloceras* is thought to be ancestral to the psiloceratid ammonites typified by *Psiloceras* (see opposite), and thus to the later very successful and diverse Jurassic ammonites. It is an involute form – which means that the spiral is tightly coiled and wraps over itself – and of small-to-medium size. Because of its compressed, smooth profile and rounded venter (the external convex, or 'belly' part, of the shell), it is thought *Phylloceras* swam about with the aid of jet propulsion, in a manner perhaps similar to the living *Nautilus*.

Name: *Phylloceras*
Meaning: Leaf horn
Grouping: Mollusc, Cephalopod, Ammonoid, Ammonite
Informal ID: Ammonite
Fossil size: 10cm/4in across
Reconstructed size: As above
Habitat: Shallow seas
Time span: Late Triassic to Early Cretaceous, 210–120 million years ago
Main fossil sites: Northern Hemisphere
Occurrence: ◆ ◆ ◆

Left: Phylloceras gets its name 'leaf-horn' from the extremely complex and frilly looking lobed, leaf-like or spatulate sutures, or joint lines. This mould fossil formed when the inside of the shell was filled by sediments, and clearly shows the internal suture pattern.

Psiloceras

Name: *Psiloceras*
Meaning: Smooth horn
Grouping: Mollusc,
Cephalopod, Ammonoid,
Ammonite
Informal ID: Ammonite
Fossil size: Slab 35cm/
13¾in long
Reconstructed size:
Individuals up to 7cm/
2¾in across
Habitat: Shallow seas
Time span: Early Jurassic,
200 million years ago
Main fossil sites: Worldwide
Occurrence: ◆ ◆ ◆

As one of the first ammonites to appear in the shallow seas of the Jurassic Period, some 200 million years ago, *Psiloceras* was probably ancestral to most of the later Jurassic ammonites. *Psiloceras* is the first widely distributed ammonite and provides a valuable insight into the extent of those shallow sea areas during Early Jurassic times. The beautiful specimens shown here have been fossilized in the form of ammolite, which is an iridescent, opal-like gemstone. Certain mollusc shells in life are made of a type of calcium carbonate called aragonite. In most cases, this material is replaced by other minerals as part of the fossilization process. In this example, however, impermeable clay sediments must have covered the shells before the replacement process could begin, thus allowing the original aragonite to be preserved as ammolite.

Below: The shale that flattened these small ammonites also allowed for their beautiful preservation. Over time, the surrounding sediments impregnated the nacreous (iridescent 'mother-of-pearl') shells with trace elements, such as iron and magnesium, and this accounts for the bright red and green colours.

Stephanoceras

Name: *Stephanoceras*
Meaning: Crown horn
Grouping: Mollusc,
Cephalopod, Ammonoid,
Ammonite
Informal ID: Ammonite
Fossil size: 6cm/2½in across
Reconstructed size:
As above
Habitat: Shallow seas
Time span: Middle Jurassic,
160 million years ago
Main fossil sites: Worldwide
Occurrence: ◆ ◆ ◆

Stephanoceras was an ammonite of the shallow seas of the Mid Jurassic Period, some 160 million years ago. It had a disc-shaped, regularly spiralled shell, with a strongly ribbed pattern. Deep ribs such as those shown by many ammonites may have contributed to the strength of the shell, thus providing them with protection against predators such as fish, marine reptiles and their larger cephalopod cousins. There are many species in the genus *Stephanoceras*, and it is also widely distributed, with fossils having been found around the world. Specimens have been discovered from Europe and North Africa to the Andes, and sometimes in great abundance.

Right: The shell of Stephanoceras *has a rounded profile about the venter (the external convex, or 'belly' part, of the shell), rather than being drawn into a sharp keel, which suggests that it probably had a floating habit in life. The prominent ribs would have created drag, however, preventing it from being a fast swimmer. This specimen is from Sherbourne in Dorset, southern England.*

Prominent ribs | Venter has rounded profile | Umbilicus (first-formed central part of shell)

Younger, wider whorls of shell overlap older, smaller ones | Aperture

MOLLUSCS – AMMONITES (CONTINUED)

Cephalopod molluscs, as well as being ecologically important today, also have a fossil record going back to the beginning of complex animal life during the Cambrian. Ammonites dominated most marine environments for a period of 300 million years, from the Late Silurian to the end of the Cretaceous about 65 million years ago, when they died out with many other groups in the mass extinction of the time.

Caloceras

Above: Caloceras was an iridescent ammonite that grew in a regular, evolute spiral (its whorls are exposed and not enveloped by later ones). It has prominent ribs and is a well-known zone fossil indicating the Early or Lower Jurassic Period.

Beautiful iridescent ammonite specimens, such as the one pictured here, are much sought after by fossil collectors. Unfortunately, this demand has had a negative effect, since unscrupulous individuals have been lured by the high prices that good specimens can command. The dark shale surrounding *Caloceras* accounts for its bright colours, as described for *Psiloceras* (see previous page). The shale covered the shell in an impermeable layer before the original aragonite (a carbonate mineral) was replaced by minerals in the water, which then eventually impregnated the shell with iron, magnesium and other trace elements present in the sediment. *Caloceras* is important as a zone fossil for the Hettangian Age of the Early Jurassic Period, dating back some 200 to 196 million years ago.

Name: *Caloceras*
Meaning: Beautiful horn
Grouping: Mollusc, Cephalopod, Ammonoid, Ammonite
Informal ID: Ammonite
Fossil size: 10cm/4in across
Reconstructed size: As above
Habitat: Shallow coastal areas
Time span: Early Jurassic, 200–196 million years ago
Main fossil sites: Throughout Europe
Occurrence: ◆ ◆ ◆

Lytoceras

Lytoceras has an evolute growth pattern, meaning that all of its whorls are exposed and not enveloped or grown over by later, younger ones. The thin, often widely separated ribs are characteristic of its group, the Lytoceratida. By observing the flow of water around models of ammonite shells in flow tanks, researchers have shown that fine ribs such as these reduce drag – the resistance of water to objects moving through it. The ribs, therefore, make the animal's swimming motion more efficient and ease the effort of moving a bulky shell through the water.

Minimal contact between successive whorls

Left: In water tank tests, the low, thin ribs ornamenting the shell of Lytoceras have been shown to reduce drag and so increase swimming efficiency. The evolute growth pattern leaves almost all of the earlier, older whorls exposed. The name 'unbound horn' refers to specimens where the coils are hardly linked or joined to each other.

Reduced ribbing

Name: *Lytoceras*
Meaning: Loose or unbound horn
Grouping: Mollusc, Cephalopod, Ammonoid, Ammonite
Informal ID: Ammonite
Fossil size: 10cm/4in across
Reconstructed size: As above
Habitat: Deep water
Time span: Early Jurassic to Late Cretaceous, 200–70 million years ago
Main fossil sites: Worldwide
Occurrence: ◆ ◆ ◆

Liparoceras

Name: *Liparoceras*
Meaning: Smooth or oily horn
Grouping: Mollusc, Cephalopod, Ammonoid, Ammonite
Informal ID: Ammonite
Fossil size: 10cm/ 4in across
Reconstructed size: As above
Habitat: Shallow seas
Time span: Early Jurassic, 185 million years ago
Main fossil sites: Europe
Occurrence: ◆ ◆ ◆

The Liparoceratidae group is one of the best-studied examples of lineages, or lines of descent, among the ammonite fossils. This is because the members are very abundant and completely span the Pliensbachian Age of the Early Jurassic Period, usually dated from 192 or 190 to 183 million years ago. During this time, the typical shell shape changes from an evolute spiral (where whorls are loosely coiled and do not cover each other) to an involute spiral (where later whorls envelop, or grow over, the earlier ones). *Liparoceras* is also interesting in studies concerning evidence for ammonite sexual dimorphism. This is the difference in size and shape between males and females of the same species. In some ammonites, the female form is larger than the male, and it or its shell is termed the macroconch. Its fossils can be as much as a hundred times more abundant than the male form, or microconch, with its smaller shell.

Above: This specimen of Liparoceras *is L. contractum, from the coast of Charmouth, Dorset, in southern England. It has the involute shell pattern. The smaller male form, or microconch, of* Liparoceras *is sometimes called by a different scientific name, Aegoceras.*

Amaltheus

Name: *Amaltheus*
Meaning: From Amalthea, ancient Greek symbol for 'horn of plenty'
Grouping: Mollusc, Cephalopod, Ammonoid, Ammonite
Informal ID: Ammonite
Fossil size: 6cm/2½in across
Reconstructed size: As above
Habitat: Hardground sea bottoms
Time span: Early Jurassic, 185 million years ago
Main fossil sites: Throughout Europe
Occurrence: ◆ ◆ ◆

Amaltheus is one of the few ammonites from the fossil record in which colour has occasionally been preserved, in the form of longitudinal brown stripes on a white background. The thin disc shape and narrow, sharp keel (the outer edge of the shell spiral) suggest that it was a fast swimmer. *Amaltheus* lived in 'hardground' marine environments – cemented (hardened) sea beds recognized by the presence of borings and incrustations. Cemented beds or bottoms came about when the settling or deposition of sediment occurred very slowly. Dissolving of the molluscan aragonite shells on the sea floor was followed by calcium carbonate coming out of solution into the sediment. This event acted as a cement to bind the general sea floor material into a type of concrete.

Right: Amaltheids are an extremely polymorphic group, meaning that the different species vary greatly in shape. This is Amaltheus subnodosus, *from Early Jurassic rocks near Goppingen in West Germany. It has almost straight ribs that branch near the outer part of the whorl to give a comb or rope-like effect to the keel.*

Sharp comb-effect keel | Ribs | Involute form

Coloured stripes

MOLLUSCS – AMMONITES (CONTINUED)

*Ammonites were at their most diverse during the Mesozoic, which corresponds roughly on land to the
Age of Reptiles and especially dinosaurs. Ammonites have been extensively studied and are so well
known that they are often used as symbols of the fossil record. They are particularly important as index
fossils used to identify geologic periods because of their widespread distribution and rapid evolution.*

Austiniceras

Faintly
S-shaped
interval ribs

Flattened
sides

Rounded
venter

Light
intermediate
ribs

Relatively
evolute (loose-
coiled) shell

Ammonites ranged from smaller than a fingernail, even when
fully grown, to as large as a dining table. *Austiniceras* was one
of the bigger types, with some specimens more than 2.5m/8¼ft
across. It is a relatively rare find from the Late
Cretaceous Period, mainly in Britain and other
European sites. *Austiniceras* has an evolute
spiral shell, which may be smooth or lightly
ribbed, with slightly more pronounced
interval ribs. Its sides are almost flat or
gently convex. The narrowly rounded
venter suggests that it led an active
swimming lifestyle despite its great size.

Name: *Austiniceras*
Meaning: Austin's horn
Grouping: Mollusc,
Cephalopod, Ammonoid,
Ammonite
Informal ID: Ammonite
Fossil size: 15cm/6in across
Reconstructed size: Some
specimens exceed 2m/6½ft
in diameter
Habitat: Shallow seas
Time span: Late
Cretaceous, 95–70 million
years ago
Main fossil sites: Throughout
Europe
Occurrence: ◆ ◆

Left: This small specimen of Austiniceras
austeni, *from the Late Cretaceous Lower Chalk
of Sussex, England, is about 15cm/6in in diameter.
But examples of* Austiniceras *have been known to grow
to more than 2m/6½ft across. The generally flattened shell shape (from
side to side), low ribs and narrowly rounded venter suggest an active
lifestyle, 'jetting' through the water in the manner of a modern squid.*

Dactylioceras

Snakes of the sea
Evolute ammonites were
once believed to be coiled
snakes turned to stone.
The shell opening was
often carved to resemble
a snake's head. The
fossils were then sold to
pilgrims as serpents that
had been petrified by a
local saint.

Dactylioceras is a common find in Jurassic bituminous
shales. These shales formed when limited water circulation
allowed stagnant (still, oxygen-poor) conditions to develop
in dense sediments on the sea floor. This was favourable for
preservation of ammonites and other shells in various ways.
The impermeable nature of the sediment prevented the
shell's structure of aragonite material from dissolving away.
In addition, the stagnant conditions encountered by the
shells when they sank to the bottom meant that
burrowing animals or currents
would not disturb them as
the fossilization process
occurred. Several
individuals are preserved in
the block shown here,
discovered in Germany. This
suggests that *Dactylioceras*
had gregarious (group-living)
habits. Possibly, like many
modern cephalopods, such as
squid, they congregated in large
swarms or schools to breed.

Name: *Dactylioceras*
Meaning: Finger horn
Grouping: Mollusc,
Cephalopod, Ammonoid,
Ammonite
Informal ID: Ammonite
Fossil size: Slab length
15cm/6in
Reconstructed size:
Individuals 2–5cm/
¾–2in across
Habitat: Open sea
Time span: Early Jurassic,
200–175 million years ago
Main fossil sites: Worldwide
Occurrence: ◆ ◆ ◆

Left: The shell of Dactylioceras *is
evolute in form, rather than the
larger whorls enveloping the
smaller, older ones. The ribs
branch towards the outside of the
whorls to give a braid-edge effect.*

Hamites

Name: *Hamites*
Meaning: Hook-like
Grouping: Mollusc, Cephalopod, Ammonoid, Ammonite
Informal ID: Uncoiled or heteromorph ammonite
Fossil size: Length 6cm/2⅜in
Reconstructed size: Length 8cm/3⅛in
Habitat: Relatively deep sea floor
Time span: Middle Cretaceous, 110–100 million years ago
Main fossil sites: Africa, Eurasia, North America
Occurrence: ◆ ◆ ◆

Not all ammonites or ammonoids have the familiar coiled or spiral shell form that is seen in so many specimens. *Hamites* is a heteromorph, or uncoiled type. It lived alongside *Euhoplites* (see below) in a soft-bottom marine community that has been preserved in detail in Gault Clay, found in Kent, England. In addition to ammonite specimens, other molluscs discovered in the Gault Clay include nautiloids, such as *Eutrephoceras*; gastropods, such as *Nummocalcar* (which is superficially ammonite-like); and the carnivorous snail *Gyrodes* (which fed on the abundant bivalves by boring small circular holes in their shells with its specialized file-like 'tongue', or radula). Other creatures found at this English site include echinoderms, such as the crinoid *Nielsenicrinus*, and crustaceans, such as the lobster *Hoploparia*. (See also *Macroscaphites* on the following page.)

Below: This is a section of the heteromorph ammonite Hamites, *from the Gault Clay of Folkestone in Kent, south-eastern England. It is an internal mould, showing the pattern of joint, or suture, lines on the shell's inner surface. Many Gault Clay specimens of the actual shells retain their original aragonitic material and still show the nacreous 'mother-of-pearl' lustre.*

Younger end (nearer aperture)

Suture moulds

Euhoplites

Name: *Euhoplites*
Meaning: Good Hoplite (a heavily armoured ancient Greek soldier), from the related genus *Hoplites*
Grouping: Mollusc, Cephalopod, Ammonoid, Ammonite
Informal ID: Ammonite
Fossil size: 3cm/1¼in across
Reconstructed size: As above
Habitat: Probably sea floor
Time span: Middle Cretaceous, 110–100 million years ago
Main fossil sites: Throughout Europe
Occurrence: ◆ ◆ ◆

Euhoplites is a strongly ribbed example of an ammonite, with the ribs giving way to tubercles (lumps) on the inside of the curvature and with a double-row of ribs around the outside at the venter (the external convex, or 'belly' part, of the shell). *Euhoplites* is a common ammonite in the Gault Clay of Folkestone, as described above for *Hamites*. From the assemblage of fossils, experts can describe a community of animals that lived together and were preserved in their original environment – a relatively deep, calm marine location. *Euhoplites* lived alongside other ammonites, such as the tiny *Hysteroceras*, just 1.8cm/¾in in diameter, as well as *Hamites*. Other animals preserved include the belemnite *Neohibolites*, and there is also evidence for sharks in the form of fossil sharks' teeth.

Right: Euhoplites *is almost pentagonal (five-sided) in cross-section and slightly evolute, with a distinctive deep and narrow ventral groove. As with most ammonites, the creature itself lived in the last-formed, largest chamber and could withdraw into this for safety. The pronounced ribs probably helped to strengthen the shell against predator attack, but they would have caused drag, reducing swimming speed.*

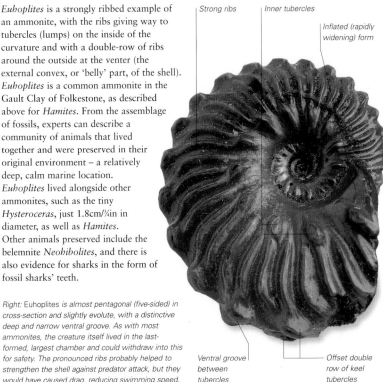

Strong ribs

Inner tubercles

Inflated (rapidly widening) form

Ventral groove between tubercles

Offset double row of keel tubercles

MOLLUSCS – AMMONITES (CONTINUED)

Ammonites are usually reconstructed with large eyes and long tentacles similar to a squid. Some are assumed to have been speedy, predatory swimmers. The thousands of types are distinguished by features such as the coiling of the shell – from evolute to involute – as well as the shell's width in its coils and umbilicus (the central first-formed region), zigzag lines, surface ribs and other ornamentations.

Hyphoplites

Umbilicus

Fine inner ribs

Broad outer ribs

Hyphoplites is a beautiful, elaborately sculptured ammonite from the Cenomanian Age of the Mid to Late Cretaceous Period, around 95 million years ago. Sculpturing like this probably contributed to strengthening of the shell. However, these deep ribs and tubercles (bumps), along with the flattened venter ('belly' region of the shell) suggest this ammonite was not an active swimmer. Instead, it probably led a more sluggish lifestyle, on or near the sandy sea bottom, where its remains were preserved. *Hyphoplites* is an important component of the sand communities of its time, along with echinoderms, bryozoans, other ammonites and the strange coiled oyster *Exogyra*.

Left: Hyphoplites has a mix of pronounced, wide ribs with large and small tubercles (bumps) around the outer part of the whorl, and fine oblique (diagonal) ribs along the inner region of the whorl. Its umbilicus (central, oldest part of the shell) is wide and shallow.

Name: *Hyphoplites*
Meaning: Under Hoplite (a heavily armoured ancient Greek soldier), from the related genus *Hoplites*
Grouping: Mollusc, Cephalopod, Ammonoid, Ammonite
Informal ID: Ammonite
Fossil size: 5cm/2in across
Reconstructed size: Up to 10cm/4in across
Habitat: Sandy sea floor
Time span: Middle to Late Cretaceous, 95 million years ago
Main fossil sites: Throughout Europe
Occurrence: ◆ ◆

Macroscaphites

Macroscaphites was an unusual-looking heteromorph (not completely spiral-shaped) ammonite from the Early Cretaceous Period, mainly in Europe. Heteromorph ammonites (see also *Hamites* on the previous page) have long puzzled palaeontologists. Early researchers thought that the strange shapes were the result of 'evolutionary decadence', when features become more exaggerated and outlandish, usually just prior to extinction – which, for the ammonites, would have been at the end of the Cretaceous Period. However, it is now known that such ammonites had a long history that began at least in the Early Triassic and lasted until the very end of the Cretaceous. They coexisted with normally coiled ammonites and were even more numerous than coiled types in some habitats.

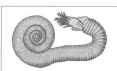

Coiled early part of shell

Living chamber

Left: This example of the strongly ribbed Macroscaphites was discovered in the French Alps. Most heteromorph ammonites had a coiled shell when young, but this grew straighter as the animal aged.

Name: *Macroscaphites*
Meaning: Large hoe or shovel
Grouping: Mollusc, Cephalopod, Ammonoid, Ammonite
Informal ID: Uncoiled ammonite
Fossil size: Length 10cm/4in
Reconstructed size: Length as above
Habitat: Calm seas
Time span: Early Cretaceous, 135–95 million years ago
Main fossil sites: Europe, North America
Occurrence: ◆ ◆ ◆

Ludwigia

Name: *Ludwigia*
Meaning: After Ludwig
Grouping: Mollusc,
Cephalopod, Ammonoid,
Ammonite
Informal ID: Ammonite
Fossil size: 11cm/4½in across
Reconstructed size:
As above
Habitat: Shallow seas
Time span: Middle Jurassic,
175–165 million years ago
Main fossil sites: Worldwide
Occurrence: ◆ ◆ ◆

Ludwigia was a stout-whorled, involute ammonite with a broad, strongly keeled venter ('belly' region of the shell). The genus *Ludwigia* is important in stratigraphy – the study of the deposition and age of sedimentary rock strata (layers or beds). Ammonites of this genus are found abundantly in the Murchison beds of the Swiss Jura Mountains – the location after which the Jurassic Period was originally named. Finding the same species in other locations helps to date and correlate the rock layers to the Aalenian Age of the Jurassic, about 175 million years ago.

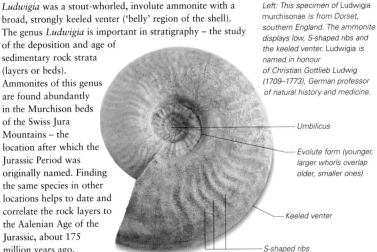

Left: This specimen of Ludwigia murchisonae is from Dorset, southern England. The ammonite displays low, S-shaped ribs and the keeled venter. Ludwigia is named in honour of Christian Gottlieb Ludwig (1709–1773), German professor of natural history and medicine.

Umbilicus

Evolute form (younger, larger whorls overlap older, smaller ones)

Keeled venter

S-shaped ribs

Predator and prey

Active and fast-swimming ammonites such as *Macrocephalites* and *Cardioceras* (9cm/3½in across, in the specimen shown here) usually had a moderately compressed form – in other words, the shell was flattened from side to side. They also had a strongly carinated venter, which means that the 'belly' part of the shell was drawn into a ridged or sharpened keel. The ridges in the shell may have helped reduce drag in the water, making them more efficient swimmers. Fossils associated with *Cardioceras* show other, larger marine reptiles such as ichthyosaurs, plesiosaurs and marine crocodiles. Bite marks are sometimes found on preserved ammonite shells. The size, spacing and pattern of the indentations can sometimes be attributed to a specific predator.

Macrocephalites

Macrocephalites had quite a wide and bulky shell covered in thin ribs, which branched into two (bifurcated) around each side. As with other fine-ribbed ammonites, this ornamentation would reduce drag and help the animal move its cumbersome shell through the water. *Macrocephalites* has been found in fossil assemblages all over the world, including the Ellsworth Mountains in Antarctica. It is an important index fossil for the Callovian Age of the Middle Jurassic Period, especially in Northern Europe from Britain to southwest Germany. The Callovian Age is dated at about 160 million years ago.

Name: *Macrocephalites*
Meaning: Like a large head
Grouping: Mollusc,
Cephalopod, Ammonoid,
Ammonite
Informal ID: Ammonite
Fossil size: 6cm/2⅜in across
Reconstructed size: Some specimens up to 2m/6½ft in diameter
Habitat: Shallow seas
Time span: Middle Jurassic, 165–160 million years ago
Main fossil sites: Worldwide
Occurrence: ◆ ◆ ◆

Right: This specimen of Macrocephalites, from Porta Westfalica, near Hanover, Germany, could easily fit into the palm of the hand. The genus could, however, reach gigantic proportions – in fact, almost 2m/6½ft in diameter. The fine ribbing pattern probably aided in swimming. The shell is extremely involute, with each coil overlapping and obscuring the previous, older one.

Rib bifurcations

Extreme involute form (outer whorls obscure preceding ones)

MOLLUSCS – NAUTILOIDS

The great cephalopod ('head-foot') group of molluscs encompasses ammonoids, actinoceratoids, bactritoids, belemnoids, the living squid and octopus and cuttlefish – and nautiloids, both living and extinct. The surviving genus Nautilus *includes the Indo-Pacific pearly nautilus,* Nautilus pompilius, *plus four or five other extant species in two genera,* Nautilus *and* Allonautilus. *They are the only living cephalopods with a true external shell, and sole remnants of a once enormous mollusc group. Knowledge of their soft-tissue anatomy and mode of life allows detailed reconstructions of fossil nautiloids and their marine communities.*

Orthoceras

Below: The shell chambers of Orthoceras *are known as concavo-convex, having a concave, or in-curved, surface facing to the rear (older end of the shell) and a convex, or out-bulging, surface directed to the front (the living chamber end). The structure is often likened to a row of contact lenses. This species, identified as* Orthoceras canaliculatum, *is from the Silurian Wenlock Beds of a quarry near Cardiff, Wales.*

This well-known nautiloid is extremely abundant in certain European localities, especially from the Middle to Late Ordovician Period. The first-formed portion of the shell was rounded. The shell then grew straight but gradually increased in diameter to form a gently widening cone shape. In nautiloids, belemnoids and similar cephalopods the chambered portion of the shell is termed the phragmocone, as opposed to the large living compartment where the main body of the creature is located and which ends at the aperture. The siphuncle (inner tube passing through the chambers) was centrally placed. In life, *Orthoceras* probably swam with its shell horizontal, parallel to the sea bed, as it chased small prey or scavenged across the ocean floor.

Name: *Orthoceras*
Meaning: Straight horn
Grouping: Mollusc, Cephalopod, Nautiloid
Informal ID: Nautiloid
Fossil size: Length 12cm/4¾in
Reconstructed size: Length up to 20cm/8in
Habitat: Seas
Time span: Ordovician–Silurian, 460–430 million years ago
Main fossil sites: Throughout Europe
Occurrence: ◆ ◆ ◆

Eutrephoceras

Remains of this nautiloid come mainly from Late Cretaceous deposits found in the Midwest of the USA. At that time, the region was covered by a shallow sea, the Western Interior Seaway, which harboured not only nautiloids, but also a vast array of other marine life, including the ferocious sea-going reptiles known as mosasaurs (ancient relatives of today's monitor lizards). Many nautiloid and ammonoid shells bear grooves or cracks that correspond well with mosasaur tooth shape and spacing. The shell of *Eutrephoceras* was involute – that is, tightly coiled – and rapidly enlarging in cross-sectional area. The central, or first-formed, part of the shell known as the umbilicus, in the middle of the spiral, is likewise narrow.

Name: *Eutrephoceras*
Meaning: Well fed horn
Grouping: Mollusc, Cephalopod, Nautiloid
Informal ID: Nautiloid
Fossil size: Shell 7cm/2¾in across
Reconstructed size: Diameter up to 12cm/4¾in
Habitat: Shallow seas
Time span: Late Cretaceous, 75–65 million years ago
Main fossil sites: North America
Occurrence: ◆ ◆

Umbilicus hidden within matrix

Living chamber

Venter (rounded ventral surface)

Left: Identified as Eutrephoceras dekayi, *this nautiloid from the Fox Hills Formation of South Dakota, USA, is dated to the Maastrichtian Age, about 70–65 million years ago – which was the last time span of the Cretaceous Period. It has a wide shell with a rounded shape, like a partial doughnut. The smaller scattered shells resembling mussels or clams are not molluscs but brachiopods.*

Cenoceras

Name: Cenoceras
Meaning: Recent horn
Grouping: Mollusc,
Cephalopod, Nautiloid
Informal ID: Nautiloid
Fossil size: 5cm/2in across
Reconstructed size: Up to
15cm/6in across
Habitat: Seas
Time span: From Late
Triassic to Middle Jurassic,
220–160 million years ago
Main fossil sites: Worldwide
Occurrence: ◆ ◆ ◆

Different species of *Cenoceras* show varying contours on the shell, from simple, gently curving sutures (as in this example), to narrow ribs following the curling spiral of the shell. Characteristic of the genus are an involute, or tightly coiled, shell form and a very narrow umbilicus (the central, earliest-grown region of the shell). Inside the shell, the siphuncle (which is not visible in this photograph) is not central within the dividing walls, or septa, rather it is offset towards the dorsal side, which is the inner portion of the whorl. When the animal swam, the shell would have been in much the position shown here, with the eyes and tentacles at the shell opening facing to the right. The inner surface of each whorl is the upper or dorsal side of the animal, and the outer surface the ventral side or belly.

Narrow umbilicus | Dorsal surface of opening

Sharp-rimmed sutures | Ventral surface of opening

Right: This species Cenoceras inornatum *dates from the Bajocian Age of the Mid Jurassic Period, about 170 million years ago. It was recovered from loose material in a road cutting in Dorset, southern England. The sutures show a sharp-margined, slightly overlapping pattern similar to that of fish scales.*

Septa, sutures, siphon and siphuncle

A nautiloid lives in the largest, last compartment of its many-chambered shell. The chambers are formed by dividing cross-walls, septa, usually shaped like shallow bowls. Where their edges join the main shell they form lines, sutures, visible on the outside. Nautiloid sutures are usually plain and ring-like, in contrast to the elaborate sutures of ammonoids.

The nautiloid's rear body tapers into a long fleshy stalk, the siphon. This passes though an opening in the most recent septa, and then though similar openings in each of the septa in turn. Where the siphon passes through, it is surrounded by a collar-like structure, the neck. Successive necks are linked by tube-shaped connecting rings, forming a long passageway with the siphon inside. The series of necks and rings is called the siphuncle. In many species it was thickened with aragonite and preserved well. Some nautiloids are identified by the shape and arrangement of necks and rings in the siphuncle.

Right: This specimen from north Wales shows the inner shell region of Lituites, with the shell coiled in a loose spiral – so loose, that successive whorls were not in contact on their dorsal-ventral surfaces. As the animal aged, the shell would straighten up as it lengthened to give a walking stick or shepherd's crook effect. The umbilicus at the centre, and the close-set ridged sutures – indicating the concavo-convex septa, or dividing walls, within the shell (see above) – are clearly visible. The large, straight living chamber is mostly missing.

Lituites

An early and aberrant nautiloid – that is, a departure from the standard type – was *Lituites* from the Ordovician and Silurian Periods. In its younger stages it grew as a loosely coiled, or evolute, spiral. However, with increasing age from juvenile to adult, the shell straightened and grew as a slowly enlarging straight or slightly curved tube, which could achieve lengths of 30cm/12in or more. The result looked similar to the 'walking stick' ammonite *Baculites*, which could reach even greater lengths of up to 1m/3¼ft. (See also *Cyrtoceras*, page 177.)

Name: Lituites
Meaning: Like a trumpet,
curved staff, crook
Grouping: Mollusc,
Cephalopod, Nautiloid
Informal ID: Nautiloid
Fossil size: Slab 9cm/
3½in across
Reconstructed size: Total
shell length 30cm/12in plus
Habitat: Seas
Time span: Ordovician to
Silurian, 460–420 million
years ago
Main fossil sites: Asia
(China), northern Europe
Occurrence: ◆ ◆

Broken-away area of shell

MOLLUSCS – NAUTILOIDS (CONTINUED), BELEMNOIDS

Nautiloids are among the most primitive cephalopods, and one of the earliest groups to appear, with Plectronoceras dating to the Late Cambrian Period, some 500 million years ago. Nautiloids dominated the Palaeozoic seas, with many hundreds of well-described fossil genera. Their shell shapes vary from straight and almost tube-like to conical, hooked, or spiralled as in the living species. Rare glimpses of soft-tissue preservation suggest that some early nautiloids had fewer arms (tentacles), perhaps only ten or so, compared with the living nautilus, which may possess up to 90. (Note that the two specimens shown opposite are not nautiloids but belemnoids – see following pages.)

Nautilus

Numerous species of the living genus *Nautilus* are known from fossils dating back tens of millions of years. The gently curved shell sutures are characteristic. The living nautilus has a zebra-like pattern of brownish stripes on a pale background and, in rare cases, marks on fossils suggest extinct species could have been likewise patterned.

The living nautilus makes a new dividing wall, or septum, about every two weeks as its aragonite-reinforced shell gradually extends and widens at the open end, or aperture. To move, the nautilus sucks in water and squirts this out through a muscular funnel as a fast-moving jet. (Squid have a similar system, but this involves movements of the fleshy 'cloak', or mantle, around the main body.) The fleshy siphon running through the siphuncle within the shell can alter the amount of gases inside the shell chambers and so control the nautilus's buoyancy, allowing it to hang in mid-water, rise or sink.

The chambered part of the shell, or phragmocone, is gas-filled and light, while the living compartment containing the animal is relatively heavy. This is why the nautilus floats with its body lowermost. The genus *Nautilus* is known from Oligocene times (about 30 million years ago), but its nautiloid subgroup, Nautilida, first appeared in the Devonian Period some 400 million years ago.

Above: This Cretaceous Nautilus has a deep, narrow umbilicus (the central, first-grown region of the shell) and, as with other members of its genus, is involute, or tightly coiled, with younger, later whorls partly obscuring older, smaller ones. Specimen 3cm/1in in diameter.

Umbilicus

Name: *Nautilus*
Meaning: Sailor
Grouping: Mollusc, Cephalopod, Nautiloid
Informal ID: Nautilus
Fossil size: See text
Reconstructed size: Some species exceeded 50cm/20in
Habitat: Seas
Time span: Genus *Nautilus*, Oligocene, 30 million years ago, to today
Main fossil sites: Worldwide
Occurrence: ◆ ◆ ◆

Left: In this specimen of the species Nautilus bellerophon, the hole known as the siphuncle (see previous page) is visible in the middle of the last dividing wall, or septum. The main living chamber has been lost. The specimen is Cretaceous and from Faxe, Denmark. Specimen 2cm/¾in in diameter.

Sutures

Septum

Siphuncle

Nautiloid lifestyle

The living nautilus, a voracious, nocturnal predator, suggests the lifestyle of fossil species. By day it rests on or near the sea bottom, at depths down to 800m/2,600ft, perhaps clinging to a rock with some of its arms. A horny protective 'hood' is drawn over most of its head, eyes and tentacles. At night, the hood tilts back and the animal becomes active, rising to around 200m/650ft deep to search by smell, feel and perhaps sight. The nautilus darts suddenly to surprise and grab victims with its tentacles, which are ridged, but not hooked or suckered as in squid or octopus. The fish, crab or other meal is ripped apart by the mouth, which is equipped with a parrot-like beak at the centre of the tentacles.

Nautiloid 'hooks'

Cyrtoceras (Meloceras) was a finger-size, hook-like nautiloid from Silurian–Carboniferous times. It demonstrates the way that nautiloid evolution explored many different patterns of shell growth and shape (see also Lituites, shown previously, which changed from a youthful, loosely coiled spiral to become a straight or slightly curved adult). This specimen is from Silurian deposits in the Bohemian 'Cephalopod Quarry' region of Lochkow, Czech Republic. Fossil length 8cm/3¼in.

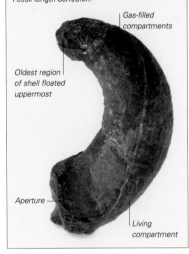

Gas-filled compartments

Oldest region of shell floated uppermost

Aperture

Living compartment

Hibolithes

One of the most classically shaped 'belemnite bullets', this fossil of the belemnoid Hibolithes is of the body part called the guard. (For general information on belemnoids, see next page.) The guard was the usually pointed structure within the rear end of the squid-like body. Since belemnoids, like squid, presumably often jetted backwards, the guard provided strong internal support when the animal bumped 'tail-first' into an obstacle while shooting through the water. The long, slender shape of the whole guard and its attached internal shell, or phragmocone, suggest that Hibolithes was a slim, streamlined belemnoid that could swim at speed. It has given its name to a family of belemnoids, the Hibolithidae.

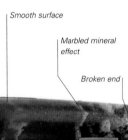

Name: Hibolithes
Meaning: Stick stone
Grouping: Mollusc, Cephalopod, Belemnoid
Informal ID: Belemnoid
Fossil size: Length 6cm/2¼in
Reconstructed size: Whole animal exceeded 30cm/12in
Habitat: Seas
Time span: Middle to Late Jurassic and Cretaceous, 160–70 million years ago
Main fossil sites: Northern Hemisphere
Occurrence: ◆

Right: This specimen is the rearmost end part of the guard from the species Hibolithes jaculoides. *It dates from the Hauterivian–Barremian Ages of the Early Cretaceous, 135–125 million years ago. These fossils occur in abundance in the Speeton Clay of North Yorkshire, England. More complete specimens show that the whole guard was long and slender and would extend to the right in the view shown here.*

Smooth surface

Marbled mineral effect

Broken end

Pachyteuthis

Name: Pachyteuthis
Meaning: Thick squid
Grouping: Mollusc, Cephalopod, Belemnoid
Informal ID: Belemnoid
Fossil size: Length 5cm/2in
Reconstructed size: Whole animal up to 50cm/20in
Habitat: Seas, usually deeper water
Time span: Middle to Late Jurassic, 170–145 million years ago
Main fossil sites: Worldwide
Occurrence: ◆ ◆

Many belemnoids were finger-, hand- or foot-size but Pachyteuthis, at 50cm/20in or perhaps more, was almost arm-length. The proportions of the rear part of the guard show that the restored creature was a stoutly built heavyweight. This is reflected in its name, which means 'thick squid' – 'teuthis' is a common element of squid names, such as Architeuthis, the living giant squid. Fossils found with its remains indicate that it hunted or scavenged in relatively deep waters, probably using size and strength to overwhelm its prey, rather than surprise and sudden bursts of speed. Pachyteuthis belonged to the Cylindroteuthididae family of belemnoids. Specimens originally named as Boreioteuthis are generally reassigned to Pachyteuthis. For general information on belemnoids and Cylindroteuthis, see next page.

Below: This specimen of Pachyteuthis densus *is from the Sundance Formation of Late Jurassic rocks in Wyoming, USA. The whole guard would extend to the left, forwards, to surround the phragmocone – the belemnoid's chambered internal shell.* Pachyteuthis *is well known from various fossil sites, especially in the USA (the Dakotas, Wyoming, Montana) and in Europe (in particular, Germany). It was prominent during the late Mid Jurassic, from about 160–155 million years ago. Its remains are often mixed with those of the sea-going, dolphin-shaped reptiles known as ichthyosaurs, which may have dived deep to prey on these and other belemnoids.*

Relatively blunt posterior end

Broken surface

MOLLUSCS – BELEMNOIDS (CONTINUED)

The belemnoids – a name derived from the Greek for a thrown dart or javelin – were members of a vast group of cephalopod molluscs that began their rise in the Carboniferous, and swarmed in their millions in Jurassic and Cretaceous seas, but declined in the Late Cretaceous. Their kind did not survive the end-of-Cretaceous mass extinction of 65 million years ago, although a few squid-like types are claimed for the Eocene Epoch, 50 million years ago. Belemnoids belonged to the group of cephalopods known as coleoids. Also in this group are extinct and living teuthoids or squid, octopods or octopuses, and sepioids or cuttlefish. Coleoids have two gills, whereas other cephalopods, such as nautiloids and ammonoids, had four. (Two belemnoids are shown on the previous page.)

Belemnitella

The distinctive guard of this belemnoid – one of the last of the group, from the end of the Cretaceous Period – is nearly tube-shaped for much of its length. The rear end curves around as it narrows and the rearmost tip has a nipple-like structure, the mucron. A network of small, shallow grooves can be seen on the surface of many specimens. These may have been occupied by blood vessels and/or nerves in the living animal. Various species of *Belemnitella* are well known from locations across the Northern Hemisphere, especially eastern North America and Europe, where massive accumulations occur in some rocks. One member of the genus, *B. americana*, is the state fossil of Delaware, USA.

Below: This specimen of the species Belemnitella mucronata *is from Late Cretaceous deposits in Holland. The 'nipple', or mucron, is at the rear tip. The alveolus is the 'socket' that housed the rear part of the animal's chambered internal shell, the phragmocone. The broken surface indicates where the guard would have continued forward, becoming much thinner and more fragile as it surrounded the phragmocone.*

Name: *Belemnitella*
Meaning: Small dart
Grouping: Mollusc, Cephalopod, Belemnoid
Informal ID: Belemnoid
Fossil size: Length 8cm/3⅛in
Reconstructed size: Whole animal up to 45cm/18in
Habitat: Shallow seas
Time span: Late Cretaceous, 80–65 million years ago
Main fossil sites: Northern Hemisphere
Occurrence: ◆ ◆ ◆

Main body of guard

Break line at alveolus

Mucron (tip)

Curved taper

Surface network of fine grooves

Belemnoid guards and phragmocones

The most common fossils of belemnoids are their guards (rostra). These are variously shaped like darts, bullets, cigars, swords and daggers, and are known in folklore as 'devil's fingers' or 'thunderbolts', from the belief that they were cast down by the gods during thunderstorms. The guard was in the belemnoid's rear body, with its tapering end or apex pointing backwards. At the front end in some belemnoids was a deep socket, the alveolus, into which fitted the phragmocone, an internal shell with a chambered structure, not unlike that of the nautiloid shell, but generally conical or funnel-shaped. The animal altered the balance of fluids and gases in the phragmocone to adjust its buoyancy. In other belemnoids the phragmocone simply butted on to the front end of the guard. Phragmocones were fragile, and therefore easily disrupted during preservation. In addition, many guards broke at the place where they became very thin as they arched around the narrow end of the phragmocone. So, in general, only the rear, solid part of the guard is found preserved as a fossil.

Above: Passaloteuthis, *Early Jurassic, Dorset, southern England. Fossil length 10cm/4in.*

Below: Hastites, *Late Jurassic, Austria. Fossil length 9cm/3½in.*

Above: Oxyteuthis, *Early Cretaceous, Hanover, Germany. Fossil length 8cm/3⅛in.*

Cylindroteuthis

Name: *Cylindroteuthis*
Meaning: Cylinder squid
Grouping: Mollusc,
Cephalopod, Belemnoid
Informal ID: Belemnoid
Fossil size: Length 10cm/4in
Reconstructed size: Whole
animal up to 80cm/32in
Habitat: Seas, usually deeper
shelving areas
Time span: Jurassic,
165–145 million years ago
Main fossil sites: North
America, Europe
Occurrence: ◆ ◆ ◆

The main guard of *Cylindroteuthis* is long and pointed, like a poker, and is a very characteristic fossil. The rear end, or apex, tapers to a sharp tip. The front end expands at the alveolus, or socket, which can occupy up to one-quarter of the guard's total length. This housed the phragmocone – the animal's internal chambered shell – and the guard became very thin as it covered the rear portion of this structure. The phragmocone was broad and conical, expanding towards its front end, which was roughly in the centre of the animal's body. The guard length can reach 25cm/10in in this genus. Working on the assumption that the complete guard can occupy one-quarter to one-third of the animal, this gives a suggested head–body length of 70–80cm/ 28–32in, making *Cylindroteuthis* one of the larger belemnoids.

Below: This Cylindroteuthis *specimen from near Chippenham, Wiltshire, west England, is dated to the Callovian Stage of the Late Middle Jurassic Period, about 155 million years ago. It was found in the Oxford Clays, which have provided many thousands of similar specimens.*

Fractured
remains of
chambered
phragmocone

Alveolus of
guard

Posterior sharp tip of guard

Cylindrical main body of guard

Actinocamax

Life and death of belemnoids
Rare soft-tissue fossils, especially from Solnhofen, Germany, show that belemnoids were very similar to living squid. They had ten tentacles armed with small, strong hooks, a beak-like mouth at the centre of the tentacles, two large eyes, a torpedo-shaped body covered by a fleshy mantle tapering to a point at the 'tail' end, and two fleshy side fins near the rear. They swam by jet propulsion, taking water into the mantle and squirting it out through a funnel-like siphon. Some soft-tissue remains even show an ink sac, allowing the belemnoid to discharge a water-clouding pigment when in trouble. Huge accumulations of belemnoid guards occur in some localities. These 'belemnite graveyards' or 'battlefields' may be the result of a sudden mudslide burying a swarm of them, or semelparity – mass death following breeding – as in some types of squid today.

The guard of this belemnoid has a distinctively long groove in the ventral (lower) side. The guard also expands towards the rear end before curving in, a shape known as lanceolate. The apex, or rear, forms a nipple-like tip, the mucron. If a belemnoid guard is broken or sliced open, its inner structure is seen as concentric onion-type layers, light and dark, made of calcite crystals radiating outwards like spokes. The overall pattern is similar to the growth rings of a tree trunk. Assuming these guard layers were true growth rings, estimates show that a typical belemnoid lived for about four years. The solid, heavy, mineralized guard probably acted as a counterweight at the rear end of the animal, to the head and tentacles at the front. This allowed stable swimming as the chambered, partly gas-filled phragmocone in the middle was adjusted for buoyancy.

Below: This view of the underside of an Actinocamax *guard shows the long ventral groove. The specimen comes from Late Cretaceous chalk deposits along the coat of Sussex, southern England. The Plenus Marls of the 'White Cliffs' along Kent and Sussex coasts are named from the many specimens of the species shown here,* Actinocamax plenus.

Name: *Actinocamax*
Meaning: Not known,
possibly radiating or
spoke-like
Grouping: Mollusc,
Cephalopod, Belemnoid
Informal ID: Belemnoid
Fossil size: 9cm/3½in
Reconstructed size: Whole
animal 40cm/16in
Habitat: Shallow seas
Time span: Late Cretaceous,
90–70 million years ago
Main fossil sites:
Northern Hemisphere
Occurrence: ◆ ◆

ECHINODERMS – CRINOIDS (SEA LILIES, FEATHER STARS)

The crinoids are members of the phylum Echinodermata – creatures that have been common in the oceans since the Cambrian (500 million years ago). All echinoderms possess wheel-like radial symmetry usually based on the number five and a 'skeleton' of countless hard, small plates, termed ossicles.

Encrinus

Crinoids appeared in the oceans in the Early Ordovician Period, 480 million years ago, and thrived throughout the Palaeozoic Era. Their plant-like body plan has led to them being given the common name of sea lily, and consists of a crown of radiating arms mounted on an elongated stalk. In order to feed, the crown of the animal is raised above the surface on the stalk, and the arms of the sea lily open out to gather any food particles floating past. These are then passed along the arms towards the mouth by finger-like fleshy extensions of the water-filled hydrostatic system, known as tube feet. Crinoids still thrive in the oceans today, though mainly in the deep sea, and there are more than 600 living species known to science.

Below: Crinoids, such as Encrinus, *have a tendency to close the arms of the crown after death, due to muscle contraction and decay of the water-pressurized hydrostatic system. This makes them resemble a flower with its petals folded up – as though just emerging from a bud. Crinoids are often preserved in this state.*

Name: *Encrinus*
Meaning: Lily-like
Grouping: Echinodermata, Crinoidea
Informal ID: Sea lily
Fossil size: 13cm/5in
Reconstructed size: Up to 30cm/12in
Habitat: Sea floor
Time span: Middle Triassic , 230 million years ago
Main fossil sites: Throughout Europe
Occurrence: ◆ ◆ ◆

Marsupites

Below: Complete cups of Marsupites *are relatively common crinoid fossils, perhaps because they were almost ready-buried in the sediment when the animals were alive. The arms, however, are never retained intact.*

Many crinoids looked like flowers on stalks. *Marsupites*, however, lacked a stalk and so is known as a stemless crinoid. This creature apparently lived with its bulbous, pouch-like cup, or calyx, planted on the sea floor and its elongate arms extended into the water above. The mouth faced upwards and was located at the centre of a sheath, or tegmen, stretched over the top of the cup. *Marsupites* flourished briefly in the Late Cretaceous and the distinctive polygonal (many-sided) plates of its cup act as a worldwide marker fossil for rocks of that age. The closely related *Uintacrinus* apparently lived as large colonies on the sea floor. Rock layers bearing hundreds of associated individuals occur in the Cretaceous Chalks of Kansas, USA.

Name: *Marsupites*
Meaning: Pouch-like
Grouping: Echinodermata, Crinoidea
Informal ID: Sea lily
Fossil size: 2cm/¾in
Reconstructed size: Calyx 3–5cm/1–2in; arms up to 1m/3¼ft
Habitat: Sea floor
Time span: Late Cretaceous, 85 million years ago
Main fossil sites: Worldwide
Occurrence: ◆ ◆ ◆ ◆

Eucalyptocrinites

The arms of the crinoid's crown attach to a plated cup-like main body, or calyx, which contains the bodily organs. These organs comprise mainly a looped stomach and intestine. The stem extends from the base of the cup and bears regular branching structures, termed cirri, which give the crinoid anchorage. A nervous system runs along the arms and stem and is controlled by a central 'brain' within the cup. Many modern crinoids live on the deep-sea floor, but most groups in the fossil record preferred shallow water. Well-preserved specimens of *Eucalyptocrinites* from the Waldron Shale rocks of Indiana, USA, show other creatures living on their stems, including brachiopods (lampshells), tabulate corals, tube or keel worms, such as *Spirorbis*, and bryozoans (sea-mats).

Below: The columnals of the crinoid stem, here of Eucalyptocrinites, are the skeletal plates or ossicles covering the stem or stalk. They are common fossils and come in all shapes and sizes. Many are flattened discs, some are five-pointed stars and others are elongate rods.

Name: *Eucalyptocrinus*
Meaning: Covered cup lily
Grouping: Echinodermata, Crinoidea
Informal ID: Sea lily
Fossil size: Ossicles each 2cm/¾in wide
Reconstructed size: 40cm/16in across
Habitat: Sea floor
Time span: Middle Silurian to Middle Devonian, 420–390 million years ago
Main fossil sites: Europe, North America, Siberia, Australia
Occurrence: ◆ ◆ ◆

Saccocoma

Stalked crinoids were hugely successful in the Palaeozoic Era and their remains form thick limestone layers from the shallow sea beds of that time. During the Mesozoic Era stalked crinoids declined and stemless forms, known as feather stars or comatulids, began to dominate instead. These still survive and are free roaming, able to walk along the sea floor, climb corals and swim in the water. Although they have lost the stem, comatulids have retained a ring of hair-like cirri (tassel-like filaments) that enable them to anchor themselves once they have found a suitable location. *Saccocoma* has flared, paddle-like ossicles (skeletal plates) at the base of its arms and was evidently a swimmer. Specimens are commonly found in the famous Jurassic Lithographic Limestones of Solnhofen, Germany, which were laid down in a shallow lagoon. Evidently, individuals were periodically swept into the lagoon where they succumbed to the inhospitable, extremely salty waters.

Name: *Saccocoma*
Meaning: Hairy pouch
Grouping: Echinodermata, Crinoidea
Informal ID: Feather star
Fossil size: 3cm/1in
Reconstructed size: Calyx less than 1cm/½in; arms less than 5cm/2in long
Habitat: Various marine habitats
Time span: Jurassic to Cretaceous, 160–70 million years ago
Main fossil sites: Europe, North Africa
Occurrence: ◆ ◆

Bourgueticrinus

These worm-like crinoids anchored themselves by a branching root network, known as a radix, at the base of their stem. The fossilized calyx and columnals are commonly found intact, though articulated material, such as arms, are rarely retained. Other crinoids have structures similar to the root bulbs of plants, coiled whips and grappling hooks.

Left: The skeletons of feather stars such as Saccocoma were not robust and so quickly disarticulated (fell apart or were pulled to pieces) after death. Whole specimens of these creatures are found only in unique circumstances – where the sea floor was free of disruptive scavengers, for example.

ECHINODERMS – ASTEROIDS (STARFISH), OPHIUROIDS (BRITTLESTARS)

Starfish and brittlestars appear as fossils in the Ordovician Period, 450 million years ago, and are presumably related. They are usually placed in a single group of echinoderms termed the Asterozoans, as they both share the familiar five-armed body plan, but the two groups are different structurally.

Crateraster

Below: The skeleton of a goniasterid starfish such as Crateraster comprised a mosaic of small ossicles on the upper side and undersurface, and an outer edging or marginal frame of larger, blocky ossicles, which extend along the arms.

Small inner ossicles

Marginal frame

Arm

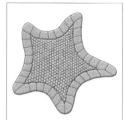

Although asterozoans have been common since the Palaeozoic Era, they are very rarely found whole as fossils. The flexible skeleton is a jigsaw of countless small, often brick-like calcareous plates, or ossicles, that are weakly bound together in life, and so quickly fall apart after death. The arms of living individuals are easily detached, a feature that serves as a defence mechanism, and can be subsequently regenerated. *Crateraster* was a typical goniasterid starfish whose isolated ossicles are commonly found in Cretaceous chalky limestones. Articulated remains are very scarce, although bedding planes littered with complete individuals occur in the Austin Chalk of Texas, USA. Specimens are often found as pellets of regurgitated ossicles, spat out by a predator that was unable to digest them. Such predators included larger starfish.

Name: *Crateraster*
Meaning: Pitted star
Grouping: Echinoderm, Asteroid
Informal ID: Starfish
Fossil size: 4cm/1½in
Reconstructed size: 3–10cm/1–4in across
Habitat: Sea floor
Time span: Late Cretaceous, 90–70 million years ago
Main fossil sites: Europe, North America
Occurrence: ◆ ◆ ◆ ◆

Metopaster

The underside of a starfish has a central mouth and five radiating rows of suckers mounted on its fleshy tube-feet. These move the creature along the sea floor and also enable it to grip its prey. Starfish feed mainly on molluscs, including larger bivalves, such as mussels and clams, by pulling apart the valves (two halves of the shell) and then turning their stomach inside out in order to digest the soft parts. Many starfish differ from the familiar five-pointed-star body plan. For example, the modern crown-of-thorns starfish comprises a large, spiny disc with up to 20 arms, while cushion-stars are simple, rounded domes. *Metopaster* had highly reduced arms and complete fossilized specimens are biscuit-(cookie-)like, with a circular profile.

Right: The simple and robust marginal frame of Metopaster was often relatively well preserved. However, the smaller ossicles (skeletal plates) of the upper and undersurfaces are typically lost.

Name: *Metopaster*
Meaning: Forehead star
Grouping: Echinoderm, Asteroid
Informal ID: Starfish
Fossil size: 5cm/2in
Reconstructed size: 3–10cm/1–4in across
Habitat: Sea floor
Time span: Late Cretaceous to Eocene, 90–35 million years ago
Main fossil sites: Europe, North America
Occurrence: ◆ ◆ ◆ ◆

Urasterella

Name: *Urasterella*
Meaning: Tailed star
Grouping: Echinoderm, Asteroid
Informal ID: Starfish
Fossil size: 10cm/4in
Reconstructed size: Up to 15cm/6in across
Habitat: Sea floor
Time span: Ordovician to Permian, 450–250 million years ago
Main fossil sites: Canada, Europe, Russia
Occurrence: ◆ ◆

Right: The basic body plan of the asterozoans, with a central disc and radial arms, has remained unchanged since the Early Palaeozoic Era. This allows even ancient forms, such as Urasterella, *to be easily recognized, and so they are rarely confused with other echinoderms or other creatures.*

The seven modern orders (main groups) of starfish all arose in the Early Mesozoic Era and are viewed as distinct from those of the preceding Palaeozoic. The Devonian (400-million-year-old) Hunsrück Slate of Germany provides a rare window into the world of those Palaeozoic asterozoans. Scarce but spectacular echinoderm fossils preserve the finest details of the anatomy, including replacement of the soft, fleshy body parts by iron-sulphide minerals. This mode of preservation allows the delicate specimens to be analyzed by X-ray photography while they are still encased in their rock matrix.

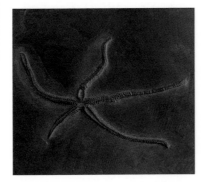

Sinosura
In exceptional circumstances, many asterozoans may be preserved together intact within a single bedding plane of rock. Such 'starfish beds', as they are known, usually result from the rapid burial of live individuals on the sea floor by an influx of gravity-driven sediment – in other words, an underwater landslide or submarine avalanche. The smooth arms of *Sinosura* distinguish them from specimens of *Ophiopetra*, which have distinctly spiny arms.

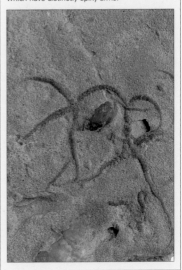

Palaeocoma

Name: *Palaeocoma*
Meaning: Ancient hair
Grouping: Echinoderm, Ophiuroid
Informal ID: Brittlestar
Fossil size: 7cm/3in
Reconstructed size: Less than 10cm/4in
Habitat: Sea floor
Time span: Early to Middle Jurassic, 180–160 million years ago
Main fossil sites: Throughout Europe
Occurrence: ◆ ◆

The arms of brittlestars, or ophiuroids, are built around a core of ossicles, or skeletal plates, shaped like vertebrae (backbones). This allows the arms to move freely in almost any direction. Controlled bending or flexure of the arms enables the brittlestar to move rapidly across the sea floor, and also allows it to climb structures such as branching corals. Most brittlestars today, as in ancient times, are found in the deep sea. They exist either on or within the sea-floor sediments like sand or mud, and feed on any particles of nutrients that collect there. Their informal name is well deserved, since the numerous arms are brittle and are sometimes broken off by predators.

Right: The species Palaeocoma egertoni, *from the Early Jurassic beds of Eype Cliff, Dorset. The fossils here were captured in a freak sudden burial, whereby the sea floor was rapidly smothered by a great slump of sediment, burying the inhabitants alive.*

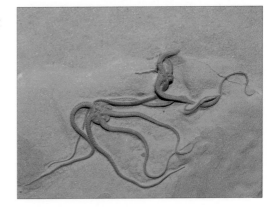

ECHINODERMS – ECHINOIDS (SEA URCHINS)

Sea urchins first appeared in the Late Ordovician, but only became successful after the end-of-Permian mass-extinction event, which eliminated many groups of plants and animals and 'remoulded' life on the sea floor. The echinoids thrived in this new world, and diversified into a variety of forms and lifestyles. They form robust fossils commonly found in shallow marine rocks of the Mesozoic and Cenozoic Eras.

Phalacrocidaris

Echinoids, or sea urchins, possess a globular or spherical shell, called the test, which is constructed from a series of interlocking plates made of calcite minerals. The outer surface of the body is also armoured, protected with a great number of spines, and in life it has flexible tube feet protruding through tiny holes in the test. 'Regular' echinoids, such as *Phalacrocidaris*, possess long spines ornamented with thorns, which they use like stilts to move along the sea floor. These spines also deter predators and often contain toxins. The area of attachment of each spine is protected by smaller spines. Most echinoids lose their spines after death as the tissues that attach them to the body quickly decay. However, rare specimens of *Phalacrocidaris* with its spines still attached are known from Cretaceous chalks around Europe. Even rarer specimens retain the five-part mouth 'jaws', which are called the Aristotle's lantern, in honour of the Greek naturalist and philosopher who first described it. The Aristotle's lantern is a highly complex beak-like structure, which extends through the mouth on the underside of the animal and can be used to scrape food off rocks or directly from the sea floor.

Name: *Phalacrocidaris*
Meaning: Bald tiara
Grouping: Echinodermata, Echinoidea
Informal ID: Sea urchin
Fossil sizes: 5 and 6cm/ 2 and 2¼in
Reconstructed size: Body with spines up to 14cm/ 5½in across
Habitat: Sea floor
Time span: Late Cretaceous, 90 million years ago, to today
Main fossil sites: Europe, Australia
Occurrence: ◆ ◆

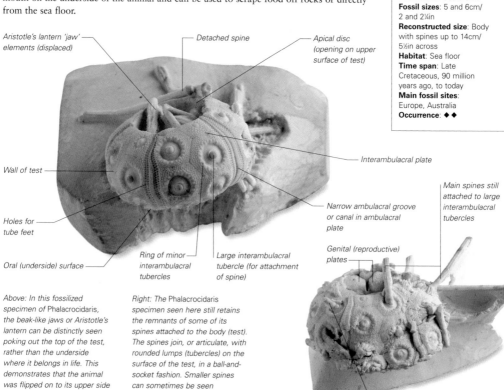

Aristotle's lantern 'jaw' elements (displaced)

Detached spine

Apical disc (opening on upper surface of test)

Wall of test

Holes for tube feet

Oral (underside) surface

Ring of minor interambulacral tubercles

Large interambulacral tubercle (for attachment of spine)

Interambulacral plate

Narrow ambulacral groove or canal in ambulacral plate

Main spines still attached to large interambulacral tubercles

Genital (reproductive) plates

Broken-off spine

Above: In this fossilized specimen of Phalacrocidaris, the beak-like jaws or Aristotle's lantern can be distinctly seen poking out the top of the test, rather than the underside where it belongs in life. This demonstrates that the animal was flipped on to its upper side before it became fossilized.

Right: The Phalacrocidaris specimen seen here still retains the remnants of some of its spines attached to the body (test). The spines join, or articulate, with rounded lumps (tubercles) on the surface of the test, in a ball-and-socket fashion. Smaller spines can sometimes be seen protecting these joints.

Hirudocidaris

Hirudocidaris belongs to the cidarids, primitive echinoids that remain hardly changed from the group that survived the end-of-Permian mass-extinction event. Cidarids are characterized by a limited number of very large spines mounted on pronounced ball-shaped bases, or tubercles, on the main shell, or test. The prolonged success and wide distribution of cidarids may be due to their simple scavenging lifestyle and omnivorous diet. The feeding trace of a 'regular' echinoid, known as *Gnathichnus*, is a distinctive star-shaped incision left in shells or on the sea floor, produced by the scraping action of its five-part jaws – the Aristotle's lantern.

Left: Echinoid tests are prone to crushing as the sediment around them is compacted before turning to rock. This specimen of Hirudocidaris most likely fell on to its side and became squashed before it was fossilized.

Name: *Hirudocidaris*
Meaning: Leech tiara
Grouping: Echinodermata, Echinoidea
Informal ID: Sea urchin
Fossil size: 11cm/4½in
Reconstructed size: Body with spines up to 16cm/6½in across
Habitat: Sea floor
Time span: Late Cretaceous, 100–70 million years ago
Main fossil sites: Throughout Europe
Occurrence: ◆ ◆ ◆

Paracidaris

Each echinoid spine, here of *Paracidaris*, is formed from a crystal of calcite and is highly resistant to weathering processes after death. For this reason, the spines are often much more common than the echinoid tests themselves. They can be an important component of sedimentary rocks.

Rows of small tubercles (pimples)

Socket at base

Tylocidaris

Echinoid spines come in all shapes and sizes, and they are often the most characteristic feature of the creature's skeleton. This is useful for fossils, since most spines are washed away from their owners before being preserved and have to be identified in isolation. *Tylocidaris* possessed a relatively small number of large and particularly distinctive club-shaped spines. The end of each spine furthest from the body is swollen, and ridges of low 'thorns' run along its length. Isolated *Tylocidaris* spines are common fossils in British Chalk, and with great luck complete individuals, with their spines still attached, can occasionally be found.

Name: *Tylocidaris*
Meaning: Knobbly tiara
Grouping: Echinodermata, Echinoidea
Informal ID: Sea urchin
Fossil size: 5cm/2in
Reconstructed size: Body with spines up to 11cm/4½in across
Habitat: Sea floor
Time span: Middle Cretaceous, 100 million years ago
Main fossil sites: Europe, North America
Occurrence: ◆ ◆ ◆

Left: This Tylocidaris specimen has been prepared using an air abrasive – a tool that 'hoses' abrasive powder over the fossil to remove the rock and expose the finest details. This preparation method works particularly well with chalk echinoids.

ECHINODERMS – ECHINOIDS (SEA URCHINS) (CONTINUED)

At the beginning of the Mesozoic Era, all echinoids had a 'regular', spherical body plan and radially arranged spines. This enabled them to roam the sea floor in search of food. However, in the Jurassic Period, many developed oblong, 'irregular' bodies with reduced spines, to help them burrow for nutrients in the sediment.

Diademopsis

Regular echinoids are classified in part by the detailed structure of their 'jaws', or mouthparts, known as the Aristotle's lantern. Four groups are recognized: cidaroid, aulodont (which includes *Diademopsis*, shown here), stirodont and camarodont. However the majority of irregular echinoids have evolved to lose their lantern. So another important feature used in echinoid classification is the structure of the ambulacra. These are five paired strip-like columns of porous plates, sometimes equally spaced, that run the vertical length of the echinoid test (body shell), in the manner of the segments of an orange. The tube feet are aligned in rows along the ambulacra, and connect to the internal water-pressurized, or hydrostatic, system through the holes, or pores, in the test. The tube feet of regular echinoids are often armed with suckers, which allow the animal to grasp food or cling to rocks.

Below: The test of Diademopsis *has broad and relatively subtle ambulacral columns. Decay has caused all of the spines to fall off, and water currents have separated them from the test.*

Name: *Diademopsis*
Meaning: Crown appearance
Grouping: Echinodermata, Echinoidea
Informal ID: Sea urchin
Fossil size: 2.5cm/1in
Reconstructed size: Body with spines up to 12cm/5in
Habitat: Sea floor
Time span: Triassic to Jurassic, 230–180 million years ago
Main fossil sites: Europe, North Africa, South America
Occurrence: ◆ ◆ ◆

Phymosoma

Below: Phymosoma had a flattened shape, somewhat like a doughnut, bearing rows of tubercules (small knobs) that curve around from bottom to top. In preserved remains, the spines sometimes associated with the test are smooth and tube-like. This specimen is seen from the underside, so the large central opening (the peristome) is for the mouth and lantern.

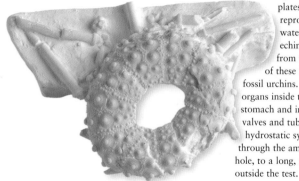

The ball-shaped shell, or test, of an echinoid has two major openings: the peristome, for the mouth, on the underside and the periproct, for the anus, on the upper side. In 'regular' echinoids, the periproct is encircled by the apical system – a ring of plates associated with reproduction and regulating water intake. In 'irregular' echinoids, the anus is separate from the apical system. Both of these features help to group fossil urchins. The main internal organs inside the test are a large, coiled stomach and intestinal system, and the valves and tubes associated with the hydrostatic system. Each valve links through the ambulacral pore, or small hole, to a long, finger-like tube foot outside the test.

Name: *Phymosoma*
Meaning: Swollen body
Grouping: Echinodermata, Echinoidea
Informal ID: Sea urchin
Fossil size: 4cm/1½in
Reconstructed size: Body with spines up to 10cm/4in across
Habitat: Sea floor
Time span: Middle Jurassic to Palaeocene, 165–60 million years ago
Main fossil sites: Worldwide
Occurrence: ◆ ◆ ◆

Conulus

The 'irregular' echinoids or sea urchins, such as *Conulus*, are characterized by spines that have been reduced into a dense coat of small, flexible 'hairs'. In some types of sea urchin this coat almost resembles fur and serves a number of specialist functions. Some of these spines maintain a burrow around the animal, while some push the animal through the sediment or beat to generate water currents within the burrow. Yet others secrete slimy sticky mucus to catch unwanted sediment. *Conulus* is a very common echinoid from the Late Cretaceous Period, but, like all irregulars, the hair-like spines are almost never found attached to the test.

Offaster
Echinoids, such as *Offaster*, often make good zone fossils for dating rocks. As they modified their tests to suit new life strategies and conditions, so they left behind an evolutionary lineage in the rock record, with each form representing a unique interval in time.

Reproductive plate

Ambulacral plate

Interambulacral plate

Name: *Conulus*
Meaning: Conical
Grouping: Echinodermata, Echinoidea
Informal ID: Sea potato
Fossil size: 3–5cm/ 1–2in across
Reconstructed size: As above
Habitat: Sea floor
Time span: Cretaceous, 135–65 million years ago
Main fossil sites: Worldwide
Occurrence: ◆ ◆ ◆ ◆

Left: The hair-like, flexible spines of irregular echinoids are mounted on numerous microscopic tubercles (socket-like joints). Although densely covering the test, the spines are barely visible to the naked eye – but they do produce a rough feel when touched. The pairs of vertical bands, or ambulacra, are particularly prominent on this specimen. Each band represents the location of a row of tube feet in life. The sea urchin has five such ambulacra.

Mouth and anus on underside

Micraster

Name: *Micraster*
Meaning: Small star
Grouping: Echinodermata, Echinoidea
Informal ID: Sea potato, heart urchin
Fossil size: 5cm/2in
Reconstructed size: 3–9cm/ 1–3½in across
Habitat: Sea floor
Time span: Cretaceous to Palaeocene, 90–60 million years ago
Main fossil sites: Europe, North Africa, Asia
Occurrence: ◆ ◆ ◆ ◆

The heart urchins are almost unrecognizable from their regular sea urchin ancestors. Their bodies are highly modified for a life within the sediment. In addition to an upper and lower surface, they have a definite front and back end, rather than a simple, circular, same-all-around body plan like regular echinoids. The mouth has been drawn to the front of the body and modified into a scoop, while the anus has moved from the top of the animal to the rear. The tube feet have certain specialized functions, such as maintaining the passage of oxygenated water through the burrow and selecting food particles.

Below: The five 'petal' depressions on top of this echinoid are modified ambulacra. In life, they carried specialized tube feet. The animal's front is to the left, at the groove.

OTHER ECHINODERMS

After their appearance in the Palaeozoic Era, echinoderms quickly diversified. They remained highly varied throughout the Palaeozoic, and so abundant at times that their remains now form entire layers of rock. Many were stalked and crinoid-like, while the edrioasteroids were small domes that encrusted hard surfaces. Most Palaeozoic groups died out before the Mesozoic and so lack any modern relatives.

Cothurnocystis

Below: This mould fossil of Cothurnocystis *is from the Late Ordovician Period. The side view shows the typical boot-like body shape of this genus, with its three-pronged cup or theca (body), tilted to the right. The stem (tail) points to the left and down and has wider stacked laminae (layers) at its upper end, where it bends towards the theca.*

Echinoderms make up the invertebrate group that is most closely related to the vertebrates, or animals with backbones, and both are classified together within a larger group, the deuterostomes. It has been suggested that the curious echinoderms known as carpoids are, in fact, the ancestors of all backboned creatures, from the most primitive fish to birds and mammals. Carpoids appeared in the Cambrian Period, about 520 million years ago, and died out in the Devonian, some 370 million years ago. Their tadpole-shaped body consists of a plated body housing, or theca, with a tail-like stem and feeler-like appendages. Some experts suggest that the flattened theca could contain slits that might work as gills, both for respiration and for filtering small food particles, while the tail-like stem could have contained the rod-like notocord, which was the evolutionary forerunner of the vertebral column or backbone.

Name: *Cothurnocystis*
Meaning: Boot pouch
Grouping: Echinoderm, Carpoid
Informal ID: Carpoid
Fossil size: Slab 7cm/2¾in across
Reconstructed size: Theca (body) 4cm/1½in across
Habitat: Sea floor
Time span: Ordovician Period, 450 million years ago
Main fossil sites: Most continents worldwide
Occurrence: ◆

Pseudocrinus

The echinoderms called cystoids are found worldwide in rocks dating from the Ordovician Period, 490 million years ago, to Permian times, about 290 million years ago. Although they are superficially similar to the carpoids (above), cystoids share anatomical details with the blastoids, such as *Pentremites* opposite. A characteristic feature of many cystoids is the possession of polygonal grille-like structures, termed pore-rhombs, variably arranged on the theca (main body housing), which is formed of skeletal plates. These connect with the inside of the theca and probably allow the passage of fluids and respiration. Pore-rhombs are located across the junction between adjoining plates of the theca, and may be hidden beneath a thin covering. Cystoids can be both bulbous and radially symmetrical, or more flattened and bilaterally symmetrical.

Left: The plated theca and stout stem of a typical cystoid were commonly preserved nearly intact. However, the delicate arms, used in life for gathering food, are usually absent.

Name: *Pseudocrinus*
Meaning: False lily
Grouping: Echinoderm, Cystoid
Informal ID: Cystoid
Fossil size: 4cm/1½in
Reconstructed size: With complete stem and arms, about 10cm/4in
Habitat: Sea floor
Time span: Silurian, 400 million years ago
Main fossil sites: Throughout Europe
Occurrence: ◆ ◆ ◆

Pentremites

Name: *Pentremites*
Meaning: Five petals or flaps
Grouping: Echinoderm, Blastoid
Informal ID: Blastoid, fossil sea bud or rose bud
Fossil size: Height 4cm/1½in
Reconstructed size: Height, including stalk and arms, about 30cm/12in
Habitat: Sea floor
Time span: Early Carboniferous, 330 million years ago
Main fossil sites: Worldwide
Occurrence: ◆ ◆

The blastoids are yet another group of stalked echinoderms from the Palaeozoic Era. Their robust body containers, or thecas, form resilient and distinctive fossils, variously referred to as 'sea buds', 'rose buds' or 'hickory nuts'. Rows of pores radiate from the summit of the theca, and open into a feature within the theca that is unique among the blastoids, termed the hydrospire. This is a delicate, folded cavity that probably functioned in both respiration and reproduction. Water entering the hydrospire via the pores could exit the theca through holes, termed spiracles, at the top. Blastoids occurred from the Middle Ordovician to Late Permian times. The genus *Pentremites* is especially common in the Carboniferous (330-million-year-old) deposits of North America.

Right: Like most preserved blastoid specimens, this example of Pentremites, *from Illinois, USA, has lost its fragile arms, known as brachioles. These projected from the ambulacra (the five rows of small holes that look like starfish arms). The brachioles in life would have gathered small items of food. A thin stem attached the base of the theca (main body casing) to seabed rock.*

Achistrum

Holothuroideans, or sea cucumbers, are related to echinoids (sea urchins), but they are virtually unrecognizable as echinoderms. The body takes the form of a leathery tube, with the skeleton of mineral plates, or ossicles, reduced to microscopic ossicles embedded in the skin. These form distinctive microfossils, shaped like wagon-wheels, anchors and hooks, and are found in rocks from the Silurian Period onwards. Holothurians are still common today, with more than 1,000 species both in shallow tropical waters and the deep sea. Some creep along the sea floor, in a manner akin to a slug, while others are free-swimming or drift with the plankton. The mouth is surrounded by tube feet modified as branching tentacles for gathering food. Rows of regular tube feet armed with suckers run the length of the body and are used for locomotion and grip.

Name: *Achistrum*
Meaning: Ancient swelling
Grouping: Echinoderm, Holothuroidean (Holothurian)
Informal ID: Sea cucumber
Fossil size: 7cm/3in
Reconstructed size: Length up to 10cm/4in
Habitat: Sea floor
Time span: Carboniferous to Cretaceous, 300–100 million years ago
Main fossil sites: Europe, Egypt, North America
Occurrence: ◆

Tentacles at head end

Left: This fossil of Achistrum *is typical of Mason Creek, Illinois, USA, which is one of the few localities in the world where whole holothuroidean remains can be found. Swift burial and the rapid formation of ironstone nodules within the sediment led to the preservation of the sea cucumber's soft parts.*

GRAPTOLITES

The hemichordates are relatively simple animals that share features with the vertebrates, such as gill slits and a dorsal nerve cord. Modern members of the Hemichordata are the acorn worms and the tiny coral-like pterobranchs. A similar skeletal structure is found in the extinct graptolites. These graptolites were highly abundant globally in rocks from the Early to Mid Palaeozoic.

Desmograptus

Name: *Desmograptus*
Meaning: Joined/linked marks in stone
Grouping: Hemichordata, Graptolithina
Informal ID: Graptolite
Fossil size: 12cm/4¾in
Reconstructed size: Up to 20cm/8in
Habitat: Sea floor, open ocean
Time span: Ordovician to Silurian, 500–410 million years ago
Main fossil sites: Worldwide
Occurrence: ◆ ◆

The first graptolites were bushy colonies that lived permanently attached to the sea floor. However, by the end of the Cambrian Period (some 500 million years ago) many had adopted a free-floating existence among the plankton. This lifestyle apparently favoured a simpler colony structure, and the general evolutionary trend was a reduction towards a stick-like form. Bushy, or dendroid, graptolites continued to exist, however, and in the end they outlived their stick-like, or graptoloid, relatives. The protein-rich graptolite 'skeleton' is most often preserved as a flattened carbon film or 'smear'. But rare three-dimensional specimens, which have been acid-etched from limestone, reveal the fine-scale structure of the colony. Evidently, the bushy dendroid graptolites had a conical form in life, as opposed to the flattened net- or leaf-like fans that they formed as fossils.

Right: Fossil graptolites such as Desmograptus *resemble hieroglyphic markings in the rocks, hence the Greek origin of their name – graptos lithos literally means 'writing [marks] in stone'. Desmograptus can resemble the corals known as sea fans.*

Network of branching stipes

Didymograptus

Below: The classic tuning-fork shape of Didymograptus *is formed by two stipes, or branches, with inward-facing thecae (cup-like containers). It is unclear how the planktonic colony would have been orientated in life.*

The colonial skeleton of a graptolite, referred to as the rhabdosome, is formed of branches (stipes) lined with inclined tubular cups called thecae. When flattened during preservation, these take on the appearance of a saw-blade. By analogy to their modern living relatives, the pterobranchs, each theca housed a minute graptolite animal called a zooid, which was perhaps similar to a tiny sea anemone. Each zooid was linked to the rest of the colony via a connective stalk. Zooids gathered food and nutrients from the water with a crown-like feeding structure of tiny tentacles, known as the lophophore. It is possible that planktonic graptolites were able actively to move up and down in the water as part of their feeding strategy.

Name: *Didymograptus*
Meaning: Paired marks in stone
Grouping: Hemichordata, Graptolithina
Informal ID: Graptolite
Fossil size: 1.5cm/½in
Reconstructed size: Up to 15cm/6in
Habitat: Open ocean
Time span: Early to Mid Ordovician, 500–450 million years ago
Main fossil sites: Worldwide
Occurrence: ◆ ◆ ◆

Monograptus clingani

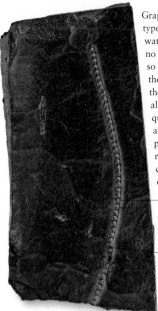

Graptolite fossils are most commonly found in the types of sediments that had been deposited in deep-water settings, such as dark shales and slates. Little or no sea-floor life was present in these environments and so the delicate graptolite skeletons that sank down from the surface waters above and settled could accumulate there undisturbed. The planktonic lifestyle of graptolites allowed them to be ocean-going and each new form quickly spread right around the globe. Their fossils are an invaluable resource for geologists and palaeontologists, since Early and Middle Palaeozoic rocks from around the world can be dated and correlated by the graptolites they contain as marker or index fossils.

Name: *Monograptus clingani*
Meaning: Clingan's single mark in stone
Grouping: Hemichordata, Graptolithina
Informal ID: Graptolite
Fossil size: 7cm/2¾in
Reconstructed size: Up to 15cm/6in
Habitat: Open ocean
Time span: Silurian to Devonian, 430–390 million years ago
Main fossil sites: Worldwide
Occurrence: ◆ ◆ ◆

Individual cup-like thecae (containers) along stipe

Stipe (branch) is straight and undivided

Left: Monograptids were among the most simply shaped graptoloids, with one stipe that varied in form, from almost straight to coiled like a spiral. They were the only graptolite group to survive into the Devonian Period, when they finally died out after 400 million years ago.

Monograptus spirilis

Name: *Monograptus spirilis*
Meaning: Spiral single mark in stone
Grouping: Hemichordata, Graptolithina
Informal ID: Graptolite
Fossil size: 2cm/¾in
Reconstructed size: Up to 10cm/4in
Habitat: Open ocean
Time span: Silurian, 435–410 million years ago
Main fossil sites: Worldwide
Occurrence: ◆ ◆ ◆ ◆

Planktonic graptolites may have used various mechanisms to remain afloat in the water. Some forms possessed a rod-like structure, referred to as the nema, which appears to have attached the colony to some kind of float. Early dendroid graptolites probably attached to naturally buoyant objects, such as floating seaweeds, but later forms may have generated their own float. Rare specimens show a number of graptolites united around a central disc, which could have been this buoyancy aid. Such associations are termed synrhabdosomes. Alternatively, colonies may have accumulated lightweight fats or gases within their own bodies to keep themselves buoyant.

Above: The spiral form of Monograptus *would have been a coiled spire, which may have caused it to twist around, slowing its descent through the water.*

Orthograptus
The action of occasional currents on the deep-sea floor often swept the remains of graptolites together into dense associations, as here with *Orthograptus*. The alignment of their stick-like skeletons records the direction of those ancient currents and helps with oceanographic studies.

ANIMALS – VERTEBRATES

Vertebrate creatures have a vertebral column or backbone, separating 'inverts' and 'verts'. However, a more scientific definition relies on the presence of a notochord – a stiffened, rod-like structure along the back, envisaged as an evolutionary forerunner of the vertebral column. The phylum (major animal group) Chordata includes vertebrates plus some vertebrateless but notochord-possessing creatures known as urochordates, hemichordates and cephalochordates (see previous chapter). Traditionally vertebrates have comprised five major classes: fish, amphibians, reptiles, birds and mammals. DNA and cladistic analysis have fragmented these into numerous subgroups. For example, fossil creatures once known as 'the first amphibians' are now more commonly called early tetrapods, 'four-legged' or 'four-footed'.

Above from left: Head of Hoplopteryx, *detail from* Hyracotherium *tooth, the fossil of an ancient bat,* Palaeochiropteryx, *showing one of the wings folded over the backbone.*
Right: Fossilized dinosaur tracks in a creek bed below the Black Mesa mountain, near Kenton, Oklahoma, USA. The mountain was named for the black lava rock which formed at the top, and is now part of a nature preserve.

FISH – SHARKS

The sharks were among the very earliest groups of fish, and their sleek, streamlined body design has changed little throughout their long history. Sharks and their close cousins the rays are together known as elasmobranchs and, like other fish, have an internal skeleton. This skeleton is unusual, however, as it is made of the tough, gristly substance known as cartilage, rather than bone, giving them and chimaeras, or ratfish, the name of cartilaginous fish (Chondrichthyes). Cartilage degrades more rapidly than bone after death, so most of our knowledge about prehistoric sharks comes from their well-preserved, abundant teeth and fin spines. These date back to the Early Silurian Period, more than 420 million years ago.

Hybodus

Name: *Hybodus*
Meaning: Healthy, strong tooth
Grouping: Fish, Chondrichthyean, Elasmobranch, Selachian, Hybodontiform
Informal ID: Shark
Fossil size: Length 16cm/6¼in (partly complete)
Reconstructed size: Head to tail length up to 2.5m/8¼ft
Habitat: Oceans
Time span: Late Permian to Cretaceous, 260–70 million years ago
Main Fossil sites: Worldwide
Occurrence: ◆ ◆

Below: This dorsal fin spine is probably from Hybodus. The portion that attached to the body is on the right. It is likely that the spine was partly embedded in the flesh of the fin for about half of its length, with the pointed end projecting freely as a deterrent.

Hybodus is one of the best-known representatives of a group of smallish, highly successful sharks that ranged from the Late Permian and Early Triassic Periods, some 250 million years ago, to the great end-of-Cretaceous mass extinction 65 million years ago. *Hybodus* grew to more than 2m/6½ft in length and, compared with many of today's modern sharks, it had a bluntish snout. Apart from this, however, it was similar in shape to its living cousins and belonged to the modern shark group, Selachii. It may have had a varied diet, suggested by two types of teeth. The sharp teeth at the front of the mouth were for gripping and slicing slippery prey, such as fish and squid, while the larger, molar-type teeth at the rear of the jaws were perhaps designed for crushing hard-shelled food, such as shellfish. Attached to the front of each of its two dorsal (back) fins was a spine that may well have served as a defence to deter predators that were larger than itself. The spines are the body parts most commonly found as fossils.

Shark jaws

Like the rest of a shark's skeleton, the animal's cartilaginous jaws were rarely preserved. Decomposition of the springy cartilage occurred readily following death, but rare examples of jaw preservation, such as the example below, show teeth in their position in life. Teeth grew continuously behind those in use, and gradually moved to the edge of the jaw. As the teeth at the front were broken off or wore away, the younger teeth moved forward to replace them.

Below: Several rows of teeth formed an effective way of holding and slicing soft, slippery prey, such as fish and squid. Most shark teeth are either triangular in general shape, with a straight base fixed to the jaw, or have a tall, dagger-like central point growing from a low base. The tooth itself is slim, like a blade, and often has tiny saw-like serrations along its exposed cutting edges.

| Oldest row of teeth in use | Length around curve of jaw 10cm/4in |

| Central point of tooth | Base of tooth |

Ptychodus

Name: Ptychodus
Meaning: Folded tooth
Grouping: Fish,
Chondrichthyean,
Elasmobranch, Selachian,
Hybodontiform
Informal ID: Shark
Fossil size: Single tooth
6cm/2½in across; slab
20cm/8in across
Reconstructed size:
Head–tail length up to 3m/10ft
Habitat: Shallow seas
Time span: Cretaceous,
120–70 million years ago
Main fossil sites: Worldwide,
especially North America
Occurrence: ◆ ◆ ◆

Not all sharks had razor-sharp teeth like blades or daggers. *Ptychodus*, for example, possessed large, ribbed, flattened crushing teeth. Hundreds of these teeth were arranged in parallel interlocking rows to form a plate-like grinding surface in the mouth. This form of dentition suggests that such sharks fed chiefly on hard-shelled invertebrates, such as crustaceans and ammonites. Associated fossils show that *Ptychodus* probably lived in shallow marine conditions, and while it attained a worldwide distribution, its remains are particularly abundant in the states of Texas and Kansas, USA.

Below right: Identified as the species Ptychodus polygyrus, *this tooth close-up shows the slightly convex (domed) main biting surface as a row of ridges surrounded by lower lumps, or tubercles. The whole tooth is roughly rectangular in shape.*

Shark vertebrae
Vertebrae are sometimes called 'backbones', but in sharks they are cartilage like the rest of the skeleton. However, some shark vertebrae may have deposits of hardened, mineralized material similar to true bone, formed by a process known as ossification. Shark vertebrae can usually be recognized by the circular centrum, or main 'body', and the ringed appearance – almost like an animal version of a sectioned tree trunk. This example is 11cm/4½in in diameter.

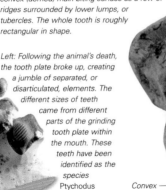

Left: Following the animal's death, the tooth plate broke up, creating a jumble of separated, or disarticulated, elements. The different sizes of teeth came from different parts of the grinding tooth plate within the mouth. These teeth have been identified as the species Ptychodus mammillaris *from the Late Cretaceous Period.*

Margin of crown

Convex biting surface

Coarse ridges

Tubercles (pimple-like lumps)

Fish coprolites
Coprolites, or fossilized droppings (faeces), are important for determining the diet of extinct animals. The remains of creatures eaten by sharks, such as shell fragments, bones and scales, can be preserved within the coprolite, showing exactly what these prehistoric creatures were eating. Shark coprolites often take on the spiral or helical pattern of a part of the shark's digestive tract (intestine) called the spiral valve, making them look like pine cones or squat corkscrews.

Below: Shark coprolite, or enterospirae, Late Cretaceous, length 6cm/2½in.

Left: Fish coprolite, Triassic, length 2.5cm/1in.

FISH – LOBE-FINNED BONY FISH

Most fish species today, and those found in the fossil record, have skeletons made of bone, not cartilage, and belong to the fish group Osteichthyes. Devonian times saw a major group of these fish, known as lobe-fins, or sarcopterygians. Lobe-fins include lungfish and coelacanths, and also long-extinct fish closely related to the ancestors of tetrapods – amphibians and other four-legged vertebrates.

Osteolepis

The tetrapods – backboned animals with four limbs, including amphibians, reptiles, birds and mammals – almost certainly evolved from some form of Devonian lobe-finned fish or sarcopterygian. This would have possessed the same pattern of bones in its fin bases as found in limbs of terrestrial vertebrates. *Osteolepis* was a relative of such a fish. This is not only because of the structural similarity between its fin bones and a tetrapod's limb bones, but also because of other features found in the first amphibian-type tetrapods. These include an internal link between the nose and throat, termed the choanae, which most fish lack, but all tetrapods have. *Osteolepis* lived in shallow bodies of fresh water, feeding on any prey it could find, and was able to breathe air as well as obtaining oxygen through its gills.

Name: *Osteolepis*
Meaning: Bony scaled
Grouping: Fish, Osteichthyan, Crossopterygian, Rhipidistian, Osteolepiform, Osteolepid
Informal ID: Lobe-finned Devonian fish
Fossil size: Head–tail length 18cm/7in
Reconstructed size: Head–tail length 20cm/8in
Habitat: Shallow lakes and rivers
Time span: Middle to Late Devonian, 380–360 million years ago
Main fossil sites: Antarctica, Europe, Asia
Occurrence: ◆ ◆

| Rounded snout | Eye orbit (socket) | Fleshy-based pectoral fin | Caudal fin (tail) |

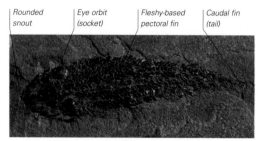

Left: Osteolepis was a slim-bodied, multi-finned rhipidistian, or fan-sail, and belonged to the subgroup of lobe-fins called crossopterygians, or tassel-fins, which also included coelacanths. It had large, shiny, squarish-shaped scales of the type known as cosmine, which had a surface layer of spongy bone. Cosmine also covered the bones of the head.

Coccoderma

Within the sarcopterygian (lobe-fin) group, coelacanths belong to the crossopterygians, or tassel fins. Coelacanths first appeared in the Middle Devonian Period and were believed to be extinct for some 70 million years until they were rediscovered in 1938. This specimen of the fossil coelacanth *Coccoderma* came from the famous Solnhofen limestone rocks of Bavaria, southern Germany, which have yielded many spectacular fossils, including the earliest known bird, *Archaeopteryx*, and the very small dinosaur *Compsognathus*.

Name: *Coccoderma*
Meaning: Berry skin
Grouping: Fish, Osteichthyan, Sarcopterygian, Crossopterygian, Coelacanth (Actinistian)
Informal ID: Coelacanth
Fossil size: Head–tail length 32cm/12½in
Reconstructed size: As above
Habitat: Shallow marine lagoons
Time span: Late Jurassic, 150 million years ago
Main fossil sites: Throughout Europe
Occurrence: ◆

Left: Coccoderma is smaller than, but otherwise very similar to, the living coelacanth Latimeria. It had a deep body and fleshy bases to its main fins. Visible as a diagnostic feature of coelacanths is the third lobe of the caudal fin, or tail – the smaller rearmost 'tassel', projecting backwards from between the tail's main upper and lower lobes. (This specimen was prepared using a technique called acid transfer and mounted on a polygonal glass-fibre block.)

Dipterus

Name: *Dipterus*
Meaning: Two wings
Grouping: Fish,
Osteichthyan, Sarcopterygian,
Dipneustian
Informal ID: Lungfish
Fossil size: 20cm/8in
Reconstructed size:
Head–tail length 30cm/12in
Habitat: Seas
Time span: Devonian,
360 million years ago
Main fossil sites: Europe,
North America
Occurrence: ◆ ◆

*Right: This well-preserved fossil
of the species* Dipterus
valenciennesi, *from Scottish Old
Red Sandstone, shows clearly the
asymmetrical tail fin. Also visible
are the part-rounded hexagonal
scales, known as cosmoid scales,
characteristic of extinct lungfish
and the coelacanths.*

Lungfish, or dipneustians, first appeared in the Devonian Period, some 400 million years ago. *Dipterus* is one of the oldest and most primitive lungfish genera. It originated some 370 million years ago, obtained a worldwide distribution in the fossil record, and although it went extinct, it may have been an ancient ancestor or cousin of the living African lungfish, *Protopterus*. Like all but the very earliest lungfish, *Dipterus* possessed specialized teeth, which were fan-shaped and ridged, to grind down hard prey, such as molluscan and crustacean shellfish. Lungfish were among the first vertebrate animals to develop air-breathing organs, lungs, by modifying a type of swim bladder to allow the absorption of oxygen.

Anal fin | Cosmoid scales | Skull

Asymmetrical
tail

Ceratodus

Name: *Ceratodus*
Meaning: Horn tooth
Grouping: Fish,
Osteichthyan, Sarcopterygian,
Dipneustian
Informal ID: Lungfish
Fossil size: Width 7cm/2¾in
Reconstructed size:
Head–tail length 50cm/20in
Habitat: Shallow seas
Time span: Early Triassic to
Early Tertiary, 240–55 million
years ago
Main fossil sites: Worldwide,
especially Europe and Africa
Occurrence: ◆ ◆ ◆

The living Australian lungfish, *Neoceratodus*, is regarded as the most primitive existing member of the group – that is, it is least changed from the original lungfish body plan. It reaches 1.8m/6ft in length and weighs more than 40kg/88lb. *Ceratodus* is one of its ancient cousins, but it attained only about one-third the size. Like other lungfish, it could breathe air and had large, plate-like teeth for grinding shelled invertebrates. Early evidence of *Ceratodus* comes from the Triassic Period, some 240 million years ago. The genus went extinct in the Early Tertiary Period after a very long-lived existence of more than 180 million years.

Below: The genus Ceratodus *was
named after its distinctive horn-
like teeth, which were grouped to
form two upper and two lower
plates within the animal's mouth.
This view shows a single tooth,
which in life would have been
growing in a row or stack with
several others.*

Wave-like outer
margin

Lateral margin

Convex shape
to body of tooth

Base of tooth

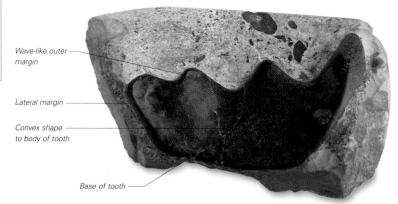

FISH – PRIMITIVE AND RAY-FINNED BONY FISH

Most fish today belong to the osteichthyan (bony fish) subgroup – ray-fins, or actinopterygians. In these, the spine-like fin rays, which hold each fin open like the ribs of a fan, emerge directly from the body, rather than from a fleshy or lobe-like base. However, before the ray-fins developed, there were earlier groups, including the jawless fish, or agnathans, and the long-extinct placoderms, or 'flat-plated skins'.

Cephalaspis

Below: This Cephalaspis head shield shows the animal's shovel-shaped head used for lying on and ploughing into bottom sediments. The eyes are set close together and face upwards. The pineal opening, sometimes called a 'third eye', would have been able to detect changes of light levels but probably not form clear images.

The very first fish had no true fins and no jaws either, and are known as agnathans. Their history stretches back more than 500 million years into the Cambrian. Today fewer than 100 species survive, as eel-like, sucker-mouthed lampreys and hagfish. *Cephalaspis* was an armoured agnathan with a prominent flattened head shield, suggesting it was a bottom-dweller. Its lack of biting jaws meant a diet of soft-bodied animals small enough to be swallowed whole. *Cephalaspis* also lacked mobile true fins and, instead, possessed fleshy 'flaps' for clumsy swimming. Its skull shows slightly depressed areas – sensory plates or fields. These suggest nerve endings in the cheek and forehead that could detect water currents, ripples from the movement of prey or perhaps tiny electrical signals from the active muscles of prey, as in sharks today.

Name: Cephalaspis
Meaning: Head shield
Grouping: Fish, Agnathan, Osteostracan
Informal ID: Armoured jawless fish
Fossil size: Head shield width 12cm/4¾in
Reconstructed size: Head–tail length up to 30cm/20in
Habitat: Rivers, estuaries, perhaps also shallow sea coasts
Time span: Early Devonian, 400 million years ago
Main fossil sites: Throughout Europe
Occurrence: ◆ ◆

Pterichthyodes

Below: The body shield of Pterichthyodes dominates the fossil, although the smaller head is also clearly visible and would have formed an effective defence against larger predators. The unusual wing-shaped, arm-like appendages would provide additional movement by pushing through the sediment. This specimen comes from the famed Devonian Period Old Red Sandstone, near Caithness, in Scotland.

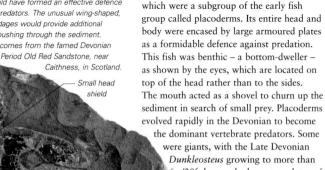

— *Small head shield*

— *Large body shield*

— *Wing-like appendage*

Pterichthyodes was one of a number of heavily armoured fish called antiarchs, which were a subgroup of the early fish group called placoderms. Its entire head and body were encased by large armoured plates as a formidable defence against predation. This fish was benthic – a bottom-dweller – as shown by the eyes, which are located on top of the head rather than to the sides. The mouth acted as a shovel to churn up the sediment in search of small prey. Placoderms evolved rapidly in the Devonian to become the dominant vertebrate predators. Some were giants, with the Late Devonian *Dunkleosteus* growing to more than 6m/20ft long – the largest predator of its time. However, they had died out by the Early Carboniferous Period.

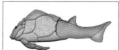

Name: Pterichthyodes
Meaning: Like a winged fish
Grouping: Fish, Placoderm, Antiarch
Informal ID: Armoured or tank fish
Fossil size: Length 8cm/3¼in
Reconstructed size: Head to tail length up to 20cm/8in
Habitat: Bottom of shallow lakes
Time span: Middle Devonian, 380 million years ago
Main fossil sites: Throughout Europe
Occurrence: ◆ ◆ ◆

Palaeoniscus

Name: *Palaeoniscus*
Meaning: Ancient small fossil
Grouping: Fish,
Actinopterygian,
Palaeonisciform, Palaeoniscid
Informal ID: Predatory
freshwater fish
Fossil size: Length 23cm/
9¾in
Reconstructed size: Head to
tail length 20–30cm/8–12in
Habitat: Fresh water
Time span: Middle Devonian
to Late Triassic, 370–210
million years ago (but most
abundant in Carboniferous
Main fossil sites: Europe,
Greenland, North America
Occurrence: ◆ ◆

The strong, fusiform (spindle-shaped) build of *Palaeoniscus* indicates that it was a powerful swimmer rather than a bottom-dweller. Its large, forward-placed eyes also suggest that vision was its most important sense. It had proportionately very large jaws, lined with rows of short, sharp teeth that continuously replaced themselves (as in sharks). *Palaeoniscus* is an early or basal actinopterygian (ray-fin). Its deeply forked, strongly heterocercal tail (the two lobes unequal in size) is entirely fleshy to the tip of its upper lobe – while, in more derived ray-fins, only the bony rod-like rays support the tail, which is often homocercal (with equal lobes). Additionally, *Palaeoniscus* regulated its buoyancy using a pair of air sacs connected to the throat, instead of the swim bladder as in most later ray-finned fish, which develops as an outgrowth of the digestive tract.

Dorsal (back) fin | Caudal fin
Body | Tail base

Above: Although anatomical details are obscured on this Palaeoniscus specimen, the animal has obviously been rapidly buried, preserving all features, down to each scale, in their precise life arrangement.

Lepidotes

Name: *Lepidotes*
Meaning: Covered with
scales, scaly
Grouping: Fish,
Actinopterygian,
Semionotiform, Semionotid
Informal ID: Ray-finned
cosmopolitan fish
Fossil size: Scale slab
25cm/10in long
Reconstructed size:
Head–tail length up to
2m/6½ft
Habitat: Lakes, shallow
coastal waters
Time span: Middle Triassic to
Cretaceous, 230–100 million
years ago
Main fossil sites: Worldwide
Occurrence: ◆ ◆ ◆

An extremely successful Triassic-to-Cretaceous genus of ray-finned fish, the *Lepidotes* group was related to the modern gars. Around a hundred species have been listed from Mesozoic sediments laid down around the world, although some badly preserved specimens have probably been mistakenly identified as entirely new species. Different forms of *Lepidotes* have been found in a wide variety of environments, including rivers, lakes and shallow coastal sea areas. The various species range in length from 30cm/12in up to 2m/6½ft or more. The jaws had developed a new mechanism for shaping themselves into a tube that could suck in prey from a distance, and its flatenned or peg-like teeth were capable of crushing molluscan prey. Some of the recognizably thick scales of *Lepidotes* have been found in the fossilized chest region of the large dinosaur *Baryonyx*; the fish-eater perhaps scooped them up with its large claws, like a bear.

Below: Lepidotes scales were about thumbnail-sized, rhomboid or diamond-shaped and arranged in rows. Each scale was composed of layers of bone, dentine and enamel (as in our own teeth). The enamel often gives its fossils the shiny, jet-black appearance as seen here. These scales were probably from the side, or flank, of the body.

Rhomboid (diamond or kite) shape | Dorsal scales
Preserved black enamel
Ventral (belly) scales

FISH – TELEOSTS

Most of today's fish are in the ray-fin (actinopterygian) group called teleosts, or 'complete bone', where few, if any, parts of the skeleton are made of cartilage (gristle). The teleosts include the vast majority of living fish, with more than 20,000 species. They arose in the Triassic Period and underwent rapid evolution in the Middle Cretaceous, when many of the modern families became established.

Leptolepis

Above: This specimen, from the famed Late Jurassic limestone of Solnhofen, Germany, shows the protractible mouth, which had shorter jaws than earlier fish, but could gape more widely, forming a tube-like structure to suck in small food. The vertebrae of the backbone, as well as the deeply forked homocercal (equally lobed) tail, are visible.

Leptolepis is usually classed as an early teleost. In particular, this herring-like swimmer possessed a fully ossified (bony) vertebral column, or backbone. In addition, its scales lacked a heavy enamel coating and were much thinner and lighter than in more primitive fish, as well as being more flexible and more cycloidal, or rounded, in shape. *Leptolepis* remains are most abundant in Jurassic rocks, where entire fossilized schools of hundreds of individuals can be found on single slabs. Other, more fragmentary remains indicate that the genus persisted throughout almost the whole Mesozoic Era. These relatively small, warm-sea fish fed on the small planktonic organisms.

Name: *Leptolepis*
Meaning: Thin scale
Grouping: Fish, Actinopterygian, Teleost, Leptolepiform, Leptolepid
Informal ID: Extinct 'herring'
Fossil size: Head–tail length 8cm/3⅛in
Reconstructed size: Head–tail length up to 25cm/10in
Habitat: Warm coastal seas
Time span: Middle Triassic to Late Cretaceous, 230–80 million years ago
Main fossil sites: Europe, Africa, North America, Australia
Occurrence: ◆ ◆ ◆

Eurypholis

Below: This fossilized specimen of Eurypholis illustrates the species' large head, the narrow, streamlined body and the long, fine, ragged-looking teeth. Several of the fins are also visible in this specimen, including the front paired fins (or pectorals), the rear paired fins (or pelvics), and the unpaired back (or dorsal) fin.

Eurypholis – also called the 'viper fish' – was a Cretaceous euteleost with no living close relatives, whose fossils come chiefly from the region of Hadjoula, Lebanon. Its common name reflects its long, thin, 'ragged' teeth, reminiscent of the living sand tiger shark. The scientific name refers to the row of three large, bony scales superimposed behind its skull on its back. The dentition, wide eyes and very large mouth give *Eurypholis* a fearsome appearance and indicate its predatory lifestyle. *Eurypholis* fossils have been recovered with other fish in their stomach region – signs of their last meal. These fish lived in the warm, shallow seas of the Mesozoic Era. Individuals are found alone in 'mass mortality layers' known from Lebanon, indicating that they were solitary rather than shoaling fish.

Name: *Eurypholis*
Meaning: Broad scale
Grouping: Fish, Actinopterygian, Euteleost, Aulopiform, Eurypholid
Informal ID: Extinct viper fish
Fossil size: Head–tail length 12cm/4¾in
Reconstructed size: Head–tail length up to 20cm/8in
Habitat: Shallow coastal seas, lagoons
Time span: Middle to Late Cretaceous, 100–70 million years ago
Main fossil sites: Europe, Middle East, North Africa (especially Lebanon)
Occurrence: ◆

Dorsal fin

'Snaggle-tooth' dentition

Vertebral column (backbone)

Hoplopteryx

Name: Hoplopteryx
Meaning: Armoured wing
Grouping: Fish,
Actinopterygian, Teleost,
Beryciform, Trachichthyid
Informal ID: Sawbelly,
slimehead
Fossil size: Each specimen
about 13cm/5in long
Reconstructed size:
Head–tail length 30cm/12in
Habitat: Warm, shallow
coastal seas
Time span: Late Cretaceous,
80–70 million years ago
Main fossil sites:
Northern Hemisphere
Occurrence: ◆ ◆

A relative of modern perch-like fish,
Hoplopteryx is from the Late Cretaceous
Period and it showed many anatomical
characteristics that are seen today in the
living ray-finned fish group Berciformes,
which includes roughies, squirrelfish,
pinecone fish and the unpleasantly named
slimehead fish. The protractible mouth of
Hoplopteryx, which was lined with
minuscule teeth, would suck in a small
volume of water when it was speedily
opened, thereby capturing prey from a
distance. The upturned mouth is typical
of surface feeders, making it a probable
predator of small creatures in shallow
coastal waters. It had large eyes, small
pectoral fins, forward-placed pelvic fins,
a homocercal tail and a narrow body.

Beryx
Beryx superbus, like *Hoplopteryx* (see left), was
a Late Cretaceous member of the Berciformes
group. Its genus is still represented by two
species found almost worldwide today – the
common alfonsino (*B. decadactylus*) and
the splendid alfonsino (*B. splendens*). Beryx
are relatively large fish, up to 70cm/27½in in
length, and feed on small fish, cephalopods
and crustaceans on the coastal sea floor.

*Below: This specimen shows the skull and thoracic
(chest) region and the vertebral column (backbone)
with the vertebral spines projecting above it.*

*Right: This spectacular
specimen is beautifully
preserved in three dimensions
within the chalk deposits typical
of Late Cretaceous marine rocks.*

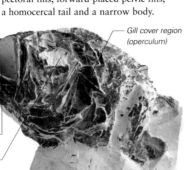

Gill cover region
(operculum)

Mouth

Eye orbit (socket)

Belonostomus

Name: Belonostomus
Meaning: Arrow mouth
Grouping: Fish,
Actinopterygian, Teleost,
Aspidorhynciform,
Aspidorhynchid
Informal ID: Needlefish
Fossil size: Jaw 16.5cm/6½in
Reconstructed size: Head–tail
length up to 40cm/16in
Habitat: Warm coastal seas,
possible also brackish and
fresh water
Time span: Late Jurassic to
Late Cretaceous, 150–65
million years ago
Main fossil sites: Europe,
Middle East, South and
North America
Occurrence: ◆ ◆

Superficially similar to the living needlefish (*Belone belone*),
Belonostomus was a long, slender, ray-finned fish of the
latter half of the Mesozoic Era. It had a long, pointed
rostrum (or snout) packed with closely spaced teeth.
Its dorsal and anal fins were positioned far back along the
body, and it possessed recognizably deep, elongated flank
scales. Most fossils of this fish have been found in rocks
that were deposited in shallow coastal marine areas.
However, some specimens from North America are known
from what were freshwater habitats, and although most
remains are Mesozoic, one jaw fragment is known from
the Early Tertiary Period.

*Below: This is a fossil of the long,
pointed, upper jaw (or rostrum)
of Belonostomus, showing some
of the teeth sockets. This fish
was probably a speedy predator
of small surface fish, such as
herring (clupeomorphs). Fins set
near the rear of the body signify a
fast-accelerating fish.*

Anterior (front) end
of jaw bone

Teeth

Tooth
sockets

FISH – TELEOSTS (CONTINUED)

Among the modern ray-finned bony fish, teleosts, the largest subgroup, include the perciforms, or perch-like fish, such as Mioplosus. Together with their close relatives, teleosts make up the Acanthopterygii, which includes more than half of all kinds of living fish. Their characteristic features include stiff bony spines in or near the front dorsal fin, giving the whole group the common name of spiny-rayed fish.

Mioplosus

Below: The fine-grained calcite limestones in which fossils such as this specimen have been found suggest that Mioplosus frequented areas similar to those of perches today – mainly upper and middle lake zones. This specimen is from Wyoming, USA, its main area of occurrence.

The spiny-fin, or perciform, *Mioplosus* has been found, although relatively rarely, in the exceptionally well-preserved Green River Formation rocks of Wyoming, USA. Its two dorsal (back) fins, and the comparable size of the second (rearmost) of these to the anal fin, which is directly beneath, are identifying features. The body is quite variable in proportions, but its length and strong build give it an overall perch-like appearance. Specimens of *Mioplosus* often seem to have died while trying to swallow, and choking on, fish up to half their own size. This suggests *Mioplosus* was a voracious predator, while the isolated nature of the finds indicate that it was solitary rather than shoaling.

Name: *Mioplosus*
Meaning: Small plosus
Grouping: Fish, Actinopterygian, Teleost, Acanthopterygian, Perciform
Informal ID: Extinct perch
Fossil size Head–tail length 28cm/11in
Reconstructed size: Head–tail length up to 40cm/16in, and rarely up to 50cm/20in
Habitat: Warm temperate to subtropical freshwater lakes
Time span: Eocene, 50 million years ago
Main fossil sites: North America (especially Wyoming, USA)
Occurrence: ◆

Second dorsal fin ⏤
⏤ First dorsal fin
⏤ Mouth line
⏤ Anal fin

Diplomystus

This member of the herring family, Clupeidae, is recognized by its anal fin extending to its tail, and its deep body. *Diplomystus* also possessed two rows of scutes (bony plates) behind its head, dorsally (on its back) and ventrally (on the belly), extending to its paired fins. It lived from the Cretaceous Period through to the Early Tertiary Period, therefore surviving the mass extinction of 65 million years ago. Its fossils have been found worldwide, in both fresh water and marine habitats. It is especially abundant in the Green River Formation rocks of Wyoming, USA (see *Mioplosus*, above), where it grew to lengths in excess of 60cm/24in. *Diplomystus* fed on surface-water fish, as indicated by specimens fossilized with their prey still in their mouths or guts.

Name: *Diplomystus*
Meaning: Double recess, twice hidden
Grouping: Fish, Actinopterygian, Teleost, Clupeiform, Clupeid
Informal ID: Extinct herring
Fossil size: Head–tail length 43cm/17in
Reconstructed size: Head–tail length up to 65cm/26in
Habitat: Varied, seas and lakes
Time span: Mid to Late Cretaceous to Early Tertiary, 80–50 million years ago
Main fossil sites: Europe, Middle East, Africa, North and South America
Occurrence: ◆ ◆ ◆

Left: Diplomystus had a drastically upturned mouth, a characteristic typical of surface-feeding fish. The extremely long anal fin on the underside of the rear body extends right to the deeply forked, homocercal (equal-lobed) tail fin.

Knightia

Name: Knightia
Meaning: After Knight (Wilbur Clinton Knight, Wyoming's first state geologist)
Grouping: Fish, Actinopterygian, Teleost, Clupeiform, Clupeid
Informal ID: Extinct herring
Fossil size: Head–tail length 9cm/3½in
Reconstructed size: Head–tail average length 10cm/4in, up to 25cm/10in
Habitat: Warm temperate to subtropical fresh water
Time span: Mainly Eocene, 50 million years ago
Main fossil sites: North and South America (especially Wyoming, USA)
Occurrence: ◆ ◆ ◆

Knightia has the distinction of being the vertebrate fossil most often found completely articulated – that is, with its structural parts still attached or aligned as in life. A herring and relative of *Diplomystus* (see opposite), it can be distinguished from the latter by its smaller size, shorter anal fin and slender body. *Knightia* is frequently found in mass mortality layers, in which thousands of individuals have died virtually simultaneously. This clearly suggests shoaling or schooling, but often the cause of death remains unclear – perhaps sudden temperature changes, or water stagnation with falling oxygen content, or rising levels of toxins due to algal blooms. Its small size, and common presence in the jaws or guts of larger fish, suggest that *Knightia* was near the beginning of the food chains and probably fed on plankton. Its phenomenal abundance in the Green River Formation rocks (see opposite) have led to it being appointed as Wyoming's state fossil.

Right: Soft-tissue preservation and perfect articulation of Knightia *fossils, as seen here, is sometimes observed in thousands of specimens packed densely together, with up to several hundred fish per square metre.*

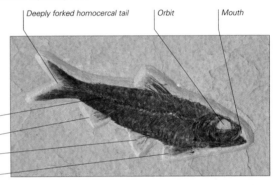

Deeply forked homocercal tail | *Orbit* | *Mouth*

Vertebral column

Short anal fin

Pelvic fin

Pectoral fin

Dastilbe

Name: Dastilbe
Meaning: Not known
Grouping: Fish, Actinopterygian, Teleost, Ostariophysian, Gonorynchiform
Informal ID: Extinct milkfish
Fossil size: Head–tail length 10.5cm/4in
Reconstructed size: Head–tail length of largest individuals in excess of 20cm/8in, average 10cm/4in
Habitat: Fresh to salty water, including inland salt lagoons
Time span: Early Cretaceous, 120 million years ago
Main fossil sites: South America (Brazil), Africa (Equatorial Guinea)
Occurrence: ◆ ◆ ◆

Dastilbe was a relation of today's milkfish, a member of the major teleost group called the Ostariophysi, which includes more than 6,000 living species, such as catfish and carp. Their fossil history shows such features as modified hearing parts, termed Weberian ossicles, which link the swim bladder to the inner ear. This means that the swim bladder acts as a resonating chamber to improve underwater hearing. *Dastilbe* did not spread particularly far or last very long, but wherever it was present it was abundant, especially in the shallow tropical lakes of what is now Brazil. Fossil specimens are found with prey still in their mouths, indicating that *Dastilbe* was a predator – and when fully grown it was a cannibal, since some were eating young of their own kind.

Below: Fossilized Dastilbe *remains have been found in rocks from Brazil's Cretaceous Crato Formation, which were deposited as the beds of brackish lagoons. Most specimens were small juveniles, such as the example shown here, which could suggest that the adults were migratory and perhaps even marine. The young died when the water's salt level rose and became too high, and the fish were not sufficiently large to leave the protective waters of their nursery lagoon.*

Deeply forked homocercal tail

TETRAPODS – AMPHIBIANS

Tetrapods were and are vertebrates with four limbs – which today includes amphibians, reptiles, birds and mammals (although some, such as snakes, have lost limbs during their more recent evolution). The first air-breathing tetrapods probably evolved from fleshy-finned fish resembling Eusthenopteron *and* Panderichthys *into creatures such as* Ventastega *and* Acanthostega, *some 380–360 million years ago.*

Branchiosaurus

Below: The wedge-shaped skull, slim limbs (one front limb is missing due to slab fracture) and long tail are clearly visible in this example of Branchiosaurus from Rotleigend in northern Germany – an area famous for its Permian rocks, fossils and mineral reserves, such as natural gas. Total specimen length 9cm/3½in.

Tail   Rear limb

Front limb   Skull

Not to be confused with the massive dinosaur *Brachiosaurus*, which was some 26m/85ft long, *Branchiosaurus* belonged to the group of tetrapods known as temnospondyls. These appeared during the Early to Mid Carboniferous Period and included newt-like aquatic forms as well as large, powerful, land-going predators, such as *Eryops* (see overleaf) and *Mastodonsaurus*, which had scaly or bony plates on the skin and bore a vague outward resemblance to crocodiles. *Branchiosaurus* was a smallish, fully aquatic form, about 30cm/12in in length, that in some ways resembled the modern salamander-like axolotl. It had four weak limbs for walking in water, a long finned tail for swimming, and feathery external gills. Its family date from the Late Carboniferous Period through to the Permian. Usually only the young or larval forms of amphibians, known commonly as tadpoles, have external gills. ('Amphibian' is a commonly used though imprecise term usually applied to tetrapods that breathe using gills when young, and by gills and/or lungs when adult.) Keeping the larval gills as the rest of the body became sexually mature is an example of a well-known phenomenon in animal development termed paedomorphosis – retention of juvenile features into adult life – something that it shares with the Mexican axolotl. *Branchiosaurus'* way of life as a sharp-toothed aquatic predator was similar to that of *Micromelerpeton*, opposite.

Name: *Branchiosaurus*
Meaning: Gill lizard
Grouping: Vertebrate, Tetrapod, Temnospondyl, Dissorophoidean, Branchiosaurid
Informal ID: Amphibian, prehistoric newt or salamander or axolotl
Fossil size: See text
Reconstructed size: Total length up to 30cm/12in
Habitat: Tropical fresh water, swamps
Time span: Permian, 290–260 million years ago
Main fossil sites: Europe
Occurrence: ◆ ◆

Below: This specimen of Branchiosaurus, also from Germany, measures 8cm/3⅛in in length. The front limbs are unclear. The gills of Branchiosaurus would have been very soft and fragile in life, and preserved only rarely. They would be positioned just behind the rear lateral angle, or backward-facing 'cheek', of the skull.

The Mexican axolotl
The rare Mexican axolotl salamander is said 'never to grow up'. This description comes about because it retains its feathery external gills, which most modern amphibians have only when they are larvae (immature young), throughout its adult life.

Micromelerpeton

Name: *Micromelerpeton*
Meaning: Tiny *Melerpeton* (another proposed tetrapod genus)
Grouping: Vertebrate, Tetrapod, Temnospondyl, Dissorophoidean
Informal ID: Amphibian, prehistoric newt or salamander or axolotl
Fossil size: Total length 18cm/7in
Reconstructed size: Total length up to 25cm/10in
Habitat: Tropical fresh water, swamps
Time span: Permian, 290–260 million years ago
Main fossil sites: Europe
Occurrence: ◆

In many ways similar to *Branchiosaurus* (see opposite), *Micromelerpeton* was a temnospondyl amphibian from the Permian Period. Its fossils are best known from Germany, such as in the Saar region, and France. Like *Branchiosaurus*, and modern salamanders and newts, it was an aquatic predator of small creatures, such as young fish, insect larvae and worms. It had sharp teeth not only in the jaws, but also on the palate (mouth roof). It, too, showed the phenomenon of paedomorphosis, retaining its larval feature of feathery external gills as the rest of its body metamorphosed into the sexually mature adult. At one time its remains were thought to be the larva of an unknown land amphibian. Some features of its shoulder girdle and other skeletal parts suggest that its ancestors may have been land-dwellers, after which *Micromelerpeton* returned to the water.

Below: This specimen of Micromelerpeton *distinctly shows the small, sharp teeth along the animal's jaw bone used for grabbing and impaling slippery prey, such as fish and worms. The rear limbs were slim and weak. They were not strong enough for walking on land, but they were suitable for manoeuvring among waterweeds or walking along the bed of a stream or lake. This species,* Micromelerpeton credneri, *is named in honour of German palaeontologist Hermann Credner (1841–1913).*

Snout
Teeth
Jaw bone

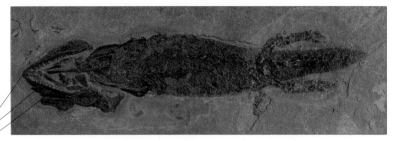

Diplocaulus

Name: *Diplocaulus*
Meaning: Two-stemmed (double-stalked)
Grouping: Tetrapod, Lepospondyl, Nectridean
Informal ID: Newt-like amphibian
Fossil size: Width of skull 40cm/16in
Reconstructed size: Head–tail length 1m/3¼ft
Habitat: Streams and lakes
Time span: Early Permian, 290–270 million years ago
Main fossil sites: North America, also North Africa
Occurrence: ◆ ◆

One of the most distinctive of all animal fossils is the skull of the 'giant Permian newt' *Diplocaulus*. The skull is immediately recognized from its boomerang-like shape, with two long, backswept, pointed 'horns', on either side, smallish eye sockets (orbits) set relatively close together near the front, and two much smaller nostrils just on top of the blunt snout. Associated backbones (vertebrae) and limb bones show that *Diplocaulus* was probably newt-like in shape and about 1m/3¼ft in length. The function of *Diplocaulus*'s extraordinary head shape is much debated. One suggestion is that it was a defensive adaptation – a predator would need a very large mouth gape to engulf the head. Or the skull may have been hydrodynamic, working like the wing of an aircraft, but in water, to provide a lifting force as *Diplocaulus* swam with its relatively weak limbs.

Nostril
Eye orbit (socket)
Lateral 'horn' tip of skull
Cervical (neck) joint
Vertebrae (backbones)

Right: This specimen of Diplocaulus *is from Baylor County, Texas, USA – the region of the famed Texan 'Red Beds', which have provided marvellous fossils of amphibians, reptiles and many other life-forms from Permian times. It shows the distinctive skull, most of the vertebral column and part of the shoulder girdle for the front left limb.*

TETRAPODS – AMPHIBIANS (CONTINUED)

In the past, some types of amphibian were perfectly at home on dry land and, presumably, needed water only to lay their jelly-covered eggs in when spawning. Living amphibians are known in modern classification schemes as lissamphibians. The three main groups are frogs and toads, the tailless anurans; salamanders and newts, the tailed urodeles; and the legless, worm-like caecilians or apodans.

Eryops

A temnospondyl amphibian, like *Branchiosaurus*, *Eryops* was a strong, stoutly built and powerful predator. Its sturdy limbs probably allowed it to move reasonably well on dry land, and the tall spinal processes along the vertebrae of its backbone suggest effective back muscles that swished its body and tail from side to side when walking and swimming. Its way of life, however, was probably semi-aquatic. Both its eyes and nostrils were on top of the head, allowing it to lurk almost hidden in water yet still see above and breathe air. Or it may have skulked along the banks of rivers and lakes, on the lookout for likely prey. The temnospondyl group had died out by the Late Jurassic or perhaps the Early Cretaceous Period, more than 100 million years ago.

Name: *Eryops*
Meaning: Long eye
Grouping: Vertebrate, Tetrapod, Temnospondyl
Informal ID: Giant prehistoric amphibian
Fossil size: Total length 2m/6½ft
Reconstructed size: As above
Habitat: Rivers, lakes and swamps with dry ground
Time span: Late Carboniferous to Permian, 300–280 million years ago
Main fossil sites: North America
Occurrence: ◆ ◆

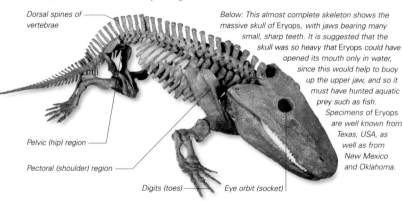

Dorsal spines of vertebrae

Pelvic (hip) region

Pectoral (shoulder) region

Digits (toes)

Eye orbit (socket)

Below: This almost complete skeleton shows the massive skull of Eryops, with jaws bearing many small, sharp teeth. It is suggested that the skull was so heavy that Eryops could have opened its mouth only in water, since this would help to buoy up the upper jaw, and so it must have hunted aquatic prey such as fish. Specimens of Eryops are well known from Texas, USA, as well as from New Mexico and Oklahoma.

Eye socket (orbit)

Skull

Front limb

Ribs

Rear limb

Long tail

This unidentified Miocene salamander shows the bony processes in the tail that held up a ridge of skin, for propulsion in the water.

Salamanders

The urodeles are commonly known as newts (mostly aquatic) and salamanders (mainly terrestrial). However, usage of these common names varies around the world, leading to potential confusion, and encompasses salamanders with names such as congo-eels, olms, axolotls and mudpuppies. They are mostly speedy swimmers and voracious hunters of varied small prey, from worms, grubs and insect larvae to fish and the tadpoles (larvae) of fellow amphibians. Although many invertebrates have the ability to regrow body structures, urodeles are the only examples of vertebrates that can completely regenerate limbs as adults. The fossil history of the salamander can be traced back to forms such as *Karaurus* from the Late Jurassic Period in Kazakhstan, Central Asia. Their design has changed little in almost 150 million years, with a long body and tail, and legs that project almost sideways. This specimen is dated to the Middle Miocene Epoch, about 10 million years ago.

Rana (R. pueyoi)

Name: Rana pueyoi
Meaning: Frog of Pueyo
Grouping: Vertebrate,
Tetrapod, Lissamphibian,
Anuran, Ranid
Informal ID: Frog
Fossil size: Head–body
length 10cm/4in
Reconstructed size:
As above
Habitat: Ponds, marshes
and streams
Time span: From Early
Oligocene Epoch, 30 million
years ago, to today
Main fossil sites: Worldwide
Occurrence: ◆ ◆

The huge genus *Rana* (typical or 'green' frogs) contains numerous species of living frogs, including the familiar common frog of Europe, *R. temporaria*, and the American bullfrog, *R. catesbeiana*. The fossil history of frogs and toads, the Anura, stretches back 200 million years, to the Early Jurassic Period. About 40 million years before this, the very frog-like *Triadobatrachus* is known from Early Triassic rocks of Madagascar. 'Modern' frogs of the genus *Rana*, with their relatively large, wide-mouthed, pointed skull, shortened, compact body, small shock-absorbing front legs for landing and large rear limbs and feet adapted for leaping, have remained essentially unchanged through most of the Tertiary.

Right: This specimen of Rana pueyoi *is from Late Miocene rocks (8 to 6 million years old) near Teruel in the mountainous, east-central region of Aragon, Spain – a locality also noted for its Early Cretaceous dinosaur fossils. It is very similar to living frogs of the same genus, with large eyes and an extensive eardrum behind each of these.*

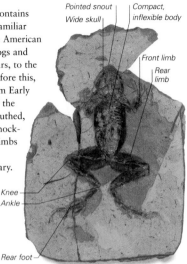

Pointed snout | Compact,
Wide skull | inflexible body

Front limb
Rear limb

Knee
Ankle

Rear foot

Nanopus

Name: *Nanopus*
Meaning: Tiny foot
Grouping: Vertebrate,
Tetrapod, possibly
Temnospondyl
Informal ID: Amphibian
footprints
Fossil size: Print size
1–2cm/½–¾in
Reconstructed size: Animal
length estimates 20–30cm/
8–12in
Habitat: Fresh water,
marshes, rivers, lakes, ponds
Time span: Late
Carboniferous to Early
Permian, 310–290 million
years ago
Main fossil sites: North
America, Europe
Occurrence: ◆ ◆

Nanopus is an ichnogenus – evidence for a creature based only on the traces it left, such as droppings, burrows or, in this example, footprints. The shape of the prints differ between the manus (the 'hand' of the front limb) and the pes (the 'foot' of the rear limb). Particularly well-known prints ascribed to the ichnogenera *Matthewichnus* and *Nanopus*, along with footprints and trackways made by many other vertebrates and invertebrates, are known from sites such as the Union Chapel mine of Walker County, Alabama, USA. These fossils are dated to the Westphalian (Moscovian) part of the Late Carboniferous Period, just more than 300 million years ago. Studies of these and other prints, including their spacing and progress pattern, the way the toes splay, and associated tail drags, give clues to the walking and swimming abilities of tetrapods such as *Nanopus*, *Limnopus* and *Matthewichnus* from Carboniferous times.

Above: The size of Nanopus *and similar prints is generally on the order of 1–2cm/½–¾in. Some were left in the damp sand or mud in quiet backwaters where the currents did not disturb them. The water receded and the sediments were baked hard by the sun before fossilization. Expert analysis suggests several species of the genus* Nanopus, *including N. caudatus, N. obtusus, N. quadratus, N. quadrifidus and N. reidiae.*

Left: These prints were made by the animal walking from right to left in soft sand. The placement can suggest if the animal was walking slowly or hurrying, as here. Blank areas between prints may suggest that the animal was partly floating – perhaps kicking its feet to move forward.

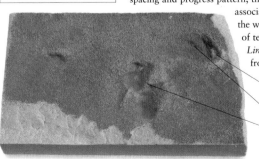

Heel area

Toe impression

Two prints close together

REPTILES

One of the most significant of evolutionary events was the amniotic egg – an egg sealed in an amniotic sac, usually enclosed in a tough outer shell. It first appeared with the tetrapods we call reptiles more than 300 million years ago. Its strong, encased structure allowed the reptiles to free themselves from the water, which the amphibians – dominant land vertebrates at the time – needed to lay their jelly-coated spawn.

Hylonomus

Often referred to as the 'first reptile', *Hylonomus* lived about 310 million years ago in the Late Carboniferous Period. Its remains come from the famed site of Joggins in Nova Scotia, Canada. *Hylonomus* outwardly resembled a lizard, but the lizard group of reptiles would not appear for many millions of years after this time. There has been much discussion about the circumstances of preservation of *Hylonomus*. Huge tree-like *Sigillaria* clubmosses lived and died in the area, snapping off their trunks low down as they fell, leaving stumps behind. Floods brought mud that built the ground up to the same level of the snapped-off *Sigillaria* stumps. These, in time, rotted from within to form hollows. Insects, millipedes and other small creatures fell into these 'pitfall traps'. Small predators, such as *Hylonomus*, followed them in to feed, but became trapped themselves and were buried in later sediments.

Below: The preservation detail of Hylonomus *fossils is remarkable, with almost every body part present, even skin scales. The jaws shown here bear many conical teeth suited to snapping up small prey such as insects, grubs and worms.*

Name: *Hylonomus*
Meaning: Forest mouse
Grouping: Reptile, Captorhinid
Informal ID: First reptile, 'lizard'
Fossil size: Jaw length 2cm/¾in
Reconstructed size: Total length 20cm/8in
Habitat: Swampy forests
Time span: Late Carboniferous, 310 million years ago
Main fossil sites: North America
Occurrence: ◆

Elginia

Below: Elginia *had an elaborate head shape with knobs, spikes and two long horns formed by outgrowths of the skull bones. This skull's larger side opening is the eye socket, the smaller one near the front is the nostril, and the central one on the forehead is the pineal, or 'third eye', which was possibly used to help regulate temperature.*

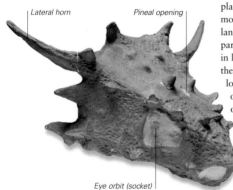

Lateral horn   Pineal opening

Eye orbit (socket)

The captorhinids were the earliest main reptile group to appear, led by *Hylonomus* (above). During the Middle Permian one of the subgroups, the pareiasaurs, began to spread and evolve into larger, more powerful forms. They were strongly built plant eaters and some reached the size of a modern buffalo, being among the largest land animals of the time. *Elginia* was a pareiasaur, but a dwarf form about 1.5m/5ft in length – one of the smallest and last of the group. It is named after its discovery location of Elgin, Scotland. Like many other pareiasaurs, it had bony growths over its head. Their function is not clear, but they may have been for defence against predators of the time, or for show and display to partners of their own kind when breeding. The pareiasaurs became all but extinct at the end of the Permian Period.

Name: *Elginia*
Meaning: Of Elgin
Grouping: Reptile, Captorhinid, Pareiasaur
Informal ID: Pareiasaur, prehistoric reptile
Fossil size: Skull length 25cm/10in
Reconstructed size: Head–tail length 1.5m/5ft
Habitat: Mixed scrub and plant growth
Time span: Late Permian, 270–250 million years ago
Main fossil sites: Europe
Occurrence: ◆

Stereosternum

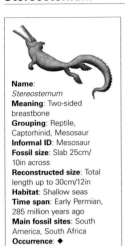

Name:
Stereosternum
Meaning: Two-sided breastbone
Grouping: Reptile, Captorhinid, Mesosaur
Informal ID: Mesosaur
Fossil size: Slab 25cm/10in across
Reconstructed size: Total length up to 30cm/12in
Habitat: Shallow seas
Time span: Early Permian, 285 million years ago
Main fossil sites: South America, South Africa
Occurrence: ◆

Soon after reptiles had developed their protective, tough-shelled amniotic egg and scaly skin to reduce water loss when on dry land, some types went back to the water. The first mesosaurs date from the Early Permian Period, approximately 290 million years ago, but the group did not last until the end of the period. Their fossils are known only from the Southern Hemisphere. Superficially resembling crocodiles, they are in a very different group of reptiles, usually linked to the 'primitive' captorhinids (see opposite). *Stereosternum* was a typical member of the mesosaur group and was adapted for an aquatic lifestyle. It had a long, slim neck, body and tail for sinuous swimming, and short limbs (rear ones larger than forelimbs), probably with webbed feet for paddling and steering.

Below: This beautifully preserved specimen from Brazil clearly shows the detailed skeleton of Stereosternum, including the girdle bones, shoulder and hip, for both sets of the animal's limbs. Mesosaurs had long, thin, delicate teeth, which may have worked like a comb or sieve, to filter small creatures, such as shrimps or similar crustaceans that were plentiful at the time, from the ocean water.

Hyperodapedon

Name: *Hyperodapedon*
Meaning: Ground-hugging, short-legged reptile
Grouping: Reptile, Archosauromorph, Rhynchosaur
Informal ID: Rhynchosaur
Fossil size: Skull length 22cm/8⅔in
Reconstructed size: Total length 1.4–1.8m/4½–6ft
Habitat: Dry scrub with seed ferns
Time span: Late Permian, 260–250 million years ago
Main fossil sites: Europe, Asia
Occurrence: ◆

The rhynchosaurs, or 'beaked lizards (reptiles)', were a spectacularly successful, although short-lived group from the Triassic Period. They were mostly stout animals with a barrel-shaped body with strong limbs, a hook-ended upper jaw and blunt teeth for crushing plant food. Their fossils are found so commonly in some localities, especially the southern continents, that they have been described as dotting the landscape and munching on plants like 'Triassic sheep'. Like most other rhynchosaurs, *Hyperodapedon* had several rows of teeth set in each side of the upper jaw, with a furrow or groove between them. The singe row of teeth on each side of the lower jaw fitted into this furrow to give the animal a powerful crush–shear action when chewing.

Cheek teeth of upper jaw

Bony Y-shaped projection of lower jaw

Lower jaw

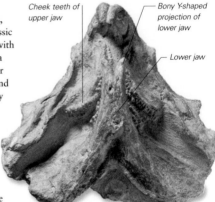

Above: This view from below shows the tooth rows of Hyperodapedon in the upper jaw, and the much narrower lower jaw with its Y-shaped, or forked, tip.

Eye orbit (socket)

Snout

Down-curved 'beak' (rostrum) of upper jaw

Left: The distinctive shape made by the downward-curving tip of the upper jaw of rhynchosaurs such as Hyperodapedon may have been a food-gathering device. The creature might have used it to hook plant material towards its batteries of crushing teeth. The dished area to the upper middle-left is the eye socket, while the dished area to the upper right is a skull 'window', or fenestra. This may have allowed the jaw muscles to pass through or bulge easily as they contracted while chewing.

REPTILES – CHELONIANS, PHYTOSAURS

One of the most distinctive, long-lived reptiles groups is the chelonians – turtles, tortoises and terrapins. They appeared during the Triassic and have changed little in basic body form in more than 200 million years. The phytosaurs were also reptiles and from the same time. However, they are linked to a different group, the archosaurs ('ruling reptiles'), which included true crocodiles, dinosaurs and pterosaurs.

Emys

The family Emydidae of 'typical' freshwater and semi-aquatic turtles includes more than 90 living species, as well as many more extinct ones, and it makes up not only the largest, but also the most diverse of the turtle families, being found in both North and South America, Europe, Northern Africa and Asia. Although emydid species live mainly in fresh water, some species are also found in brackish waters or are terrestrial in habitat. The genus *Emys* is represented by well-known living species, including the European pond turtle (*Emys orbicularis*), the water terrapin (*E. elegans*) and the western pond turtle (*E. marmorata*). Early members of the *Emys* group are known in the fossil record from Nebraska, in the central USA, dating back to the Barstovian (Langhian) Age of the Middle Miocene Epoch – approximately 15–13 million years ago. However, other fossils, which have been found both in North America and Asia, and the geographic spread of these remains, suggest an origin for the group in the Late Eocene. For further details of turtle anatomy see below.

Name: *Emys*
Meaning: Turtle
Grouping: Reptile, Chelonian, Emydid
Informal ID: Turtle
Fossil size: Fragments 2–3cm/¾–1in across
Reconstructed size: Total length 50cm/20in
Habitat: Fresh water
Time span: Late Eocene, 35 million years ago, to today
Main fossil sites: Worldwide
Occurrence: ◆ ◆

Broken edge of plate

Junction line between plates

Left: These fragments of shell are probably from a representative of the turtle genus Emys. The dividing lines between the plates, where they are joined firmly together, form a characteristic 'paving' effect. Sometimes the vertebrae (backbones) and ribs are also preserved, firmly fixed to the inner side of the upper shell, or carapace.

The turtle shell

Chelonian anatomy has changed little since the group appeared relatively suddenly in the Late Triassic Period. The skull of the animal is box-like, with large eye sockets (orbits) but no openings or 'windows' behind them – a distinctive skull structure known as anapsid. The jaws lack teeth and form a horny sharp-edged beak for chopping food. The shell consists of a dome-like carapace above and a flatter, shelf-like plastron on the underside. The vertebrae, ribs and limb girdle bones are all fused to the inside of the carapace. The shell, in fact, has two layers, each made up of flat sections fused together. The inner layer has bony plates and the outer one has horny scutes that form the visible observed pattern of the shell. The carapace pictured here, from the Purbeck Beds of Dorset, southern England, is dated to the Late Jurassic Period or Early Cretaceous Period, about 140–130 million years ago.

Vertebral column (backbone)

Main area of carapace

Lateral struts

Lateral plates form edging 'skirt'

Phytosaurus

Name: *Phytosaurus*
Meaning: Plant lizard/
reptile
Grouping: Reptile, Archosaur,
Crocodylotarsian, Phytosaur
Informal ID: Phytosaur,
crocodile-like extinct reptile
Fossil size: Tooth length
4.5cm/1¾in
Reconstructed size: Total
length 5m/16½ft
Habitat: Fresh water, rivers
and lakes and swamps
Time span: Late Triassic,
220–210 million years ago
Main fossil sites:
North America
Occurrence: ◆ ◆

The phytosaurs (parasuchians) were one of several groups of crocodile-like reptiles whose fossil record dates them from the Triassic Period. They were among the main semi-aquatic predators found in the Northern Hemisphere at that time, while their similar cousins, the rauisuchians, prowled more on dry land, and a third related group, the aetosaurs, became plant-eaters. All three of these groups have been placed within the crocodylotarsians, or 'crocodile ankles'. This is because fossils of their limbs show that their feet could be turned so that the toes faced more to the side, rather than being restricted to just facing forwards. *Phytosaurus*, which gave the phytosaur group its name, was misleadingly named 'plant lizard (reptile)', since its sharp teeth clearly show that it was a carnivore. The name came from the parts that were first studied as fossils. These were cast fossils from the blunt-tipped empty tooth sockets that acted as moulds, and these were mistaken at the time for the crushing teeth typical of a herbivore. (See also *Rutiodon*, below.)

Below: The conical tooth of Phytosaurus is recurved: that is, bent backwards towards the animal's throat, to prevent slippery prey such as fish from wriggling free. This specimen showing wear marks from struggles with victims is from Texas, USA.

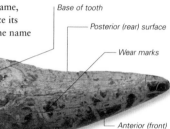

Base of tooth

Posterior (rear) surface

Wear marks

Anterior (front) surface

Rutiodon

A member of the phytosaur group (see *Phytosaurus*, above), *Rutiodon* – which may include specimens known as *Leptosuchus* – is known from many fossil sites across North America and Europe. Like most phytosaurs it was armoured over its body with bony plates known as scutes, similar to those of a crocodile, which form characteristic fossils even when they fall away from the decayed skin. Its snout was very long, low and narrow, similar to the modern-day crocodilian known as the gharial from the Indian region. This design may be adapted to swishing sideways through the water with minimal resistance when snapping at prey. The skulls of phytosaurs such as *Rutiodon* and *Phytosaurus* can be distinguished from true crocodiles especially by the presence of nostrils high up on the forehead, just in front of and between the eyes, rather than on the top of the tip of the snout as in crocodilians.

Name: *Rutiodon*
Meaning: Wrinkled tooth
Grouping: Reptile, Archosaur,
Crocodylotarsian, Phytosaur,
Angistorhininan
Informal ID: Phytosaur,
crocodile-like extinct reptile
Fossil size: Tooth length
5cm/2in
Reconstructed size: Total
length 3m/10ft
Habitat: Fresh water
Time span: Late Triassic,
220–215 million years ago
Main fossil sites: Europe,
North America
Occurrence: ◆ ◆

Below: The gharial is one of the largest living crocodilians, growing to lengths in excess of 6m/20ft. With weak legs and webbed feet, it is also one of the most aquatic, both catching and eating prey – chiefly fish – in the water.

Below: This specimen of a Rutiodon tooth from Arizona, USA, shows the characteristically prominent vertical grooves, or striations – the genus name means 'wrinkled tooth'. The root is flat and 'cut-off'. Like crocodilians, phytosaurs lost their teeth regularly and, as this happened, new ones grew from the jaw, so the mouth was usually filled with different-sized teeth of various ages.

Wrinkles or grooves

Base of tooth

Convex front surface

REPTILES – CROCODILIANS

Crocodiles, alligators, caimans and gharials are semi-aquatic predators around the warmer parts of the world. Yet the 23 or so living species of crocodilians are a small remnant of a once large and diverse group dating back more than 220 million years. They may have started as lizard-like terrestrial animals. Crocodilians are included with dinosaurs and pterosaurs as archosaurs, or 'ruling reptiles'.

Goniopholis

Supratemporal fenestra (skull opening)

The typical body design of a crocodilian such as the Late Jurassic–Early Cretaceous *Goniopholis* is for ambush predation. The skull was adapted for lurking in water. The eyes and nostrils are on the upper surface, so that the animal can see, breathe and smell while floating almost submerged. (Crocodilian nostrils are at the tip of the snout, differing from the position in phytosaurs already covered.) The snout is long and low, the body thick-set and powerful and the legs usually project sideways for a sinuous, slithering gait. The tail is narrow and tall and provides the main thrust for fast swimming, when the limbs are usually held against the body; the webbed feet may be used as paddles for slower movement and manoeuvring in water. Crocodilians have protective bony slabs called scutes that grow embedded in the skin, especially along the upper surface and sides of the animal (see below), and provide plentiful fossils.

Right: Goniopholis had a single nostril opening, an undivided naris, at the upper tip of the snout. The bone surface is ornamented with a waffle-like texture. The eye sockets, or orbits, are smaller than the gaps above them in the skull, known as the supratemporal fenestrae.

Nostril

Name: *Goniopholis*
Meaning: Angled scutes
Grouping: Reptile, Archosaur, Crocodilian
Informal ID: Crocodile
Fossil size: Skull length 70cm/27½in
Reconstructed size: Head–tail length 3–4m/10–13ft
Habitat: Rivers, lakes and swamps
Time span: Late Jurassic to Early Cretaceous, 150–130 million years ago
Main fossil sites: Europe, North America
Occurrence: ◆ ◆

Diplocynodon

Below: This is a preserved piece of the body armour of Diplocynodon, from the bony plates called scutes (see Goniopholis, above). Each type of crocodilian has a characteristic pattern of scute sizes, shapes and surface textures – the one here being squarish and dimpled.

Crocodiles can be distinguished from alligators principally by the structure of their teeth. In alligators, for example, the fourth tooth in the lower jaw fits into a corresponding socket, or pit, in the upper jaw, and so cannot be seen when the mouth is closed. In crocodiles, however, this tooth slides into a notch on the side of the jaw, and so the tooth is readily visible when the animal's mouth is closed. This key identifying feature is useful when unknown fossil material of the jaws and teeth are available, in which case the relevant part of the upper jaw can distinguish between them. In addition, the snout shape of an alligator such as *Diplocynodon* is generally broader, more foreshortened and more rounded at the tip than that of a crocodile. *Diplocynodon* remains are found especially from swampy and marshy habitats in Europe about 30–20 million years ago, during the Oligocene Epoch, although remains of *Diplocynodon* from the Bridger beds of Wyoming, USA, have also been discovered.

Name: *Diplocynodon*
Meaning: Double dog tooth
Grouping: Reptile, Archosaur, Crocodilian
Informal ID: Alligator
Fossil size: 4cm/1½in across
Reconstructed size: Head–tail length 3m/10ft
Habitat: Lakes, rivers and swamps
Time span: Eocene to Pliocene, 45–5 million years ago
Main fossil sites: North America, Europe
Occurrence: ◆ ◆

Metriorhynchus

Name: *Metriorhynchus*
Meaning: Moderate snout
Grouping: Reptile, Archosaur, Crocodilian
Informal ID: Marine crocodile
Fossil size: 22cm/8¾in
Reconstructed size: Head–tail length 3m/10ft
Habitat: Shallow seas
Time span: Middle Jurassic to Early Cretaceous, 160–120 million years ago
Main fossil sites: South America, Europe
Occurrence: ◆ ◆

This crocodile was highly adapted for life at sea, and may have come ashore only to lay eggs, in much the same way that marine turtles do today. Its limbs were paddle-shaped with extensive toe webbing. The tail end of the backbone (vertebral column) angled downwards and supported a large fish-like fin that provided sideways, sweeping propulsion through the water. The snout was very slim, long and pointed, in the style of the living crocodilian known as the gharial (gavial). This species is mainly a fish-eater, swiping its snout sideways to catch slithering prey with its many sharp teeth; *Metriorhynchus* probably did the same. Although shorter than modern crocodiles, *Metriorhynchus* would have been a formidable hunter, with a powerful, streamlined body ideally suited for swimming down a variety of prey. An adaptation to its fast-swimming way of life meant that it lost most of its protective armour, leaving it vulnerable to attack from larger and more powerful reptiles.

Below: The vertebrae of Metriorhynchus, *seen here from above, had characteristic joints that distinguished modern crocodiles from more primitive ones. The large lateral processes projecting to either side would have anchored powerful back muscles along the sides of the body and tail, that arched them left and right when swimming. Specimen length 22cm/8¾in.*

Right: The teeth of Metriorhynchus *were slimmer and more pointed than the sturdier, conical teeth of land-dwelling crocodilians. Tooth length 3cm/1in.*

Conical tip

Convex anterior (front) surface

Recurved posterior (rear) surface

Tooth base

Dorsal spines or processes (projections)

Transverse, or lateral, processes (projections)

Zygapophyseal prongs

Intervertebral joint

Centrum (body) of vertebra

Body of rib

Distorted fossil femur

These femurs (thigh bones) of *Metriorhynchus* contrast a healthy one (on the left) with a diseased, arthritic one (on the right). In a land crocodilian, where the walking weight is borne solely by the limbs, this disfiguring condition may have been a much more considerable handicap compared with the same condition in a swimming *Metriorhynchus*. The rear limbs of *Metriorhynchus* were larger than the front pair. Femur length 28cm/11in.

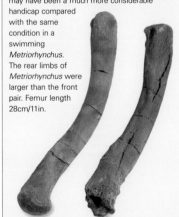

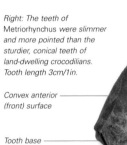

Above: The ribs of Metriorhynchus *were slim and lightweight. Despite this marine crocodile's highly modified adaptations, it remained an air-breather and so the ribcage and the lungs within would function in the normal reptilian way. Rib length 18cm/7in.*

Joint with thoracic vertebra (backbone in chest)

REPTILES – NOTHOSAURS, LIZARDS AND SNAKES

Several groups of reptiles took to the seas during the early Mesozoic, including the semi-aquatic placodonts, nothosaurs such as Lariosaurus, *their later cousins the plesiosaurs and also the ichthyosaurs. Meanwhile, on land the lizards had appeared, but snakes did not evolve until the end of the Mesozoic.*

Lariosaurus

Above: This fine juvenile specimen of Lariosaurus from Como, Italy is dated to the Mid Triassic, about 225 million years ago. Its fossils are also known from Spain and other European locations. The large spread fingers may have been encased in tough skin and connective tissue in life, to form flipper-like structures. The skull is wedge-shaped and the neck is flexible but relatively short.

The nothosaurs are named after their best-known member, the 3m/10ft *Nothosaurus* of Europe and West Asia. *Lariosaurus* was much smaller, just 60cm/24in long. Some dwarf types of nothosaurs were just 20cm/ 8in long. Nothosaurs had partly webbed feet. Larger nothosaurs probably lived in a similar way to seals today, swimming fast after prey such as fish, which they seized in their long, pointed, fang-like teeth. Then they would haul out to rest on land. *Lariosaurus* was less aquatic than other types. It may have foraged among rockpools or shallow seaweed beds, slithering and paddling after small victims such as young fish and shrimps.

Name: *Lariosaurus*
Meaning: Lario (Lake Como) lizard or reptile
Grouping: Reptile, Nothosaur, Nothosaurid
Informal ID: Nothosaur
Fossil size: Slab width 25cm/10in
Reconstructed size: Head–tail length up to 60cm/24in
Habitat: Coastal waters
Time span: Middle Triassic, 225 million years ago
Main fossil sites: Europe
Occurrence: ◆ ◆

Kuehneosaurus

Vertebrae (3) —

A type of 'flying lizard' or 'gliding lizard', *Kuehneosaurus* fossils come mainly from England. The ribs were long and hollow and directed sideways, being longest in the middle of each side. This produced a wing-like framework that in life was probably covered by tough skin, to give a gliding surface. The modern flying lizard of Southeast Asia, *Draco volans*, probably leads a similar lifestyle. It uses its gliding ability to swoop from the upper part of one tree to the lower part of a nearby one, in order to find fresh feeding areas and, especially, to escape from danger. However the ribs of the modern *Draco* are jointed with the vertebral column so the wings can be folded against the sides of the body. The 'wingspan' of *Kuehneosaurus* is estimated at about 30cm/12in, being half its total length.

Left: This specimen of Kuehneosaurus shows mainly the long, slim, hollow, light ribs, plus a femur, or thigh bone. This genus is regarded as a primitive member of the group, not advanced enough to belong to the 'true' lizards.

Femur

Ribs

Name: *Kuehneosaurus*
Meaning: Kühne's (Kuehne's) reptile
Grouping: Reptile, Squamate, Kuehneosaurid
Informal ID: Flying lizard
Fossil size: Slab 15cm/ 6in across
Reconstructed size: Head–tail length 60cm/24in
Habitat: Woodland, scrub
Time span: Late Triassic, 210 million years ago
Main fossil sites: Europe
Occurrence: ◆

Ardeosaurus

Name: *Ardeosaurus*
Meaning: Water lizard/reptile
Grouping: Reptile,
Squamate, Lacertilid,
Ardeosaur
Informal ID: Gecko
Fossil size: Slab 9cm/
3½in across
Reconstructed size: Total
length 20cm/8in
Habitat: Woods, forests
Time span: Late Jurassic,
150–140 million years ago
Main fossil sites: Throughout
Europe
Occurrence: ◆ ◆

The ardeosaurs are better known as geckos – lizards named from their sharp, bark-like calls. Today, the gecko family is huge, with approaching 700, mainly tropical, species around the world. The geckos were also one of the first modern lizard groups to appear, in the Late Jurassic Period, along with others, such as skinks, iguanas and monitor lizards, or varanids. However, lizard-like reptiles had been around since the Early Triassic Period and even the Late Permian, more than 250 million years ago. *Ardeosaurus* probably lived largely nocturnally, very much like its present-day equivalents. The large orbits (eye sockets) in the skull show that it had big eyes, probably to enable it to see well at night as it snapped up insects, spiders, grubs and similar small prey.

Above: This type specimen cast from Bavaria, southern Germany, is dated to the Late Jurassic Period, some 150 million years ago. It has been preserved in the very fine-grained 'lithographic' limestone that also trapped the early bird Archaeopteryx *and the tiny dinosaur* Compsognathus. *Most of the tail of this individual is missing.*

Anapsids, diapsids and synapsids

Reptiles, both living and extinct, have been classified partly according to openings in the skull bone behind the orbits (eye sockets). This is a useful feature often preserved in fossils, but some authorities doubt its true value in determining evolutionary relationships.
• Anapsids, chiefly chelonians – turtles, terrapins and tortoises – have no such openings. This is regarded as the primitive state.
• Diapsids typically have two openings (fenestrae) on either side behind the eye socket, one above the other. However, in some types such as snakes further evolution has merged these two into one.
• Diapsids include most living and extinct reptiles, such as crocodiles, dinosaurs (and, therefore, birds), ichthyosaurs, plesiosaurs, lizards and snakes.
• Synapsids had one opening low down on the skull behind the orbit. They include the mammal-like reptiles (pelycosaurs, therapsids) and their descendants, the mammals.

Columber

The snake group, Serpentes, is placed with lizards in the major reptile group Squamata. The fossil history of snakes is far shorter than that for lizards, stretching back to the Late Cretaceous Period about 80 million years ago. The group origins are obscure: two suggestions include evolution from some type of burrowing lizard, hence the loss of limbs; or evolution from a form of aquatic lizard. The snake skull is usually low and squat, with a flattened forehead and loose jaw articulation (joint). This allows a very wide gape and 'dislocation' of the jaws to permit swallowing large prey whole, since the teeth are slim and fang-like and cannot bite off lumps or chew.

Name: *Columber kargi*
Meaning: Kargi's whip-snake
Grouping: Reptile,
Squamate, Serpent
Informal ID: Whip-snake
Fossil size: Slab width
30cm/12in
Reconstructed size: Total
length 80–90cm/32–36in
Habitat: Forests
Time span: (This specimen)
Late Miocene, 8 million years
ago. Genus continues today.
Main fossil sites: Europe
Occurrence: ◆

Right: This specimen, Columber kargi, is in Late Miocene rocks from Oenigen, Switzerland. The snake skeleton has typically just a skull and a very elongated spinal column of many vertebrae (backbones), sometimes more than 400, mostly with arched ribs.

Ribs

Skull

Cervical (neck) vertebrae

Caudal (tail) vertebrae

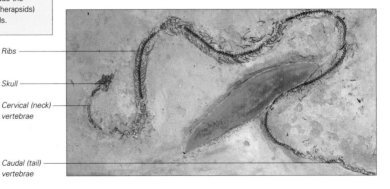

MARINE REPTILES – ICHTHYOSAURS

The ichthyosaurs, or 'fish-reptiles', were the reptiles most highly adapted to aquatic life. They appeared abruptly in the Early Triassic Period and by the Late Triassic to Late Jurassic they were among the dominant large predators in many seas. However, they declined during the Cretaceous and had all but disappeared by the end-of-Cretaceous (K-T) mass extinction that marked the end of the Mesozoic Era.

Ichthyosaurus

This group of marine reptiles is named after the medium-sized *Ichthyosaurus*, which grew up to 3m/10ft in length. Many species have been assigned to this genus, sometimes on the flimsiest of fossil evidence. The genus is said to have persisted in a variety of different forms from the Early Jurassic Period to the Early Cretaceous Period, a time span covering more than 80 million years. A 'typical' *Ichthyosaurus* was shaped like a fish or dolphin – making it an example of 'convergent evolution'. This is when different organisms come to resemble each other due to a similar habitat and/or lifestyle. The jaws of *Ichthyosaurus* were very long, slim and pointed – similar to a dolphin's beak, only more exaggerated. These predators were armed with many small, sharp teeth for impaling slippery prey such as fish and squid. The eyes of many types were large, indicating that they hunted at night or deep in the gloomy water where light penetration was poor. All four limbs were modified as paddles, with the front pair usually larger than the rear ones. These were used mainly for steering, manoeuvring and braking. A dolphin-like fin on the back prevented the animal leaning or rolling to the side. The caudal vertebrae (tail backbones) angled down at the end to support a large upright fin, similar to the tail of a fish. Swishing this from side to side provided the thrust for speedy swimming.

Name: *Ichthyosaurus*
Meaning: Fish reptile (fish lizard)
Grouping: Reptile, Ichthyosaur
Informal ID: Ichthyosaur
Fossil size: Slab length 1m/3¼ft
Reconstructed size: Total length up to 3m/10ft
Habitat: Seas
Time span: Chiefly Jurassic, 200–150 million years ago
Main fossil sites: Worldwide
Occurrence: ◆ ◆ ◆

Below: This Early Jurassic ichthyosaur is Stenopterygius, and it is from the Early Jurassic Posidonia Shale of Holzmaden, Germany. Some of the ring-like vertebrae have been displaced during preservation, as has the end of the rear (pelvic) flipper. Long, thin ribs have also been scattered across the main body region. The front flipper shows numerous digit bones set closely together, which in life would have been bound with muscle and connective tissue.

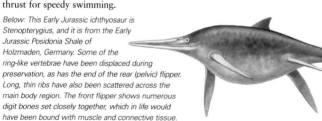

Left: Shonisaurus *from the Late Triassic was one of the largest ichthyosaurs, reaching lengths of 15m/50ft – as big as some great whales of today.*

| Long, slim jaws | Small sharp | Large orbit | Shoulder girdle | | Hip girdle | Displaced | Rear flipper |
| Pointed snout | teeth | (eye socket) | Front flipper | Ribs | | vertebrae | Angle in tail |

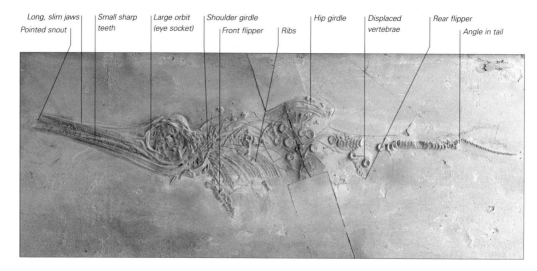

Ophthalmosaurus

One of the larger ichthyosaurs, *Ophthalmosaurus* was more than 3m/10ft long. (Some ichthyosaurs reached huge sizes, in excess of 15m/50ft in length.) The genus was named after its remarkable distinguishing feature – its huge eyes. Each eyeball was more than 10cm/4in across and was housed in a large orbit whose deepest recess almost touched that of the orbit in the other side of the animal's skull. Around the orbit was a ring arrangement of rectangular to wedge-shaped bony plates, known as the sclerotic ring (see also below right). All ichthyosaurs had this structure, which probably protected the soft eyeball tissues from excessive water pressure at depth. However, the ring was very large and pronounced in *Ophthalmosaurus*.

Below: Ichthyosaur vertebrae (backbones) have a characteristically disc-like construction, with pronounced dished (concave) surfaces. The two larger fossil specimens shown here have a slight constriction around the side, producing an hour-glass shape, and are from Peterborough, England, and they are probably from Ophthalmosaurus itself. The smaller one for comparison is from an unidentified species of ichthyosaur.

Name: *Ophthalmosaurus*
Meaning: Eye reptile (eye lizard)
Grouping: Reptile, Ichthyosaur, Ichthyosaurid
Informal ID: Ichthyosaur
Fossil size: Eye ring 16cm/6¼in across, largest vertebra 8cm/3⅛in across
Reconstructed size: Length 3.5m/11½ft
Habitat: Seas
Time span: Middle to Late Jurassic, 160–140 million years ago
Main fossil sites: Chiefly North and South America, Europe
Occurrence: ◆ ◆

Ichthyosaur details and lifestyle

Ichthyosaurs were air-breathers like other reptiles. Their nostrils were placed just in front of their eyes, and they would hold their breath while diving to locate and chase prey. Many details are known about their soft body tissues due to the remarkable preservation of specimens at sites such as Holzmaden, Germany. Slow decay has produced carbon film outlines, which delineate the shapes of the flippers and the outline of the dorsal (back) and caudal (tail) fins, all as they were in life. Preserved skin shows that it was smooth, not scaly. In addition there is evidence for live birth rather than egg-laying, with many fossils of young developing within their mother's body. There are even remarkable specimens of babies being born tail-first (as in modern whales and dolphins).

Above: Furrow-surfaced coprolites – fossilized droppings – of ichthyosaurs contain remains of fish scales and bones, as well as the hard parts such as the 'beaks' of molluscs such as squid.

Below: This ichthyosaur skull clearly shows the protective sclerotic ring around the eye (see above and right) and the very long and sharp-toothed jaws resembling needle pliers. Specimen length 50cm/20in.

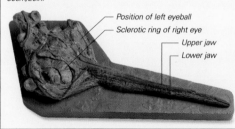

— Position of left eyeball
— Sclerotic ring of right eye
— Upper jaw
— Lower jaw

Below: The sclerotic ring of Ophthalmosaurus probably formed an anti-pressure guard around the exposed part of the eyeball. Such huge eyes were probably an adaptation for hunting prey either at night or at depth.

MARINE REPTILES – PLESIOSAURS AND THEIR KIN

Plesiosaurs were the greatest ocean-going reptiles of the Jurassic and Cretaceous seas at the time when dinosaurs ruled the land. There were two groups. The plesiosaurs were long-necked with smallish heads and hunted smaller prey than the pliosaurs. The pliosaurs had much larger heads and mouths armed with sharp teeth. All died out with the dinosaurs, some 65 million years ago.

Pliosaur

A typical plesiosaur or pliosaur had a tubby body, four paddle-like limbs, and a shortish, tapering tail. An Early Jurassic pliosaur was *Macroplata*, and a Later Jurassic one *Peloneustes*, both 3–4m/ 10–13ft in overall length. During the following Cretaceous Period, some pliosaurs reached massive proportions. One was *Liopleurodon*, whose size estimates range up to 15–20m/50–65ft plus from nose to tail, and its weight a staggering 50 or even 100 tonnes. If so, this would place it as the largest predator ever to live on Earth – larger even than today's record-holder, the sperm whale. Pliosaurs seized substantial prey, such as big ammonites and fish, as well as other marine reptiles, too, with their rows of sharp, back-curved fangs.

Above: A vertebra (backbone) from a large pliosaur, dated to the Middle Jurassic, showing the rounded cotton-reel-like shape that is common in many Mesozoic marine reptiles.

Name: Pliosaur (genus unknown)
Meaning: Further lizard
Grouping: Reptilia, Plesiosaur, Pliosaur
Informal ID: Pliosaur, short-necked plesiosaur
Fossil size: Thigh bone 50cm/20in; tooth 10cm/4in
Reconstructed size: Nose–tail length 5–10m/ 16½–33ft
Habitat: Seas and oceans
Time span: Much of Mesozoic, 250–65 million years ago
Main fossil sites: Worldwide
Occurrence: ◆ ◆ ◆

Plesiosaurs

These marine dinosaurs did not reach the massive size of pliosaurs. However, they did develop amazingly long necks. *Elasmosaurus* from eastern Asia and North America reached 14m/46ft in length, and more than half of this was its neck. This is a vertebra from the plesiosaur (long-necked type) *Plesiosaurus*, which grew to about 2.2m/7¼ft in total length. This is a similar size to many modern dolphins.

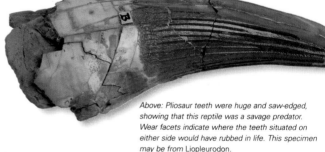

Above: Pliosaur teeth were huge and saw-edged, showing that this reptile was a savage predator. Wear facets indicate where the teeth situated on either side would have rubbed in life. This specimen may be from Liopleurodon.

Below: One of several possible paddle limb bones of a pliosaur from the Middle Jurassic Period. It may be the femur (equivalent to the thigh bone) at the base of the left rear paddle.

Head of bone

Shaft of bone

Articular (joint) surface

Coniasaurus

Coniasaurs were probably aquatic reptiles similar in overall appearance to a small mosasaur or lizard. Their relationships with the mosasaurs and aigialosaurs are not clear, but from various skull and skeletal features they are thought to be members of the larger squamate group, which included lizards and snakes as well as mosasaurs. Coniasaurs were probably predators on small fish, young ammonites and similar animals. Their remains were once known only from England, but from the 1980s they have been discovered in North America, in the Eagle Ford Group of Texas (Travis, Bell and McClennan counties in the Balcones Fault zone and farther north in Dallas County).

Name: *Coniasaurus*
Meaning: Cretaceous reptile
Grouping: Reptile,
Squamate, Coniasaur
Informal ID: Coniasaur
Fossil size: 10cm/4in
Reconstructed size:
Nose–tail length 50cm/20in
when adult
Habitat: Seas
Time span: Late
Cretaceous, 85–65 million
years ago
Main fossil sites: Europe,
North America
Occurrence: ◆

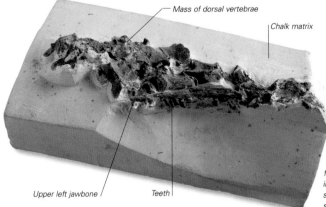

Mass of dorsal vertebrae

Chalk matrix

Upper left jawbone

Teeth

Left: The upper left maxilla (jawbone) of a juvenile of the best-studied (although still poorly known) species, Coniasaurus crassidens. *The animal's upper front teeth are pointed, but those situated behind are increasingly rounded and blunt or bulbous. This specimen is from the Cretaceous chalk beds of Sussex, southern England.*

Mosasaurus

Mosasaurs were large, four-flippered, slim, long-tailed, predatory marine lizards, named after the Meuse region of the Netherlands where the first scientifically described fossil specimen was dug from a chalk mine in the 1770s. They were close cousins of the varanids, or monitor lizards, of today, which include the Nile monitor and huge Komodo dragon. Mosasaurs, along with pliosaurs, dominated the Late Cretaceous seas, and although the two look similar, they were from different reptile groups.

Below: This is the lower jaw bone, with teeth in place, from the species Mosasaurus gracilis, meaning 'slender mosasaur'. Its teeth are well spaced, like a crocodile's today, but they are much sharper. The V-shaped patterns of mosasaur tooth marks appear on many prey creatures of the time, including the shells of ammonites.

Name: *Mosasaurus*
Meaning: Meuse
lizard
Grouping: Reptile,
Squamate, Lacertid, Varanid
Informal ID: Mosasaur
Fossil size: Lower jaw
38cm/15in long
Reconstructed size:
Nose–tail length up to
10m/33ft
Habitat: Seas
Time span: Mid to Late
Cretaceous, 100–65 million
years ago
Main fossil sites: Europe,
North America
Occurrence: ◆ ◆

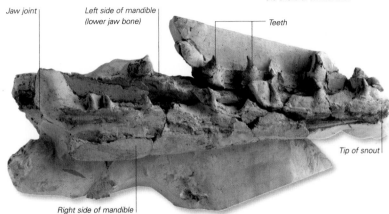

Jaw joint

Left side of mandible
(lower jaw bone)

Teeth

Tip of snout

Right side of mandible

DINOSAURS AND THEIR KIN

Dinosaurs were members of the reptile group called archosaurs and dominated the land from the Mid to Late Triassic Period, around 225 million years ago, to the sudden end-of-Cretaceous mass-extinction event of 65 million years ago. One of their key features was legs held directly below the body, as in birds and mammals, rather than angled out to the side, like other reptiles such as lizards and crocodiles.

Chirotherium

Chirotherium looked similar to a dinosaur, and probably belonged to the same major group of reptiles as the dinosaurs, called the archosaurs, although it lived just before the dinosaur group appeared. It had a large mouth with sharp teeth for catching varied prey, including smaller reptiles. *Chirotherium* usually walked on all fours, although its rear legs were larger and stronger than the front ones, with its tail held out behind, rather than dragging. Its legs were straight, in the upright posture of dinosaurs. Fossil bones of *Chirotherium* have not been found. Its restoration comes from the remains of *Ticinosuchus*, which had similar feet.

Right: The print is a mould fossil, where sediment filled in the impression and then hardened, and so is shown here effectively upside down. It is a rear right foot with four smaller claw-tipped toes. What looks like the big toe is the smallest one set at an angle.

Claw of outer digit
(smallest toe)

Claws of four
larger digits

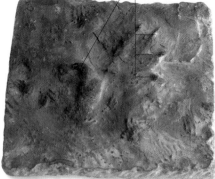

Name: *Chirotherium*
Meaning: Hand beast (footprint is similar to the impression of a human hand)
Grouping: Reptile, Archosaur, possibly Pseudosuchian
Informal ID: Chirotherium, 'pre-dinosaur'
Fossil size: Print about 15cm/6in across
Reconstructed size: Nose to tail length 2–2.5m/6½–8¼ft
Habitat: Dry scrub
Time span: Triassic, 250–203 million years ago
Main fossil sites: Throughout Europe
Occurrence: ◆

Grallator (dinosaur footprint)

Below: This 10cm-/4in-long specimen is dated to 207–206 million years ago. The relative length of the toes suggests a Coelophysis-type carnivore, which would have had a smallish head, flexible neck, slim body, long rear legs and a very long tail.

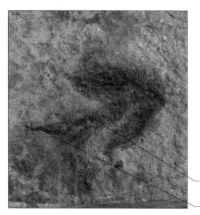

Long central toe

Claw impression

Grallator is an ichnogenus – in other words, it is named from trace fossils rather than from the remains of the creature itself. The footprints known as *Grallator* were made by an unknown dinosaur. However, the size and the shape of the prints allow scientists to make certain assumptions, and indicate that the creature was probably an early meat-eating or theropod-type of dinosaur. It would have measured around 3m/10ft in length and weighed in at some 35–40kg/77–88lb, similar to the well-known *Coelophysis*, which lived about 20 million years earlier. The prints of several individual animals often occur in lines or trackways, showing that this was probably a group-dwelling or herding dinosaur.

Name: *Grallator* (print fossil)
Meaning: Stilt walker
Grouping: Reptile, Dinosaur, Theropod
Informal ID: Grallator
Fossil size: Prints up to 17cm/6¾in long
Reconstructed size: Nose–tail length 3m/10ft
Habitat: Varied land habitats
Time span: Late Triassic and Early Jurassic, around 200 million years ago
Main fossil sites: North America, Europe
Occurrence: ◆ ◆ ◆

Gastroliths

Gastroliths, or stomach stones, are from the digestive system of larger plant-eating dinosaurs, especially members of the sauropod group, such as *Diplodocus*, *Brachiosaurus* and *Apatosaurus* ('Brontosaurus'). Such dinosaurs had a very small head and weak, rake-like teeth that could only pull in vegetation, which was swallowed without chewing. Stones were swallowed, too. In the stomach (gizzard), powerful muscular writhing actions worked like a grinding mill to make the stones crush and pulp the food for better digestion. In the process, the stones became rounded and shiny. In some fairly complete dinosaur skeletons, a pile of gastroliths is located in the position where the stomach would have been in life. Some crocodilians also swallow stones, to alter their buoyancy.

Below: This gastrolith is from Early Cretaceous rock called Paluxy Sandstone, from Carter County, Oklahoma, USA. It was associated with dinosaur fossils and shows the typical polished surface with worn, rounded corners.

Name: Gastroliths (trace fossils)
Meaning: Stomach stones
Grouping: Usually associated with large plant-eating sauropod dinosaurs
Informal ID: Stomach stones
Fossil size: From pea-sized to as large as soccer balls
Reconstructed size: —
Habitat: Dinosaur gizzard/stomach
Time span: Mainly Jurassic and Cretaceous, 200–65 million years ago
Main fossil sites: Worldwide
Occurrence: ◆ ◆ ◆

Diplodocus

Name: *Diplodocus*
Meaning: Double beam
Grouping: Reptile, Dinosaur, Sauropod, Diplodocid
Informal ID: Diplodocus
Fossil size: Skull length 60cm/24in
Reconstructed size: Nose–tail length 27m/88ft
Habitat: Scattered woodlands, shrubs
Time span: Late Jurassic, 150–140 million years ago
Main fossil sites: North America
Occurrence: ◆ ◆

The sauropod dinosaurs were mostly huge, with a small head, long neck, bulky body, four column-like legs and a long, whippy tail. *Diplodocus* was one of the slimmer types, weighing 'only' 15–20 tonnes. But it is also one of the longest dinosaurs for which relatively complete fossils are known. It lived in North America during the heyday of the sauropods, the Late Jurassic Period, around the same time as the mega-predator *Allosaurus*. Finds of numerous individuals preserved together suggest that sauropods lived and travelled in herds of young and adults. *Diplodocus* is named 'double beam' for the two ski-like chevrons on the undersides of the caudal vertebrae – the bones in the middle section of its tail.

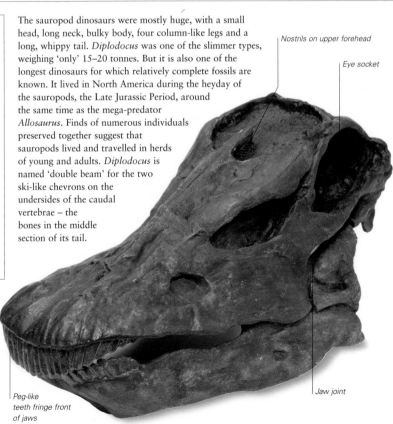

Nostrils on upper forehead

Eye socket

Jaw joint

Peg-like teeth fringe front of jaws

Right: The skull of Diplodocus is low and rather horse-like. Slender, peg- or pencil-like teeth formed a fringe at the front of the mouth, but there are no rear chewing teeth. The front teeth probably worked like a garden rake to strip leaves from branches.

PREDATORY DINOSAURS

The dinosaurs shown here were all members of the theropod group, which was almost exclusively carnivorous, or meat-eating. Tyrannosaurus *had long enjoyed fame as the largest predator to walk the Earth. Recently, however,* Carcharodontosaurus *and the even bigger* Giganotosaurus *had taken this record. The dromaeosaurs were much smaller but their fossils suggest that they hunted in packs.*

Tyrannosaurus

Name: *Tyrannosaurus*
Meaning: Tyrant lizard
Grouping: Reptile, Dinosaur, Theropod, Tetanuran
Informal ID: T-rex
Fossil size: Phalanx 8cm/3¼in; tooth tip 5cm/2in; centrum 6cm/2⅓in
Reconstructed size:
Nose–tail length 12m/40ft
Habitat: Varied land habitats
Time span: Late Cretaceous, 75–65 million years ago
Main fossil sites:
North America
Occurrence: ◆ ◆

The symbol of a mighty hunting dinosaur, *Tyrannosaurus* weighed 6 tonnes or more, yet could probably run faster than any human today, as suggested by the spacing of its preserved footprints. It was one of the very last dinosaurs, surviving to the great end-of-Cretaceous extinction 65 million years ago. Bite marks of its teeth have been found on the plant-eating dinosaur *Triceratops*. Its large, strong teeth and thick, powerful neck suggest that it tackled living prey, biting with incredible power and pulling or 'sawing' its head from side to side to slice out chunks of flesh.

Below: This phalanx, or toe bone, comes from the famous Hell Creek Formation rocks in Harding County, South Dakota, USA. Many Tyrannosaurus remains have been located in the area.

Ball-shaped proximal joint (towards toe tip)

Shaft

Hole for nerve or blood vessel

Medial joint socket (nearest to limb)

Left: The centrum is the central part of a vertebra, or backbone. In many dinosaurs the end caudal, or tail, vertebra lacked the usual muscle-anchoring flanges of the other vertebrae within the main body, and were reduced to simpler, almost cylindrical shapes. This specimen is probably from a juvenile's tail.

Joint surface with neighbouring vertebra

Big teeth
The mouth of *Tyrannosaurus* probably contained anywhere between 50 and 60 teeth at any one time. The longest projected some 15cm/6in above the jaw, with the same length, or more, beneath, firmly anchored within the jaw bone itself. As the animal's old teeth wore down or were broken, new ones grew to replace them, giving the mouth something of a gappy appearance.

Broken lower tooth merged into root

Carcharodontosaurus

Even larger than *Tyrannosaurus* (opposite), this species is named *Carcharodontosaurus saharicus*, since its original fossils, found in 1927, come from the Sahara Desert. In 1996, larger and more complete remains were discovered in the Tegana Formation region of K'Sar-es-Souk Province, south of Taouz, Morocco. These specimens reveal a very large predator indeed, but from a slightly different meat-eater group, being a closer cousin of the North American, Late Jurassic carnivore *Allosaurus*.

Below: The tooth of Carcharodontosaurus is curved backwards (recurved), pointing to the rear of the mouth, to prevent struggling prey from slipping out. As with the Tyrannosaurus *tooth, this is only the end of the visible portion, probably a shed (discarded) specimen.*

Name: *Carcharodontosaurus*
Meaning: Shark-tooth lizard
Grouping: Reptile, Dinosaur, Theropod, Allosaur
Informal ID: Carcharodontosaurus
Fossil size: Tooth tip 6cm/2¼in
Reconstructed size: Nose–tail length 14m/46ft
Habitat: Floodplains, marshes, swamps
Time span: Middle Cretaceous, 110–100 million years ago
Main fossil sites: North Africa
Occurrence: ◆

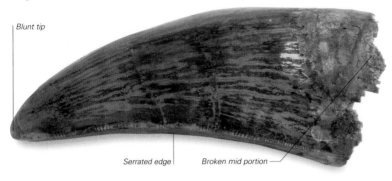

Blunt tip

Serrated edge | Broken mid portion

Dromaeosaurus

Name: *Dromaeosaurus*
Meaning: Running or swift lizard
Grouping: Reptile, Dinosaur, Theropod, Dromaeosaur
Informal ID: Raptor
Fossil size: Claw length 5cm/2in
Reconstructed size: Nose–tail length 2m/6½ft
Habitat: Varied land habitats, mainly woodlands
Time span: Middle to Late Cretaceous, 110–65 million years ago, for the group
Main fossil sites: Mostly Northern Hemisphere
Occurrence: ◆

The dromaeosaurs were medium-sized carnivorous dinosaurs of the Mid to Late Cretaceous Period, which were often called raptors, meaning 'hunters' or 'thieves'. They include the well-known *Velociraptor*, the human-sized *Deinonychus*, whose name means 'terrible claw', and the larger, 5m-/16½ft-long *Utahraptor*, which had large eyes and long, grasping hands. Most of these dinosaurs ran quickly on their back legs and had strong arms with long-clawed fingers. *Dromaeosaurus* was the first of the group to be named, but it is among the least well known from the fossil record. Remains of several *Deinonychus* have been found together, indicating that it may have hunted in packs, as the dinosaur version of today's wolves. The exciting feature of the group is the 'terrible claw' or 'killing claw' on each foot.

Below: The extremely effective 'killing claw' was found on the second toe of each rear foot. Usually it was held up, clear of the ground. But it could be swung down fast in an arc at the toe joints as the dinosaur kicked out, to slash wounds in its prey or to inflict terrible injuries on its enemies.

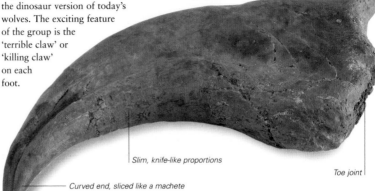

Slim, knife-like proportions

Toe joint

Curved end, sliced like a machete

OSTRICH- AND BIRD-FOOT DINOSAURS

The ostrich-dinosaurs, or ornithomimosaurs, appeared late in the Age of Dinosaurs. Their skeletons are remarkably similar in size and overall proportions to the largest living bird, the ostrich, so they were probably the fastest runners of their time. Bird-foot dinosaurs, or ornithopods, were plant-eaters and included one of the best-known and most-studied dinosaurs of all, Iguanodon.

Ornithomimus

Built for speed, *Ornithomimus* walked and ran on its two long, slim, yet powerful rear legs. The legs' proportions were typical of a sprinter, with a shortish, well-muscled thigh, longer shin and lengthy foot bones, but comparatively short, stubby, clawed toes. Like other ostrich-dinosaurs, *Ornithomimus* had a long, low head, large eyes and a beak-like mouth that lacked any teeth. The dinosaur probably snapped up any kind of food available, from plant seeds and leaves to small creatures, such as insects, worms and little lizards. The ostrich-dinosaurs evolved fairly late in the Age of Dinosaurs.

Below: This bone is the terminal phalanx at the toe-tip. The claw is flattened and narrow, rather than sharp, probably to provide good traction as the dinosaur sped along, rather than for slashing at prey. Only the three middle toes of each rear foot touched the ground, with the central toe being longest.

— Terminal joint

| Flattened base of claw

| Joint with medial phalanx

Name: Ornithomimus
Meaning: Bird mimic
Grouping: Reptile, Dinosaur, Theropod, Ornithomimosaur
Informal ID: Ostrich-dinosaur
Fossil size: Bone and claw 11cm/4⅓in long
Reconstructed size: Nose–tail length 4m/13ft
Habitat: Open scrub
Time span: Ostrich-dinosaurs: Mainly Late Cretaceous, 85–65 million years ago
Main fossil sites: Chiefly Asia, North America
Occurrence: ◆ ◆

Thescelosaurus

A medium-sized plant-eater, *Thescelosaurus* was probably a cousin of *Iguanodon*, although it has also been linked to another family of ornithopods called the hypsilophodonts. It had a smallish head, strong body, shorter front legs, powerful rear legs and a long, tapering tail. The beak-like front of its mouth indicates that it snipped and cropped vegetation, which it chewed with long rows of crushing cheek teeth. One celebrated specimen of *Thescelosaurus*, nicknamed 'Willo', supposedly has its heart preserved as a fossil, an incredibly rare instance of soft-tissue preservation. However, the 'heart' may be a natural mineral formation.

Left: The well-preserved vertebra (backbone) buts up against those in front and behind mainly at the centrum (broad part). Just above this is a hole, the spinal canal, through which the animal's spinal cord (main nerve) ran. The dorsal and transverse processes were mainly attachment surfaces for the animal's back muscles.

— Dorsal process

— Transverse, or lateral, processes

— Zygapophysis joint

— Spinal canal

— Centrum

Name: Thescelosaurus
Meaning: Marvellous or wonderful reptile
Grouping: Reptile, Dinosaur, Ornithopod
Informal ID: Thescelosaurus
Fossil size: Vertebra 6cm/2¼in long
Reconstructed size: Nose–tail length 3–4m/ 10–13ft
Habitat: Woods, scrub
Time span: Late Cretaceous, 70–65 million years ago
Main fossil sites: North America
Occurrence: ◆

Iguanodon

A large dinosaur fossil at an Early–Mid Cretaceous site in Western Europe may well be from *Iguanodon*. Large herds of these big plant-eaters roamed the region for tens of millions of years. *Iguanodon* probably stooped down to carry its 5-tonne bulk on all fours, but it might also have reared up to run mainly on its larger back legs. One of its special distinguishing features was a bony spike on the thumb (the first digit of the front paw), which it might have used as a weapon with which to jab at enemies. As part of *Iguanodon*'s original reconstruction in the nineteenth century, this spike was erroneously placed on the animal's nose!

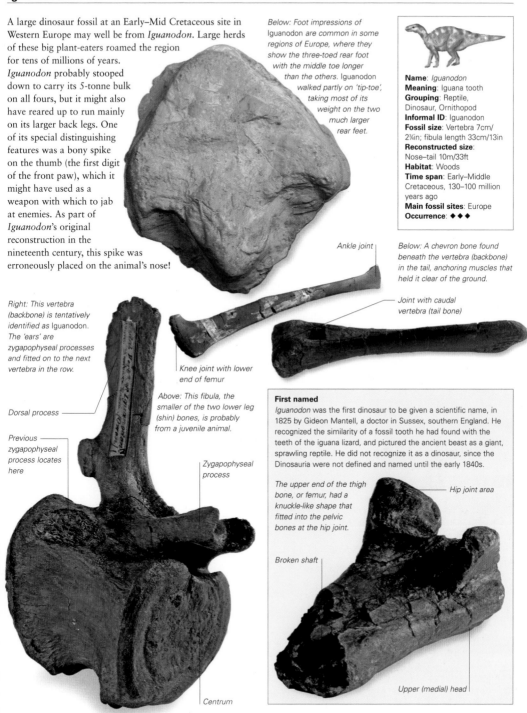

Below: Foot impressions of Iguanodon *are common in some regions of Europe, where they show the three-toed rear foot with the middle toe longer than the others.* Iguanodon *walked partly on 'tip-toe', taking most of its weight on the two much larger rear feet.*

Name: *Iguanodon*
Meaning: Iguana tooth
Grouping: Reptile, Dinosaur, Ornithopod
Informal ID: Iguanodon
Fossil size: Vertebra 7cm/2¾in; fibula length 33cm/13in
Reconstructed size: Nose–tail 10m/33ft
Habitat: Woods
Time span: Early–Middle Cretaceous, 130–100 million years ago
Main fossil sites: Europe
Occurrence: ◆ ◆ ◆

Ankle joint

Below: A chevron bone found beneath the vertebra (backbone) in the tail, anchoring muscles that held it clear of the ground.

Joint with caudal vertebra (tail bone)

Right: This vertebra (backbone) is tentatively identified as Iguanodon. The 'ears' are zygapophyseal processes and fitted on to the next vertebra in the row.

Dorsal process

Previous zygapophyseal process locates here

Knee joint with lower end of femur

Above: This fibula, the smaller of the two lower leg (shin) bones, is probably from a juvenile animal.

Zygapophyseal process

First named
Iguanodon was the first dinosaur to be given a scientific name, in 1825 by Gideon Mantell, a doctor in Sussex, southern England. He recognized the similarity of a fossil tooth he had found with the teeth of the iguana lizard, and pictured the ancient beast as a giant, sprawling reptile. He did not recognize it as a dinosaur, since the Dinosauria were not defined and named until the early 1840s.

The upper end of the thigh bone, or femur, had a knuckle-like shape that fitted into the pelvic bones at the hip joint.

Hip joint area

Broken shaft

Upper (medial) head

Centrum

DINOSAURS AND PTEROSAURS

Among the last of the dinosaurs were the hadrosaurs, or duck-bills, which probably evolved from
Iguanodon-like ancestors. They flourished especially in North American and Asia. Pterosaurs have been
traditionally regarded as flying 'reptiles', but most had furry bodies and were probably warm-blooded.
Different types lived all through the Mesozoic Era and perished at its end.

Edmontosaurus

Joint with finger

Joint with wrist

Ossified tendon

Name: *Edmontosaurus*
Meaning: Edmonton lizard
Grouping: Reptile, Dinosaur, Hadrosaur
Informal ID: Duck-billed dinosaur
Fossil size: Tooth battery 6cm/2¼in long; metacarpal 31cm/12¼in
Reconstructed size: Nose–tail length 13m/42½ft
Habitat: Wooded areas, valleys, hillsides
Time span: Late Cretaceous, 75–65 million years ago
Main fossil sites: North America
Occurrence: ◆ ◆

Below: Viewed from inside the mouth, the lower part of this jaw bone is missing, which reveals new teeth growing and pushing up to replace the old ones. This renewal was a continuous process. The teeth have sharp ridges for grinding plant matter.

Above: This metacarpal (hand bone) has ossified tendons – the tough, stringy ends of muscles that have, themselves, became mineralized like bone during life.

One of the largest of the hadrosaurs, *Edmontosaurus* had the typical flattened, toothless, duck-beak-like front to its mouth, with batteries of hundreds of huge cheek teeth behind for grinding its tough plant food. Fossils of many individuals of this dinosaur have been found together, and remains come from widely spaced locations in North America, from Colorado to as far north as Alaska, leading to suggestions that it migrated in huge herds.

Triceratops

The largest of the ceratopsians, or horned dinosaurs, was the well-known *Triceratops*. It was probably hunted by the meat-eating *Tyrannosaurus*, and both were among the very last of the dinosaurs, surviving right up to the mass-extinction event of 65 million years ago. Its 50 or so cheek teeth were very small compared with the size of the dinosaur's massive head, with its nasal horn, twin eyebrow horns and wide, ruff-like neck frill. The front of *Triceratops'* mouth was a toothless beak used for snipping and plucking vegetation. The remains of several *Triceratops* of different sizes found in the same location indicate that this dinosaur herded in mixed-age groups.

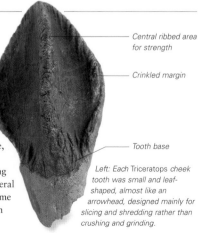

Central ribbed area for strength

Crinkled margin

Tooth base

Left: Each Triceratops *cheek tooth was small and leaf-shaped, almost like an arrowhead, designed mainly for slicing and shredding rather than crushing and grinding.*

Name: *Triceratops*
Meaning: Three-horned face
Grouping: Reptile, Dinosaur, Ceratopsian
Informal ID: Triceratops
Fossil size: Tooth 3.5cm/1½in tall
Reconstructed size: Nose–tail length 9m/30ft
Habitat: Woodlands, forests
Time span: Late Cretaceous Period, 70–65 million years ago
Main fossil sites: North America
Occurrence: ◆ ◆

Pterosaur (unidentified)

Pterosaurs were the principal flying creatures during much of the Mesozoic Era (birds evolved at the end of the Jurassic Period but did not appear to attain great size or numbers until the Tertiary Period). Some pterosaurs, such as *Pteranodon* and *Quetzalcoatlus*, were the largest flying creatures ever, with wingspans in excess of 12m/40ft. The front limbs had evolved into wings, held out mainly by the very elongated bones of the fourth finger. A pterosaur's body had many weight-saving features, including tube-like, hollow bones – as in modern birds – so their remains are very rare and fragmentary.

Name: Pterosaur
Meaning: Wing lizard
Grouping: Pterosaur
Informal ID: Pterodactyl
Fossil size: Fragment length 4cm/1½in
Reconstructed size: Wingspan 2m/6½ft
Habitat: Coastal regions
Time span: Group spanned almost the whole Mesozoic Era, 225–65 million years ago
Main fossil sites: Worldwide
Occurrence: ◆

Right: This may be a fragment from the ulna, one of the lower arm bones, which would have been found at the front of the wing. The arm, wrist and hand bones held out the inner section of wing, but the outer half of each wing's span was supported by the creature's fourth finger. The fossil, from near Oxford, England, dates from the Bathonian age of the Mid Jurassic Period, about 160 million years ago.

Fragmented end ————————

———— Shaft

Rhamphorhynchus

Name: *Rhamphorhynchus*
Meaning: Beak snout
Grouping: Pterosaur, Rhamphorhynchoid
Informal ID: Pterodactyl
Fossil size: Total width approx 1m/3¼ft
Reconstructed size: Wingspan up to 1.8m/6ft
Habitat: Coasts, lagoons
Time span: Late Jurassic, 170–140 million years ago
Main fossil sites: Throughout Europe
Occurrence: ◆ ◆

Right: This is not an original fossil, but a cast of a Solnhofen specimen. The contrast between the bones, sharp teeth (which suggest a fish diet), and the preserved soft tissues of the wing and tail membranes has been etched using special paint.

This genus has given its name to the first of the two main groups of pterosaurs, the Rhamphorhynchoidea. They were the earliest types, living mainly to the end of the Jurassic Period, and each had a long trailing tail, unlike the tail-less Pterodactyloidea that succeeded them in the Cretaceous. Various species of *Rhamphorhynchus* are known, varying in wingspan from 40cm/16in to almost 2m/6½ft. Many of their fossil remains occur in the fine-grained limestone of Solnhofen, southern Germany, along with those of the earliest bird, *Archaeopteryx*, and the small dinosaur *Compsognathus*. Long ago, this area was a shallow lagoon into which various creatures fell, died, sank and then quickly became buried for detailed fossilization.

Wing membrane | Fourth finger bone | Skull Tail membrane | Tail bones

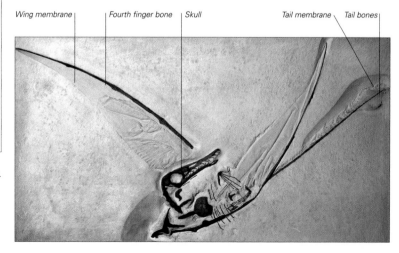

BIRDS

The first known bird is Archaeopteryx, dating to the Late Jurassic Period, 155–150 million years ago. During the Cretaceous, several further groups of birds appeared, but most died out with the dinosaurs. The only survivor is the Neornithes, to which all present-day 9,000-plus species belong. Bird fossils are rare because their bones were lightweight, fragile and hollow, and were soon scavenged or weathered.

Archaeopteryx

Among the world's most prized and precious fossils are those of *Archaeopteryx*, the earliest bird so far discovered. Its remains come only from the Solnhofen region of Bavaria, Germany. There, the very fine-grained Lithographic Sandstone (so named because it was formerly quarried for printing) has preserved amazing details, including the patterns of feathers, which are very similar to those of modern flying birds. *Archaeopteryx* had dinosaurian features, such as teeth in its jaws and bones in its tail, but also bird features, including proper flight feathers (rather than fuzzy or downy ones). It probably evolved from small, meat-eating dinosaurs called maniraptorans or 'raptors', but it was perhaps a side-branch of evolution and left no descendants.

Right: One of only seven known fossils of Archaeopteryx, this is termed the 'London specimen'. The neck is arched over its back, a common death pose for reptiles, birds and mammals. The wings show their spread feathers and the legs were strong, with three weight-bearing toes on each foot.

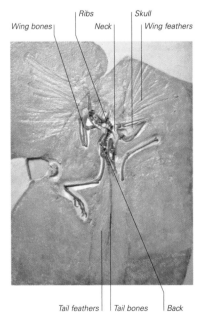

Ribs | Skull
Wing bones | Neck | Wing feathers

Tail feathers | Tail bones | Back

Name: *Archaeopteryx*
Meaning: Ancient wing
Grouping: Aves, Archaeornithes
Informal ID: First bird, early bird
Fossil size: Total width 30cm/12in
Reconstructed size: Nose–tail length 50–60cm/20–24in
Habitat: Wooded areas, tropical islands
Time span: Late Jurassic Period, 155–150 million years ago
Main fossil sites: Europe
Occurrence: ◆

Phalacrocorax

Freshwater and marine birds, such as ducks, geese, gulls, cormorants and waders, are more likely to be preserved than many woodland species, whose remains were quickly scavenged or rotted. A bird that falls into water may quickly be covered by current-borne sand, mud or other sediments. This keeps away oxygen so that aerobic decomposition cannot occur, but fossilization can. Many bird fossils are of species that live around lakes or along seashores. This specimen belongs to the same genus, *Phalacrocorax*, as modern cormorants and shags.

Humerus
Wrist
Hand
Fingers
Keel
Radius and ulna

Left: The cormorant has powerful wing bones for swimming underwater after its food, and a long, hook-tipped, sharp-edged beak for grabbing slippery prey, such as fish.

Name: *Phalacrocorax*
Meaning: Finger raven
Grouping: Aves, Pelicaniform
Informal ID: Cormorant
Fossil size: Beak–tailbone length 60cm/24in
Reconstructed size: Beak–tail length 80cm/32in
Habitat: Seashores, inland waters
Time span: Tertiary Period, Pliocene Epoch, about 2 million years ago
Main fossil sites: Worldwide
Occurrence: ◆

Feathers, nests, eggs and prints

Bird nests and footprints have been preserved as trace fossils in many parts of the world. This process may also occur with the nesting ground burrows of birds such as penguins, and tree holes, such as those made by woodpeckers. The nest shown below is still complete with its eggshells. It may have been raided by a predator or suffered some other sudden catastrophe just after the young hatched, since the empty shells are usually removed by the parent bird or trampled into fragments by the hatchlings. Moulted feathers are another relatively common fossil find for birds, having been shed, fallen into shallow freshwater or marine sediments and then quickly been buried to prevent decomposition. This tends to happen in habitats with still or slow-flowing water, where the sediments are less disturbed.

Below: This nest is a pseudofossil – a relatively recent specimen that has become infiltrated and mineralized (petrified, or 'turned to rock') due to the action of water, probably from a splashing spring in a limestone area. It is the typical cup-shaped nest of a small songbird, perhaps in the tit family. The nest diameter is 8cm/3⅛in.

Above: These trace fossils of bird footprints, from Utah, USA, date to the Eocene Epoch, 53–33 million years ago. They were probably made by a presbyoniform, an early type of bird related to the duck and goose group, Anseriformes. Presbyornis itself looked like a combination of duck and flamingo, and stood 1m/3¼ft tall.

Left: Moulted feathers were often preserved in the fine sediments of lake mud, such as this one from the Oligocene Epoch, about 25 million years ago. Feather width 2cm/¾in.

— *Separated barbs*

Below: Preserved examples of bird eggs include those from waterfowl, such as ducks and geese. Their nests are usually built low, just above the water's surface, and the eggs may fall in and down into the soft, muddy bottom intact if a predator upsets the nest. This may be a duck's egg from the Oligocene Epoch about 25 million years ago. Length 4.5cm/1¾in.

SYNAPSIDS (MAMMAL-LIKE REPTILES)

Synapsids get their name from the pattern of openings, or windows, on the sides of the skull bone, with one main opening in each upper side. Synapsids appeared about 300 million years ago and during the Permian Period they were the main large land animals, with both plant- and meat-eaters. They faded as the dinosaurs came to domination in the Triassic, but some of their kind gave rise to the first mammals.

Dimetrodon

One of the early carnivorous synapsids, *Dimetrodon* is well known from the many remains that have been discovered in the Red Beds of Texas, USA. All parts of its skeleton have been found and they show a long, low predator with big, powerful jaws and sprawling legs, which could probably run rapidly. The most unusual feature of *Dimetrodon* was a tall flap of thin skin on its back, held up by a series of spine-like bony rods from the backbone. This has led to its common names, such as 'sail-back' or 'fin-back'. The skin may have helped to absorb heat from the sun, allowing *Dimetrodon* to warm up faster and move more quickly than its contemporaries. A similar reptile from the same time and place, plant-eating Edaphosaurus, also had the feature. During the later Mesozoic Era, various dinosaurs, such as the huge predator *Spinosaurus*, had a similar feature.

Below: This piece of jaw from Oklahoma, USA, shows the powerful teeth with which Dimetrodon seized its prey. In life, sharp, full-grown teeth would be more than 10cm/4in long.

Name: *Dimetrodon*
Meaning: Two forms of teeth
Grouping: Reptile, Synapsid, Pelycosaur
Informal ID: Sail-back (sometimes incorrectly called 'dinosaur')
Fossil size: Jaw piece length 5cm/2in
Reconstructed size: Nose–tail length 3m/10ft
Habitat: Mosaic of scrub and swamp
Time span: Early Permian, 295–270 million years ago
Main fossil sites: North America, Europe
Occurrence: ◆ ◆

Diictodon

Dicynodonts were squat, barrel-shaped, strong-legged creatures, in body bulk not unlike modern pigs. But they had typical reptile scales and the front of the mouth was extended into a hooked 'beak', probably used for plucking bits of plant food from trees and bushes. Their name means 'two tusk teeth' and most types had two large, tusk-like teeth in the upper jaw. These were probably for defence against enemies, or display at breeding time. *Diictodon* is one of the first vertebrates for which fossils suggest sexual dimorphism: that is, males and females have different features. In this case, of about a hundred skeletons found, only some had tusks – presumably the males.

Below: This fossil skull from Beaufort West District, Cape Province, South Africa, clearly shows large tusks and was presumably a male. Some Diictodon remains have been found in burrows, perhaps excavated by the beak-like mouth or blunt-clawed feet. The tusks lack digging-type wear marks.

Name: *Diictodon*
Meaning: Two tusk teeth
Grouping: Reptile, Synapsid, Dicynodont
Informal ID: Mammal-like reptile
Fossil size: Skull length 14cm/5½in
Reconstructed size: Nose–tail length 1m/3¼in
Habitat: Mixed
Time span: Late Permian, 260–250 million years ago
Main fossil sites: Regions of southern Africa
Occurrence: ◆

Beak-like front of mouth ——

Tusk ——

—— Eye socket

Lystrosaurus

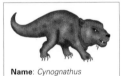

Name: *Lystrosaurus*
Meaning: Shovel or spoon reptile
Grouping: Reptile, Synapsid, Therapsid, Dicynodont
Informal ID: Lystrosaurus, herbivorous mammal-like reptile
Fossil size: Skull length 22cm/8⅝in
Reconstructed size: Total length 70cm–1m/28in–3¼ft
Habitat: Riverbanks, lakesides, shallow fresh water
Time span: Early Triassic, 245–230 million years ago
Main fossil sites: Southern Africa, Asia, Antarctica
Occurrence: ◆ ◆ ◆

Lystrosaurus was a type of small 'reptilian hippopotamus'. With its barrel-like body, short tail and stubby limbs it probably spent its time wading in shallow water. Here it would feed on lush aquatic foliage that it pulled up and gathered into its mouth using the paired tusks projecting from the upper jaw. The distribution of fossils from this dicynodont (see also *Diictodon*, opposite) encompasses southern Africa, Russia, China and India, and in 1960 its remains were also discovered in Antarctica. This is compelling evidence for the union of most of these landmasses at the time – the Permian Period – into the one great southern supercontinent known as Gondwana.

Left: Lystrosaurus *fossils, such as this skull, are very common in certain parts of southern Africa, including the Karoo, where they give their name to the* Lystrosaurus *Zone of the Early or Lower Triassic. The rocks are sandstones and shales, which indicate a moist climate with regular flooding. The local distribution of* Lystrosaurus *remains suggests that these herbivores lived in groups, or herds, and grazed in freshwater shallows. In this skull, the eye socket is upper left and the snout is to the right.*

Cynognathus

Name: *Cynognathus*
Meaning: Dog jaw
Grouping: Reptile, Synapsid, Therapsid, Theriodont
Informal ID: Cynognathus, mammal-like reptile
Fossil size: Skull length 40cm/16in
Reconstructed size: Nose–tail length 1.8m/6ft
Habitat: Open country, scrub, semi-desert
Time span: Early Triassic, 240–230 million years ago
Main fossil sites: Southern Africa, South America
Occurrence: ◆

One of the Early Triassic synapsids, and also one of the largest in its group called the cynodonts, *Cynognathus* was a strongly built carnivore with powerful jaws. It had three types of teeth, similar to those of the Carnivora mammals that would evolve some 200 million years later. These teeth consisted of small front incisors for nipping and nibbling, large pointed canines for ripping and stabbing, and molar teeth with coarse serrations for chewing and shearing. The cynodonts, 'dog teeth', were among the longest-surviving of all the synapsids, living from the Late Permian to the Middle Jurassic. They were mammal-like in many features and deserve their casual name of 'mammal-like reptiles' – especially since some of their kind probably gave rise to the true mammals.

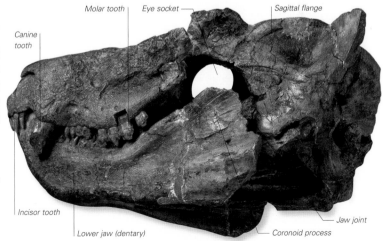

Right: The skull shows a large flange on top where powerful jaw muscles were anchored. The jaws could open wide partly due to an upward-angled component at the rear of the lower jaw, the coronoid process, which formed the jaw joint.

Molar tooth | Eye socket | Sagittal flange
Canine tooth
Incisor tooth
Lower jaw (dentary)
Coronoid process
Jaw joint

EARLY MAMMALS

The first mammals appeared almost alongside the first dinosaurs, more than 200 million years ago.
However, throughout the Mesozoic Era they were mostly small, vaguely shrew-like hunters of insects and
other small creatures. Only a few of them exceeded the size of a modern domestic cat, one being
the recently discovered koala-sized Repenomamus.

Megazostrodon

Below: This fossil specimen shows the main body or trunk region with the pelvis (hip) bone, rear limb and foot bones. In overall appearance, Megazostrodon and other very early mammals probably looked like the tree-shrews or tupaids of today, although they belonged to a very different mammal group, the triconodonts, which all became extinct.

Tibia (shin)

Femur (thigh)

Vertebrae (backbones)

Pelvis

Foot bones

One of the earliest known mammals is *Megazostrodon*, the remains of which are known from Late Triassic rocks in Southern Africa. Around the same time, similar small mammals were appearing on other continents. When studying fossils, the key features of a mammal include the bones that form the lower jaw (dentary/mandible) and the jaw joint, and the alteration of what were formerly jaw bones to the three tiny bones, called auditory ossicles, in each middle ear. Large eye sockets indicate *Megazostrodon* was nocturnal, at a time when the day-active dinosaurs were beginning to dominate life on land. Its teeth show it probably hunted insects in the manner of today's shrews.

Name: *Megazostrodon*
Meaning: Large girdle tooth
Grouping: Mammal, Triconodont
Informal ID: Early mammal, shrew-like mammal
Fossil size: 3cm/1¼in
Reconstructed size: Nose–tail length 12cm/4¾in
Habitat: Wooded areas, scrub regions
Time span: Late Triassic to Early Jurassic, 210–190 million years ago
Main fossil sites: Regions of southern Africa
Occurrence: ◆

Monotreme

Today there are just a handful of monotremes (egg-laying mammals), including the duck-billed platypus, *Ornithorhynchus*, of Australia, and the echidnas (spiny anteaters), *Tachyglossus* and *Zaglossus*, of Australia and New Guinea. Of all living mammal groups, the monotremes have the most ancient fossil record, stretching back 100 million years. The living platypus shows reptilian traits, such as limbs angled almost sideways from the body, and of course egg laying. However, its defining mammal features include its three middle ear bones, warm-bloodedness, a fur-covered body and feeding its young on milk.

Left: A monotreme fossil molar tooth is compared with the teeth in a skull of a modern duck-billed platypus, Ornithorhynchus. *There is great similarity in the cusp (point) pattern. The fossil tooth is dated to 63 million years ago, just after the mass extinction at the end of the Cretaceous Period.*

Name: *Ornithorhynchus* (living platypus)
Meaning: Bird beak or bill
Grouping: Mammal, Monotreme
Informal ID: Platypus
Fossil size: Fossil tooth 1cm/½in across
Reconstructed size: Unknown, possible head–body length 50cm/20in
Habitat: Unknown, possibly fresh water
Time span: Early Tertiary, 65–60 million years ago
Main fossil sites: (This specimen) South America; Australia
Occurrence: ◆

Diprotodon

About one-fifteenth of all living mammal species are marsupials, or pouched mammals, with the biggest being the red kangaroo of Australia. Many other species lived during the Tertiary and Quaternary Periods. One of the largest was *Diprotodon*, which became extinct relatively recently, perhaps just 30,000 years ago. It was a plant-eater resembling a wombat, with a large snout and stocky body. But it was huge, almost the size of a hippo. The protruding nasal area may have supported very large nostrils or the muscles for an elongated snout or shortish, mobile trunk, similar to the modern tapir. Various diprotodontids came and went from the Oligocene Epoch onwards, and their living relations include the wombats themselves, as well as kangaroos and koalas.

Below: An important distinguishing feature of the diprotodonts, as seen in this fossilized skull, was a single pair of lower front incisor teeth, which pointed forwards, and from which the name is derived. There was also a long gap, or diastema, as seen in rodents living today, between the front teeth and rear chewing teeth.

Name: *Diprotodon*
Meaning: Two prominent/ forward teeth
Grouping: Mammal, Marsupial, Diprotodont
Informal ID: Giant wombat
Fossil size: Skull length 50cm/20in
Reconstructed size: Head–body length 3m/10ft
Habitat: Woods, forests
Time span: Pleistocene to 30,000 years ago
Main fossil sites: Australia
Occurrence: ◆ ◆

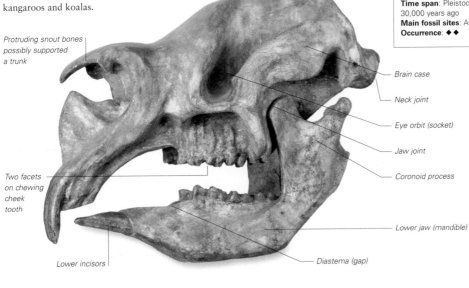

Protruding snout bones possibly supported a trunk

Brain case

Neck joint

Eye orbit (socket)

Jaw joint

Coronoid process

Two facets on chewing cheek tooth

Lower jaw (mandible)

Lower incisors

Diastema (gap)

Protungulatum

The ungulates are the hoofed mammals, which today include horses, rhinos, giraffes, hippos, deer, cattle, sheep and goats. One of the earliest examples was *Protungulatum*. Its fossils have been associated with those of dinosaurs. But the dinosaur fossils from the end of the Mesozoic Era may have been eroded from earlier rocks and then mixed with *Protungulatum*'s remains during the start of the Tertiary Period, about 60 million years ago. *Protungulatum* may have had claw-like 'hooves', but very few remains of this animal are known, other than teeth, which show the trend towards the broad, crushing teeth of later ungulates, designed to masticate tough, fibrous plant foods.

Right: This tiny tooth is from the Hell Creek Formation of Montana, USA. It has two larger pointed cusps, a broken section where other cusps would have stood, and a double-root anchored in the jaw bone. Protungulatum probably fed on fruits and soft plants, but could still chew small creatures, such as insects, as its ancestors had done.

Cusps

Root

Root

Name: *Protungulatum*
Meaning: Before ungulates
Grouping: Mammal, Condylarth
Informal ID: Early hoofed mammal
Fossil size: 5mm/³⁄₁₆in
Reconstructed size: Nose–tail length 40cm/16in
Habitat: Woodland
Time span: Late Cretaceous, 70–65 million years ago, or early Tertiary (see main text)
Main fossil sites: Regions of North America
Occurrence: ◆

SMALL MAMMALS

The original mammals hunted insects and similar small creatures. The second-largest group of living mammals are bats, with about one-fifth of all mammalian species. They appeared almost fully evolved early in the Tertiary Period. Other small mammal groups moved from eating insects to mainly plants, including the rats, mice and other rodents, and rabbits and hares, called lagomorphs.

Palaeochiropteryx

Bats have lightweight, fragile bones and fossils are rare. *Palaeochiropteryx* is known from beautiful specimens in the Messel fossil beds of Germany. The front limbs have become wings, with arm and hand bones holding out what would have been a very thin, stretchy flying membrane, or patagium. The first digit (thumb) was a claw for grasping and grooming, the second digit was also clawed (unlike most modern bats) and the very long bones of the third digit extended to the end of the wing. The hip area had become small, with the rear limbs used mainly for hanging.

Below: This specimen has been prepared from the front side (skull lowermost), then that side embedded in resin and the other, rear side likewise cleaned and prepared. It shows the whole skeleton with one wing folded over the backbone. The resin prevents the fragile oil-shale fossil, typical of Messel specimens, from degenerating.

Name: *Palaeochiropteryx*
Meaning: Ancient hand wing
Grouping: Mammal, Chiropteran
Informal ID: Bat
Fossil size: Whole specimen about 7cm/2¾in across
Reconstructed size: Nose–tail length 5–6cm/ 2–2¼in; wingspan 20cm/8in
Habitat: Woods
Time span: Eocene, 50 million years ago
Main fossil sites: Throughout Europe
Occurrence: ◆

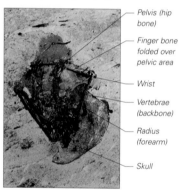

— Pelvis (hip bone)
— Finger bone folded over pelvic area
— Wrist
— Vertebrae (backbone)
— Radius (forearm)
— Skull

Wing shapes
The wings of *Palaeochiropteryx* were relatively short in span, but broad from front to back, indicating a fast, manoeuvrable flier. Bats that soar and swoop more, without sudden directional changes, have longer, narrower wings. The same principles apply to the wings of birds.

Leptictidium

Most insectivores eat not only insects, but also worms, spiders and other small creatures. *Leptictidium* was a ground-dwelling animal that could bound along at speed, something like a modern rat-kangaroo, using its powerful rear legs and extremely elongated hind feet (as in a real kangaroo). Its long, pointed skull suggests an animal with a lengthy, fleshy snout, which was probably equipped with long whiskers for probing, feeling and sniffing food. The large eye sockets indicate a nocturnal lifestyle. The leptictid group began to expand just before the end of the Cretaceous Period and became common and diverse during the early part of the following Tertiary Period.

Name: *Leptictidium*
Meaning: Delicate/ Graceful weasel
Grouping: Mammal, Insectivore
Informal ID: Shrew
Fossil size: Nose–tail length 65cm/25½in
Reconstructed size: As above
Habitat: Woods, Forests
Time span: Eocene, 50–40 million years ago
Main fossil sites: Europe
Occurrence: ◆

Left: This well-preserved skeleton of Leptictidium has been caught in a very lifelike, bounding pose, showing the enormously long tail that in life would have helped it with balance. The tail was flicked to one side to twist the body to the other side when darting about and changing direction at great speed.

Palaeolagus

Rabbits and hares are often confused with rodents, but they are a separate group, known as the lagomorphs, or 'leaping shapes'. A lagomorph has two pairs of gnawing or nibbling teeth in the upper and lower front of the skull, rather than one main pair, as in rodents. The jaw joint allows chewing by side-to-side motion using the five or more pairs of molar (cheek) teeth (seen in living rabbits), rather than the up-and-down motion of rodents. *Palaeolagus* was one of the earliest rabbits, after the hares and rabbits split off from the other main group of lagomorphs, called the pikas.

Below: This fossilized skull of a young Palaeolagus *clearly shows the sharp gnawing teeth, which were tipped with ridges of enamel, prominently situated at the front of the animal's skull. The femur is the thigh bone and the tibia is the main shin bone, and both of these are greatly elongated in lagomorphs to provide them with the power they require for jumping and running to avoid being taken as prey. This specimen is from South Dakota, USA.*

Name: *Palaeolagus*
Meaning: Ancient leaper
Grouping: Mammal, Lagomorph
Informal ID: Rabbit
Fossil size: Skull length 4cm/1½in
Reconstructed size: Nose–tail 25cm/10in (adult)
Habitat: Woods
Time span: Oligocene, 30–25 million years ago
Main fossil sites: North America
Occurrence: ◆

Gnawing incisors
Gap (diastema)
Eye socket
Molars

Ankle joint end of tibia

Tibia

Hip joint end of femur

Knee joint

Lepus

Hares are generally bigger than rabbits, with a body form even further adapted to leaping and jumping. The rear leg bones are long for greater leverage as powerful muscles extend the leg joints to fling the animal forward. The genus *Lepus* includes modern hares such as the common or brown hare and mountain hare. Early lagomorphs probably lived in woodlands, since the grasslands where most rabbits and hares live today did not begin to spread until the Miocene, from about 25 million years ago.

Below: This recent subfossil of a lower leg or shin bone (tibia), shows details such as the foramina (tiny holes) for blood vessels and nerves passing into the bone's interior. It was found in a cave, suggesting that the hare could have been sheltering. If it had been a prey item, the bone may well have been cracked and gnawed.

Enduring design
Lagomorph design has proved to be very successful, with changes in their dental and skeletal development mostly occurring only very gradually. Although worldwide in distribution now, lagomorphs were naturally absent from only a few regions of the world: most of the islands of Southeast Asia, Australia, New Zealand, the island of Madagascar, southern South America and Antarctica.

Name: *Lepus*
Meaning: Leaper
Grouping: Mammal, Lagomorph
Informal ID: Hare
Fossil size: Length 14cm/5½in
Reconstructed size: Nose–tail length 45cm/18in
Habitat: Open scrub, grass, moor
Time span: Quaternary, within the last 2 million years
Main fossil sites: Worldwide
Occurrence: ◆ ◆

Head (knee joint end)

Shaft

Ankle joint end

RODENTS AND CREODONTS

Rodents make up almost half of all the living mammal species and first appeared as squirrel-like creatures some 60 million years ago. Creodonts were the main carnivorous mammals from about 60 to 30 million years ago. Different types looked like bears, wolves, cats and hyaenas. However, they had all but faded away by 10 million years ago, to be succeeded by the Carnivora of today.

Mimomys

The vole genus *Mimomys* had shown rapid evolution during the past five million years, with 40 or more species being recognized based on features including their molar teeth. *Mimomys* was widespread, especially across Europe, but seems to have died out about half a million years ago. The many species of *Mimomys* are described mainly from the shape and features of the teeth, especially the lower first molar and the upper third molar. The molars had roots, which are lacking in the modern equivalent of *Mimomys* – the water vole, *Arvicola*.

Below: This Pleistocene specimen is from Mimomys savini, a type of water vole, from the West Runton Gap, near Cromer, Norfolk, England.

High crown formed of prisms

Lower right first molar

Toothless gap between molars and incisors

Lower jaw (mandible)

Vole clock
Remains of *Mimomys* are very common in the fossil record and have been accurately dated in some well-studied rocks. Because of this, they can be used as a 'vole clock' to date zones of unfamiliar rocks and the fossils they contain.

Name: *Mimomys*
Meaning: Mouse-like
Grouping: Mammal, Rodent, Myomorph
Informal ID: Vole, Water vole
Fossil size: Length of jaw fragment 8mm/⅓in
Reconstructed size: Head–body length 5–8cm/2–3⅛in
Habitat: Woods, wetlands
Time span: Quaternary Period, Pleistocene Epoch, within past 1.75 million years
Main fossil sites: Worldwide
Occurrence: ◆ ◆

Rodent teeth

Long, curved, sharp teeth are the common remains of many rodents, from mice, voles and rats, to larger types, such as beavers. They are the front teeth, or incisors, and in the rodent group they keep growing throughout the animal's life. As the rodent gnaws and nibbles, the teeth are continually worn down. The layer of enamel on the front is hardest and shows least wear, with the dentine just behind being eroded faster. This gives an angle to the tooth tip, which forms a self-sharpening cutting ridge. Rodents have two pairs of incisors – one pair in the top jaw and one pair in the lower – which distinguishes them from similar gnawing-nibbling herbivores, such as rabbits.

Cutting tip

Crown

Root end

Left: This rodent, a coypu (nutria), shows the upper of its two pairs of long, gnawing, continuously growing, self-sharpening front teeth, incisors, which are characteristic of the group. They are used for tackling woody or nutty foods and also for defence – they can inflict severe wounds on breeding rivals or predators.

Left: These Quaternary Period specimens came from a cave in Mid Glamorgan, Wales. Most of the length of the tooth is root, anchored in the maxilla (upper jaw) or mandible (lower jaw).

Name: Incisors
Meaning: Cutting
Grouping: Mammal, Rodent
Informal ID: Rodent front teeth
Fossil size: Length around curve 1.3cm/½in
Time span: Palaeocene, 60 million years ago, to today
Main fossil sites: Worldwide
Occurrence: ◆ ◆ ◆

Hyaenodon

The creodont genus *Hyaenodon* was long-lasting, widespread and varied. Some species were as small as stoats, others as big as lions – however, they were not closely related to stoats or lions, since these hunters belong to the more modern Carnivora group. The *Hyaenodon* genus originated in the Late Eocene Epoch, probably in Asia or Europe. Some members spread to North America and possibly Africa, and one Asian kind survived into the Pliocene Epoch, some five million years ago – then the whole creodont group went extinct. See the next page for a comparison with the jaws and teeth of a 'true' hyaena.

Below: This specimen of Hyaenodon comes from Oligocene rocks in Wyoming, USA. The skull is long and low, with a large snout indicating a good sense of smell. It is deep-jawed, with immensely strong jaw bones. These would be able to crack and chew tough food, such as gristle and bone, in the manner of the modern scavenging hyaena.

Name: *Hyaenodon*
Meaning: Hyaena tooth
Grouping: Mammal, Creodont, Hyaeonodont
Informal ID: Ancient 'hyaena'
Fossil size: Skull length 15cm/6in
Reconstructed size: Head–body length 1.2m/4ft
Habitat: Wood, scrub
Time span: Oligocene, 30–25 million years ago
Main fossil sites: Europe, Asia, North America
Occurrence: ◆ ◆

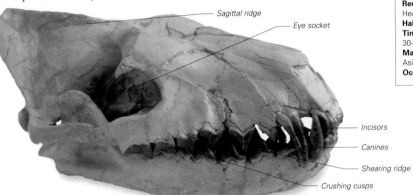

Sagittal ridge

Eye socket

Incisors

Canines

Shearing ridge

Crushing cusps

Hesperocyon

Name: *Hesperocyon*
Meaning: Western dog
Grouping: Mammal, Canid
Informal ID: Hesperocyon, prehistoric mongoose, 'first dog'
Fossil size: Skull length 15cm/6in
Reconstructed size: Total length 80cm/32in
Habitat: Mixed
Time span: Oligocene to Early Miocene, 30–20 million years ago
Main fossil sites: North America
Occurrence: ◆ ◆

This vaguely mongoose-like animal was an early canid, or member of the mammal family Canidae. This embraces wolves, dogs, foxes, jackals and their kin. Modern canids tend to be long-legged, dogged pursuit specialists. *Hesperocyon* had a long, bendy body and short legs, more like those of a weasel or stoat. Perhaps it lived like a mustelid, squirming through dense undergrowth and following prey animals such as rodents into their burrows. Its fossils come mainly from Nebraska, USA. The species is usually named as *Hesperocyon gregarious*, since the distribution of remains suggests they lived in groups.

Below: Hesperocyon's skull is long and low, with an elongated snout. The shape is suited for movement in restricted places, such as tunnels. Complete specimens show 42 teeth rather than the usual 44, due to a missing molar on each side in the rear of the upper jaw. Details of the inner ear region and the small ear bones (ossicles) mark this as a true canid rather than another type of carnivorous mammal.

Brain case

Eye socket

Molar teeth

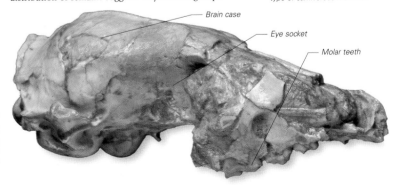

CARNIVORES (MAMMALIAN)

A 'carnivore' is generally any flesh-eating or predatory creature. However, Carnivora is also the official name for the mammal group containing hunters ranging from weasels, stoats and otters, through civets, raccoons, foxes, wild dogs and wolves and hyaenas to cats and bears. Many other prehistoric mammal groups had carnivorous members, especially the credonts, but these were not members of the Carnivora.

Hyaena/Crocuta

The hyaena of the Carnivora should not be confused with *Hyaenodon* of the Creodonta. These two groups differed in several important features, including the bones of the ear and foot, the pattern of teeth, and a relatively smaller brain among the creodonts. In the Carnivora, the rearmost upper premolar tooth moves down against the first lower molar tooth so that their sharp edges work together like shearing blades – this is called the carnassial pattern. Hyaenas have a slight variation on this pattern, with certain teeth missing. The massive jaws, with fairly tall-crowned but blunt teeth, exert 'spots' of pressure – essential for cracking gristle and bone.

Below: This section of mandible (lower jaw) shows the massive crunching cheek teeth, and the sharp shearing surface. The specimen may be from the cave hyaena, Hyaena spelea, or the modern spotted hyaena of Africa, Crocuta crocuta, but at a location from which hyaenas have long since disappeared – Devon, England.

Name: *Hyaena/Crocuta*
Meaning: Hyaena
Grouping: Mammal, Carnivore, Hyaenid
Informal ID: Hyaena
Fossil size: Jaw section length 10cm/4in
Reconstructed size: Nose–tail length 1.6m/5¼ft
Habitat: Scrub, plains
Time span: Pleistocene, within the past 1.75 million years
Main fossil sites: Europe, Africa
Occurrence: ◆

Smilodon

Name: *Smilodon*
Meaning: Knife tooth
Grouping: Mammal, Carnivore, Felid
Informal ID: Sabre-tooth cat, sabre-tooth 'tiger'
Fossil size: Canine length 17cm plus/6½in plus
Reconstructed size: Head–body length 2m/6ft
Habitat: Varied terrain, mainly wooded
Time span: Pliocene, to 12,000 or even 10,000 years ago
Main fossil sites: North America
Occurrence: ◆ ◆ ◆

One of the best-known and most recent sabre-tooth cats, *Smilodon*, was approximately the size of a modern lion. Its massively elongated canines were wide from front to back, but were narrower from side to side, giving them an oval cross-section. The rear edge of each canine was serrated to cut through hide and flesh more easily. *Smilodon*'s jaws opened extremely wide – to an angle of 120° – allowing the animal to use its canines as effective stabbing or slashing weapons. The chest, shoulders and neck were all heavily muscled to give great power for its deadly lunges. The cat may have sliced open the belly of a larger victim, causing it to bleed to death, or it could have severed the spinal cord or windpipe of smaller prey.

Left: The remains of many hundreds of Smilodon have been recovered from Rancho La Brea in Los Angeles, California, USA. In Pleistocene times, surface 'lakes' of oozing tar trapped many creatures, from huge herbivores like mammoths and bison, to predators attracted by their struggles, including dire wolves and sabre-tooth cats.

Shearing (carnassial) cheek teeth

Stabbing canine teeth

Ursus

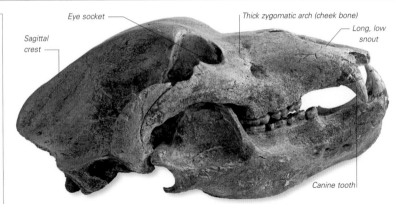

Sagittal crest

Eye socket

Thick zygomatic arch (cheek bone)

Long, low snout

Canine tooth

Name: *Ursus spelaeus*
Meaning: Cave bear
Grouping: Mammal, Carnivore, Ursid
Informal ID: Cave bear
Fossil size: Skull length 50cm/20in
Reconstructed size: Head–body up to 3m/10ft
Habitat: Varied
Time span: Pleistocene, within the past 2 million years, to today (for the genus)
Main fossil sites: Throughout Europe
Occurrence: ◆ ◆

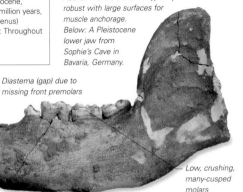

Above: The ursid skull is typically robust with large surfaces for muscle anchorage.
Below: A Pleistocene lower jaw from Sophie's Cave in Bavaria, Germany.

Incisor

Diastema (gap) due to missing front premolars

Low, crushing, many-cusped molars

The ursids, or bears, make up one of the smallest living families within the mammal group Carnivora, but it contains the largest and most powerful members. *Ursus spelaeus* was the fearsome-looking European cave bear that our prehistoric ancestors would have encountered across Central and Southern Europe during the most recent Ice Ages, perhaps less than 10,000 years ago. Its probable diet was chiefly plants rather than meat. Its remains are often found in caves where the bears regularly rested, sheltered, gave birth and hibernated, sometimes in large numbers – but never woke up. The bones and teeth were used in rituals and as decoration by Neanderthal people more than 30,000 years ago.

Canid

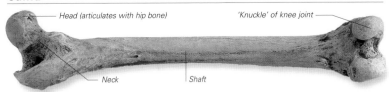

Head (articulates with hip bone)

'Knuckle' of knee joint

Neck

Shaft

The canids are the wolf, dog and fox family of the mammal group Carnivora. They are characterized by having long snouts and they are long-legged running specialists, built for 'dogged' pursuit of prey, rather than a stealthy stalk-and-pounce like the cats. Canids first appeared in the fossil record in the Eocene Epoch, some 40 million years ago. Many species have come and gone, including the dire wolf, *Canis dirus*, of North America – many specimens of which have been excellently preserved in La Brea Pits of tar pools in Los Angeles (see opposite). The grey wolf (common wolf), *Canis lupus*, has a long fossil history and is the ancestor of all breeds of modern domestic dog.

Above: This well-preserved Quaternary-dated specimen is from Mid Glamorgan, Wales and is less than 2 million years old. The femur, or thigh bone, shows the typical ball-shaped head that fitted into the bowl-like socket of the animal's hip bone, or pelvis. The ball is carried on an angled neck, as is the case in most mammalian species.

Name: Canid femur
Meaning: Dog thigh bone
Grouping: Mammal, Carnivore, Canid
Informal ID: Wolf or fox
Fossil size: Length 13cm/5in
Reconstructed size: Head–body length 50–60cm/ 20–24in
Habitat: Mixed
Time span: Pleistocene, within past 1.75 million years, to today
Main fossil sites: Worldwide
Occurrence: ◆ ◆

HERBIVOROUS MAMMALS – EQUIDS

Many types of mammals eat plants, from tiny voles and mice to huge elephants. The main group of large herbivores is the ungulates, or hoofed mammals. Their toe-tips evolved from claws into hard hooves, and most have become alert, swift browsers or grazers. The perissodactyls – odd-toed ungulates, with an odd number of toes per foot – include the equids, which are horses and zebras, and also rhinos and tapirs.

Hyracotherium

Name: *Hyracotherium*
Meaning: Hyrax beast
Grouping: Mammal, Perissodactyl, Equid
Informal ID: Early horse
Fossil size: Length of teeth section 2.5cm/1in
Reconstructed size: Head–body length 60cm/24in
Habitat: Woods
Time span: Early Eocene, 50 million years ago
Main fossil sites: Northern Hemisphere
Occurrence: ◆ ◆

The evolution of horses is probably one of the best-studied of all prehistoric mammal sequences. One of the early members was *Hyracotherium* from the Eocene Epoch, some 50–45 million years ago. The reason that this name refers to the hyrax, a smallish African mammal said to be the elephant's closest living relative, rather than a horse, is because of a mistaken identity that occurred back in the nineteenth century. A more apt alternative has occasionally been proposed, *Eohippus*, meaning 'dawn horse'. *Hyracotherium* was a small woodland herbivore, about the size of a fox terrier, widespread across North America, Europe and Asia. It had four toes on each front foot and three on each back foot.

Below: This specimen of three molar teeth embedded in their jaw bone is from the Willwood Formation rocks near Powell, Wyoming, USA. It is dated to the Wasatchian Age (Stage), at the start of the Eocene Epoch. The molars are low-crowned, suited for chewing soft forest leaves.

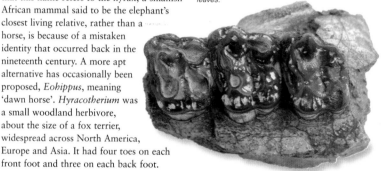

Miohippus

Below: The skull shows the incisors for nipping and nibbling leaves, and the premolars and molars for shredding. The snout has become longer than in previous horse types, with a slightly dished upper surface, and the deep lower jaw was operated by large chewing muscles.

By the Oligocene Epoch some horses were becoming larger, able to run swiftly through open woodlands. There were no wide-open grassy plains as yet – grasses were only just beginning to evolve. *Miohippus* lived from 30 to less than 25 million years ago and had three toes per foot, all of which touched the ground. However, the middle toe was larger than the other two and bore most of the weight. *Miohippus* was about the size of today's sheep, standing some 60cm/24in at the shoulder, and had a longer, dished snout, a longer neck and longer legs that earlier horses. It lived at the same time as another horse genus, *Mesohippus*, with probably the former giving rise to further, larger types of horses.

Name: *Miohippus*
Meaning: Lesser horse
Grouping: Mammal, Perissodactyl, Equid
Informal ID: Early horse
Fossil size: Skull length 18cm/7in
Reconstructed size: Head–body 1m/3¼ft
Habitat: Open woodland regions
Time span: Oligocene, 30–23 million years ago
Main fossil sites: North America
Occurrence: ◆ ◆

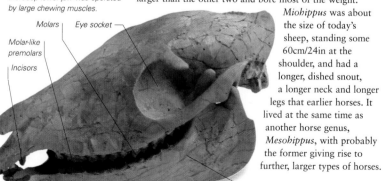

Molars   Eye socket

Molar-like premolars

Incisors

Deep mandible (lower jaw)

Merychippus

Continuing the horse trend in increased body size, *Merychippus* appeared about 17 million years ago in North America, and stood about 1m/3¼ft at the shoulder – the same height as a 10-hand pony of today. This coincided with the appearance of grasses and their spread to form wide-open plains in the drier climate of the Miocene. The neck and legs of *Merychippus* were even longer than its ancestors. There were still three toes on each foot, but the central one (digit 3) was now much larger and the two outer ones hardly touched the ground at all and bore no weight. The position of the eyes allowed better all-round vision to scan the open habitat for enemies.

Name: *Merychippus*
Meaning: New-look horse
Grouping: Mammal, Perissodactyl, Equid
Informal ID: Prehistoric horse
Fossil size: Skull length 26cm/10¼in
Reconstructed size: Head–body length 1.5m/5ft
Habitat: Open grassy plains
Time span: Miocene, 17–15 million years ago
Main fossil sites: North America
Occurrence: ◆ ◆

Right: The overall proportions of the skull of Merychippus *were approaching those of the modern horse, with the jaw deeper and eyes set farther back, partly to accommodate the long roots of the molar teeth. The brain was also larger in relation to body size, allowing it to process information from the keen senses of sight, smell and hearing.*

Higher snout profile

Higher-crowned molar teeth

Enlarged nasal chamber

Equus

Name: *Equus caballus*
Meaning: Work horse
Grouping: Mammal, Perissodactyl, Equid
Informal ID: Modern horse
Fossil size: Tooth length 5cm/2in
Reconstructed size: Head–body 2m/6½ft
Habitat: Grasslands, open woodland
Time span: Quaternary, within past 1.75 million years, to today
Main fossil sites: North America, then almost worldwide
Occurrence: ◆ ◆

Right: This skull of a modern horse, Equus caballus, *is from Pleistocene rocks in Germany. The nipping and nibbling incisors are separated by a long gap from the row of powerful chewing cheek teeth. There are signs of damage to the sinus area, perhaps caused by an injury.*

By the late Miocene Epoch, the *Merychippus* line had undergone 'explosive radiation' and quickly produced several new branches of the horse evolutionary tree. One of these led to the genus *Equus*, which includes the modern horse, *Equus caballus*, as well as zebras and asses. About 1 million years ago there were more than 20 *Equus* species on almost every continent, except Australia and Antarctica, but many went extinct. The modern horse carries all its weight on only one large hoof-capped toe per foot, with small 'splints' representing the toes to either side.

Left: The horse's cheek or molar teeth are high-crowned, or hypsodont: that is, adapted for lengthy chewing of abrasive, low-nutrition foods. The teeth grow continually, with strong cement-covered crests to resist wear.

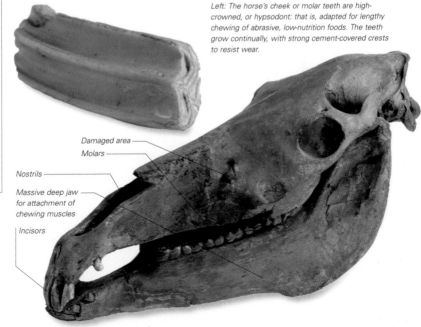

Damaged area

Molars

Nostrils

Massive deep jaw for attachment of chewing muscles

Incisors

HERBIVOROUS MAMMALS (CONTINUED)

Many mammal groups contained herbivores during their prehistory, such as the xenarthrans – sloths, anteaters and armadillos. The elephant group have always been plant-eaters. Like the rhinos, they were once more numerous, diverse and widespread. Over millions of years, scores of species of rhinos and elephants ranged greatly in a wide variety of habitats, compared with the very few living species today.

Glyptodon

South America was cut off as a giant island for much of the Tertiary Period, and many animals evolved there that were found nowhere else. The glyptodonts were big, heavily armoured, armadillo-type creatures that mostly wandered the pampas regions of grassy scrub over the past few million years. They had no teeth at the front of the mouth, and the rear or molar teeth lacked hard enamel covering, but they grew continuously to replace the wear from grinding up tough grasses and other plant food. The most recent glyptodonts survived until a few thousand years ago.

Right: The dome-shaped 'shell' consisted of bony polygonal (many-sided) plates or scales fused together to make a rigid covering, like an upturned bowl.

Name: *Glyptodon*
Meaning: Sculptured or grooved tooth
Grouping: Mammal, Xenarthran
Informal ID: Prehistoric armadillo
Fossil size: Overall width 15cm/6in
Reconstructed size: Nose–tail length 2m/6½ft
Habitat: Plains
Time span: Pleistocene, within past 2 million years
Main fossil sites: South America
Occurrence: ◆ ◆

Mammuthus

Root

There were several types of mammoth, all members of the elephant family. Most widespread was the woolly mammoth, which ranged across all northern continents and grew a very long, thick, hairy coat to keep out the bitter cold of the recent Ice Ages. It may have used its long, curving tusks to sweep away drifted snow to get at plants beneath. This mammoth is known from mummified and/or frozen specimens in the ice of Siberia, Northern Asia. Prehistoric Neanderthal people and those of our own species hunted mammoths and used their tusks and bones for building, tools, utensils and ornaments.

Chewing surface

Above: A milk (deciduous) molar tooth of a young mammoth, shed to make room for the adult tooth.

Right: Adult shoebox-sized tooth, composed of a stack of plates of enamel-covered dentine, bound together by dental cement, which wore into a series of sharp ridges. This is known as the loxodont or 'washboard' form of dentition.

Name: *Mammuthus primigenius*
Meaning: Earth-burrower (from old Russian 'mammut')
Grouping: Mammal, Proboscid
Informal ID: Woolly mammoth
Fossil size: Adult tooth 24cm/9½in long
Reconstructed size: Head–body length 3.5m/11½ft, excluding trunk and tail; tusks up to 4m/13ft
Habitat: Tundra, steppe, open plains
Time span: Pleistocene, within past 2 million years
Main fossil sites: Throughout Northern Hemisphere
Occurrence: ◆ ◆

Protitanotherium

Brontotheres, meaning 'thunder beasts' (also called titanotheres), were relatives of horses and rhinos, which made their appeared during the Early Eocene Epoch, about 50 million years ago, but then died away after 20–15 million years. Brontotheres were mainly large to very large browsing mammals, feeding on the soft, juicy leaves and other plant matter of mixed woodlands and forests. *Protitanotherium* probably led something of a rhino-like existence.

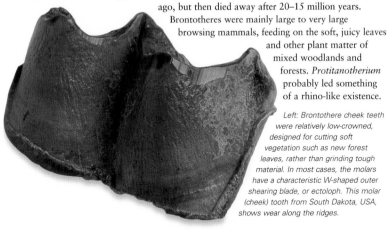

Left: Brontothere cheek teeth were relatively low-crowned, designed for cutting soft vegetation such as new forest leaves, rather than grinding tough material. In most cases, the molars have a characteristic W-shaped outer shearing blade, or ectoloph. This molar (cheek) tooth from South Dakota, USA, shows wear along the ridges.

Name: *Protitanotherium*
Meaning: Before titanic beast
Grouping: Mammal, Perissodactyl, Brontothere
Informal ID: Brontothere
Fossil size: Tooth 8cm/ 3in long
Reconstructed size: Head–body length 3m/10ft
Habitat: Mixed woodland and forests
Time span: Middle Eocene, 45 million years ago
Main fossil sites: North America, East Asia
Occurrence: ◆ ◆

Coelodonta

The woolly rhinoceros, *Coelodonta*, is well known from plentiful fossil, subfossil and mummified remains, as well as from specimens frozen in ice, and also the cave paintings and remnant tools, utensils and ornaments of Neanderthal people and our own prehistoric ancestors. Like the woolly mammoth, its long, coarse hair kept out the snow and wind on the tundra and steppe of the recent Ice Ages. The woolly rhino probably originated in East Asia about 350,000 years ago and spread to Europe, but it never reached North America. It survived in some areas to perhaps just 10,000 years ago. The front horn reached a length of more than 1m/3¼ft in older males.

Left: The woolly rhino vertebra (backbone) has a massively strong build with large processes (flanges) for muscle attachment. The deeply dished centrum (main body) fitted into the corresponding bulge of the next vertebra, all along the vertebral column. This meant great strength, but little flexibility, of the back.

Name: *Coelodonta*
Meaning: Hollow tooth
Grouping: Mammal, Perissodactyl, Rhinocerotid
Informal ID: Woolly rhino
Fossil size: Vertebral body width 6cm/2⅓in; tooth length 6cm/2⅓in
Reconstructed size: Head–body length 3.5m/11½ft
Habitat: Cold grassland, scrub, steppe, tundra
Time span: Pleistocene, within the past 1 million years
Main fossil sites: Europe, Asia
Occurrence: ◆ ◆

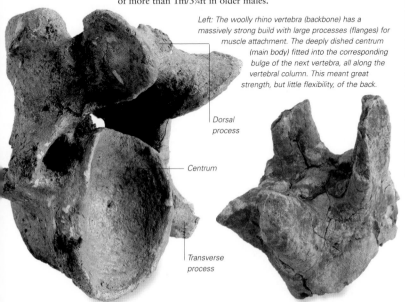

Dorsal process

Centrum

Transverse process

Left: This fossil of an upper molar tooth has been positioned with its chewing surface facing down – as it would have been in life – showing the roots.

HERBIVOROUS MAMMALS (CONTINUED)

By far the largest living group of ungulates (hoofed animals) are even-toed ungulates or artiodactyls, with an even number of hoof-tipped toes per foot. They include pigs (suids), hippos, camels and llamas (camelids), deer (cervids), giraffes (giraffids) and the enormous bovid family of antelopes, gazelles, cattle, sheep and goats. All have a rich fossil history across all the continents except Australia and Antarctica.

Merycoidodon

This sheep-like browser from the Oligocene Epoch, some 30 million years ago, had a mixture of features reflecting pigs and camels. It also had a body shape reminiscent of a short-legged early horse, but with four toes on each foot. It has also been known as *Oreodon*, meaning 'mountain tooth', after the region where its early fossils were found. *Merycoidodon* gave its name to a group of similar plant-eaters that were successful in North America during the Oligocene Epoch. They evolved into various forms, including squirrel-like tree-climbers and bulky, hippo-shaped swamp-dwellers. However, the group declined during the Miocene and became extinct soon after.

Below: The teeth of Merycoidodon *were medium- to high-crowned and had a characteristic crescent shape, suited for slicing and chewing soft forest vegetation.*

Name: *Merycoidodon*
Meaning: Ruminant tooth
Grouping: Mammal, Artiodactyl, Merycoidodont (Oreodont)
Informal ID: Merycoidodont, sheep-pig
Fossil size: Four-tooth section length 3cm/1⅛in
Reconstructed size: Head–body length 1.5m/5ft
Habitat: Woodlands, forested areas
Time span: Oligocene, 30–25 million years ago
Main fossil sites: North America
Occurrence: ◆ ◆

Sus

The living wild boar or wild pig, *Sus scrofa*, is one of the widest-ranging of all wild hoofed animals, being found in woods and forests across most of Europe and Asia. It is also the ancestor of the domestic pig, which is now one of the world's most common larger mammals, distributed with humans in almost every habitable corner of the globe. Along with deer and similar creatures, wild boar feature in the cave art of prehistoric humans, and their tusks were valued in decorative and ornamental items, such as necklaces and headdresses. The genus *Sus* first appeared in Asia during the Miocene, and several different species arrived in Europe at various times. These included the wild boar itself in the Late Miocene. It also spread to Africa, but disappeared there in Neolithic (New Stone Age) times.

Below: Male boar have nibbling incisors and long, curving tusks, which are the lower canines, used for defending themselves as well as battling with rival males at breeding time. This Pleistocene tusk specimen is from Burwell in Cambridgeshire, England.

Root

Name: *Sus*
Meaning: Pig, swine
Grouping: Mammal, Artiodactyl, Suid
Informal ID: Boar, Pig
Fossil size: 12cm/4¾in around curve
Reconstructed size: Head–body length 1.5m/5ft
Habitat: Forested areas, open woodlands
Time span: Quaternary, within past 1 million years
Main fossil sites: Europe, Asia, North Africa
Occurrence: ◆ ◆

Macrauchenia

During South America's time as an isolated island continent through much of the Tertiary Period, many types of ungulates, known as meridiungulates, evolved there. They resembled various hoofed mammals in other regions, such as horses, camels, pigs and wild cattle. The litopterns, or 'simple ankles', were mostly like camels and horses, and showed the same trend to fewer toes per foot, usually the odd number of three or one. However, there were differences from true horses in the foot and ankle bones and, particularly, in the paired lower leg bones, of radius/ulna and tibia/fibula, which did not fuse as in horses. *Macrauchenia*'s nostrils were high on its skull, suggesting it may have had a trunk.

Left: This particularly historic specimen was collected in Argentina in 1834 by naturalist Charles Darwin, on his around-the-world voyage on the Beagle. It is the right front foot, showing the three-toed structure for standing on the 'tip toe' hooves.

Original Royal College of Surgeons registration number

Phalanges (toe bones)

Name: *Macrauchenia*
Meaning: Big llama, large neck
Grouping: Mammal, Meridiungulate, Litoptern
Informal ID: Prehistoric camel-llama
Fossil size: Height 30cm/12in
Reconstructed size: Head–body length 3m/10ft
Habitat: Open woodlands
Time span: Pleistocene, within past 2 million years
Main fossil sites: South America
Occurrence: ◆ ◆

Bison

There are two living species of the hulking, sharp-horned wild cattle called bison, in America and Eastern Europe. Formerly, other species roamed most northern lands, being hunted by prehistoric people and featuring in their cave art and rituals. Various types of bison have inhabited North America and Europe since Pliocene times. The horns are true horns – that is, they grow continually with a bony core covered by an outer horny material, unlike the antlers of deer, which are shed yearly.

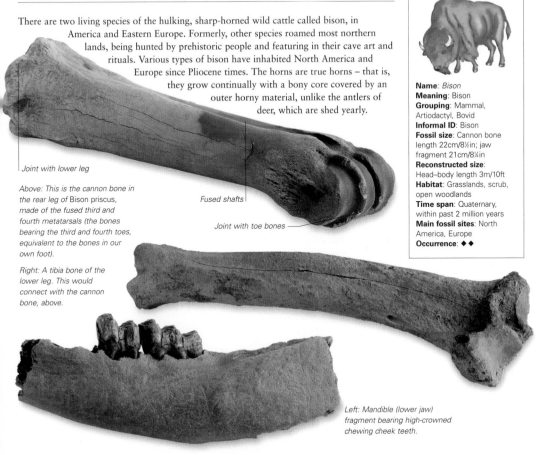

Joint with lower leg

Above: This is the cannon bone in the rear leg of Bison priscus, made of the fused third and fourth metatarsals (the bones bearing the third and fourth toes, equivalent to the bones in our own foot).

Right: A tibia bone of the lower leg. This would connect with the cannon bone, above.

Fused shafts

Joint with toe bones

Left: Mandible (lower jaw) fragment bearing high-crowned chewing cheek teeth.

Name: *Bison*
Meaning: Bison
Grouping: Mammal, Artiodactyl, Bovid
Informal ID: Bison
Fossil size: Cannon bone length 22cm/8½in; jaw fragment 21cm/8¼in
Reconstructed size: Head–body length 3m/10ft
Habitat: Grasslands, scrub, open woodlands
Time span: Quaternary, within past 2 million years
Main fossil sites: North America, Europe
Occurrence: ◆ ◆

HERBIVOROUS MAMMALS (CONTINUED), MARINE MAMMALS

The deer family, Cervidae, was one of the last main groups of large herbivorous mammals to evolve, in the Miocene Epoch from some 13 million years ago. In contrast, the whale and dolphin family, Cetacea, was one of the first mammal groups to take to the sea, becoming fully aquatic over 50 million years ago.

Megaloceros

Megaloceros is known as the 'Irish elk' because many of its remains have been discovered in Irish peat bogs, and its spreading antlers resemble those of the modern elk (moose). However, it is, in fact, a closer relative of today's fallow deer and its remains have been found across most of the north of Europe and Asia. The antlers spanned almost 4m/13ft, weighed an incredible 50kg/110lb and – unlike the horns of bovids (cattle, sheep and goats) – they grew anew each year. In most living species, only the male deer possess antlers, and this was the case in *Megaloceros*. It is possible that the 'giant elk' *Megaloceros* survived until less than 10,000 years ago in parts of Central Europe, as it was pictured and hunted by early people.

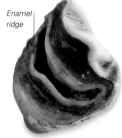

Left and below: The high-crowned molars have complex wavy lines. These are formed by cusps that have become elongated in a front-rear direction and folded, giving extra cutting and grinding ridges of enamel. Deer and some cattle have this tooth pattern, known as the selenodont dentition.

Root

Enamel ridge

Name: *Megaloceros*
Meaning: Gigantic large horn
Grouping: Mammal, Artiodactyl, Cervid
Informal ID: Giant elk, Irish elk
Fossil size: 2.5cm/1in
Reconstructed size: Head–body length 2.5m/8¼ft
Habitat: Woods, scrub, moor
Time span: Pleistocene, within the past 400,000 years
Main fossil sites: Europe, Asia
Occurrence: ◆ ◆

Rangifer

Name: *Rangifer*
Meaning: Single-file walker
Grouping: Mammal, Artiodactyl, Cervid
Informal ID: Reindeer (Europe), Caribou (North America)
Fossil size: Length 25cm/10in
Reconstructed size: Head–body length 2m/6½ft
Habitat: Tundra, steppe, cold forests
Time span: Quaternary, within past 1 million years
Main fossil sites: Throughout the Northern lands
Occurrence: ◆ ◆

Among the modern deer species living today, only the reindeer, or caribou (*Rangifer*), has antlers in the females as well as in the males. *Rangifer* fossils from almost one million years ago crop up in Alaska, North America, and in Europe the fossils date to nearer half a million years ago. In more recent times, *Rangifer*'s fossils are associated with those of mammoths, woolly rhinos and similar Ice Age mammals around the north of the Northern Hemisphere. Neanderthal people of 40,000 years ago fashioned reindeer antlers, bones and other parts into tools and utensils. They are also depicted in cave art around 15,000 years old. Domestication may have occurred in the Aerhtai Shan (Altai Mountains) region – now in west Mongolia close to the Russian border – some 5,000 years ago.

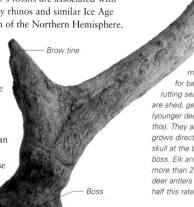

Main beam

Brow tine

Left: Deer antlers grow each year, and are mainly used by males for battles during the rutting season, after which they are shed, generally in the spring (younger deer slightly later than this). They are made of bone that grows directly from the skull at the blunt lower end or boss. Elk antlers can grow at more than 2.5cm/1in in a day; deer antlers lengthen at less than half this rate.

Boss

Cetacean

After the end-of-Cretaceous mass-extinction event of dinosaurs and many marine reptiles, mammals lost no time in taking to the seas and becoming highly evolved as marine hunters. The first cetaceans – members of the whale, dolphin and porpoise group – date from the Eocene Epoch, more than 50 million years ago. All are meat-eaters, with toothed cetaceans – such as dolphins, porpoises and sperm whales – specialized as hunters of fish and squid, and the great whales as filter-feeders of much smaller prey, such as shrimp-like krill. The fossil record of cetaceans shows loss of rear limbs and extreme adaptation of the skull and jaws, especially in the great or baleen whales. In these animals, all teeth are lost, the skull bones form long curved arches and prey is sieved from the water by fringe-edged, comb-like baleen plates, which rarely survive preservation.

Name: Cetacean, skeleton of Mysticete
Meaning: Mysticete refers to the upper lip (as in moustache)
Grouping: Mammal, Cetacean, Mysticete
Informal ID: Baleen whale skeleton
Fossil size: Length 9m/30ft
Reconstructed size: As above
Habitat: Seas, oceans
Time span: Eocene, 50 million years ago, to today
Main fossil sites: Worldwide
Occurrence: ◆ ◆

Tail region | Main vertebrae (backbones) | Rib cage | Cervical vertebrae (neck bones) | Brain case area of skull | Front upper skull (rostrum)

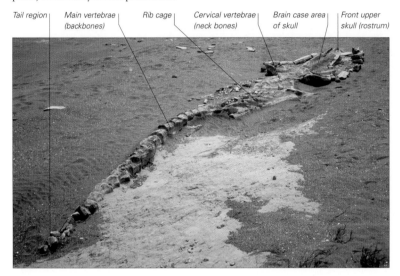

Left: These in situ remains are from near Sacaco, Peru, and show most of the fossilized skeleton of a 9m/30ft great whale from the Tertiary Period. Once located on the ocean bed, the region is now a desert.

Cetacean tympanic bone

The ears of most whales are very different from those of other mammals. There is no ear flap, or even an ear canal opening, as we have. In water, sounds travel as ripples of water pressure that vibrate a channel of fat and bone in the whale's lower jaw – this is the route for sounds entering the ear. These vibrations are passed on to tympanic bones (rather than our own flexible skin-like eardrum), which, in turn, pass them to the nerve centre of the inner ear. Whales use many types of sounds for communication, especially when males 'sing' at breeding time. In addition, toothed whales – from dolphins to sperm whales – use them, like bat squeaks and clicks in the air, for the echo-location of prey and obstacles.

Name: Cetacean tympanic bone
Meaning: Whale 'ear bone'
Grouping: Mammal, Cetacean
Informal ID: Whale ear bone
Fossil size: Length 10cm/4in
Reconstructed size: Total animal length 20m/65ft
Habitat: Seas, oceans
Time span: This specimen Early Pleistocene, almost 2 million years ago
Main fossil sites: Worldwide
Occurrence: ◆ ◆

Right: The ear bones of a large whale are stout and bulky, passing vibrations from the lower jaw area to the inner ear. They are made of very hard, dense bone and fossilize well, being common in some marine deposits. Each specimen has a unique shape.

PRIMATES

The two main groups of living primates are prosimians, or strepsirhines – lemurs, lorises, pottos and bushbabies – and the anthropoids, or haplorhines – all monkeys (including marmosets and tamarins), the lesser apes or gibbons, the great apes and humans. Main group features are grasping hands and often feet with nails rather than claws, flexible shoulders, forward-facing eyes, and a large brain for body size.

Plesiadapis

A profusion of *Plesiadapis* fossils in north-east France, in the Cernay region, indicate that this was once a common creature. Remains are also frequent in North America. *Plesiadapis* had the primate hallmarks of gripping fingers and toes suited for a life in the trees, and a long tail for balancing. Its body and hands were primate-like, but its tooth pattern was more similar to that of the rodents, with large incisors and a gap, or diastema, between these and the chewing molars at the rear. With other features, this had led to debate over whether *Plesiadapis* was a true early primate or close relative. It was relatively long-limbed and could probably move fast and with agility, both through the branches and across the ground.

Diastema (gap)

Molar tooth

Above: This is a section of the left side of the mandible (lower jaw). The large incisor teeth were procumbent – angled forwards, as in some rodents – and were perhaps used for digging into bark to get at wood-boring grubs or release the sticky sap.

Name: *Plesiadapis*
Meaning: Near Adapis (another primate genus)
Grouping: Mammal, Primate, Prosimian, Plesiadapid
Informal ID: Lemur
Fossil size: Length 3.3cm/1¼in
Reconstructed size: Head–tail length 80cm/32in
Habitat: Woods, forests
Time span: Late Palaeocene and Eocene, 55 to 45 million years ago
Main fossil sites: North America, Europe
Occurrence: ◆ ◆

Megaladapis

Below: This Quaternary specimen comes from near Ampoza, in southwest Madagascar. It has prominent incisors with a small gap (or diastema) to the rear of these. The mandible (lower jaw) is deep and strong with large areas for anchoring powerful chewing muscles. The probable diet of this creature was leaves and fruits.

The giant lemur *Megaladapis* was the size of living great apes today, such as the orang-utan or perhaps even the gorilla. Like all living lemurs, its fossils come from the island of Madagascar, off the east coast of Africa, although earlier members of the lemur group occurred across North America and Europe as well as Africa. *Megaladapis* had a stout body and relatively short limbs. Weighing in at more than 50kg/110lb, it probably clambered between large branches in the slow, deliberate manner of a sloth. There is evidence that this huge lemur survived to at least 2,000 years ago, and possibly less than 1,000 years ago – perhaps humans played a part in its eventual extinction.

Cranium (braincase)

Large nostril area possibly supported a small trunk

Prominent canine

Orbit not completely enclosed by bone

Deep mandible

Name: *Megaladapis*
Meaning: Big Adapis (another primate genus)
Grouping: Mammal, Primate, Prosimian, Lemurid
Informal ID: Giant lemur
Fossil size: Skull length 29cm/11¼in
Reconstructed size: Head–body length 1.5m/5ft
Habitat: Woods, forests
Time span: Pleistocene, less than 2 million years ago
Main fossil sites: Madagascar
Occurrence: ◆

Australopithecus afarensis

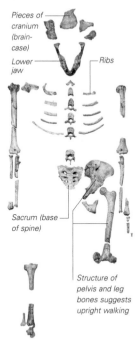

Pieces of cranium (braincase)

Lower jaw

Ribs

Sacrum (base of spine)

Structure of pelvis and leg bones suggests upright walking

A combination of fossil, DNA and biochemical evidence suggests that human lines of evolution separated from those of our closest living relatives, the chimpanzees, sometime around 6–8 million years ago. Early fossil finds of the human family, hominids, indicate that through time they gradually became taller, more upright and larger-brained. However, newer finds show that a mix of species came and went over the past few million years. Some of the earlier ones were more like recent humans, while some of the later ones 'reverted' to being more ape-like. The australopithecines included several species that lived from about 4 to 1 million years ago, all in Africa. They ranged from large and powerful, or robust, types with massive jaws and teeth, to smaller and more slender, or gracile, types, such as the famous 'Lucy'. She was once thought to be female, but in fact 'she' could have been a male, 'Lucifer'. *Australopithecus afarensis* is a relatively well-known species of early human, with fossilized remains coming from more than 300 different individuals. The remains exhibit many ape-like features and an average brain size equivalent to that of a modern chimpanzee.

Left: The 'Lucy' specimen (AL 288-1) of Australopithecus afarensis was found near Hadar, Ethiopia, in 1974 by Donald Johanson and his team. At a remarkable two-fifths complete, it is dated to just over 3 million years old.

Name: *Australopithecus afarensis*
Meaning: Southern ape from Afar
Grouping: Mammal, Primate, Hominid
Informal ID: 'Lucy', ape-man, ape-woman
Fossil size: Femur (thigh bone) length 25cm/10in
Reconstructed size: Overall height 1m/3¼ft
Habitat: Open woodland, open savannah
Time span: Pliocene, from 4 to 3 million years ago
Main fossil sites: Africa
Occurrence: ◆

Homo neanderthalensis

Name: *Homo neanderthalensis*
Meaning: Human from Neander (in Germany)
Grouping: Mammal, Primate, Hominid
Informal ID: Neanderthal, 'cave-man'
Fossil size: Skull front–rear 20cm/12.5in
Reconstructed size: Adult height 1.5–1.65m/5–5½ft
Habitat: Open woodland, steppe, tundra, rocky areas
Time span: Pleistocene, from 250,000 years ago, to perhaps 30,000 years ago
Main fossil sites: Europe, West Asia
Occurrence: ◆ ◆

Following the australopithecines such as 'Lucy', and in some cases overlapping them in time and place, came members of our own genus, *Homo*. *Homo neanderthalensis* was named after the Neander Valley region of Germany, the discovery site in 1856 of the first fossil skeleton to be scientifically described. Neanderthal people were strong-limbed, large-torsoed, stocky and powerful, and they were generally adapted to surviving the intense cold of the Ice Ages that swept down from the north through the Pleistocene Epoch. Their fossils and artefacts are known from about 250,000 to as recently as less than 30,000 years ago. They made a range of tools as well as decorative objects, used fire, perhaps carried out ceremonies and lived in extended family groups, often favouring the protection of caves.

Below: This skull of a female Homo neanderthalensis is from Tabun at Mount Carmel, Israel. It is dated to around 100,000 years ago. Most Neanderthals had brains as large as, or even bigger than, our own.

Sloping forehead

Projecting brow ridge

Broad nose

Projecting upper jaw

Receding chin

GLOSSARY

abdomen Rear or lower part of the body in many animals

absolute dating Estimating the age of rocks and fossils by physical means, such as the radioactive minerals they contain

agnatha Literally 'without jaws', usually applied to fish that lack jointed jaws, including the first fish and modern lampreys and hagfish

amber The hardened fossilized resin or exudate from certain plants, mainly coniferous trees

ambulacra Curved plates associated that make up the shell or test of an echinoid (urchin)

aptychi In fossils, plate like structures that were possibly the 'jaws' or 'teeth' of molluscs such as ammonoids

articulated In fossils, as in life, when parts are found still attached to each other at joints

binomial nomenclature The traditional system of two names, genus and species, for identifying organisms, both living and extinct

byssal threads Strong threads by which various invertebrates, such as mussels, attach themselves to a firm surface

calcareous Consisting predominantly of calcium-rich minerals such as calcium carbonate, as in limestones and chalks

carapace The hard outer covering over the head and body, especially in crustaceans

Carnivora The mammal group that includes dogs, bears, otters, mongooses, civets, cats and similar hunting members

cartilage A tough, springy substance that forms the skeleton of sharks, and parts of the skeleton in other vertebrates

caudal To do with the tail or rear end of the body, as in the caudal or tail fin of fish

cladistical analysis Determining the relationships of living things and grouping them according to the possession of unique characters derived from a common ancestor

cladogram A branching diagram showing relationships between living things determined according to cladistical analysis

comparative anatomy Studying the structure or anatomy of living things and comparing their parts, organs and tissues to suggest origins, groupings and evolutionary relationships

convergent evolution When two dissimilar organisms come to resemble each other superficially, due to adaptation to similar conditions and lifestyles

coprolites Fossilized droppings or dung

cusp A mound-like projection or point, as might appear on a tooth

DNA De-oxyribonucleic acid, the genetic substance that contains the instructions for life, passed from generation to generation

dorsal To do with the upper side or back

erosion Wearing away of rocks and other materials by the forces of weather such as rain, sun, wind, snow and ice

exoskeleton A body casing or framework on the outside, as in insects and shelled animals

frond The leaf of a fern

foramen A gap, hole, opening or window in a surface or object

gastroliths 'Stomach stones', swallowed by animals such as sauropod dinosaurs into the digestive tract, to help grind tough plant food

guard The pointed, often bullet-shaped structure in the rear of a belemnoid's body

heterocercal In fish, when the tail (caudal fin) has two unequal lobes

homocercal In fish, when the tail (caudal fin) has two equal lobes

ichnogenus A genus known only from trace fossils or signs it has left, such as footprints or droppings, rather than fossils of bodily matter

igneous rocks Rocks which have melted and then cooled and become solid, such as lava

labial To do with lips or the front of the mouth

leaflet Segment of a compound leaf or frond

macro/microconch Molluscs in which one sex (usually male) is small, with a reduced shell, while the other sex (usually female) is larger

mass extinction When a large proportion of organisms die out at a particular time, usually due to some form of rapid global change

matrix In palaeontology, the rock and other material in which a fossil is embedded

metamorphic rocks Rocks which have changed their crystalline and mineral make-up via great pressure and heat, without melting

mummification When preservation of dead organisms is aided by severe drying out

neural To do with nerves, or the upper parts of bones or plates

operculum The door-like cover to the shell opening certain molluscs, such as snails

oral To do with the mouth or feeding area

paedomorphosis When the adult retains features or characteristics usually seen only in the young or juvenile phase

palaeomagnetism The study of the Earth's magnetism, and how it affected and aligned magnetic minerals in rocks as they formed

pectoral To do with the front limbs or front side area of an animal (in humans, the shoulders)

pelagic Living in the open sea

pelvic To do with the rear limbs or rear side area of an animal (in humans, the hips)

permafrost Ground which never unfreezes, as found in the far north of Asia today

permineralization When certain substances, such as the tissues of a once-living organism,

are replaced by inorganic minerals, as happens during certain forms of fossilization

petrification Turning to stone or rock

phloem The tiny tubes in a vascular plant that transport sap and similar fluids

phragmocone The cone-like inner shell in molluscs such as belemnites

planktonic Floating with the ocean currents

pleural To do with the lungs or breathing anatomy of animals; a pleural spine is the body spine of a trilobite

predator An animal that gains its food by active hunting

proboscis A long, flexible, snout- or trunk-like part on the head of an animal

punctuated equilibrium A form of evolution where long periods of stability are interrupted by times of rapid change, in contrast to the traditional view of slow, gradual change

relative dating Estimating the age of fossils from the rocks they are contained within, and from the rocks and fossils in adjacent layers

radula The file-like tongue of certain animals, especially the snail and slug group of molluscs

sedimentary rocks Rocks formed by laying down of particles or sediments, usually on the bed of a sea or lake

scutes Protective hard, bony, shield-like plates or scales found in some fish and reptiles

semelparity When an organism reproduces only once in its lifetime, often dying soon after

sexual dimorphism When the male and female of a species exhibit different physical characteristics (other than reproductive parts)

soft tissues Nerves, blood vessels, muscles and similar soft parts of a body

sporangia The spore-producing units found on many seedless plants, such as ferns

sutures Firm, tight joints, usually marked by lines, as in the shell of an ammonoid or the skull of a vertebrate

taphonomy The study of how an organism decays over time and produces a fossil

taxonomy Grouping or classifying organisms, living or extinct, along with the reasons and principles underlying their classification

tetrapod Four-legged, usually referring to vertebrate animals with four limbs

thoracic To do with the chest or the front or upper body of an animal

trace fossils Fossils which record the signs, marks or parts left by a living thing, rather than being actually part of the living thing

vascular To do with tubes, pipes and vessels, as in the sap and water tube systems in a vascular plant, or the blood vessel network of an animal

ventral To do with the underside or belly

whorl A complete turn of a shell or casing, such as in a snail or ammonite shell

xylem The tiny tubes in a vascular plant that transport water and dissolved minerals, usually up from the roots

PICTURE ACKNOWLEDGEMENTS

Note: t=top; b=bottom; m=middle; l=left; r=right. Further detail of image is given where position on page might be difficult to clarify.

Artworks

Andrey Atuchin 35br (*Giganotosaurus*); Peter Barrett 10bl (Jurassic scene); 28b (freshwater scene); 29 (panel); 29br (dinosaur tracks); 34mr (*Baryonyx*); 52br (*Pteranodon*); 63bl (*Nautilus*); 63 (panel, left, modern coelacanth); Stuart Carter 32bl (*Iguanodon*); Anthony Duke 13 ('recording geological time'), 22b ('how a fossil forms'); 29br (dinosaur footprints map); 65tr (human migration map). All panel reconstructions as credited below; 87br (panel); Denys Ovenden all artworks on pages 62–3 except for Nautilus and modern coelacanth (see Peter Barrett, above); 65 (panel).

Reconstructions of fossils appearing in the panels on pages 74–249 were drawn by Anthony Duke, except for the following which were drawn by Samantha J. Elmhurst www.livingart.org.uk: 217t; 219b; 222; 223t; 224; 225t; 226; 230t; 233b; 234b; 235; 236; 237b; 238t; 239; 240–241; 242t; 243b; 244t; 244b; 245b; 246

Photographs

The following photographs are © Corbis (www.corbis.com):

2, 8/9, 12 (panel), 14tr, 14bl, 18bl, 21tr, 26tr, 27tl, 30tl, 30tr, 31 (panel), 34bl, 35tr, 36tr, 37tr, 38tr, 45tr, 55tr, 55br, 56tl, 56bl, 57tr, 57mr, 58tr, 58mr, 61bl, 61br, 63tr, 64bl, 64br, 193

The following photographs are © Natural History Museum Picture Library, London (www.piclib.nhm.ac.uk):

6tr, 6bl, 6br, 7b, 11tr, 16tr, 16bl, 24bl, 25tl, 30br, 31tl, 31tr, 32tl, 32tr, 33tl, 33tr, 33 (panel), 34tr, 36bl, 37 (panel), 38tr, 38bl, 39bl, 39 (panel), 40tr, 42bl, 43tl, 43bl, 43 (panel), 44/5 (all photographs except 45tr), 51tr, 51br, 51 (panel), 53br, 53 (both images in panel), 54tr, 56tr, 57 (panel), 58bl, 60tr, 60bl, 61tr, 61mr, 61 (panel), 62bl, 63tl, 64t, 71b, 75t, 78t, 80b, 88, 89b, 98t, 98b, 109t, 109b, 109 (panel), 123t, 123b, 136t, 149t, 149b, 151t, 157 (panel), 188t, 189t, 196b, 205b, 206t, 207t, 208/9 (all photographs), 214/15 (all photographs except 214t), 221b, 227b, 228t, 231, 232t, 233t, 237b, 238b, 245t, 248/9 (all photographs)

The following photographs are © NHPA (www.nhpa.co.uk):

66/7, 73, 78 (panel), 79 (panel), 82 (panel), 83 (panel), 84 (panel), 88 (panel), 101 (panel), 107, 138 (bottom-left photograph of *Eryma*), 176 (panel), 204 (panel), 211b (left-hand photograph of *Rutiodon*), 236 (coypu)

33bl (Crystal Palace dinosaurs) © Mary Evans Picture Library (www.maryevans.com)

The following photographs are © The Science Photo Library, www.sciencephoto.com: 70/71 (all photographs except 71b), 206 (panel),

232b, 247t

The following photographs are © Anness Publishing Ltd, and feature specimens from the following locations:

Museum of Wales, Cardiff, Wales
11bl (all images except 11tr), 20tr (claw and tooth), 21tl (bivalves), 21 (panel), 21mr (leaf), 22tr (trilobite), 23 (panel), 24ml (ammonite), 25 (panel), 25b (fish), 27bl (frog skull), 28tr (vertebrae), 41tr, 42tr, 43br, 46 (panel), 47tl, 47tr, 49tl, 49 (panel), 50tl, 50tr, 50b (shoal), 52tl (display), 52tr (toe and hoof), 72 (all), 74t, 74b, 75b, 76/7 (all photographs), 79t, 79bl, 80t, 81t, 81b, 82b, 83t, 85t, 86/7 (all photographs), 89t, 90t, 91t, 91br, 92b, 93b, 94/5 (all photographs except panel), 96/7 (all photographs except 97tr), 99b, 100/101 (all photographs except panel), 102/3 (all photographs), 104/5 (all photographs except panel), 106 (all), 108t, 111t, 112b (both of *Raphidonema*), 113b, 114b (both of Ediacaran medusoid), 115b, 118t, 119 (all photographs), 120t, 121t, 122t, 122b (all photographs of *Archimedes*), 127b, 128t, 129 (all photographs except 129tr), 131t, 132 (panel), 133b, 140t, 140b, 141b, 142b, 149 (panel), 150 (all photographs), 151b, 152 (panel), 154/5 (all photographs), 156t (both photographs of *Lopha*), 157 (all photographs of *Gryphea* except largest in centre), 158/9 (all photographs), 160b, 161t (top photograph of *Viviparus*), 162/3 (all photographs except 162t), 164/5 (all photographs), 166t, 167t, 167b, 168/9 (all photographs), 170/71 (all photographs except 170t), 173 (all photographs), 174/5 (all photographs), 176b (bottom photograph of *Nautilus*), 177t, 177 (panel), 178b, 178 (panel), 179t, 183t, 183 (panel), 185 (panel), 186t, 187b, 188b, 189b, 190/91 (all photographs), 192m, 192r, 194bl, 195 (panel), 196t, 197t, 197b, 198t, 198b, 200t, 200b, 202/3 (all photographs except 203b), 204br (bottom image of *Branchiosaurus*), 205t, 207 (both photographs of *Nanopus*), 210t, 210 (panel), 211t, 211br, 212/13 (all photographs except 212t), 214t, 217 (all photographs), 218 (all photographs), 220b, 221t, 222/3 (all photographs), 224 (all photographs), 225 (caudal vertebra), 226/7 (all photographs except 227b), 229 (moulted feathers and bird eggs), 233b, 236/7 (all photographs except 237b), 239 (all photographs except 239mr), 240/41 (all photographs except 241mr), 242 (all photographs), 243t, 244 (all photographs), 245 (top and bottom photographs of bison), 246/7 (all photographs except 247t)

Booth Museum of Natural History, Brighton & Hove City Council, England
6mr (hyaena jaw), 10tm (trilobite), 20bl (fish), 26ml (fern), 29tb (pond snails), 46tr, 47ml, 47mr, 48 (all photographs except 48tr), 49br, 50ml, 50mr, 50b, 59br, 59 (panel), 84t, 85b, 90bl, 90br, 99t, 99m, 110t, 110 (panel), 112t, 113t, 120b, 129 (top photograph of *Calymene*), 134t, 135b, 136t, 137t, 142t, 144t (all

photographs except 144b), 146b, 147t, 148t, 152t, 152b, 153 (all photographs), 156b, 157t (largest photograph of *Gryphea* in centre), 161 (bottom photograph of *Viviparus*), 170t, 172t, 179b, 180b (both photographs of *Marsupites*), 181 (panel), 182 (all photographs), 184/5 (all photographs except panel), 186b, 187t, 187 (panel), 192l, 194/5 (all photographs except *Hybodus*, bottom-left), 199 (all photographs), 201 (all photographs), 212t, 216b, 219 (all photographs), 225 (all photographs except caudal vertebra), 229bl (pseudofossil), 238t, 239m, 241m, 243bl, 243br, 245 (middle photograph of bison)

Manchester Museum, England
18tm (sponge), 24tr (chain coral), 63bl (nautiloid), 79 (middle photograph of *Calamites*), 84b (both photographs of *Neuropteris*), 91 (bottom photograph of *Stigmaria*), 92t, 111b, 114t, 116/17 (all photographs), 118b, 121 (all photographs of *Spirorbis* worm casts), 124/5 (all photographs), 126/7 (all photographs except 127b), 128b, 130/31 (all photographs except 131t), 132t, 132b (both photographs of *Agnostus*), 133t, 134 (panel), 135t, 137b, 138 (both photographs of *Eryma*), 139 (all photographs), 141t, 143 (all photographs except panel), 144b, 146t, 147t (two smaller photographs of *Trichopterans*, bottom), 147b (*Cupedid*), 148t, 160t, 162t, 166b, 172b, 176t (top photograph of *Nautilus*), 177b, 178 (middle and bottom photographs in panel), 180t, 181t (both photographs of *Eucalyptocrinites*), 181b, 203b, 204t, 220t

Additional photography credits

Photograph of *Sequoia* fossil appearing on page 27 (panel) © Rich Paselk, Natural History Museum, Humboldt State University, CA, USA

Photograph of Dorothy Hill appearing on page 35 (panel) © The Physical Sciences and Engineering Library, University of QLD, Australia

Photograph of Kings Canyon appearing on p53bl © Amy-Jane Beer/Origin Natural Science

Photograph of balloon vine appearing on page 104 (panel) © Jackie Miles and Max Campbell

Photographs of amber appearing on pages 143 and 147 (panel, top-left) © John Cooper

Photograph of fossil operculum appearing on page 161 (panel) © Dr Bill Bushing, Starthrower Educational Media, www.starthrower.org

Photograph of brittlestar appearing on page 183b © R. Shepherd

INDEX